From Big Bang to Big Mystery

Brendan Purcell is Adjunct Professor in Philosophy at Notre Dame University, Sydney. Having studied philosophy at University College Dublin, theology at the Pontifical Lateran University Rome, and psychology at the University of Leuven, he lectured in logic, psychology and philosophical anthropology at University College Dublin, retiring as Senior Lecturer in the School of Philosophy in 2008. He was ordained a priest of Dublin diocese in 1967 and is at present assistant priest at St Mary's Cathedral, Sydney. He wrote *The Drama of Humanity: Towards a Philosophy of Humanity in History* (1996), and with Detlev Clemens edited and translated *Hitler and the Germans*, volume 31 of *The Collected Works of Eric Voegelin* (1999).

Brendan Purcell

From Big Bang to Big Mystery

Human Origins in the Light of Creation and Evolution

VERITAS

Published 2011 by
Veritas Publications
7–8 Lower Abbey Street
Dublin 1, Ireland
publications@veritas.ie
www.veritas.ie

ISBN 978 1 84730 2717
Copyright © Brendan Purcell, 2011
10 9 8 7 6 5 4 3 2 1

'Race Memory (by a dazed Darwinian)' by G.K. Chesterton is reprinted from
Collected Poetry, Part I (Ignatius Press, 1994) by permission of A P Watt Ltd
on behalf of The Royal Literary Fund.

All Les Murray extracts are reprinted from *New Collected Poems* (Carcanet,
2003) by permission of Carcanet.

Every effort has been made to trace copyright holders and to obtain their
permission for the use of copyright material. Should any errors or omissions
occur please notify the publisher and corrections will be incorporated in
future reprints or editions of this book.

The material in this publication is protected by copyright law. Except as
may be permitted by law, no part of the material may be reproduced
(including by storage in a retrieval system) or transmitted in any form or by
any means, adapted, rented or lent without the written permission of the
copyright owners. Applications for permissions should be addressed to the
publisher.

A catalogue record for this book is available from the British Library.

Designed by Norma Prause-Brewer, Veritas

Printed in the Republic of Ireland by Hudson Killeen, Dublin

Veritas books are printed on paper made from the wood pulp of
managed forests. For every tree felled, at least one tree is planted,
thereby renewing natural resources.

Praise for **From Big Bang to Big Mystery**

Brendan Purcell has given philosophical anthropology a new lease of life. *From Big Bang to Big Mystery* seamlessly weaves together the best that science can tell us about human origins with the deepest insights human beings have gained upon themselves in the course of history. It is a comprehensive guide to what it means to be human. Purcell moves easily from the latest debates in evolutionary genetics to mystical affirmations of God without skipping a beat. It is an astonishing, learned, and profoundly moving tale of the journey in which we are all travellers.
David Walsh, Professor of Politics, The Catholic University of America

Purcell has achieved a remarkable synthesis: he has brought together Bernard Lonergan's philosophical concept of 'emergent probability' and Eric Voegelin's philosophy of participatory (and not just perceptual) consciousness with an immense and ever-growing literature dealing with the hominid sequence. This book is a must-read for philosophers and theologians and especially for paleoscientists. Their sciences will never be the same.
Barry Cooper, Professor of Political Science, University of Calgary

This is a profound, challenging and erudite book, offering a fresh and constructive approach to issues and debates that affect us all. Highly recommended.
Conor Cunningham, Assistant Director, Centre of Theology and Philosophy, University of Nottingham and author of Darwin's Pious Idea: How the Ultra–Darwinists and Creationists Both Get it Wrong

Brendan Purcell has given us a study of human origins that is comprehensive, wise, and of startling philosophical clarity. He combines the latest discoveries in paleoanthropology, genetics, neuroscience, linguistics, and other sciences with the insights of thinkers from Xenophanes and Aristotle to Eric Voegelin and Bernard Lonergan to produce a deeply impressive and convincing synthesis.
Stephen M. Barr, Professor of Theoretical Physics, University of Delaware, and author of Modern Physics and Ancient Faith

Purcell paints an enormous canvas, ranging from the Big Bang to human consciousness. He draws on a wide range of authoritative sources to compose a gracefully written scholarly synthesis. The book is full of valuable insights … the author proposes that a sensible relation of complementarity should exist between science, religion and philosophy rather than a confrontational interaction where one discipline tries to refute and supplant the explanations of the others.
William Reville, Professor of Biochemistry, University College Cork and science columnist with the Irish Times

From Big Bang to Big Mystery

Human Origins in the Light of Creation and Evolution

Introduction

Part One: A conversation between myth, philosophy and revelation on the human and on nature

Part Two: The scientific partners in the conversation: what science is and how it can complement rather than replace or invalidate philosophy and revelation

Part Three: How we belong and yet – because of the 'human revolution' – don't fully belong to the hominid sequence

Part Four: The seven grace notes in the 'Sonata for a Good Man'

Part Five: Meeting you face to face – the human person as Communion

Introduction

1. The Quest

These lines from Australian poet Les Murray's 'A Walk with O'Connor' are perhaps a good way to start:

> I looked at O'Connor
> and he spoke to me,
> but there were as many aspects of our quest,
> I mean the Quest that summons all true men,
> as that evening's light
> permitted us to see.[1]

Murray's notion of the Quest that summons all true human beings gets to the heart of the human mystery – we're not answers, but rather summoned to a quest, where even the source of that summons isn't clear to us. Fyodor Dostoevsky felt summoned by the same quest when he wrote to his brother Michael in 1839, the year of their father's murder: 'Man is a mystery. One must solve it. If you spend your entire life trying to puzzle it out, then do not say that you have wasted your time. I occupy myself with this mystery, because I want to be a man.'[2] He undertook this through a magnificent sequence of dramatic explorations, beginning with *Notes from Underground* and not really finishing with his last novel, *The Brothers Karamazov*.

This book is about one way of 'occupying ourselves' with the quest. I'll be inviting you to join me in the quest I've been on for many years, and to find out for yourself if your questions lead you closer to understanding the mystery of human origins. My own background is in philosophy, but exploring human origins involves a lot more than philosophy, and includes biology and the study of the remains of hominids, the creatures closest to us. That means we must consider the evolutionary context for understanding where we come from.

Still, the philosophical questions don't go away, and I'll also be discussing that evolutionary context in the light of a philosophy of creation. Since Judeo-Christian revelation is inextricably interwoven in the rich fabric of Western culture, the relation between revelation, the natural sciences and

---

1 Les Murray, *New Collected Poems*, Manchester: Carcanet, 2003, p. 31.

2 Konstantin Mochulsky, *Dostoevsky: His Life and Work*, tr. Michael A. Minihan, Princeton, NJ: Princeton University Press, 1971, p. 17.

philosophy will be discussed from time to time, although the primary focus of our inquiry will be philosophical.

If our topic, then, is the quest for human origins, there'll also be an underlying theme, which is that human beings are both continuous with evolutionary process and discontinuous with it. Steven Pinker, a philosopher of language, writes in *The Blank Slate* (2002) that we can't establish a clear boundary between human and animal existence. I'd like to contrast what he's saying with the viewpoint of another philosopher of language, Walker Percy (who was also a novelist). Speaking of the kind of communication only human beings have, which is permeated by self-consciousness, he argues that there's more difference between a human and an animal – let's say an orang-utan – than between the animal and the planet Saturn.[3] So, this book will be making a case for our massive belongingness to, along with our massive difference from, the rest of the material universe.

2. Who's questing?

Who we are very much enters into the kind of quest we undertake, so I'd better say something about my philosophical background. I hope it will explain why the quest I'm writing about here takes the kind of twisting and turning path it does. I suppose the beginning of my search to unravel what makes us human was the doctoral thesis I began at the Catholic University of Leuven in 1969 and finished in UCD in 1980. It was eventually called 'Wewards: Towards a Theory of Interpersonal Relations' – 'eventually' because it was only towards the end of all those years of slogging away that I realised what I'd been looking for. The thesis tried to work out a framework for exploring the full range of human relationships: friendship; deepening love; its opposite, enmity; and finally, going beyond enmity in reconciliation. But it was only after I'd finished it that I understood that, all along, I'd been trying to get inside what is meant by the word 'we'.

What led me from psychology back to philosophy was a sense that, as a human being, I myself wasn't really, at least not exclusively, 'an object', the kind of a thing a science could wholly encompass and explain. Fundamentally, I realised I'm something other than a world-immanent thing – a subject – and that there's an inexhaustibility to the within-ness that marks me out as a human being as distinct from a galaxy, an ecosystem or an animal.

---

3 Walker Percy, *Lost in the Cosmos: The Last Self-Help Book*, New York: Washington Square Books, 1983, p. 97.

I was in search of a way to explore that exclusively inner dimension that characterises us as human beings, and the quest presented here tells the story of how I found a thousand and one mirror quests in the unanticipatable multiplicity and variety of quests other individuals and cultures have undertaken throughout history. Socrates made the typically provocative remark that the unexamined life is hardly worth living and Aristotle gives as a sort of thumbnail definition of human beings, that we all desire by nature to know. What has driven forward the quest narrated in the pages that follow is the repeated, surprised recognition that this, that or the other human creation or artefact is an expression of the quest of another human being – uniting us as members of the same human family no matter how far apart we are in time and space, and in the style or medium of our expression.

What this quest has shown me is that the self-appropriation of the questing nature of our humanity, through meditative re-enactment of the expressions of the quests of others animates our existence with a heightened sense of the worth of human existence – our own and others' – and grounds a sense of human family that is universal across space and time: showing us that we human beings are a big mystery, both individually, and as a humankind that's one, yet has to become much more so.

While I was in Leuven, working on 'Wewards' in the Psychology Department's impressively named Research Center for Motivation and Time Perspective, I had chased up the three volumes then published of the major work of a philosopher of history called Eric Voegelin. Since his work was more in philosophy than psychology, I didn't think it was right to read it during my days at the research centre. Instead I began shaving my way through them instead. Shaving? I always accompanied my morning shave with reading – in this case, Voegelin's multivolume *Order and History*. As time went on I realised I was shaving my face off as I didn't want to leave Voegelin's work down. So I gave up and made him part of my daily research in the little room in the basement of the psychology building, which had a grille letting in the sunshine from the garden of the Higher Institute of Philosophy.

I began to see that sooner or later I'd have to change my whole approach to understanding what it is to be human to take into account Voegelin's work on the ancient near Eastern world, the Old Testament, and the Greek experience from Homer to Aristotle. Still, I wanted to know where the rest of *Order and History* was – he'd promised three further volumes. So I wrote to him asking (a) if he was still alive, (b) if so, where the other volumes were, and (c) – the kind of thing young doctoral students are good at – pointing out to him some errors I'd found in his work. His reply included a typed-out version of my handwritten screed, a few comments on it, his explanation of why he'd interrupted his work on *Order and History* and two or three of his most recent published articles. Not long after, he asked me what hotel I could recommend for his visit to Dublin.

When he came to Ireland in September 1972 to see the Irish Neolithic sites for himself, particularly Newgrange and what later became known as the Céide Fields in North Mayo, I had to ask him why on earth, as a philosopher, he was doing this? 'Because I'm an empirical anthropologist,' he said. In other words, for him, philosophy had to go back in time to the earliest expressions of the human if we were ever to have a grasp of the full story of our humanity. That got me interested in the earliest archaeological evidences that were available, like Egyptian myths of order and Australian aboriginal experiences. But Voegelin was pushing me back to the so-called pre-historic period, which of course wasn't so pre-historic any longer, since archaeology was telling us more and more about it.

I wrote to Voegelin in late 1976, suggesting (though not sure how he'd take it, as he didn't really belong to any particular church) that the prayer in St John's Gospel, 'That all may be one', was something he was helping to bring about at a philosophical level by his reaching out to all of humanity, from the paleolithic period to our own. He replied in a letter of 21 December, 1976: ' ... you have gotten the point of my work. If we don't respect those who have gone before us, who will respect us when we are gone? If we exclude the community of mankind, the community will exclude us.'[4]

3. The drama of humanity

Having met Voegelin in person and studied his works, I spent years developing and teaching courses on what has been called the Greek discovery of mind: the odyssey of the human spirit from Homer to the mystic philosophers before Plato, through the Greek tragic poets. That discovery gained momentum and clarity in those dialogues of Plato that focus on what constitutes the essence of the human, and achieved its clearest articulation in the more systematic works of Aristotle.

---

4 Eric Voegelin, *Selected Correspondence 1950–1984*, ed. Thomas A. Hollweck, Columbia, MO: University of Missouri Press, 2007, p. 816. (While I'm quoting from Voegelin's works throughout in the form I have them, they're all available since 2000 from the University of Missouri Press, Columbia, MO, in the thirty-four volumes of *The Collected Works of Eric Voegelin*.)

But Voegelin didn't just push me thousands of years back to the early great civilisations of Egypt and Mesopotamia, or to the Irish Neolithic period of around 3200 BC. He also made me reach outwards beyond the core civilisations of the West – ancient Israel, the Greco-Roman world, and Christianity. Early on in teaching philosophical anthropology I realised the quest for an understanding of the human couldn't be limited to the Western philosophical world, so I taught classes on the Chinese Tao Te Ching, the Indian Bhagavad Gita, and the Old and New Testament revelation on the meaning of human existence in Job and the Gospel of St John.

Not only the good sides of being human have to be investigated, however. Ever since my early teens I had wondered how had great countries like Russia and Germany got it so wrong in the twentieth century? Now, many years later, aware that understanding the human mystery meant facing the fact of evil, of our systematic failure to be human, I had to engage with ideological experiences of the left and right in twentieth century Russia and Germany. This left me looking for the foundations for the human condition that'd take the weight not just of its articulation in terms of myth, philosophy and revelation, but would also make sense of twentieth-century ideological mass movements like Communism and National Socialism, along with the recovery of human reality after such attempts to reduce it to economic or racist terms.[5] Eric Voegelin's articulation of order, drawing particularly on classic philosophy, had offered a way of uniting all of these multiple sources of human meaning. I published an attempt at summarising a lot of this teaching in 1996 called (borrowing the first part of the title from the title of a lecture series Voegelin gave in 1967) *The Drama of Humanity: Towards a Philosophy of Humanity in History*.[6]

4. When did the drama begin?

The German writer, Thomas Mann explored the limitations of his own late-nineteenth-century origins in his novel, *Buddenbrooks* (1901), then expanded that quest to an analysis of European culture in *The Magic Mountain* (1924), with his diagnosis of the specific ills of German culture that had led to National Socialism in *Doktor Faustus* (1947). But it was in the prologue to *Joseph and his Brothers* (1933–1942) that Mann spelt out

---

5 David Walsh has brilliantly explored this recovery in his *After Ideology: Recovering the Spiritual Foundations of Freedom*, San Francisco: HarperCollins, 1990.

6 Brendan Purcell, *The Drama of Humanity: Towards a Philosophy of Humanity in History*, Frankfurt: Peter Lang, 1996.

the background quest to all other quests, that search for the first search of our own humanity Les Murray called 'the Quest that summons all true men':

> Deep is the well of the past. Should we not call it unfathomable? That indeed may be so, if and perhaps only if, it is the past of that human essence that is being spoken of and questioned; that enigmatic essence ... whose mystery very understandably forms the Alpha and Omega of all our speaking and questioning, bestowing stress and fire to all speech, on all questioning its urgency.
>
> For the deeper we sound, the further down into the underworld of the past we grope towards and arrive at, the more the beginnings of the human, its history, its culture, prove to be completely beyond our grasp, and no matter what agelengths we unspool our plumblines to, they always recede again and further into fathomlessness.[7]

I was already thrown into a full exploration of all the expressions of humanity I could find – on the basis that it's only when you see all the good and bad that human beings are capable of that you can begin to understand what's at the core of the human condition. That exploration, for me, had always stopped where written records began – say, at 3000BC with the ancient Near Eastern materials from Egypt and Mesopotamia. But along with those written records, we're finding out more and more about the unwritten expressions of the human quest.

Not long after Voegelin's visit to Newgrange, I went up there for the first time with some friends. In those days you had to get hold of the sometimes erratic caretaker to open the gate into the passageway. Once you got into the site you could still climb all over the mound – built as a sacred mountain uniting heaven and earth. Voegelin had awoken in me the awareness that the Boyne Valley people had created Newgrange as an expression of their yearning to outlast death through focusing on the rebirth of their world. At my first contact with it, everything there – the symbols, the stone circle, the just discovered fact that the sun entered the mound at the dawn of the first and shortest day of the new year – suddenly seemed to be speaking to me. With Mircea Eliade's invaluable *Patterns in Comparative Religion* as my guidebook, I felt as if I had been sent a love letter in a foreign language – I could make out the most important words. As I wrote some years afterwards:

---

7 Thomas Mann, *Joseph und seine Brüder: Die Geschichten Jaakobs*, Frankfurt: Fischer, 1964, p. 7.

In and through their loving-suffering agon of attunement to the central place of the cosmos, at its own anxiously awaited time of rebirth, the Boyne people touched ecstatically for a few boundless timeless moments the everlasting cosmic oneness at the heart of being. Radiating outwards from that oneness, renewing their kingship, sanctifying every corner of the earth's four quarters, eternalising every moment of cosmic time, bestowing hope and dignity to the people's otherwise mere mortality, was the happiness of belonging to the ultimately kind cosmic ground, the source of peace beyond the struggle between life and death.[8]

Another time, I went off the beaten track over miles of dust roads to the huge 1200AD Pueblo people's temple complex at Chaco Canyon, New Mexico, to experience their own quite different way of capturing midwinter sunrise. Closer to home, I took trips to the perhaps 7,000-year-old Neolithic burial grounds at Carrowmore and Carrowkeel, all centred around Queen Maeve's tomb on top of Knocknarea, in Co. Sligo, which transform an area of well over a hundred square miles through a kind of spiritual geography into a meditation on the passage from life to death to further life. Some years ago, with some friends, I visited caves in the Lascaux area, with carvings going back perhaps to 17,000 years ago, and Kakadu national park in Australia's Northern Territory, where quite recent cave paintings speak of a human tradition of transfiguring stone to make it point towards the beyond. But, to take up Thomas Mann's meditation on human history, just how 'deep is the well of the past'? And the further back we go, will we indeed find that 'the more the beginnings of the human, its history, its culture, prove to be completely beyond our grasp ... they always recede again and further into fathomlessness'?

5. Falling into the well of the past

The best thing that happened to me on my last sabbatical was slipping coming out of the Harper Library of the University of Chicago in October 2001. A few weeks earlier I'd had to preach the sermon of my life in St Thomas the Apostle Church, just beside the university, the Sunday after the 9/11 attack. The church was packed to the doors, and since the horror

---

8 Brendan Purcell, 'In Search of Newgrange: Long Night's Journey into Day.' In Richard Kearney, ed., *The Irish Mind: Exploring Intellectual Traditions*, Dublin: Wolfhound Press, 1985, pp. 39–55, at p. 55.

of that event, which I'd heard unfolding on someone's car radio as I'd made my way to the library that morning, I'd been struggling to find the words that would help me and the congregation make sense of such murderous evil. That put my merely breaking my leg and ending up on crutches into perspective.

I normally managed to get to the cinema once a week, sometimes meeting some former students and friends on a Sunday in downtown Chicago. I couldn't get on a bus for a while, so a confederate (Father Fitzsimons from New Zealand) would ask the patient congregation at St Thomas if anyone going into town that day could give me a lift. Invariably some parishioners would offer to take the moviegoer into town, and one Sunday, a kind parishioner said he'd be free to take me in. The good Samaritan was Tony Mahowald, Louis Block Professor and Chair of the Department of Molecular Genetics and Cell Biology at the University of Chicago. Once I heard the word 'genetics' I asked him would he ever explain a new development in the understanding of evolution called 'evo-devo' – I'd kept coming across these words, but having always been a scientific duffer whose study of biology ended after my first year at UCD, felt they were very important but didn't know why. It turned out that Professor Mahowald was right in the thick of that new development. Not only did he give me a brilliant lecture during the twenty-minute drive into town, he presented me with some key texts which I did my best with in between the hours of physical exercises I'd been told to do every day. In chapter four, we'll look at just why a range of new discoveries rock the foundations of evolutionary theory and have implications for human origins. But if I hadn't broken my leg I'd have already left Chicago and I'd have remained cheerfully ignorant of this huge biological breakthrough.

I had another, quite different experience on my next port of call during that sabbatical, this time at the University of Melbourne. I called on Professor Jim Bowler, an Australian geologist proud of his Irish roots. He told me how he'd stumbled upon the earliest cremated human burial in Lake Mungo in the far southwest of New South Wales in 1968. Surveying the fossil-rich shores of the long dried-out lake, these were the deliberately cremated bones now called Mungo I or Mungo Lady – which, after a few discussions and careful testing, have been dated to around 41,000 years ago. That great discovery should have been enough to make his reputation.

Then, in 1974, after heavy rains had exposed layers of the sandy dunes to the east of Lake Mungo, he spotted what turned out to be the skeletal remains of a male human, now called Mungo III or Mungo Man. The bones had been daubed with red ochre – traditionally an aboriginal sign of life – and turned out to be the earliest non-cremated burial of a human being ever found, dating to the same enormous age as Mungo Lady. Not only were the bones undeniably belonging to the human race, the careful positioning in burial of Mungo Man showed that from the very beginning human beings haven't accepted death as final. For them, the blood-coloured ochre was a sign of hope or belief in some kind of lastingness beyond death – at least that's a standard understanding of archaic burial rites. So such burials don't just convey factual information, they ask questions of you and me about who we think we are and what we think we're for.

I knew before I took the long train and bus trip to Mildura, in northwestern Victoria, the nearest big town to Lake Mungo, that neither these ancient remains nor even the actual site – on the southern edge of Lake Mungo – were accessible to tourists. Still, this trip, organised and interpreted by local aboriginal tribesmen, was for me a kind of quest to get as near as I could to one of the earliest sites where my fellow human beings had been living on this earth. Our aboriginal guides helped evoke in us the awe and respect they felt for their own people of over 40,000 years earlier (indeed, they continued to use similar burial rites until only a century ago).

On the trip back to Mildura, as we lumbered out of Lake Mungo National Park, I could just make out lots of kangaroos hanging about the left side of the track in the twilight. Both our aboriginal guides and the kangaroos, emus and other wildlife we spotted during the day seemed to bring me slap up against 'that enigmatic essence … whose mystery very understandably forms the Alpha and Omega of all our speaking and questioning, bestowing stress and fire to all speech, on all questioning its urgency'.

6. Making philosophical sense of the mystery of human origins

It became obvious that any adequate philosophical understanding of what makes human beings human would have to deal with our very beginnings in time. But aren't there many books already available that deal with this?

Certainly, and I've learned from all of them.[9] Still, one of my favourite quotes is from the American-based philosopher of evolution, Michael Ruse, who has said that: 'Unfortunately, there is simply nothing in the literature by philosophers on human origins.'[10] This book will try to make up for that lack. What we'll be doing here is reflecting philosophically on the huge heap of materials relevant to the question of human origins that are being continually unearthed. Still, important developments in philosophy have also taken place – it seemed to me that what was needed was to bring these two sets of developments together. That's why I think philosophy needs to enter into the dialogue a little less timidly. But there are different kinds of questions. There are the vitally important factual questions to do with the bones of Mungo Man – do they belong to our species; if so, how old are they; were they deliberately buried; and so on. But there are also issues that go beyond these natural scientific questions: why would humans deliberately bury their dead, what – in the words of Arnold van Gennep's famous anthropological study – do 'rites of passage' mean? Even more basically, when we speak about human origins, what does the word 'human' mean for us? It's this kind of question that philosophers raise explicitly and try to answer.

Apart from my contact with people like Eric Voegelin and their work, there was another mighty pressure on my taking up this inquiry. This was the (always for me slightly frightening) fact that up to five hundred students had signed up for a course in what was rather grandly called philosophical anthropology (the part of philosophy dealing with what makes a human being human). And the English-speaking world I and the students are living in is far more likely to focus on that question in the context of science, ethics, politics, and of course, human origins, than on more specifically philosophical topics like metaphysics or theory of knowledge. So, spurred

---

9 For example, Juan Luis Arsuaga and Ignacio Martínez, *The Chosen Species: The Long March of Human Evolution*, Oxford: Blackwell, 2006; Glenn Conroy, *Reconstructing Human Origins: A Modern Synthesis*, New York: Norton, 1997; Robin Dunbar, *The Human Story: A New History of Mankind's Evolution*, London: Faber & Faber, 2004; Jan Klein and Naoyuki Takahata, *Where Do We Come From? The Molecular Evidence for Human Descent*, Berlin: Springer, 2002; Richard G. Klein, *The Human Career: Human Biological and Cultural Origins*, Chicago: University of Chicago Press, 1999; Richard Leakey and Roger Lewin, *Origins Reconsidered: In Search of What Makes Us Human*, New York: Anchor Books, 1993; Chris Stringer, and Robin McKie, *African Exodus: The Origins of Modern Humanity*, London: Pimlico, 1997; Ian Tattersall, *Becoming Human: Evolution and Human Uniqueness*, New York: Harcourt Brace, 1998.

10 Michael Ruse, 'Philosophy and Paleoanthropology: Some Shared Interests?' in G. A. Clark and C. M. Willermet, eds., *Conceptual Issues in Modern Human Origins Research*, New York: Aldine de Gruyter, 1997, pp. 423–35, at pp. 426–7.

on by my earlier interest in psychology, then in an applied philosophy of humanity in history, and aware of the questions the culture around me asks regarding human origins, I began to work up a course on the topic.

My first efforts in this investigation were expressed in a set of student notes for which I borrowed the title of Walker Percy's *Lost in the Cosmos*.[11] I realised how closely intertwined our understanding of the unfolding of the cosmos, biological evolution, and human emergence were. That meant I'd need to go back to the beginning, to what we know as the Big Bang, 13.7 billion years ago. And once the process that began with the Big Bang moved on to living things, I'd have to see just how human origins fitted into that long process of evolutionary development. As a philosopher I'd be asking further questions about how the whole process started, whether human beings simply derive from that process or if their existence poses questions of a different sort to the questions asked by natural scientists.

So in this book I will be writing about human origins in the context both of evolution and of creation – later on, I'll be talking about the difference between creation, which is a standard topic in what's called natural or philosophical theology, and 'creationism', which is a very particular take on creation that smuggles into natural science what I think is a misunderstanding of theism. Behind that topic will be the main argument of this book, which is that human beings are both continuous with evolutionary process and discontinuous with it.

7. Why the 'big mystery' and why 'origins', plural?

The book's title makes a nod to Australian neurologist John Eccles' book, *The Human Mystery*.[12] We'll be referring to at least one event – the Big Bang – occurring at the limits of the natural sciences' ability to explain it as posing a boundary or threshold question. I'll also be suggesting here that there's another event, occurring at the limits of anthropology's ability to explain it – the coming into existence of each human being and of the whole human family.

The book's subtitle is 'human origins in the light of creation and evolution'. Why the plural 'origins'? We'll explore as fully as possible the evolutionary side of our origins in terms of the almost 7-million-year-long sequence of those beings we're most closely related to, called hominids, who themselves belong to the over 550-million-year-long sequence of multi-

---

11 See note 3.

12 John Eccles, *The Human Mystery*, Berlin: Springer, 1979.

cellular animals. As we'll suggest later, everything that exists has a question about its existence as such attached to it. But what makes human beings different is that we ourselves are aware of this questionability of existence. Asking and to some extent receiving an answer to that question enters into the very definition of what it is to be human. If we're to be faithful to the evidence of our own consciousness then we'll have to explore another kind of origin along with our evolutionary one.

8. The story this book will be telling

When I went to update my work in this area at the University of Chicago a few years ago, I was pleasantly surprised. I had thought I'd have to argue my philosophical case against materialist or exclusively biological preconceptions of the experts in the area. Quite the contrary: again and again I was struck by the overall consensus among the most prominent scientists that the emergence of *Homo sapiens* requires a radical shift in intellectual perspective, even if they themselves did not follow up the philosophical implications of that shift. This encouraged me to take up the questions raised or prompted by this consensus and explore human origins from the perspective of philosophical anthropology, building on the tremendous work done by the leading paleontologists (specialists in hominid studies) and paleoanthropologists (specialists in the earliest human skeletal and archaeological evidence).

Since I'd like to think of this book as an invitation to join in the quest of 'the Quest that summons all true men' (need I say, meaning all true human beings, female and male), I've tried to have each chapter focus on a set of questions we need to ask in order to get closer to an understanding of the human mystery. There's no hope in a book with such a wide sweep as this that the many issues touched on are anything close to fully worked out: I can only invite readers to make what corrections are needed and carry on the quest themselves, following the hints given here. I've divided that quest into five parts – the first a conversation with myth, philosophy and revelation on what it is to be human, and on nature; the second continues that conversation with the natural sciences, especially biology; the third and fourth parts advance the dialogue on human origins between the natural sciences and philosophy; the final part focuses on the human person as requiring a deeper dimension of the dialogue.

Part One: A conversation between myth, philosophy and revelation on the human and on nature: This conversation will continue right through the book, particularly with the natural sciences that deal with evolution and paleoanthropology (we'll take up those important partners in the dialogue in Part Two). It's a dialogue that's necessary firstly because each of these partners in the conversation about the truth of human existence explores different dimensions of the human with its own methods, strengths and limits. Secondly because our contemporary culture, while it respects science, can sometimes suffer from a historical amnesia about the validity and value of the other ways of exploring reality, thereby hindering us from 'ascending the humane' – Wallace Stevens' memorable phrase in what he called his 'poem about tradition'.[13]

Chapter One: 'Is there a barcode for humanity?' We'll begin our quest with the question: what do we mean by 'human'? Because if we don't know what we're looking for, there's a fair chance we won't recognise it if we find it. It might seem strange, but the self-understanding of what it is to be human was a real discovery, and we'll trace that discovery, which happened with full clarity just three times in history – in classical Greece from Homer up to Aristotle, in biblical Israel, and in New Testament Christianity. I should say here that our inquiry is primarily philosophical, not theological, so I'm not presuming readers are believers. Still, like Eric Voegelin's philosophy of politics and history and his underlying philosophical anthropology, no serious exploration of these issues can ignore the empirical data to be found in the revelational texts of Judaism and Christianity, nor their formative influence on all later Western culture, including philosophy and the natural sciences.

Chapter Two: 'In the beginning ... ' Here we'll reflect on how the natural world has been regarded in myth, philosophy, revelation and art, as a reminder that the natural scientific approach occurred and still occurs within that much richer context.

---

13 Wallace Stevens, 'Recitation after Dinner' in *Opus Posthumous*, New York: Vintage, 1990, pp. 114–15.

Part Two: The scientific partners in the conversation: what science is and how it can complement rather than replace or invalidate philosophy and revelation: To prepare the way for the exploration of human origins later, we'll need to examine the nature of scientific thinking, along with the particular area of science that deals with the theory of evolution in biology and zoology.

Chapter Three: 'The universe must have known we were coming' was physicist Freeman Dyson's summarising insight into the human significance of the material universe. Here we'll have a look at the steps in existence that lead to human beings, particularly the first two steps, the astrophysical and the chemical. We'll examine the notion of boundary questions – that is, questions which arise within, though at the edge of, 'each of the natural sciences, but which can't be answered from within them.[14] After checking out how the natural sciences presuppose a theory of knowledge and of reality, and arise out of a rich cultural matrix, we'll see how the sequence of natural sciences dovetails with the sequence of different levels in reality. The chapter will finish by noting that while science can sometimes lose its way, it can complement the other ways of knowing, particularly here, philosophy.

Chapter Four: Darwin and the evolution of evolution will begin by outlining the scientific strength of Charles Darwin's evolutionary theory, and – what may be a surprise – his awareness of an order of reality wider than that of biology. His failure, however, to allow for what's been called natural theology has had a few unfortunate consequences. One of these has been the later development of what we'll have to call 'evolutionism' as a secular religion, which itself bears at least some of the blame for what's called 'creationism' (not at all the same as 'creation' as we'll see). On the base of the High Cross at Monasterboice are two gentlemen eternally tugging at each other's beards, and the similar tug of war between evolutionists and creationists suggests that the way ahead is a deeper look at both evolution and creation. We'll go on to explore the 'evolution of evolution' in some of the contemporary modifications of the theory of evolution, and a philosophical notion of development to

---

14 I found the notion of 'threshold question' in Robert P. George and Patrick Lee, 'Acorns and Embryos,'*The New Atlantis*, Number 7, Fall 2004/Winter 2005, pp. 90–100, at pp. 90–1, in their discussion of the humanity of the human embryo.

be found in Bernard Lonergan's *Insight*. We'll conclude with the notion of complementarity introduced in the previous chapter, but now applied to the ongoing conversation between biology, philosophy and revelation.

Part Three: How we belong and yet – because of the 'human revolution' – don't fully belong to the hominid sequence: Having clarified some of the strengths and limits of science and of biological science, we're in a better position to take up our topic of human origins – at least one aspect of those origins. That aspect can firmly be placed within the amazingly swift evolutionary sequence from the first hominids up to the human body plan. But do we quite fit into that evolutionary context? The next two chapters will give these questions an airing.

Chapter Five: Hanging by our ancestors' tails? We're strikingly close anatomically to the later hominids. In this chapter we'll recall the development that took place among all the hominids, starting with the first chimpanzee-sized ones in Chad nearly 7 million years ago. Because there's more known about the Neanderthals than any of the other late hominids, most of the chapter will focus on what they could and couldn't do, particularly their lack of symbolisation. And a key question we'll be asking will be whether we should study the pre-human hominids under zoology as animals, or under anthropology as early modern humans.

Chapter Six: On the threshold of the Human Mystery: was there a human revolution? This chapter will discuss how paleoanthropologists define the human, then take a look at two competing approaches to when humans first emerged: there's an approach which sees us emerging gradually, called the multiregional theory, while another approach insists that human emergence was a sudden and one-off event, called by some paleoanthropologists 'the human revolution'. Sally McBrearty and Allison Brooks countered this with a celebrated book-length article called 'The Revolution that Wasn't', so we'll note these different views, and end by asking whether human emergence is fully explicable by paleontology and archaeology.

Part Four: The seven grace notes in the 'Sonata for a Good Man': What it is exactly that has to be to be present in the remains of a once-living being for the paleontologist or paleoanthropologist to pronounce it 'human' is, not infrequently, less than adequately explored by the scholars themselves, so we'll devote five chapters to filling out empirically just what makes a human being 'human' and why. Our focus will be on seven characteristics or grace notes in what we'll call 'the sonata for a good man'.[15] All of which lead us – while emphatically embodied in the space-time universe – both to depths within ourselves and each other, as well as on principle beyond the edge of the observable universe, about 46 billion light years away. As David Walsh puts it: 'We do not live within the physical universe; we live within the human community.'[16] Or in Martin Buber's language of *I and Thou*:

> Every *It* is bounded by others; *It* exists only through being bounded by others. But when *Thou* is spoken, there is no thing. *Thou* has no bounds ... And just as prayer is not in time but time in prayer, sacrifice not in space but space in sacrifice, and to reverse the relation is to abolish the reality, so with the man to whom I say *Thou*. I do not meet with him [primarily] at some time or place or other.[17]

Chapter Seven: The first three grace notes in the human sonata: (1) the genetic 'African Eve & Adam', (2) our culture-oriented body plan, and (3) our meaning-oriented brain and vocal tract. Now we're on the last leg of our 'Journey to the Centre of the Person', exploring what makes human beings radically different from all others on this earth. We'll see how genetic factors, along with their expression in the human body plan, and the human brain and vocal tract, constitute the material basis for that radical difference paleontologists have discussed in terms of 'the human revolution'.

Chapter Eight: Two more grace notes in the human sonata: (4) symbolisation and (5) language. Since our capacity for symbolisation and language are what most paleontologists and archaeologists take as the first unmistakeable and observable indications of a radically new

---

15 Lest the use of 'man' gives offence, the reference is to a scene from a German film, where of course *Mensch* means man and woman – the meaning intended here.

16 David Walsh, 'The Unattainability of What We Live Within: Liberal Democracy' in Anton Rauscher, ed., *Die fragile Demokratie – The Fragility of Democracy*, Berlin: Duncker & Humblot, 2007, pp. 133–56, at p. 139.

17 Martin Buber, *I and Thou*, Edinburgh: T. & T. Clark, 1966, p. 4, p. 8.

species *Homo sapiens*, we'll spend some time exploring what in fact is a single capacity for shared meaning. The discussion of symbolisation will lead us through Mircea Eliade's and Marie König's articulation of the very earliest human symbols, along with what we'll call Eric Voegelin's 'depth grammar' of (archaic) human symbolisation. We'll apply their analyses to some of the earliest instances of symbolisation in 'cave art' and early human burials. The section on language will touch on a few theories on the origins of language, outline language as a carrier of meaning and conclude that while animals communicate, they don't use language.

Chapter Nine: The last chords in the human sonata: (6) understanding and (7) freedom. Traditionally, philosophers have focused on these two areas as the primary indications of what constitutes our humanity. We'll examine Lonergan's understanding of understanding, and go on from the cognitive aspect of understanding to the existential, taking John Henry Newman, Socrates and Sophie Scholl as paradigms of what living the truth can mean. We'll finish with a note on the problem of living in untruth. In the section on freedom, we'll see how Richard Dawkins, Daniel Dennett and Stephen Hawking seem to explain freedom away, then go on to Lonergan on freedom, and conclude with a reflection on the mystery of evil.

Chapter Ten: The human person's limitless orientation to horizons of beauty, meaning, truth and goodness. All along we've been following the lead of prominent scientists whose engagement with the data raised questions that seemed to point beyond a reductively and exclusively biological view of what it is that makes human beings 'human'. In this chapter we continue along that arc of inquiry, taking up what we've named the last four notes of the human sonata and reformulating them as capacities which by their nature go far beyond the limits of the animal needs of survival and reproduction. Again we'll propose actual human beings – Jewish Auschwitz victim Etty Hillesum and leading Nazi Albert Speer – as examples of human good and evil that can't be explained in less than moral terms.

Part Five: Meeting you face to face – the human person as Communion: The 'Sonata for a Good Man', focused on the characteristics that make a human being human. Our last chapter will touch on why the human person – while of course measurable and weighable, and very much part of this universe – if not *Lost in the Cosmos*, is certainly not bound by it.

Chapter Eleven: From Big Bang to Big Mystery. Our long journey will arrive at something like a mountain top here, as we explore the 'Big Mystery' of the book's title, namely, the mystery that each of us is and the mystery that the human family as a whole is. Of the human person we'll ask three questions: 'Who am I?', and answer it in terms of the intrinsic youwardness and wewardness that we are. Then we'll ask, 'What am I?' and draw on Lonergan's notion of a unity-identity-whole to in some way articulate the nature of the human person. Thirdly we'll ask 'How do I come into existence?' This will lead to a brief review of the current scientific understanding of the human zygote and embryo, followed by a reflection on the two origins of the human mentioned in the book's title, through the cooperative action of creation and pro-creation. The broader question of the origins of humankind will see the human family as originating both in creation and in the wider 'pro-creation' of the cosmos and evolutionary process.

Part One: A conversation between myth, philosophy and revelation on the human and on nature

Chapter One: Is there a barcode for humanity?

The basic problem of our inquiry is: how do we know if something is human or not? If you're reading about human origins, the word 'human' simply jumps out at you from the book titles – *The Human Revolution*, *Principles of Human Evolution*, *The Origins of Modern Humanity*, or phrases like 'early modern humans.' There are lots of words deriving from the Latin word, *Homo*, for human being, starting with 'hominids' (more recently changed to 'hominins') for the whole range of beings with body plans rather like our own, who show up from perhaps over 6 million years ago. Among these are the later hominids, with names like *Homo erectus*, *Homo heidelbergensis*, *Homo neanderthalensis*, dating back to around 2 million years ago, all seen as different species of the overall genus *Homo*. It's as if Noah was rushed on the gangway by an enormously diversified bunch of would-be travellers, all insisting on first-class seats. Certainly, in terms of paleontology, or the study of all of these human-like beings, the cabins reserved for 'humans' on the Ark would have been seriously overcrowded.[1] The reason this chapter is important is that it will narrow down the philosophical meaning of 'human' (or *Homo*) so that it refers to human beings and nothing else.

We badly need a clear understanding of what we mean by 'human', otherwise the question of human origins remains confused. I'll be following Eric Voegelin's understanding of the drama of humanity in suggesting that the notion of what it is to be human emerges only three times in history – in the Hebrew Bible, in classic Greek philosophy, and in the New Testament.[2] Karl Jaspers (1883–1969) wrote of the 'axis time of humanity',

---

1 The culprit for at least some of this is the taxonomist Carl Linnaeus (1701–1778) from Sweden. His hard work in tidying up biological, botanical and zoological classification included combining the notion of genus or 'kind' used by an earlier Swiss classifier, Konrad von Gesner (1516–1565) with the seventeenth-century English zoologist and comparative anatomist, John Ray's notion of species, so that he could apply the notions of genus and species to all plant and animal types. But when he tried out his categories of genus and species on human beings, what he got was the genus '*Homo*', with ourselves belonging to the '*Sapiens*' or 'knowing' species, and a few other species of '*Homo*' thrown in for good measure. This presumed there was a range of different species of humans as there is, for, say, the cat genus, from ferocious Siberian tigers down to Felix the Cat. For background on this issue, see B. A. Wood, 'The History of the Genus Homo', *Human Evolution*, Vol. 15, 1–2, Jan–Jun 2000, pp. 39–49, or the first chapter, 'The Path of Human Evolution', in Ian Tattersall and Geoffrey H. Schwartz's *Extinct Humans*, New York: Westview Press, 2000. Since his approach has had enormous implications for paleoanthropology, we'll return to him later.

2 In the introductory part of the first of his 1967 'Drama of Humanity' lectures at Emory

in which a whole series of spiritual outbursts occurred from the Pacific to the Atlantic. What these 'spiritual outbreaks' were superseding was what Voegelin understood as the compact or undifferentiated experience where the major partners in being – gods and humans, society and the natural world – are all so closely interwoven in a single pattern of existence that it's almost impossible to separate them. In that experience, the regular recurrence of what we'd see as the cycles of the natural world are the primary sources of the order of all the other partners.

In each of these outbreaks there occurred what Henri Bergson (1859–1941) called 'the opening of the soul'. This opening or self-discovery of the soul in Israel began around 1300BC with Moses, and continued and deepened with the Jewish prophets Isaiah, Jeremiah and Ezekiel, dating from around 700 BC. In Greece the discoveries were made by Xenophanes, Parmenides and Heraclitus, around 500 BC, and later developed by Socrates, Plato and Aristotle from about 400 BC. It was the period when human beings first reflected explicitly on their own nature and origins, breaking more or less decisively with the myth. Within this rich cultural context, both of Athens and Jerusalem, occurred the New Testament revelation of the human.

Along with these differentiations of the human there were the less clear breaks with the myth in the great Eastern religions, all about or after 500 BC.[3] In China, Confucius exhorts us to develop as the humane man – what he considered himself to be; Lao Tzu exalted the wise man or sage as someone at least as important as the emperor. In India, the Hindu Upanishads speak of cultivating our Atman, or self; also in India there emerged the Buddhist notion of becoming a *boddhisattva*, an enlightened one.

All of these breakthroughs, partial or complete, happened against the understanding of human existence within the context of the myth. Myth

---

University, Voegelin explained the title, with 'humanity' referring to the underlying constant of human self-understanding and 'history' referring to the vicissitudes that self-understanding undergoes: '*Humanity* means man in a mode of understanding himself in his relation to God, world, and society, and those modes change. History would be the drama (if a meaning in it can be discovered), of humanity, of the self-understanding of man.' See Eric Voegelin, 'The Drama of Humanity', in *The Drama of Humanity and Other Miscellaneous Papers, 1939–1985*, eds. William Petropulos and Gilbert Weiss, Columbia, MO: University of Missouri Press, 2004, p. 186.

3 Voegelin borrows the word 'differentiation' from biology where it refers to the process by which a less specialised cell becomes a more specialised cell type. He uses it to refer to the intellectual and spiritual clarification of the major partners in reality – human, social, historic, natural and divine – from the more 'compact' myth where all of these realities are experienced as a whole. The differentiations of philosophy, revelation and the natural sciences gradually develop more adequate symbols to explain the separate natures and roles of the partners.

was the default form of human experience for 150,000 years or more, so in a later chapter when we're considering the first humans we will set out a framework rich enough to include both mythic and post-mythic forms of experience. But our investigation is primarily philosophic, so we'll begin with the Greek odyssey of the human spirit, before exploring examples from the Hebrew Bible and the New Testament. I should warn the reader that it's only if we carry on these dialogues within ourselves that they can have any relevance for our quest for human origins. Awareness of our humanity isn't a matter of drawing a conclusion to an argument, but of rising to a level of self-reflection within the person doing the seeking. So, let's call these examples 'exercises in meditation'. I've always liked what seems a rash remark of Voegelin's, that in the search for truth about human existence, the test of truth will be its lack of originality.[4] So these meditations shouldn't end with results we don't recognise as reminders of what we mean by human.

1. The Greek discovery of human nature

During his visit to Ireland to see the Irish Neolithic sites at Newgrange and Céide Fields in 1972, I asked Eric Voegelin which books had most helped him in his development of a philosophy of history. To my surprise he put classical philologist Bruno Snell's 1946 *The Discovery of the Mind* high up on his list. The point was that the 'mind' – *'Geist'* is the German word for both 'mind' and 'spirit' – the essential component of our humanity, was a discovery, one that was made in classical Greece in what we can characterise as a questing odyssey from Homer through the Greek mystic philosophers, the tragic poets, and the classic philosophers, Socrates, Plato and Aristotle.[5] That odyssey has been best explored, in my opinion, in Voegelin's 1957 *The World of the Polis*, but all that's needed here is to mention some of its high points.

Let's keep an eye on what we're trying to clarify in this chapter: what should we be looking for when we're looking for the origins of the first human beings? In the world of the myth, humans find their meaning beyond themselves in what they consider the more unchanging and majestic rhythms of the cosmos. What's going on during the emergence of philosophy in classical Greece is a gradual discovery of the difference

4 Eric Voegelin, 'Equivalences of Experience and Symbolisation in History', in *Published Essays 1966–1985*, ed. Ellis Sandoz, Baton Rouge: Louisiana State University Press, 1990, p. 122.

5 Voegelin deals with the parallel discovery in ancient Israel of what it is to be human in his *Israel and Revelation*.

between what Voegelin called the partners in being: divine reality, human beings, human society and the natural world. So Plato first coined the word 'theology' for God, and to Aristotle we owe the first technical use of the terms 'ethics' for humans, 'politics' for human society, and 'physics' for the natural world. It'll be important to get hold of what the Greeks came to mean by human, since that technical understanding is still a key component of our usage of the word 'human' today.

For many years my MA students worked through Voegelin's *The World of the Polis* as a text for their weekly seminars – each week a student would introduce a chapter, on Hesiod, Heraclitus, Parmenides, Aeschylus, and so on, until we'd covered the 350-year period from Homer to Thucydides.[6] Of course I gained more than they did, as I had the advantage, year by year, of listening in on their own discovery of what was going on: the emergence both of the Greek understanding of the autonomous individual under God, and of the social and political reality that was formed by such individuals under God. Remembering what we're looking for here – the earliest discovery by human reason of itself as the characteristic mark of the human – I'll pick out three moments of that centuries-long process: the three great 'mystic philosophers', as Voegelin calls Xenophanes, Heraclitus and Parmenides, all roughly from around 500 BC, and conclude with a few remarks on the better-known Plato and Aristotle. Of course, more relevant than simply recovering their texts is the task each of us has to recover the experiences underlying them. As Voegelin remarks in his essay 'On Classical Studies':

> The Greek differentiation of reason in existence has set critical standards for the exploration of consciousness behind which nobody is permitted to fall back. This achievement, however, is not a possession forever, something like a precious heirloom to be handed on to later generations, but a paradigmatic action to be explored in order to be continued under the conditions of our time.[7]

So, these texts will work for us if we allow them to push our own self-exploration as far as the mystic philosophers went themselves.

---

6 Eric Voegelin, *The World of the Polis*, Baton Rouge, Louisiana State University Press, 1964, referred to in the text here as *OH2*.

7 Eric Voegelin, 'On Classical Studies', in *Published Essays 1966–1985*, p. 264.

1.1 Xenophanes (c. 565–470BC) – human existence as capacity for wisdom reaching out to the One divine reality. What we find in Xenophanes is the emergence both of a deeper understanding of the nature of the divine, and of the human being who participates in that divine. So, for the first time in Greek experience there's an indication of the divine as the One, rather than the many gods of the Greek myth. Aristotle quotes Xenophanes as saying:

> Looking up at the expanse of the Heaven, 'The One,' he said,' is the God.' (*OH2*, 181)

This comment always brings back to me my wonder at the huge handfuls of stars I remember seeing in the incredibly bright southern skies over Kakadu in Northern Territory, Australia. The awe I felt – especially as a city dweller who rarely gets to see the majesty of a starry night any more – nudged me towards Xenophanes' conclusion that underlying all those galaxies upon galaxies is not only the oneness of a single universe, but their transparency in tumbling into existence from One transfinite source.

Voegelin understands Xenophanes' discovery of the transcendent One as correlative with an incipient articulation of our common humanity based on our capacity through our shared wisdom to recognise that One. We can take this as Xenophanes' contribution to our understanding of what makes us human.

Some of my students were atheists, so I asked if they'd ever had anything like Xenophanes' over-arching experience of the One. One student spoke of watching dawn breaking over the ocean from a mountain in Hawaii as the nearest to an experience of transcendence she'd had, which I thought wasn't that far from Xenophanes' formulation, 'Looking up at the expanse of the Heaven ... '

Along with that correlative set of insights into the human and the divine there's a clearing away of the human-all-too-human characteristics of those earlier gods. Xenophanes was very much aware of the limitations of the mythic way of articulating transcendent existence, criticising inadequate ways of symbolising the One:

> Homer and Hesiod have ascribed to the gods all things that are a shame and disgrace among men, such as stealing, adultery and cheating each other (B11, *OH2*, 172). Ethiopians make their gods flat-nosed and black, the Thracians let theirs have blue eyes and red hair. (B16, *OH2*, 172)

Rather,

> One God is greatest among gods and men, not like mortals in body or thought. (B23, *OH2*, 179).

The divine is a living being though not of articulated form, for 'all through it sees, all through it thinks, all through it hears'. (B24, *OH2*, 172)

> Without effort it sways all things through its thought (B25, *OH2*, 172). It ever abides in the self-same place and never moves; nor is it seemly [*epiprepei*] for it to go now hither now thither. (B26, *OH2*, 172)

The Xenophanes who has experienced the One is aware of the difference this insight makes, not just for him, but for every human being. With justified indignation, he criticises his society for rewarding people, not on the basis of the very quality which marks out the human – wisdom – but the merely physical attributes which were more highly regarded:

> If a man through swiftness of foot should gain victory ... /Or if he should hold his own in painful boxing ... /He would become glorious in the view of the citizens, /He would gain a front seat of honour at the games ... /And he would not be worthy to have it as I! ... /For better than the strength /Of men or horses is our wisdom [*sophie*]! Senseless indeed is custom in such matter; it is not right [*dikaion*]/To judge strength higher than holy wisdom. (B2, *OH2*, 184)

For Voegelin, *sophie* refers to 'the differentiation of personality, together with [its] correlative body of knowledge'. Xenophanes was fully aware that his discovery of this capacity of wisdom wasn't merely an individual matter. 'He had discovered new areas of experience; and he knew that the differentiation of such experiences was an actualisation of the common essence of man' (*OH2*, 185, 186).

Along with his attack on the earlier mythic conception of the gods, Xenophanes criticises the merely military qualities of physical strength as a standard for judging the human. So he does two things: (1) He rules out the mythic language for the gods as not 'seemly', and (2) he rejects the merely conventional language for human excellences as not 'right'. The new human being doesn't find his meaning in tribal gods but in the universal

One, to whom all human beings are related and in relation to whom they find their meaning.

This discovery of what it is to be human as intrinsically rooted in the transcendent divine One will remain as the enduring Greek insight into human nature to be continued by Parmenides and Heraclitus. It's not unlike the classical Chinese experience where, in relation to the Way of Heaven, *T'ien*, there is also the reign of heaven, literally what's under heaven, *T'ien hsia*, so what unites everyone in the Middle Kingdom is their shared status of being under the Way of Heaven. Xenophanes too can be interpreted as saying that our common experience of the One unites us into a common humanity.

1.2 Parmenides (c. 520–450BC) articulates the human mind as understanding exsistence beyond space and time. Parmenides was the first to formulate the experience of being-as-such. What we're interested in here is the discovery of what it is to be human, where for Parmenides the meaning of the human is buried in the mystery of existence. For the first time the immense gap between existence and non-existence is articulated:

> The one way, that *Is* and that *Not is* cannot be, is the path of Persuasion which is attendant upon Truth. (B2, *OH2*, 209)

Voegelin highlights the carefulness with which Parmenides has articulated his experience of transcendence by indicating why Parmenides chose to use what Voegelin translates as *Is*, without a grammatical subject, rather than the word Being. Parmenides wanted to make sure that the object of his experience is not considered as a thing among other things. Having safeguarded the world-transcendent nature of his experience of Existence as such, Parmenides than carves out its implications as trans-spatial and trans-temporal:

> One way only is left to be spoken of, that Is; and on this way are many signs that Is is uncreated and imperishable, whole, unmoved, and without end. And it was not, and it will not be, for it is altogether Now ... The decision on these matters depends on the following: *Is* or *Is Not* ... How could *Is* perish? ... Thus is 'becoming' extinguished and 'passing away' not to be heard of (B8, *OH2*, 209, 212).

And as Xenophanes highlighted the specific nature of the human that can experience the One, Parmenides has his own specific meaning for our capacity to experience the *Is*:

> Look with the Nous as it makes present with certainty the absent (B4, *OH2*, 208). Restrain your thought from this way of inquiry; let not much-experienced habit force you on this way, giving reign to the unseeing eye and the droning ear and the tongue, but make your decision in the much disputed inquiry by means of argument (*logos*). (B7, *OH2*, 209)

Parmenides' beginning of an explicit reflection on the nature of the human is to give a technical meaning to the words *nous* and *logos*, translated as 'mind' and 'reason,' where they stand for whatever it is in us that can reach out to the transcendent and – as the Prologue to his reflections shows – be reached into by the transcendent.

Later, when we come to speak about human language, what Parmenides has to say will be very relevant – that what our language is expressing in the first place is our experience of Being, or what he calls *Is*, and in the light of that overarching experience, that of all other beings. In other words, for Parmenides, we are Being-seekers, and human language is a web of intended meanings laced around that central experience of *Is*. However – and this is why we've left him till last, even though he probably preceded Parmenides by a few years – it's Heraclitus, of all the mystic philosophers, who most clearly focuses on what we can now call a philosophical anthropology, a philosophical reflection on the nature of the human.

But that nature primarily refers to human existence, which we can glean from Parmenides' fragment 3, 'for, what is, is the same to thinking and being'. Commenting on this, David Walsh in his forthcoming *The Politics of the Person* notes that 'The coincidence of thinking and being ... has its consummate application only in the case where thinking has become the path of being. That is the prerogative of the moral law.' In other words – and this also can be found in Parmenides' Prologue to his speculation on knowledge and being – who we are as seekers of being is only unfolded if our living is in harmony with our understanding.

1.3 Heraclitus (c. 535–475BC) – human being as possessing *logos*, reason, grounded in divine *Logos*. What we find in Heraclitus too, but more dramatically than in the other two mystic philosophers, is a correlative understanding of the nature of the divine along with the nature of the human. Heraclitus deliberately chose the aphorism as a way of communicating insights that keep us guessing, or better, meditating – as if he was aware of Saul Bellow's warning that 'we mustn't forget how quickly the visions of genius become the canned goods of intellectuals'.[8]

His first 'fragment' is the longest one, where he points towards something like the one source of all beings:

> This *Logos* here, though it is eternal, men are unable to understand before they hear it as well as when they hear it first. For, though all things come to pass in accordance with this *Logos*, they are like untried men when they try words and deeds such as I set forth, explaining each thing according to its nature and showing what the real state of the case is. But as to these other men, it escapes their notice what they do when they awake, as it escapes their memory what they do when asleep. (B1, *OH2*, 230)

And humans are characterised by our quest for the *Logos* that makes sense of our existence. So we embark on a voyage of self-discovery. Homer's Odysseus had to wander all around the Mediterranean for twenty years to discover who he was. But, for the first time in Heraclitus, we become so aware of ourselves as questionable that we make our own self the object of a quest:

> I explored [or: searched into] myself. (B101, *OH2*, 228)

And that odyssey within and beyond ourselves is a lifelong one, with the quest itself leading to a substantial deepening of who we are. Voegelin understands *logos* here to mean 'an intelligent substance with a depth of understanding' (*OH2*, 227), where the 'fragment' 45 is illuminated by fragment 115:

> You could not find the limits of the soul even if you travelled every path so deep is its *logos* (B45, *OH2*, 227). The soul has a *logos* that augments itself. (B115, *OH2*, 228)

---

8 Saul Bellow, *Herzog*, London: Penguin Classics, 2003, p. 82.

He develops Xenophanes' notion of wisdom as actualising the key human capacity, a wisdom that grasps the ground of our being:

> The one that is wise: to understand the insight that steers all things through all things. (B41, *OH2*, 225)

While the 'fragments' after the first one aren't in any particular order, they can be seen as mutually complementing and expanding each other's meaning. He recalls what can be seen as one of his central themes when he indicates how humans, as human, can be united in their common actualisation of their participation in the transcendent *Logos* or Word or Meaning:

> It is common to all [men] to understand (B113, *OH2*, 232). Listening not to me but to the *logos*, it is wise to agree [*Homologeein* = to be of the same *logos*] that all is one. (B50, *OH2*, 226)

However, Heraclitus is only too aware of how we can avoid being human. In fact, his diagnosis of this failure is so clear that Voegelin can use it to interpret why a certain percentage of the people under Hitler deliberately avoided understanding what was going on. Voegelin also uses the Austrian novelist Heimito von Doderer's term for the wilful blindness that facilitated the National Socialist dictatorship, *Apperzeptionsverweigerung*: refusal to perceive. Heraclitus says of those who refuse to ask the central questions of existence that they are (spiritually) asleep – eerily reminiscent of Hitler's own self-description: 'I go my way with all the assurance of a sleepwalker.' T. S. Eliot's choice of fragment B2 (along with another Heraclitean fragment) to open *The Four Quartets*, his key meditation in the midst of one of the twentieth-century's ideological wars – with Hitler and Nazism – is indicative of its universal diagnostic reach:

> Therefore it is necessary to follow the common [*xynon*]. But though the *Logos* is common, the many live as if they had a wisdom of their own (B2, *OH2*, 232). Those who are awake have a world [*kosmos*] one and common [*xynos*], but those who are asleep each turn aside into their private worlds. (B89, *OH2*, 232)

Some years after Voegelin had written his chapter on Heraclitus, in his lecture on the German University during the Nazi period he showed how relevant he found the mystic philosopher. There he used Heraclitus to diagnose the failure of a community to make a shared actualisation of its capacity for participating in the common *Logos*:

> Through spirit man actualises his potential to partake of the divine. He rises thereby to the *imago Dei* which it is his destiny to be. Spirit in this classical sense of nous, is that which all men have in common, the *xynon* as Heraclitus has called it. Through the life of the spirit, which is common to all, the existence of man becomes existence in community. In the openness of the common spirit there develops the public life of society. He, however, who closes himself against what is common, or who revolts against it, removes himself from the public life of human community. He becomes thereby a private man, or in the language of Heraclitus, an *idiotes*.[9]

Again, to illustrate how central Heraclitus is for an understanding of what it is to be human, Herbert Marcuse, a Jewish-born Marxist philosopher forced to emigrate under Hitler, in a letter of 12 May 1948 criticised Martin Heidegger, Germany's greatest twentieth-century philosopher, for the kind of radical closure to the common existence in truth Heraclitus wrote about:

> You write that everything I say about the extermination of the Jews applies just as much to the Allies, if instead of the 'Jews' one were to insert 'East Germans'. With this sentence don't you stand outside the dimension in which a conversation between men is even possible – outside of the *Logos*?[10]

1.4 Plato (427–347BC) – human existence as dynamically oriented to eternal beauty. Building on the work of these earlier philosophers, Plato sets out his philosophical anthropology in one of his most important dialogues, the Symposium. The participants in the dialogue discuss the origins of Love, where Love comes to represent Socrates as the standard for human existence. Love turns out to be quite a celebrity, with divine

---

9 Eric Voegelin, 'The German University and the Order of German Society: A Reconsideration of the Nazi Era', in *Published Essays 1966–1985*, p. 7.

10 Quoted in Richard Wolin, *The Heidegger Controversy: A Critical Reader*, Cambridge, MA: MIT Press, 1993, p. 163f. (Heidegger was referring to the forced expulsion of ethnic Germans from what had become western Poland after the war.)

parents – the god Plenty and the goddess Poverty – and is born on the goddess Beauty's birthday. Deliberately using the language of the myth, Plato is saying that human nature is both lack and fullness, or better, that it is a dynamic orientation towards unlimited being:

> He is neither mortal nor immortal, for in the space of a day he will be now, when all goes well with him, alive and blooming, and now dying, to be born again by virtue of his father's nature, while what he gains will always ebb away as fast. So Love is never altogether in or out of need, and stands, moreover, midway between (*metaxy*) ignorance and wisdom ... For wisdom is concerned with the loveliest of things, and Love is the love of what is lovely. And so it follows that Love is a lover of wisdom, and, being such, he is placed between wisdom and ignorance. (203e)

Plato beautifully conveys the dynamic orientation that makes human beings human in terms of a love that deepens through the three stages of what I'll call the love of outer, inner and everlasting beauty:

a) **love of outer beauty:** 'First, he will fall in love with the beauty of one individual body, so that his passion may give rise to noble discourse ... Next, he will see that if he is to devote himself to loveliness of form it will be absurd to deny that the beauty of each and every body is the same ... he must be the lover of every lovely body.'

b) **love of inner beauty:** 'Next, he must grasp that the beauties of the body are as nothing to the beauties of the soul, so that wherever he meets with spiritual loveliness, even in the husk of an unlovely body, he will find it beautiful enough to fall in love with and to cherish – and beautiful enough to quicken in his heart a longing for such discourse as tends towards the building of a noble nature. And from this he will be led to contemplate the beauty of laws and institutions.'

c) **love of everlasting beauty:** 'And now, Socrates, there bursts upon him that wondrous vision which is the very soul of the beauty he has toiled so long for. It is an everlasting loveliness which neither comes nor goes, which neither flowers nor fades ... Nor will his vision of the beautiful take the form of a face ... or of anything of the flesh. It will neither be words, nor knowledge, nor a something which exists in something else ... but subsisting of itself and by itself in an eternal oneness, while every lovely thing partakes of it ... Starting from individual beauties, the quest for the universal beauty must find him ever mounting the heavenly ladder ... until at last he comes to know what beauty is.' (210a–211c)

We can summarise Plato's definition of the human here – where he speaks of Love as a spiritual man (*daimonios aner*) – as an incarnate openness to everlasting beauty, or in the language of the Republic, an incarnate openness to the beyond (*epekeina*). I remember a student telling me of how she understood the Symposium very well, as her sister suffered from Down's syndrome. This student didn't stop at her sister's outer appearance, she'd come to appreciate over the years her sister's inner beauty. And – even though she was not a believer in the ordinary sense – somehow she could intuit that that inner beauty of soul was grounded in a beauty more than just human, an everlasting beauty.

1.5 Aristotle (384–322BC) – human existence as quest for participation in the understanding of Understanding. One of the first attempts to deal both with the issue of what is constant in all humanity and the differing stages in the drama of its unfolding, can be found in the first book of Aristotle's *Metaphysics*.[11] Aristotle opens his *Metaphysics* with the programmatic: 'All men by nature reach out for knowledge', more conventionally translated as 'All men by nature desire to know'.

If we first look at the second part of this statement, regarding what all men do, Voegelin suggests the phrase 'desire to know' seems to deserve the more active 'reach out for knowledge', where that knowledge turns out to be questioning, from minor matters to the ground of the cosmos.

Aristotle tells us that philosophy begins in wonder, and speaks of 'a wondering why things should be as they are'. So, wondering implies the quest for the ground of existence, a quest undertaken because of our consciousness of ignorance. Consequently, Voegelin suggests paraphrasing the first line of the *Metaphysics* as: 'All men are by nature in quest of the ground.'

---

11 Much of what follows is a summary of the discussion of Aristotle in Eric Voegelin, *What is History? and Other Late Unpublished Writings*, eds. Thomas A. Hollweck and Paul Caringella, Baton Rouge: Louisiana State University Press, 1990, pp. 99–110.

Now we can turn to the first part of the opening sentence, 'All men are by nature ... ' Who are these 'all'? Aristotle identifies two styles of truth, the two which were known to him (since he didn't know about the Israelite experience of revelation), myth and philosophy. He characterises what both styles have in common: wonder about the ground of being. So he can write that 'the *philomythos* (lover of myth) is in a sense a *philosophos* (lover of wisdom), for myth is composed of wonders'. And we know that he could identify with the lover of myth from a comment in a letter written in his old age: 'the more solitary and isolated I am, the more of a lover of myth I am becoming.'

For Aristotle, we humans are pure capacity or potency at the level of intelligence, a capacity we can actualise gradually in the wonder-filled knowledge either of myth or philosophy. As a philosopher he has arrived at the insight that God, both in existence and in intelligence, is pure act. Later on in the *Metaphysics* (1074 b34), his name for God is 'the understanding of understanding'. So we can say that, in an Aristotelian context, what it is to be human can be defined as the being in quest of the ground of existence, where that ground is 'the understanding of understanding'.

There's also Aristotle's complementary ethical understanding of human existence that can be gleaned from his *Nicomachean Ethics*, Book 10, chapter 7, where he advocates that humans shouldn't merely live mortally, but should 'immortalise' (*athanatizein* – Aristotle makes a verb out of the adjective for immortal, *athanatos*) as much as possible. That immortalising or living within yet beyond time is the gradual actualisation of our participation in the divine Good, so that Plato and Aristotle in the end have much the same understanding of the human.

But there are other differentiations of human existence that may have had an even greater impact on Western culture than classic Greek philosophy. We'll now look at the notion of the human person in the Book of Job and in the Gospel of St John, which received more extended treatments in chapters six and seven of my *The Drama of Humanity*.

2. An exploration of the human in the Book of Job
Les Murray asks what he entitles 'The Knockdown Question' in a short poem:

> Why does God not spare the innocent?
> The answer to that is not in
> the same world as the question

so you would shrink from me
in terror if I could answer it.[12]

Murray catches the mysteriousness of what it is to be human – that we can ask questions whose answers go beyond the space-time universe. Even more than classic Greek philosophy, does Hebrew revelation explore who we are? Certainly not in the structured way of Greek reasoning, yet its own rationality arrives at an equivalent place through a form of radical interpersonal openness. Abraham Heschel contrasted the two approaches, with philosophy emphasising man (or the human) in search of God, and revelation emphasising that God is in search of man.[13] Of course both quests can be found in the Hebrew Bible, where Job seeks to understand himself in terms of his relation to God, and where God believes that Job will come to understand Him.

The Book of Job deals with a new question which didn't arise in Genesis – the suffering of a completely innocent human being – because of course, Adam and Eve weren't all that innocent, but colluded with Satan. Not only is that question of innocent suffering an expansion of Genesis, it is also bound up with the development of the experience in Exodus both of God as I AM, and of the humans addressed by God as a Thou, as a you-for-God. The author of *Job* could draw on the surrounding literatures: Mesopotamian, Egyptian and Ugaritic. So as part of a movement towards the universalisation of the earlier differentiations of man and God, he was able to portray in *Job* a cast of non-Jewish characters.

As regards man, the biblical writers recognise that Israel as a people under God has narrowed down to the prophets as individuals. Jeremiah is the representative figure, who as a lone spiritual personality shoulders the responsibilities for the sake of the whole people of Israel. In him, the chosen people had become the chosen man. Voegelin remarks that it's in Jeremiah's own soul that the clash between the divinely willed order of history and the earlier moral-cultic requirements takes place.[14] Since mere observance of legal and cultic prescriptions could be accompanied by a

---

12 Les Murray, *New Collected Poems*, Manchester: Carcanet, 2003, p. 538.

13 Abraham Heschel, *God in Search of Man: A Philosophy of Judaism*, New York: Harper & Row, 1955. For a fuller exploration of the topic from a philosophical perspective, see Maurice P. Hogan, *The Biblical Vision of the Human Person: Implications for a Philosophical Anthropology*, Frankfurt: Peter Lang, 1994.

14 Eric Voegelin, *Israel and Revelation*, Baton Rouge: Louisiana State University Press, 1969, p. 461.

life in violation of the spirit, the prophetic critique contrasted the newly differentiated experience of the right order of the individual soul with the externals of mere behaviour. To carry out this critique, the prophets had to develop a new vocabulary for a new anthropology of personal responsibility – where humility, righteousness, knowledge and fear of God, but especially the heart, and its *hesed* or love, was understood to be the core of a new type of human being. *Job* will, in part, turn on the fact that not even the good conduct of a man in accordance with the law and the cult is sufficient.

The prologue unfolds the basic theme of the story: the clash between two ways of relationship, a first based on utilitarian calculation, a second based on the intrinsic worth of the other, for whom any sacrifice can be made.[15] The religion of Job's friends turns out to be a mere religiosity, leading them to identify social success with moral goodness and divine approval and social failure with wickedness and divine disapproval, manifested by the chastisement of Job's loss of wealth and social status. God is shown as having an unbreakable confidence that this figure, externally and physically reduced to zero, is capable of loving Him for His own sake and not at all for what he can gain from that relationship.

At the very beginning of his lament, Job has universalised his own condition to a 'tragic sense of life' for all humanity, a tragedy all the more anguished because it seems to have been willed by the personal Creator-God.

Job has everything the world regards highly, and by losing it he can be stripped down to everyman. The process is not pleasant, and Job's lament in chapter three takes the form of a series of 'Whys?' The first two 'Whys?' refer to his own condition. The following two broaden the question to include the suffering of all humans, particularly the second of these, which questions why Yahweh gives existence 'to the man whose way (*derek*) is hid, hedged around by Eloah?' (3:23) As Habel says:

> This final 'why' makes the basis of Job's complaint explicitly existential. It is not the suffering or bitterness of life as such that consumes him, but the misery of meaninglessness. The futility of existence has two clear features: (a) the *derek* of life is hidden, and (b) the one who hides it is God.[16]

---

15 Since such utilitarian rationality functions as the governing paradigm in contemporary English-language evolutionary anthropology, a figure like Job would make no sense in terms of sociobiology, which we'll be considering later.

16 Norman C. Habel, *The Book of Job*, London: SCM Press, 1985, p. 111.

In biblical wisdom literature, *derek*, meaning 'way', symbolises a cluster of meanings: one's personal destiny, the conduct of one's life, and the underlying principle of divine order. For Job all of these ways are blocked by the One who has himself created them and is supposed to be the origin and goal of ordered existence.

Perhaps the most striking symbolic vehicle for Job's deepening consciousness of personhood and confidence in God-as-personal is the law case he proposes to take out with God. Such a case presupposes that there's a common ground between man and God, a common order of being they inhabit and within which they can meet. For the Hebrew notion of law is intrinsically interpersonal – there is the Decalogue's Thou-orientation in each precept from the personal I AM WHO AM.

And for more than half a millennium before Job, the relationship between Yahweh and his people was expressed in terms of what was originally a Ugaritic term for the legal statute between a king and his subjects, the *berit*.[17] Such a covenant presupposed that 'law', in this case a 'law' of fidelity, could unite human beings (who were, after all, designated in Genesis as created 'in the image of God'), and God. So Job's gradual insistence on a law case should be understood as an insistence on relationship with God even more than a setting right of any wrongs.

For the first time he has the courage to ask to see God's face: 'Yes, though he slay me, I will not wait. I will now argue my case to his face ... no godless person would dare come before his face ... Why do you hide your face and count me as your enemy?' (13:13, 14, 24). Emmanuel Levinas speaks of 'The Idea of Infinity and the Face of Another' and of the relationship which 'opens the very dimension of infinity, of what puts a stop to the irresistible imperialism of the same and the I. We call a *face* the epiphany of what can thus present itself directly, and therefore also exteriorly, to an I.'[18] In *Etica e infinito*, he speaks of the face as signification without a

---

17 The American abstract expressionist painter, Barnett Newman (1905–1970), as Jewish, preferred not to make images of anything, yet his powerful 'zips', as he calls his vertical lines, are a contemporary way of representing the covenant between the human and the divine. His 1949 painting, *Covenant*, begun at the end of his 1948 *Onement* series, is one of the first paintings where two 'zips' appear. So the themes of the paintings move from onement to covenant. The Hebrew Covenant isn't an agreement among equals, but an act of gracious love by the more powerful One; yet man, the image of God, stands parallel to God in a relationship of thou to I. Newman expresses this by the visually more powerful bright yellow-gold zip on the right, the other zip is the black of one who is mortal, Adam or earth. The deep red which colours the huge background of *Covenant* could indicate the life of God participated in by the human being who still keeps his individuality and isn't crushed by the relationship.

18 Emmanuel Levinas, *Collected Philosophical Papers*, Dordrecht: Nijhoff, 1987, p. 55.

context, where all other significations belong within a context, stand in relation to something else:

> On the other hand, the face is meaning in itself. Thou, thou art ... It is what cannot become a content graspable by thought; it is the uncontainable, it leads you beyond ... The relation to the face is immediately ethical. The face is that which cannot be killed; or at least, that whose *meaning* consists in saying: 'thou shalt not kill'.[19]

It is this very 'asymmetry of the interpersonal' that Job seeks in his desired-for face-to-face meeting with God, each profoundly respecting the otherness of the Other.[20] For unlike his friends, Job is convinced of the utter Youness of the divine, and that he too is a you-for-God, not the abstract scarecrow the shallow generalisations of his friends have portrayed him as.

He is sure that he can stand person to person, as one authentic being to an other, in his court case against God. 'If only my case were recorded! If only it were inscribed on stone with iron stylus and lead, carved on rock forever!' (19:23–24). In the darkest night of his trial, utterly alone, Job's deepest longing is now expressed, freely, not determined by any psychological or pseudo-theological necessity. He knows that the last word in that trial will not be an unjust sentence of condemnation. His affirmation, 'I know that my redeemer lives' (19:25) is the turning point of the whole book. In Egyptian and Ugaritic sources, the affirmation 'I know' can indicate a revelation conceded by God. Who is this redeemer (*goel*) whose existence he is convinced of? Earlier (9:33; 16:19) he had spoken of a heavenly witness (*ed*), and of an arbiter (*mokiah*). So Habel regards the 'redeemer' here as a defence attorney who is the counterpart of Satan, the accuser-prosecutor.[21]

But behind his faith in such a *goel* is his utter trust that he will be guaranteed an open and fair relationship with God. This trust is so great it implies that God would not be God, if he did not ultimately recognise the innocence of his friend. Job is convinced he can be a you for the divine You, where that new clarity and depth of relation has been achieved by him precisely through his being stripped of anything to depend on, except

---

19 Emmanuel Levinas, *Etica e infinito*, Rome: Città Nuova, 1984, p. 101.

20 Emmanuel Levinas, *Totalité et infini: essai sur l'extériorité*, The Hague: Nijhoff, 1968, p. 190.

21 Habel, *The Book of Job*, p. 306. Ha-ssatan means 'the accuser'.

his bare selfhood, and his hope against hope in the personal being of God. Nor does his faith and hope remove his fragility, brought down to skin, bone, heart and dust. We glimpse here the core of that deeply excavated personhood, where Job is capable of loving an Other purely for the Other's own sake, and not for himself.

Deeper than his physical and psychological nothingness is Job's spiritual being, where he's convinced he will see Eloah [God] face to face (19:25b, 26, 27). Earlier he'd asked that God would remember him after death. Now, bursting the framework of Hebrew agnosticism regarding the afterlife, there emerges an anticipation of continuous participation in Eloah's life.

Throughout, Job has sought two things: (i) existentially, a meeting with God, and (ii) intellectually, an explanation for his sufferings. And it is to fail to understand the profoundly dialogical and interpersonal nature of biblical revelation not to see that in God's appearance to him and openly entering into the conversation Job has been directing towards him throughout the book, Job has had his desire for relationship with God vindicated. Job's greatest suffering was his experience of alienation from God, an experience which his friends' counsel exacerbated. If the book was written in a philosophic mode, one might expect a theoretical explanation by way of an answer to (ii), but in the concrete and personal mode which is that of Jewish revelation, the answer to his intellectual quest must also be sought within the theophanic encounter. As G. K. Chesterton puts it:

> All the human beings through the story, and Job especially, have been asking questions of God. A more trivial poet would have made God enter in some sense or other in order to answer the questions ... [But] in this drama of scepticism God Himself takes up the role of sceptic ... He does ... what Socrates did. He turns rationalism against itself ... The poet has made God ironically accept a kind of controversial equality with His accusers ... He asks for the right which every prosecuted person possesses; He asks to be allowed to cross-examine the witness for the prosecution ... He asks Job who he is.[22]

Martin Buber has spoken of the two qualities required in personal meeting as 'distance and relation', where without the respect for the otherness

---

22 G.K. Chesterton, 'The Book of Job', in Gilbert K. Chesterton, *G.K.C. as M.C.*, London: Methuen, 1929, p. 44f.

of the other which is what he calls the primal setting at a distance, we cannot enter into genuine relation with that other.[23]

God fully accepts Job's assertion of innocence, yet claims that He too is innocent. His first answer to Job indicated that the universe wasn't just rational, but supra-rational, a mysterious harmony of mountainous but beautiful contrasts. His second 'answer' is to indicate that not just diversity and suffering, but even chaos, and perhaps evil, can be permitted to occur in the divine plan. This second discourse gets to the heart of Job's anguish, since it tackles the black background of non-existence Job has felt seeping into his soul.

This is the significance of the two beasts, Behemoth and Leviathan, introduced in chapters 40 and 41. They are 'mythic symbols of the forces of chaos which are overcome by Baal in Canaanite traditions, by the god Marduk in the Babylonian Enuma Elish, and by Horus in Egyptian mythology'.[24] The point of the fearsome descriptions of the two beasts of chaos is that, while God does not eliminate them, he is in control of them – 'El takes [Behemoth] by the mouth with rings,' 'everything under the heavens is mine. Did I not silence [Leviathan's] boasting?' (40:24; 41:3f.). In these ancient Near Eastern myths, there was a struggle between the forces or gods of good and evil, of order and chaos, but Leviathan and Behemoth, 'whom I made' (40:15), are creatures of God, just as Ha-ssatan was.

Now Job has some glimpse into a creative wisdom that not only drenches the utterly diverse and contrasted existences and events of the universe with a higher meaning beyond his ken, but can even allow the free beings it has created in that universe the full play of their own created wills, with the chaos and evil that can result from that. Yet, because Job now trusts God in a deeper way, he knows his goodness can go beyond even that chaos/evil He has permitted. And Job's own inner development through the book, a capacity of which God was assured when he spoke to Ha-ssatan at the beginning, somehow exemplifies God's providence for a world in which the permission of chaos/evil can eventually be seen to have a meaning. Certainly by now, it is much clearer to Job that he chooses the You of God for that You's sake and not his own, which more than justifies God's choice of Job for his own unique worth as a person who can truly love. Job is representative of all human beings as free – free to love and free not to love.

---

23 Martin Buber, *The Knowledge of Man*, New York: Harper, 1965, p. 60, p. 67.

24 Habel, *The Book of Job*, p. 557.

In his essay on Job, Chesterton speaks of 'the loneliness of God' and from chapters 38–40, we know that the nature of God is self-transcendence, manifested especially in his creation of free beings.[25] If God is utter self-transcendence, Job is utter desire for self-transcendence. And his suffering is the extreme expression of his reaching beyond himself. He is then the incarnate icon of God's self-transcendence. At the end, both 'lonelinesses' meet in God's gracefulness and Job's responsive gratefulness. Although love is not a direct theme in Job, without love it's difficult to understand either Job's longing for God, or God's unshakable trust in Job's capacity for that deepest exercise of his freedom, which is the choice of an Other purely for His own sake, despite all the disasters He permits. Never before Job one might suggest, has the understanding of the capacity of a free human being for participation in a universally loving Other been so explicitly explored and expressed.

3. A New Testament insight into the human

There is no parallel in Hellenic civilisation to the passage in 1 John 4: 'Who does not love, does not know God; for God is love … We love him because he first loved us.' The development of these experiences of Johannine Christianity (which, it is my impression, were closest to St Thomas) into the doctrine of *fides caritate formata*, and the amplification of this doctrinal nucleus into a grandiose, systematic philosophy of man and society, are the medieval climax of the interpenetration of Christianity with the body of a historical civilisation. Here perhaps we touch the historical *raison d'être* of the West, and certainly we touch the empirical standard by which the further course of Western intellectual history must be measured.[26]

Voegelin is writing as a political philosopher about Aquinas's development of what he calls 'Johannine Christianity' as the criterion for assessing Western cultural history. It's an indication of what he considered to be the centrality of the Christian contribution to anthropology in any assessment of what constitutes humanity today. So we can paraphrase another remark of his we've already quoted: 'The New Testament articulation of human existence has set critical standards for the exploration of consciousness behind which nobody is permitted to fall back.' We'll focus on a few key

---

25 Chesterton, 'The Book of Job,' p. 39.

26 Eric Voegelin, *History of Political Ideas, Vol. IV: Renaissance and Reformation*, eds. David L. Morse and William M. Thompson, Columbia: University of Missouri Press, 1998, pp. 250–1.

passages from the Fourth Gospel that perhaps constitute the core of a new awareness of the intrinsic interpersonality of the human person. This will necessarily include a theological dimension, but so indeed did the Greek philosophic texts we've discussed.

3.1 'Father' and 'Son' in the gospels: John reports Jesus' statement 'I and the Father are one' (Jn 10:30), which simultaneously expresses an equality and unity of the Father and the Son.[27] Later Christian theology developed the vocabulary of person and of interpersonal relations for this reality, which gradually also became the language of human interpersonal relations.[28] Among the attributes of this unique unity of distinct persons is their relationship in terms of mutual interpersonal understanding and loving. As we'll see in the following sections, the first Christians were invited to participate in this unique unity of distinct persons, with the psychological consequences of a new awareness of the depths achievable in specifically interpersonal relationships.

3.2 *Agape* as mutual and unconditional love (Jn 13:34): Pasquale Foresi has summarised the philosophical background for the use of *agape* in the New Testament where its rare occurrence (only under the form of *agapan*) in classical Greek, and its frequency in the Septuagint translation of the Old Testament into the Koiné Greek of Alexandria, allowed for the development of a specifically biblical meaning for *agape*, love.[29] Ignace de la Potterie speaks of St John's 'spiral' mode of thinking and writing in his first letter, as 'like a winding staircase always revolving around the same centre, always recurring to the same topics, but at a higher level'.[30] This spiral style can also be found in the Fourth Gospel, and in these few sections on *agape* in St John we shall rest at some of the more important heights in the gradual ascent.

> A new commandment I give you, that you love one another; even as I have loved you, that you also love one another. (Jn 13:34)

---

27 Bernard J. F. Lonergan, *De Verbo Incarnato*, Rome: Gregorian University Press, 1964, pp. 89–99.

28 Bernard J. F. Lonergan, *De Deo Trino I, II*, Rome: Gregorian University Press, 1964; Gordon Allport, *Personality*, London: Constable,1971, p. 24ff.

29 Pasquale Foresi, *L'agape in San Paolo e la carità in San Tommaso d'Aquino*, Rome: Città Nuova, 1965.

30 Ignace de la Potterie, *Adnotationes in Exegesim Primae Epistulae S.Joannis*, Rome: Pont. Inst. Biblicum, 1967, p. 8.

The new commandment is firstly a law of mutual love. This law is not an externally imposed prescription, but an invitation to participate in the inner structure or 'law' of Jesus' own relationship of mutual love with his Father (cf.Jn 15:10).[31] Another aspect of the new commandment is that the disciples are to love one another according to the measure of the love of Jesus for them. Commenting on the *kathos*, the 'as' of 'as I have loved you', Ceslas Spicq notes its meaning of likeness, prolongation of, and assimilation to, the love of Jesus.[32]

3.3 *Agape* as personal and interpersonal love (Jn 15:9-15): That the interpersonal indwelling attained by living mutual love by no means abolishes the personal reality of those who participate in it, but rather the condition of their personal realisation is brought out in 15:4b and 5, which call for the branches to bear fruit:

> As the branch cannot bear fruit by itself, unless it abides in the vine, neither can you, unless you abide in me. I am the vine, you are the branches. He who abides in me and I in him he it is that bears much fruit ...

Like sunshine pouring through the vine and its branches, Jn 15:9-15 give us the clear source of the meaning contained in 15:4-5. With regard to Jesus' invitation to the disciples to interpersonal indwelling with him, Jesus in 15:9a gives us the model of his own relationship with the Father, and the core of that relationship, which is their mutual love: 'As the Father has loved me, so have I loved you.' So he clarifies the basis of his indwelling with his disciples in 15:9b: 'Abide in my love.' It is in mutual love that Jesus and his disciples will be inseparably bound together.

How are they to abide in him as the branches abide in the vine? Jesus remains in love with his Father by acting as his Father wishes him to act, and his disciples will remain in love with him by acting as he wishes them to act (Jn 15:10):

> If you keep my commandments you will abide in my love, just as I have kept my Father's commandments and abide in his love.

---

31 Pasquale Foresi, *Fede speranza carità nel Nuovo Testamento*, Rome: Città Nuova, 1967, p. 94.

32 Ceslas Spicq, *Agape dans le nouveau testament I*, Paris: Gabalda, 1965, p. 173f.

So that interpersonal indwelling has a personal requirement of authentic love which is proved by action.

Next, John takes us up a few steps by giving us a deeper understanding of the 'as': 'Greater love has no man than this, that a man lay down his life for his friends' (Jn 15:13). Schnackenburg refers to 1 Jn 3:16 as a commentary on this:

> By this we know love, that he laid down his life for us; and we ought to lay down our lives for the brethren.[33]

The negative side of unconditional mutual love is that under no conditions, including losing our physical life, are we prepared to break our interpersonal relationship. And we know that Jesus himself underwent the loss of the experience, even though not of the reality of his unity with his Father which impelled him to cry out 'My God, my God, why have you forsaken me?' (Mk 15:34). In this way, by losing everything for love except love, Jesus brought into history a new depth to interpersonal relationships, both as an ideal to be aimed at and as a reality for whoever wishes to respond to his invitation to make unconditional love the norm of their lives.

Jesus is a person whose life is defined in terms of his relationship of mutual love with his Father, a love offered to humans to participate in, and proved by his readiness to lay down his life for them. So that friendship with him is something quite concrete, with the practical condition, 'You are my friends if you do what I have commanded you', or as John puts it in his first letter, 'let us not love in word or in speech but in deed and in truth' (1 Jn 3:18).

The requirement for the disciples' realisation of that new relationship is living in the unconditional interpersonal love proposed by Jesus. If they do so, if they love as Jesus loves, they will begin to experience the essence of his life, which is his complete interpersonal unity with his Father; through their friendship with Jesus, they will experience the fulfilment of that unity with his Father. John leads us up to this final perspective in chapter 17.

---

33 Rudolf Schnackenburg, *The Moral Teaching of the New Testament*, New York: Herder & Herder, 1971, p. 124.

3.4 *Agape* as co-personal oneness[34] (Jn 17:11, 21–4, 26): Now we've arrived at the top of the winding staircase. For the first time, Jesus, instead of speaking further to his disciples, turns to his Father (Jn 17:1). We're somehow allowed to eavesdrop on their conversation – for it is a conversation, not a monologue, even though only Jesus is speaking, since every word he says is full with the consciousness of the Father he is addressing. The theme of that conversation is unity, the unity of the Son with the Father. Jesus wishes his disciples, who are allowed to overhear what's being spoken of, to be drawn into this same unity. Non-verbally too, the conversation conveys the quality of the unity which is its theme, in the utter respect for the Father's personal difference from the Son, who is yet utterly one with the Father:

> Holy Father, keep those in your name whom you have given me, that they may be one as we. (Jn 17:11b)

The previous two subsections have attempted to explore Jn 13:34 and 15:9-15 as setting out the quality of love as mutual, unconditional and personal-interpersonal. For John, in his Gospel, when persons love with a depth of love where they are ready to go beyond themselves utterly for the sake of the other, they become genuine friends who are living in each other. The fruit of such love is a new personal reality or unity. Jesus has already said that 'I and the Father are one' (Jn 10:30), and now he prays for this unity for the disciples. Raymond Brown remarks that John does not use the abstract noun *henotes*, 'unity' (to be found for example in Eph. 4:3, l3) but rather the concrete *hen*, 'one'.[35] The specifically co-personal nature of this unity is expressed as 'We' where the simplicity of the Johannine vocabulary should not obscure its technical brilliance.[36]

That the 'as we' in Jn 17:11b is a deliberate and technical usage – without the 'are one' often added in translations – may perhaps be gleaned from John's use of the expression *ego eimi*, 'I am'. This is extremely significant and will require of us an equivalent attentiveness to his use of 'we', 'us', and 'we are' in the only extended conversation between the Son and the Father he records, in Jn 17. Canadian philosopher and theologian Bernard Lonergan lists

---

34 We're using 'co-personal' in an attempt to express a we-dimension beyond that of inter-personality.

35 Raymond Brown, *The Gospel According to John, XIII–XXI*, London: Chapman, 1971, p. 759.

36 See Voegelin's exploration of Parmenides' *Is* earlier in this chapter.

four uses of 'I am' in John's gospel: (i) with an explicit predicate: for example 'I am the bread of life' (6:35); (ii) with an implicit predicate easily supplied from the context: 'It is I; do not be afraid' (6:20); (iii) without an explicit or implicit predicate but in the absolute sense of existence: 'before Abraham was, I am' (8:58); (iv) without an explicit or implicit predicate, and in the absolute sense of existence, where that existence is an object of faith: 'when you have lifted up the Son of man, then you will know that I am' (8:28).[37] The context for this fourth usage is given in Dodd, who shows how the Septuagint version of the Mosaic name of God as used in Isaiah is also *ego eimi*: '"You are my witnesses," says the Lord, " ... that you may know and believe me and understand that I am"'; or Is. 43:25, 'I am "I AM," who erases your iniquities.'[38]

Given this anamnetic density of 'I am' in John, there is at least a strong possibility that the use of 'We' by the one who is in some sense equivalent to the 'I am' of the Old Testament symbolises for John a new experience of divine reality under the specific aspect of a oneness of persons we may call co-personal. This seems even more likely when we notice that in every instance in which 'I am' is used absolutely, the 'I' of Jesus, the core of his self-consciousness, is immediately referred to the Father, as in 8:24-6 and 8:28a-28b: 'When you have lifted up the Son of man, then you will know that I am, and from myself I do nothing, but I speak just as my Father taught me, and he who sent me is with me.'[39]

The complete originality of the symbolism here – where a relationship between persons is communicated in terms of the 'We' of another co-personal reality – is underlined by comparison with Aristotle's theoretical model for understanding the unity of friends with each other. In Book IX, chapter 4 of his *Nicomachean Ethics*, Aristotle uses the analogy of the conscious unity of a good man's relation with himself. The later verses of Jn 17 convey Jesus' self-understanding of this 'We' he constitutes with his Father. He prays:

(a) 'That all may be one' (17:21a): that is, for the unity of the unqualified totality of humanity.

(b) 'as you Father in me and I in you' (17:21b): in Mt 11:27 the Father and the Son are spoken of as having mutual knowledge of each other, but here

37 Lonergan, *De Verbo Incarnato*, pp. 59–60.

38 C. H. Dodd, *The Interpretation of the Fourth Gospel*, Cambridge: Cambridge University Press, 1970, pp. 93–6.

39 Ibid., 1970, p. 96.

Jesus speaks of a mutual presence of each person in the other without any qualifications. So that the prayer is that the disciples and their followers will be one in the same way that the Father and the Son are interpersonally present to each other.

(c) 'that they also may be in us' (17:21c): Such an interpersonal presence would lead the disciples and their followers not only to be related to one another like the Father and the Son are, but to participate in the 'We' of Jesus and his Father: 'that they also may be in *us*'. The following verses further unfold this anthropology-theology, but for our purposes, it's enough to appreciate how East German poet Johannes Bobrowski could echo the same anthropology nearly two millennia later in the last lines of his last poem, called 'The Word Man'. He goes through various ways the word 'man' is used, but rules them all out if they lack that core Johannine quality:

> *Wo Liebe nicht ist,*
> *sprich das Wort nicht aus.*

> Where there is not love,
> do not utter that word.[40]

3.5 Wewards: towards the essence of humanity in the friendship of God: To remind the reader that biblical examples are available to all, whether believers or unbelievers, Voegelin, in the context of a study in political philosophy, makes the point that we can't simply omit huge ranges of experience that have been constitutive of Western culture, including anthropology:

> The Christian community has been, for the better part of two-thousand years, the most important political force of the Western World, and the evocative acts which created it are the basis of all later political evocations which occurred in Western history – so far as it is Christian. To omit the visions of the disciples, would be equivalent to an omission of the Declaration of Independence from a history of American political ideas.[41]

The new experience of humanity originated by Christ, and articulated by St Paul and St John, with its explicit universalism, was well-fitted to provide

---

40 Johannes Bobrowski, in 'Das Wort Mensch,' *Wetterzeichen*, [East] Berlin: Union Verlag, 1968, p. 83.

41 Eric Voegelin, *History of Political Ideas, Volume I: Hellenism, Rome, and Early Christianity*, ed. Athanasios Moulakis, Columbia, MO: University of Missouri Press, 1997, p. 164.

a spiritual foundation for what we call Western civilisation. The various tensions regarding its concrete realisation, its failures and the opposition often provoked by those failures, all make up the drama of that civilisation. And that tension has often been fruitful: for example, the origins of liberal democracy are to be found in a Trinitarian-interpersonal rather than a merely monotheistic theology.[42] Along with its trans-national, trans-civilisational ethos, such a vision is always capable of inspiring new achievements by appealing both to the uniqueness of each individual and of each ethnos, and to their underlying oneness in common humanity.

The Russian film director, Andrei Tarkovsky, illuminates the situation of contemporary humankind in the light of the co-personal symbolism we've been considering in a comment on the culminating moment of his film *Andrei Rublev*. The film leads up to the moment where we see Rublev's Troitsa, the icon expressing the artist's vision of the three mysterious beings who appeared to Abraham united in an unmoving movement of love:

> Here at last is the 'Trinity', great, serene, completely penetrated by a trembling joy from which human brotherhood springs forth. The concrete division of one alone in three and the triple union in one alone offers a wonderful perspective for the future still spread out across the centuries.[43]

Whichever notion of the human we choose to draw on – from Xenophanes to Parmenides to Heraclitus, from Plato or Aristotle, from Job or St John – in every case we're setting a standard for our own humanity, and for the derived uses of the word 'human' which we find in paleontology, archaeology and even in evolutionary biology. Yet the task of remembering, what Voegelin, using Plato's word, called 'anamnesis' is essential if we're not to lose the thread binding us to the sources of our civilisation. We're in danger of losing our humanity if we forgot those sources, as Chiara Lubich put it, drawing indeed on that 'Johannine Christianity' invoked both by Voegelin and Bobrowski:

> Love gives us our being. We do not exist only because of love; we exist because we love. If we do not love – and in all the moments in which we do not love, we no longer are – we do not exist.[44]

---

42 See Eric Voegelin, *The New Science of Politics, in Modernity Without Restraint*, ed. Manfred Henningsen, Columbia, MO: University of Missouri Press, 2000, pp. 170–4.

43 Quoted in Olivier Clément, *L'espirit de Soljénitsyne*, Paris: Stock, 1974, p. 298.

44 Chiara Lubich, *On the Holy Journey*, New York: New City Press, 1988, p. 89.

Chapter Two: 'In the beginning …'

We've called our quest towards understanding human origins *From Big Bang to Big Mystery* because our origins are bound up with the cosmic drama of the whole universe. In the previous chapter we had to sort out what we mean by 'human' so that when we get to the question of human origins we'll know what we're looking for. Echoing Genesis' 'In the beginning … ,' Psalm 90:2 says: 'Before the mountains were brought forth … ,' so for the Bible there's a question of a beginning 'before' the beginning in time. Certainly from that perspective we can say that the beginnings of the universe are our beginnings too. Another way the profoundly human implications of those remote moments have been spelt out for us is in terms of a theory known as the 'anthropic principle' (from *anthropos*, the Greek word for human being).[45] It is a theory that focuses on the amazing sequence of events from the Big Bang up to the emergence of human beings which are mathematically so improbable as to lead physicist Freeman Dyson to say that 'The universe must have known we were coming.'[46] Even Stephen Hawking in his recent *The Grand Design*, while arguing against any philosophical or theological attempt at understanding what in fact seems like a grand design, writes:

> Our universe and its laws appear to have a design that both is tailor-made to support us and, if we are to exist, leaves little room for alteration. That is not easily explained, and raised the natural question of why it is that way.[47]

In this short chapter, we'll touch on different ways human beings have responded to the wonder of the natural world, while the following chapter will discuss how the natural sciences approach it.

---

45 John D. Barrow and Frank J. Tipler, *The Anthropic Cosmological Principle*, Oxford: Oxford University Press, 1986. There are various forms of the 'anthropic principle', weak and strong, but our interest here is only in the fact that the physical universe can be seen to have an inbuilt bias to providing a favourable environment for the emergence of human beings.

46 The full quotation is: 'As we look out into the Universe and identify the many accidents of physics and astronomy that have worked together to our benefit, it almost seems as if the Universe must in some sense have known that we were coming.' Freeman Dyson, quoted in John D. Barrow and Frank Tipler, *The Anthropic Cosmological Principle*, p. 318.

47 Stephen Hawking and Leonard Mlodinow, *The Grand Design*, London: Bantam Press, 2010, p. 162.

1. The wonder of nature

> Long before bridges, the old men who are hills now were woken by
> the mopoke owl. And each had become an island ... Those blue south
> mountains were halved in height, and the sisters took their sea-digging
> sticks and camped with the Cross in the sky.[48]

As nuclear engineer and philosopher Sergio Rondinara puts it, 'the cosmos
is our home, our dwelling. Each of us is a being in space-time, living in a
given place and at a specific historic period.'[49] Our dwelling in the cosmos
has always provoked wonder. Good recent examples of wonder in the
natural sciences was the shock and surprise felt by astronomers when
they discovered that the protective magnetic bubble around our Sun and
its accompanying planets – called the heliosphere – seems to be organised
by the Milky Way galaxy's own magnetic field rather than by the Sun
itself. The discoverers spoke of the heliosphere being tied by a gigantic
ribbon of energetic neutral atoms (called ENAs) bunched together. As
one report puts it, 'The heliosphere shields the solar system from 90 per
cent of energetic cosmic rays – high-speed charged particles that would
otherwise bombard the planets and harm life.'[50] Another recent surprise
was the discovery of the Hyper-star R136a1 whose size and brightness had
been regarded as impossible until it was recorded.[51]

So the investigations of the natural sciences never leave us with less
wonder than what provoked the inquiry in the first place. It's interesting
that folk living within the experience of the myth, along with philosophers,
those influenced by Jewish and Christian revelation, and with artists, have
all shown this healthy wonder not just at the natural world, but at the
further questions that the sheer beauty and magnificence of that world
give rise to.

---

48 Les Murray, 'The Sand Dingoes', in *New Collected Poems*, Manchester: Carcanet, 2003, p. 404.

49 Sergio Rondinara, '"Dio Amore" e la nostra comprensione del cosmo', unpublished lecture,
Rome, 2009.

50 Ron Cowen, 'Solar system's edge surprises astronomers: New observations reveal a dense
ribbon structure that current models don't explain', *Science News* (Web edition), 15 October 2009;
also Tony Phillips, 'Giant Ribbon Discovered at the Edge of the Solar System', *Science@NASA*, 15
October 2009.

51 Tom Chivers, 'Universe's biggest known star discovered by British astronomers: The heaviest
known star, at its birth more than 320 times the mass of the Sun, has been discovered at the edge
of our galaxy by British astronomers', *Daily Telegraph*, London, 21 June 2010.

1.1 Nature in myth

To get a flavour of a response to the natural world in terms of mythic experience, we can recall an Australian aboriginal sense of the cosmos as weighted with a significance going beyond what can be seen within it.[52] A Cape York aboriginal, speaking of one of the wide and meandering rivers flowing into the Gulf of Carpentaria reportedly stated: 'That's not just a river. It's the coiling path of a rainbow serpent.' For him, to forget such stories of one's Dreaming turns a land to 'rubbish country'.[53] This remark, though made within the context of a mythic experience of the world, is strikingly similar to and, as we'll see, has a meaning somewhat equivalent to, Heraclitus' aphorism, that 'the most beautiful *kosmos* is like a garbage-heap strewn at random' (B124).

1.2 Nature in mytho-speculation

Those who live within the experience of the myth, or in that development of mythic experience that can be called mytho-speculation, were recognised by Aristotle as engaged in the quest for the truth of their existence. While Voegelin notes that the Hindu speculation on nature doesn't manage to break out of its mythic context, it's hard not to appreciate the depth of reflection on the cosmos and its intrinsic relatedness to an at least incipiently transcosmic reality in these examples from the Vedas and the *Mahabharata*.[54] The Vedas are some 1,000 hymns and prayers dating from c.1500 to 600 BC, collected in the *Rig Veda*. An example of speculation within the context of the myth of the cosmos is the 'Hymn of Creation':

> Non-being then existed not nor being:
> There was no air, nor sky that is beyond it ...
> Death then existed not nor life immortal;
> By its inherent force the One breathed windless:
> No other thing than that beyond existed ...

---

52 A book like Mircea Eliade's *From Primitives to Zen: A Thematic Sourcebook of the History of Religions* (New York: HarperCollins, 1978), is packed with accounts of nature and its origin from the viewpoint of myth.

53 Cathy Newman, 'The Uneasy Magic of Australia's Cape York Peninsula', *National Geographic* 189, 6 June 1996, pp. 2–33, at pp. 28. For everything considered as rubbish without the incarnate *Logos*, see St Paul's Letter to the Philippians, 3:8.

54 'The dialogues of the Upanishadic type enact the Question that leads toward the ground, but in their self-interpretation this differentiating act is a commentary within the Vedic tradition. They establish the questioning consciousness as an ordering force of existence, but they do not understand this movement beyond the myth as a break with the myth.' Eric Voegelin, *The Ecumenic Age*, Baton Rouge: Louisiana State University Press, 1974, p. 320.

Desire entered the One in the beginning:
It was the earliest seed, of thought the product.
The sages searching in their hearts with wisdom,
Found out the bond of being in non-being ...
But who knows for certain? Who shall here declare it?
Whence was it born and whence came this creation?
The gods were born after this world's creation:
Then who can know from whence it has arisen?[55]

Some centuries later, in the later chapters of the Bhagavad Gita, composed within the Hindu epic, the *Mahabharata*, there are reflections on the natural world and its relation to the divinity, Krishna. Chapter seven contrasts the *maya* of appearance with Krishna's divine reality:

With your mind attached to me, practicing yoga ... you shall know me fully ... I am the origin of all this world and its dissolution as well. Higher than I there is nothing whatsoever: on me this universe is strung like clustered pearls upon a thread. In waters I am the flavour, in sun and moon the light, in all the Vedas OM ... Pure fragrance in the earth and brightness in fire ... the eternal seed of all beings, the intelligence of the intelligent ... (7:1, 6-10)

OM is the sacred syllable, A+U+M, standing for Brahman, the whole universe. It is the syllable that begins and ends every ritual utterance.[56] What is unfolding in these chapters is the awareness of the presence of Krishna in all things, and of all things in Krishna. The limits of these things, as not Krishna, and as mere appearance, are referred to in verse 14:

This divine appearance [*daivi* ... *maya*] of mine ... is hard to overcome. But those who trust me alone shall pass beyond this *maya*. The foolish evildoers ... whose minds are carried away by *maya*, and who partake in the nature of demons, do not seek refuge in Me. (7:14-15)

---

55 Sarvepalli Radhakrishnan and Charles A. Moore, eds., *A Sourcebook in Indian Philosophy*, Princeton: Princeton University Press, 1967, p. 23.

56 R. C. Zaehner, *The Bhagavad Gita*, New York: Oxford University Press, 1973, 380f. I'm drawing here on my 'Amor amicitiae in The Bhagavad Gita', in *Amor Amicitiae: On the Love that is Friendship. Essays in Medieval Thought and Beyond, in Honor of Professor James McEvoy*, eds. Thomas Kelly & Philipp Rosemann, Leuven: Peeters, 2004, pp. 347–77.

Maya derives from the root *ma*, meaning to measure.[57] Zaehner points out that *maya* means 'material nature', and one's translation of the word will depend on what view one takes of material nature. From the viewpoint of Absolute reality, *maya* has the meaning of illusion – equivalent to Parmenides' contrast between *Is* and *doxa*, or appearance. *Maya*, then, can be both divine, as dependent on Krishna, or devilish, insofar as it distracts the individual self from Krishna.[58]

Chapter nine affirms Krishna's supremacy over all beings, creating the world from the matter which is his own lower nature:

> My Self sustains [all] beings, but does not abide in them, though I bring them forth and support them ... All beings, Arjuna, pass into nature which is my own at the end of the cycle [*kalpa*, meaning an eon or *yuga* of 4,320,000 years]; and at the beginning of the next cycle, I send them forth. (9:5, 7)

Chapter ten continues to explore the presence of Krishna in all things to the point of seeing him as their origin. Here we're told that Krishna is the highest representative of all classes of beings, including human beings and gods. Finally Krishna claims to sustain the whole of the universe with but a fraction of his own power:

> Arjuna said: You are the supreme Brahman [*param brahma*] ... the eternal, divine person [*purusam*], the divine god before all gods [*divyam adi-devam*]. (10:12)

Krishna is addressed as a Yogi 'because he controls the whole universe. The yogi controls himself, and Krishna, who is the Self of the whole creation, is the great Yogi controlling the universe.'[59] The following verses are Krishna's answer to the seeker Arjuna:

> O Arjuna, I am the Self [*atma*] seated in the hearts of all beings. I am the beginning, the middle and the end of all beings. Of the Adityas

---

57 Words like 'matter', originate in the notion of what is measured; for example, Irish *meas*, measure; 'measaim', I measure, judge. Dictionaries give *'mater'*, as mother or origin, as a source of the word.

58 Zaehner, *The Bhagavad Gita*, p. 183, p. 250.

59 Bede Griffiths, *River of Compassion: A Christian Commentary on The Bhagavad Gita*, Springfield, Illinois: Templegate Publishers, 2002, p. 189.

[that is, the Vedic gods] I am Vishnu; of the lights, the radiant sun ... of the senses I am mind [*manas*]; and in living beings I am consciousness ... Among mountains I am Meru. (10:20-3)

Meru is 'a mythical mountain, enormously high, which stands in the middle of the world'.[60]

Among lakes I am the Ocean ... among utterances the single syllable [that is, Om]; of unmovable things, the Himalayas [*hima*: snow; *alaya*: abode] ... among those who subdue I am Yama [god of death] ... Among demons I am Prahlada; among those who calculate [*kalayatam*], I am time [*kalah*]; of beasts I am the king of beasts [that is, the lion]. Among fishes I am the crocodile; among rivers I am the Ganges; among sciences [*vidyanam*], I am the science of Self [*adhy-atma-vidya*] ... Of letters I am A ... Of seasons I am flower-bearing [that is, Spring]. And what is the seed of all beings, that am I, Arjuna; nor is there anything, moving or unmoving, that can exist without Me ... But what need is there, Arjuna, for such knowledge by you? I support this entire universe pervading it with a single fraction of myself. (10: 24, 25, 29–30, 31, 33, 35, 39, 42)

In these final verses, Krishna brings together all he's been saying to identify himself with the source of all, upholding the whole world, while far transcending it in power.[61]

1.3 Nature in philosophy

At the philosophical level, Aristotle, in his treatise *On the Parts of Animals*, tells the story of Heraclitus who:

... 'when the strangers who came to visit him found him warming himself at the furnace in the kitchen and hesitated to go in, is reported to have bidden them not to be afraid to enter as even in that kitchen divinities were present' and recommends study even of the humblest animals, for the order to be found in them is itself 'a form of the beautiful'. He also speaks of 'the scanty conceptions to which we can attain of celestial things', which however gives us 'more pleasure than all our knowledge of the world in which we live; just as a half glimpse of persons that we

---

60 Zaehner, *The Bhagavad Gita*, p. 298.

61 Cf. Griffiths, *River of Compassion*, p. 199.

love is more delightful than a leisurely view of other things whatever their number and dimensions.' (644b22f.)

Heraclitus' own response to the beauty of the natural world required going further to its philosophical ground, without which it is deprived of beauty. As we've said, somewhat like the Cape Yorker, he wrote: 'The most beautiful *kosmos* is like a garbage-heap strewn at random' (B 124). Eric Voegelin comments: 'The cosmos, thus, is order only in as far as it is transparent for the invisible ordering force [that is, Heraclitus' *Logos*], while it is disorder when seen as an opaque, external arrangement of "things."'[62]

We're just touching here on philosophical approaches to nature, and Stanley Jaki's remark on Aristotle will give an indication of one aspect of the classic Greek approaches:

To see the most mature form achieved during the Hellenic times in the field of the biological sciences one must turn to the writings of Aristotle. It was he who turned zoology into a scientific discipline in his *History of Animals,* and laid lasting foundations for comparative anatomy in his *On the Parts of Animals*. His acumen as a biologist is perhaps even more brilliantly displayed in his *On the Generation of Animals* which remained until modern times the authoritative compendium on fertilisation, embryology, and the birth and raising of the offspring. Nothing shows better the value of this book than that some of its inevitable errors went undetected until the nineteenth century. Darwin, for one, felt impelled to register his admiration for Aristotle, the biologist, following his reading of *On the Parts of Animals*: 'I had not the most remote notion of what a wonderful man he was. Linnaeus and Cuvier have been my two gods, though in very different ways, but they were mere schoolboys to old Aristotle.'[63]

Of course, Aristotle complemented his years of empirical investigation with the specifically philosophic quest for the ground of reality – as he notes in his *Metaphysics*, 'it is impossible that anything should be produced if there were nothing existing before' (1032b30). We've already

---

62 See Voegelin, *The World of the Polis*, p. 235.

63 Stanley L. Jaki, *Science and Creation: From Eternal Cycles to an Oscillating Universe*, Lanham, MD: University Press of America, 1990, p. 104.

mentioned his understanding of humans as quests for the underlying truth of existence, a quest that led him to clarify the entire sequence of causes there must be a first cause of what was not existing before (*Metaphysics*, 994a1–994b7). Now let's turn to what is probably the best-known reflection on the natural world and its origin in Western culture.

1.4 Nature in Genesis

We all know the opening words of Genesis, 'In the beginning God created the heavens and the earth.' Often the first chapters of the Book of Genesis are misunderstood as mythic. However, Joseph Ratzinger, in his '*In the Beginning*' instead points to the demythologising intent of its authors (who wrote during the period of Exile in the sixth and fifth centuries BC). He notes their more than implicit critique of what would have been the familiar Babylonian cosmogenesis, where 'the world was produced out of a struggle between opposing powers ... assuming its form when Marduk, the god of light, appeared and split in two the body of the primordial dragon'. The sun and moon are not gods ruling over their subjects, nor is the sky 'full of mysterious and adversary divinities'.[64] As Stanley Jaki argues, the systematic listing of all the components in the natural world, culminating in the creation of man and woman belongs to a rather universal genre of communication of the whole by enumerating all of the parts. For Jaki, what Genesis wishes to communicate – over the multiple deities of the surrounding Babylonian-Persian world – is that God has created all that is in the world.[65]

Ratzinger goes on to discuss the mode of divine creation as occurring through God's word, 'Let there be ... ' Voegelin quotes the Buber-Rosenzweig translation, closer to the Hebrew: 'God spoke: Light be! Light became,' and continues, 'The spoken word, it appears, is more than a mere sign signifying something; it is a power in reality that evokes structures in reality by naming them.'[66] For Ratzinger, Genesis 1 is answering questions not only about the beginning, 'which points to him who had the power to produce being and to say: "Let there be ... " and it was so.' It 'goes beyond the pure "that" of being,' touching upon the so-called design of the universe ... ' The author of Genesis, though not using the word 'reason', still conveys – in the very manner of creation by the word, and in the order of the universe brought

---

64 Joseph Ratzinger, '*In the Beginning ...* ': A Catholic Understanding of the Story of Creation and the Fall, Grand Rapids, MI: Eerdmans, 1995, p. 12, p. 6.

65 Stanley L. Jaki, *Genesis 1 Through the Ages*, London: Thomas More Press, 1992, pp. 287–9.

66 Eric Voegelin, *In Search of Order*, Baton Rouge: Louisiana State University Press, 1987, p. 19.

into existence by that word – the truth that the universe 'is not the product of darkness and unreason', but of 'intelligence, freedom', and 'the beauty that is identical with love'.[67]

Writing as a philosopher of history, Voegelin sees Genesis 1 as expressing the boundary experience of Beginning, to which he relates Plato's equivalent boundary experience of the Beyond, and writes, 'We can hardly come closer to the real beginning of anything than an original act of creating everything'.[68] In his *Israel and Revelation*, again writing from a philosophical perspective, Voegelin shows how the 'I am who I am' of the Book of Exodus clarifies the meaning of the word 'God' in Genesis. He notes that John Damascene's Christian interpretation of 'HE WHO IS' 'includes being itself as an infinite and indeterminate ocean of substance'. And he agrees with Étienne Gilson's remark that, 'if there is no metaphysics *in* Exodus, there is a metaphysics *of* Exodus'. He refers to Aquinas' commentary on the HE WHO IS, which leads from what can be said about the divine nature philosophically 'into the depth of the incommunicable substance'. At that point, still following Voegelin on Aquinas, we're where 'the frontier of divine presence has become luminous through revelation', where humans become 'sensitive to the abyss extending beyond into the incommunicable substance' of the one named YHWH.[69]

Much of Jaki's *Genesis 1* is a critique of the misunderstanding of the difference between biblical and scientific accounts of the natural world. As he notes, the first readers of Genesis 'took it for an expression of the total dependence of all on God ... They did not take Genesis 1 for a physics [we could add, biological] textbook, for the very simple reason that they had no physics [nor geology, nor biology].'[70] As a result, any attempt at what's called 'concordism', that is, showing how the text of Genesis fits in with contemporary scientific evidence or conclusions, is a complete misreading of that text. This will become even more of an issue when we discuss evolution, but we can conclude these reflections on Genesis with the words of another scientist-philosopher of science, Michael Polanyi:

---

67 Ratzinger, '*In the Beginning* ... ', p. 23, p. 25.

68 Voegelin, *In Search of Order*, p. 19.

69 Voegelin, *Israel and Revelation*, Baton Rouge: Louisiana State University Press, 1960, pp. 410–11. It's in the light of that transcendent meaning of God that we should understand Genesis' portraying of every human being as the 'image' of God, as participating in God's transcendence and creativity. Our final chapter will touch on the relation between divine creation and human pro-creation in Genesis.

70 Jaki, *Genesis 1*, p. 25.

The book of Genesis and its great pictorial illustrations, like the frescoes of Michelangelo, remain a far more intelligent account of the nature and origin of the universe than the representation of the world as a chance collocation of atoms. For the biblical cosmology continues to express – however inadequately – the significance of the fact that the world exists and that man has emerged from it, while the scientific picture denies any meaning to the world, and indeed ignores all our most vital experience of this world.[71]

1.5 St Francis' mystical appreciation of nature

An example from Christian nature mysticism can be found in the life and writings of St Francis of Assisi. His 'Canticle of the Creatures' well communicates a grasp of the unity of all creatures as his brothers and sisters, all children of the same Father:

All praise be yours, my Lord, through all that you have made,
And first my lord Brother Sun,
Who brings the day; and light you give to us through him.
How beautiful is he, how radiant in all his splendour!
Of you, Most High, he bears the likeness.

All praise be yours, my Lord, through Sister Moon and Stars;
In the heavens you have made them, bright
And precious and fair.

All praise be yours, my Lord, through Brothers Wind and Air,
And fair and stormy, all the weather's moods,
By which you cherish all that you have made.
All praise be yours, my Lord, through Sister Water,
So useful, lowly, precious and pure.

All praise be yours, my Lord, through Brother Fire,
Through whom you brighten up the night.
How beautiful is he, how playful! Full of power and strength.

---

71 Quoted in Simon Conway Morris, *Life's Solution: Inevitable Humans in a Lonely Universe*, Cambridge: Cambridge University Press, 2003, p. 328.

All praise be yours, my Lord, through Sister Earth, our mother,
Who feeds us in her sovereignty and produces
Various fruits with coloured flowers and herbs ...

It's no surprise to find that the history of the natural sciences in the West begins with Franciscans in the medieval universities of Oxford and Paris.[72] We can imagine, if Francis were alive today, that he'd fill out his mystical grasp of the unity of the entire cosmos, living and non-living, with a range of studies from astrophysics through biology to zoology. These would provide him with a world even more amazing and beautiful than the one he knew. Certainly he would have felt no contradiction between the new insights of the natural sciences and his vision of creation.

1.6 Nature in art

We've touched on mythic, philosophic and revelational responses to nature, and it wouldn't have been out of place to include artistic responses too. Sometimes in fact it's these responses – a Georgia O'Keeffe flower, a Maurice de Vlaminck 'wild' glimpse of the Seine, any of the Group of Seven's or Tom Thomson's Canadian landscapes – that move us as much or more than the beauty of nature itself. For Lawren Harris, one of the Group of Seven, the Rocky Mountain summits symbolised the human reaching out for understanding and truth. He simplifies the jagged rocks into a smoothly carved surface, making the lower ridges stepping stones in the artist's and viewer's spiritual journey upward. The mountain peak was a place of encounter with the divine, with the cloud as a halo around it.[73]

Glenn Hughes in an unpublished essay, 'Artistic Symbols and Life in the *Metaxy*', quotes Voegelin in a 1965 discussion: 'All art, if it is any good, is some sort of a myth in the sense that it becomes what I call a *cosmion*, a reflection of the unity of the cosmos as a whole. The odd thing about a work of art is that it is an intelligible unit even if it is only, in the most naturalistic sense, a segment of a reality that extends around it in all directions ... How to produce such units and make them convincing models of the unity of the world – that is the problem in art.'

And Hughes notes that 'In our historical period of late modernity or postmodernity, it has become quite easy ... to suffer an eclipse of the

---

72 For background, see: James McEvoy, *Robert Grosseteste*, Oxford: Oxford University Press, 2000.

73 See Anne Newlands, *The Group of Seven and Tom Thomson*, Willowdale, ON: Firefly Books, 1995, p. 52, p. 54.

meaning of life in the *metaxy* [Plato's term in the *Symposium* for human existence in the 'in-between' of time and eternity], to succumb to what Voegelin calls the "vulgarian belief" that we are "no longer living in the cosmos but in a 'physical universe'".[74] To which one of the greatest of contemporary painters, Gerhard Richter could add:

> For me, what is missing is the spiritual foundation underlying Romantic painting. We have lost the feeling of the ubiquity of God in nature. For us everything is empty. And yet the paintings are still there, and they speak to us. We continue to love them to use them and to need them.[75]

So the artists may be seen as a continuation of the attempt by myth to convey the mystery of what, as we've seen, Voegelin called a *cosmion*, 'a reflection of the unity of the cosmos as a whole'.[76] Having made this brief reminder of other experiences of nature – mythic, philosophic, revelational, mystical and artistic – it's time to examine how the natural sciences deal with it.

---

74 Glenn Hughes deals with these issues more fully in his *Transcendence and History: The Search for Ultimacy from Ancient Societies to Postmodernity*, Columbia: University of Missouri Press, 2003.

75 Quoted in Jean-Philippe Antoine, Gertrud Koch & Luc Lang, *Gerhard Richter*, Paris: Dis Voir, 1995, p. 82.

76 Eric Voegelin, 'In Search of the Ground', in his *Published Essays, 1953–1965*, ed. Ellis Sandoz, Columbia, MO: University of Missouri Press, 2000, p. 240.

Part Two: The scientific partners in the conversation: what science is and how it can complement rather than replace or invalidate philosophy and revelation

Chapter Three: 'The universe must have known we were coming'[1]

One of the reasons for beginning our discussion of how humans respond to the natural world was so we could site the natural sciences within the human quest for understanding, rather than treat them as if they suddenly showed up from a vacuum of ignorance and superstition. Here we will look at some indications of natural scientific inquiry's underlying cognitional structure, the reality it presupposes and investigates, and finally the historical origins of the modern natural sciences. Since the understanding of the natural world achievable by the natural sciences can also be seen from a philosophical perspective, we'll go on to say something about the framework Bernard Lonergan has proposed. This will help us to understand the series of natural sciences from astrophysics to zoology as a sequence of successive higher viewpoints. After these reflections on the natural sciences, we'll conclude with some of the pitfalls that an over-reliance on the methods of the natural sciences can lead us into. We'll also suggest a way beyond the conflict through internal and external dialogue between science, philosophy and theology (and indeed the histories of science and philosophy show that revelation and theology's ongoing reflection on it have had a lot to do with the emergence of the natural sciences).

1. Epistemological, ontological and historical presuppositions of natural science

1.1 The cognitional structure underlying the natural sciences

Bernard Lonergan, in his *Insight: A Study of Human Understanding*, makes the case, drawing on his own application and development of Aristotle's and Aquinas's theory of knowledge, that inquiry in mathematics and the natural sciences has essentially the same structure as the inquiry we carry on in our ordinary common sense existence, even though scientific inquiry has its own strict empirical method.[2] Since in chapter nine we will also discuss his theory of knowledge to illustrate what human understanding is, it will be enough here to apply it to scientific knowledge.

---

1 I'm well aware the universe cannot have 'known we were coming' because it is not a who with the capacity to know. It's not even a thing at all, if it comes to that. Still the phrase rightly conveys that we're at least partly at home in the material cosmos.

2 Bernard Lonergan, *Insight: A Study of Human Understanding*, London: Longmans, 1961. All future references throughout the book will be in the text, with the short title *Insight* followed by the page number of this edition.

Let's say you're a member of the Athenian jury before which Socrates has been arraigned. To get an idea of what's involved in making a true judgment of whether he's guilty or not, we can suggest, following Lonergan, that human knowing involves many distinct and irreducible activities, falling into three groups: (i) seeing, hearing, smelling, touching, tasting, imagining, remembering; (ii) inquiring, understanding, formulating; and (iii) reflecting, weighing the evidence, judging. We can call the first group of activities, experience, the second group, understanding, and the third group, judgment. No one of these activities on its own can be called human knowing.

(i) We could look at Socrates as long as we liked, but without understanding it would just be gawking. And the same would hold for merely hearing what he said. At the same time, this first level, where we're attentive to all the relevant data, is essential. Without the presentations of sense, without listening carefully, picking up what Socrates said and how he said it, there'd be nothing to understand.

(ii) To move to the second level of understanding we need what Philip McShane and Garrett Barden called the 'What Question', that has us asking what all these data of sense mean.[3] So we'll try out the various possibilities for size and come to our best guess of what he did and why he did it.

(iii) But following on whatever answer we've arrived at by asking our 'What Question', is our 'Is Question'. Is our understanding of what happened true or false? Only when we've checked out our tentative answer by looking at the data again can we be reasonably sure that our opinion is true or false.[4]

Lonergan summarises these imperatives of human knowing as 'be attentive, be intelligent, be reasonable', since human knowing isn't experience alone, nor understanding alone, nor judgment alone, nor the combination of any two of them.[5] It only occurs as a result of all three activities. While our knowledge is materially dependent on the sense presentations or conscious data we're calling 'experience', they're not enough to constitute knowledge – we all know the difference between staring at a text we're trying to understand and actually understanding it. But then our insight – when we manage to formulate it in an idea – has to move beyond the question, 'Is it clear?' to face the second question, 'Is it true?'

---

3 Cf. Garrett Barden and Philip McShane, *Towards Self-Meaning*, Dublin: Gill & Macmillan, 1969.

4 For a more complete account, see Bernard Lonergan, 'Cognitional Structure' in *Collection*, New York: Herder & Herder, 1967, pp. 221–39.

5 Bernard Lonergan, *Method in Theology*, London: Darton, Longman & Todd, 1972, p. 20. The first chapter provides a readily accessible presentation of Lonergan's theory of knowledge.

For Lonergan, science is just one expression of the human desire to know, where the specifically scientific unfolding of that desire is expressed in terms of (i) getting hold of the data of the particular science, (ii) understanding those data in terms of hypotheses about the data, and finally, (iii) verifying the hypotheses or theories about the data by returning to them and checking to see if the hypothesis fits (as Philip McShane notes, verification involves 'a return to sense experience, but the return is intelligent and within a context of theory').[6] (Obviously this isn't strictly the order of inquiry, since most data-gathering is carried out in the light of already-formed hypotheses.) So, empirical science involves a normative – in contrast to the more spontaneous procedures guiding non-scientific inquiries – pattern of related and recurrent operations (of data gathering, hypothesis-formation and verification), yielding cumulative and progressive results.[7]

Lonergan refers to, while going beyond, the specific mathematical implications of Gödel's theorem, which showed up what Jean Ladrière later called 'the limits of formalisation'.[8] That is, every specific form of knowledge must go beyond itself for its grounding principles. Lonergan gives the example of our common sense knowledge, where we understand things in relation to ourselves, for example, that the earth is at rest and the sun rises in the morning and sets in the evening. But from the viewpoint of scientific explanation, where we aim at understanding things not in relation to ourselves but to each other, for example, 'the planets move in approximately elliptical orbits with the sun at their focus' (*Insight*, 293–5). Yet both types of knowledge are instances of the same underlying dynamic structure with its complementary aims of describing things in relation to ourselves and to each other.

Corresponding to the specific form of human knowing found in the natural sciences there's the limited nature of what is known by the natural

---

6 Philip McShane, *Randomness, Statistics and Emergence*, Dublin: Gill & Macmillan, 1970, p. 135. Lonergan entitled one essay: 'Isomorphism of Thomist and Scientific Thought' (*Collection*, pp. 142–51). He indicates there how the procedures of modern experimental science employ the same structure of human knowing he has articulated in Aquinas' cognitional theory, in its three phases of gathering data, developing hypotheses in order to understand the data, and finally verifying or falsifying those hypotheses in the data. The dictionary definition of theory given by Richard Dawkins in *The Greatest Show on Earth: The Evidence for Evolution* (London: Bantam Press, 2009, p. 9), isn't far from this: 'Theory [is] a hypothesis that has been confirmed or established by observation or experiment, and is propounded or accepted as accounting for the known facts ...'

7 See Lonergan, *Method in Theology*, p. 4.

8 Lonergan, *Insight*, xxv; Jean Ladrière, *Les limitations internes des formalismes. Étude sur la signification du théorème de Gödel et des théorèmes apparentés dans la théorie des fondements des mathématiques*, Leuven-Paris: Nauwelaerts-Gauthier-Villars, 1957.

sciences, namely the material world, itself requiring a deeper or ontological foundation in a philosophy of existence, which we'll examine in our next section.[9]

But behind those details of the structure of human knowing is the inquiring subject. The title of Michael Polanyi's magnum opus, *Personal Knowledge*, conveys his profound questioning of the notion, as Lonergan put it elsewhere, that somehow or other scientific knowledge can get along without minds, without the inquiring subject who is the scientist.[10] Sergio Rondinara points out that in quantum physics, 'the observer plays an essential role in grasping physical reality', a role profoundly explored by Patrick Heelan in his *Quantum Mechanics and Objectivity*.[11] So it's never 'science' that 'tells' us anything, but individual human beings carrying out their inquiries, attentively, intelligently and reasonably, that do so as well as they can.

1.2 What the natural sciences presuppose ontologically[12]
Probably the hardest thing to bring to the scientific table – at least in the English-speaking world – has been the reminder that science is not only an activity of human beings, a form of 'personal knowledge', but that it's an activity that takes part within a quest for understanding the truth of existence. To remind ourselves of that shock experience of the existence that underlies everything, here's a few words from a meditation on the mystery of Being (we've already come across Parmenides' first reflection on Is), to which of course all of nature belongs:

> In whatever way it is expressed in the languages of the various cultures, the fundamental statement of human thought is: being is. It is the

---

9 Stanley Jaki points out in *Is There a Universe?* (Liverpool: Liverpool University Press, 1993) that the existence of the universe as a whole is not a datum of any natural science but is a philosophical presupposition.

10 Michael Polanyi, *Personal Knowledge: Towards a Post-Critical Philosophy*, Chicago: University of Chicago Press, 1958.

11 Sergio Rondinara, *Interpetazione del reale tra scienza e teologia*, Rome: Città Nuova, 2007, p. 30; Patrick Heelan, *Quantum Mechanics and Objectivity: The Physical Philosophy of Werner Heisenberg*, The Hague: Nijhoff, 1965.

12 Józef Życiński has an excellent discussion on the natural sciences' requirement of 'methodological naturalism' – that is that scientific investigations must be conducted strictly according to their own methods and not philosophical or theological concerns. Still this shouldn't be accompanied by an 'ontological naturalism', a taking for granted of the existence of whatever they're studying. See his *God and Evolution: Fundamental Questions of Christian Evolutionism*, trs. Kenneth W. Kemp and Zuzanna Maslanka, Washington DC: Catholic University of America Press, 2006, p. 79.

acknowledgment of that great ocean of existence in which human beings are immersed in communion with everyone and everything. This is the most simple, single, and primordial certainty from which we can then proceed to penetrate the multiple and complex levels of reality. Everything can be negated, but not being. Being is offered to us by all that is around us (the various realities) and within us (our inner lives). The existence of the smallest things as of the greatest, express with all their reality: being is.

This being – which is common to all realities and through which they are not simply a nothingness – reveals, in its manifestation in nature, that Being which none of them is, but which is proclaimed in all beings. Their becoming, their limits, their very ceasing to exist is the language which states that the being of all that exists is rooted in a Being that simply and absolutely IS.[13]

While I'd suggest that natural scientists are dealing with beings with a small 'b', they are human beings like the rest of us, and can hardly help asking questions that go beyond their science, questions which in a sense are like shadows or echoes of Being. So a helpful way of approaching the problem of the relation between the natural sciences and philosophy is in terms of what we've called boundary or threshold questions, that is, questions that come up within the domain of the natural sciences but can't be answered by their own methodologies. Perhaps the most obvious boundary question is the one that arises in astrophysics. Without any evidence associated with the earliest instant of the expansion, the Big Bang theory can't and doesn't provide any explanation for such an initial condition; rather, it describes and explains the general evolution of the universe since that instant.[14]

The famous astrophysicists Stephen Hawking and George Ellis wrote of what we may see as the key boundary question posed by Big Bang theory:

The creation of the Universe has been argued, indecisively, from early times ... The results we have obtained support the idea that the universe

---

13 Chiara Lubich, *Essential Writings: Spirituality, Dialogue, Culture*, eds. Michel Vandeleene, Tom Masters and Callan Slipper, Hyde Park, NY: New City Press, 2007, p. 210.

14 Richard Dawkins' brief discussion of the event on the last page of *The Ancestor's Tale* only underlines its need for an explanation: ' ... the fact that life evolved out of nearly nothing, some 10 billion years after the universe evolved out of literally nothing – is a fact so staggering that I would be mad to attempt words to do it justice' (p. 506).

began a finite time ago. However the actual point of creation, the singularity, is outside the scope of presently known laws of physics.[15]

However, in his most popular book, Hawking proposed a view of the universe as having no boundary or edge, no beginning or end (on analogy with a sphere), and remarked of such a world: 'It would neither be created nor destroyed. It would just BE.'[16]

Here he seems not to want to ask that further question which the Big Bang theory inevitably brings up, 'Why is there something rather than nothing?' But he goes even further in his most recent book, where, answering his own question, 'how can a whole universe be created from nothing?' he continues:

Bodies such as stars or black holes cannot just appear out of nothing. But a whole universe can ... Because there is a law like gravity, the universe can and will create itself from nothing ... [17]

So, from apparently wanting to prevent the boundary question of existence from being asked, Hawking goes further, and claims (or half-claims) to be able to answer it from within astrophysics itself. But questions about existence as such while taken for granted by the natural sciences can hardly be taken for granted by human beings asking the obvious further questions. Nor is a question about existence as such answerable within astronomy or physics for the simple reason that their methodologies neither raise such questions nor have the wherewithal to answer them.

Lonergan uses the term 'internal causation' (often called 'secondary causation') for the explanatory relations within and between material objects discovered by the natural sciences, while 'external causation' (or 'primary causation') has to do with relating contingent reality to what grounds it. Again and again, many of what are treated as irresolvable conflicts between science and religion, or science and philosophy, are due

---

15 Stephen Hawking and George Ellis, *The Large Scale Structure of Space-Time*, New York: Cambridge University Press, 1973, p. 364.

16 Stephen Hawking, *A Brief History of Time*, London: Bantam Press, 1988, p. 136.

17 Stephen Hawking and Leonard Mlodinow, *The Grand Design*, London: Bantam Press, 2010, p. 180. Despite this confident assertion, surely not based on an analysis of what creation from nothing might mean, Hawking's other statements are much more tentative. While proposing 'M-theory' as 'the only candidate for a complete theory of the universe', he goes on to say: 'If it is finite – and this has yet to be proved – it will be a model of the universe which creates itself ... If the theory is confirmed by observation ... We will have found *The Grand Design*' (p. 181).

to the failure to make this distinction between two quite different levels of causal explanation.

Let's put it this way: the intelligibility 'in' things in the world can refer to the 'how' concerning the relationships that hold among the immanent elements of the world. So there are 'how' questions. But there are also questions about the sheer fact of such intelligibility being there at all (science can explain everything except why there is intelligibility in everything) and these are a different sort of question that cannot be answered in terms of 'how' but in terms of 'why' – in other words, not just questions that can be answered by understanding relationships between things in the world, but questions raised about their very existence. Distinguishing between these two types of questions, natural scientific and ontological is not an achievement of science or religion but of philosophy. As a result, not infrequently, both scientists and religious people muddle up the proper domains of the two types of questions.

Astrophysicist and philosopher William Stoeger indicates that there's no conflict between 'how' and 'why' questions, between the natural sciences and philosophy:

> As Creator, God would be the ultimate author of 'the laws of nature' as they actually function. This is God's universal creative action. The traditional model used to articulate this is that of *creatio ex nihilo*, creation from absolutely nothing. In using this term, the essential content is the absolute dependence of reality on God the Creator at every moment, not some transcendent process which rivals or replaces the processes of nature. Insofar as we can analogically attribute agency or causality to God as Creator, God is then considered 'the primary cause', the cause unlike and more fundamental than any other cause. All other causes are 'secondary' and ultimately rely on, though they are not completely determined by, the primary cause.

He notes how the increased understanding of the natural world by science confirms that God does not act:

> ... as an intervener, as a secondary cause, within creation, thus re-inforcing the formational and functional integrity of creation itself and of nature – its relative autonomy (at the level of secondary causes there is nothing missing that must be supplied by God to complete creation,

or to enable new things to emerge) ... As Thomas Tracy explicates this, the key component is that 'God's creative action includes the continuous "giving of being" to the created world in its entirety', enabling each being and system of beings within creation to function and develop according to its own capacities and dynamisms, including those of conscious, freely deciding and acting persons and communities of persons. It is through what material beings and systems of beings at all levels accomplish through the operation of their God-given potentialities that God continues to act creatively in the world – God acting in and through secondary causes. Thus, ultimately all that happens within the created world can be considered an act of God.[18]

Sergio Rondinara further notes that God's sustaining of creation isn't to be understood as an act separate from the initial act of creation, rather it is the continuation of the creative act that from our perspective extends throughout time.[19]

Because the human quest for understanding unfolds at these two distinct levels of primary and secondary causation, there will always be the possibility of boundary questions – where the question of existence is 'provoked' by the data of the natural sciences themselves. So while what Stoeger calls the 'relative autonomy' of the natural world ensures that its

---

18 William R. Stoeger, SJ, 'Reduction and Emergence: Implications for Theology', pp. 229–47, in Nancey Murphy and William R. Stoeger, SJ, eds., *Evolution and Emergence: Systems, Organisms, Persons*, Oxford: Oxford University Press, 2007, p. 236, pp. 240–1, p. 246. In 'Does a Fine-Tuned Universe Lead to God?' Robert Lawrence Kuhn interviews philosopher of science Fr Ernan McMullin, who puts the issue as clearly as I've seen anywhere: ' ... we can ask whether there should be a universe in the first place. The question of existence is a unique question. It's a question which the scientists can't address and shouldn't address. This is not a shortcoming of science, this is not a gap; this is simply a question that is of a different sort. And the religious believer has always asked it and has always given an answer to it: There is a being responsible for the fact that the universe exists, even if there are an infinity of universes or a universe which has always existed ... You have a choice between two alternatives: You either stop with the universe as given, as physicists do. Or you take the one step further and you postulate a single being and a single act of creation.' [Kuhn]: 'But this doesn't answer why there should be that kind of God in the first place?' 'There has to be a stopping point,' McMullin asserts. 'The question is: Which is the better stopping point? I myself think that it's an issue that has never come up before in the history of this discussion because, previous to this, the way in which God entered into it was as an answer to some specific of the universe, like design, for example. My argument has nothing to do with this. It is not saying, 'Look, there's something science can't explain which we can explain with God.' That's not it. What is being postulated here is a reason why there should be anything at all for physics to study in the first place. (Available online in *Science + Religion Today*, 13 May 2010. http://www.scienceandreligiontoday.com/2010/05/13/does-a-fine-tuned-universe-lead-to-god/)

19 Sergio Rondinara, '"Dio Amore" e la nostra comprensione del cosmo', where he refers to Thomas Aquinas, *Summa Theologiae*, I, q. 104, a.1.

investigation will be carried out by the relevant range of natural sciences, there will always be the 'residue' of the existence of this area of natural reality, which then remains open to the further, ontological question.

Ludwig Wittgenstein refers to the ontological issue in some trenchantly clear remarks:

> It is not *how* things are in the world that is mystical, but *that* it exists. We feel that even when all possible scientific questions have been answered, our problems of life remain completely untouched ... One keeps forgetting to go right down to the foundations. One doesn't put the question marks deep enough down.[20]

And Voegelin reminds us of the ontological question referred to by Martin Heidegger who spoke of the forgetfulness of being in contemporary culture. In response to the claim that questions about existence have no meaning from the viewpoint of the kind of evidence required in the natural sciences, Voegelin writes:

> Within the limits of the positivist horizon, the argument is valid; the questions can indeed not be answered by reference to the world of sense perception. The argument becomes invalid, however, when it goes on to declare the questions, for this reason, to be meaningless; for the people who have asked them through several thousand years of history to this day do not consider them meaningless at all, even if they find the adequate articulation of their meaning sometimes a baffling task. The denial of meaning runs counter to the empirical fact that they rise again and again as meaningful from the experience of reality.[21]

To say inquiries about existence are false requires that the person making that assessment has achieved a grasp of truth in terms of which ontological or metaphysical inquiry is false. That is to say, it presupposes an overarching experience of being, within which the distinction between reality and mere appearance can be made. And of course such an overarching experience of being is prior to the subset of reality explored by the natural sciences.

---

20 Ludwig Wittgenstein, *Tractatus Logico-Philosophicus*, London: Routledge & Kegan Paul, 1963, p. 149e; *Culture and Value*, ed. G. H. von Wright, Chicago: University of Chicago Press, 1984, p. 62e. Edward Oakes gave me the idea for these Wittgenstein references in 'Edward T. Oakes and His Critics: An Exchange', *First Things*, April 2001.

21 Eric Voegelin, *The Ecumenic Age*, Baton Rouge: Louisiana State University Press, p. 316.

The core issue remains unchanged, it seems to me – the kind of question regarding the mystery of existence raised by, say, Wittgenstein, is not removed by any assertion that the methodology of the natural sciences is the only criterion for every inquiry.[22]

1.3 The historical origins of the natural sciences

What we call the natural sciences can be seen to emerge within the Western context constituted by the experiences of Greek philosophy and Judeo-Christian revelation. How did this context make possible the emergence of the experimental natural sciences? It is possible to list three factors underlying modern scientific method, which connect with the three levels of inquiry we've been discussing. To begin any scientific investigation we have to (i) be convinced that the experienced data which prompt our inquiry is potentially meaningful – otherwise why bother to investigate?; (ii) have some control over how we're to understand those data, some kind of definition, however provisional; and (iii) acknowledge that only if the world we're in doesn't have to be the way it is, but could be otherwise, is there need for a process of verification. So, a word on each of these levels in terms of the history of natural science:

(a) **The world as potentially meaningful:** Firstly, for natural science to emerge at the level of wonder at the experience of the natural world, there had to be a belief in the meaningfulness of created reality, where that belief had its origins in faith in a rational creator. In fact, historically the experimental natural sciences only began to flourish from the late-medieval period onwards. The mathematician and philosopher A. N. Whitehead in the first chapter of his *Science and the Modern World*, discussed 'The Origins of Modern Science' and ascribed that development not only to classic Greek philosophy but also to the Jewish and Christian articulation of the rationality of God and of nature.[23] The dedivinisation of the mythic cosmos which

---

22 For example, Stephen Hawking makes this assertion at the beginning of *The Grand Design*: 'philosophy is dead' since it 'has not kept up with modern developments in science, particularly physics. Scientists have become the bearers of the torch for discovery in our quest for knowledge' (p. 5).

23 A. N. Whitehead, *Science and the Modern World*, London: Cambridge University Press, 1953, p. 15f. Stanley Jaki in his *Science and Creation: From Eternal Cycles to an Oscillating Universe* (Edinburgh: Scottish Academic Press, 1986, p. 231) refers to Whitehead's remark that 'studies in medieval science ... provided ... ample evidence that the medieval faith in the scrutability of nature had its logical justification in the medieval theology about Creator and creation, and that the faith in the possibility of science is a most conscious derivative from the tenets of medieval theology on the "Maker of Heaven and Earth".' Jaki in *Science and Creation* and in his Gifford Lectures, *The Road of Science and the Ways of God* (Chicago: University of Chicago Press, 1978) among many other publications provides a mass of material on the origins of modern science within the context of Greek philosophy and Judeo-Christian revelation.

occurred both in Genesis and the Hebrew Bible, continued emphatically with Christianity. As Voegelin notes: 'when divinity is concentrated in a world-transcendent sphere, the intracosmic [that is, within the cosmos] divine order disappears.'[24] Without the notion of a world that was not divine there couldn't be an experimental study of what's typically called 'nature'. And yet, if that natural world was either divine – as for example the Stoics considered it to be – or chaotically impenetrable to rational analysis, no one would take on the tremendous labour of investigation.[25] This, Jaki notes, underlies the failure both of the classical Greek, Indian and Chinese cultures to develop an experimental natural science.

He writes of how the phrase from the Book of Wisdom, 'You have arranged all things by measure, number and weight' (11:20) 'served as inspiration and assurance for those who in late antiquity assumed the role of champions of the rationality of the universe. A thousand years later the expression was gladly seized upon by those who daringly started out on the road to unfold the marvels of God's handiwork along the lines of quantitative inquiry.'[26] Historians of science would also include the Arab advancement of mathematics as a factor, since the ability to make controlled measurements of natural phenomena was central to the advance of the natural sciences.[27] Whatever his theological views, Einstein's famous remark, 'The most incomprehensible thing about the universe is that it is comprehensible' can be taken as a late echo of comments by scientists like Copernicus, Galileo, Kepler and Newton, all explicitly referring to the Creator as the underlying source of the world's meaningfulness for scientific investigation.[28]

(b) **The world as actually defined:** Secondly, at the level of what we've been calling the 'what question', the Greek discovery of definition was a key component in the emergence of scientific thinking, or of controlled reasoning in the history of humanity. Lonergan discusses this Greek component, where the 'classic expression of the effort to control meaning is found in the early Platonic dialogues'. Socrates' questions aimed at

---

24 Eric Voegelin, *The Drama of Humanity and Other Papers, 1939–1985*, eds. William Petropulos and Gilbert Weiss, Columbia, MO: University of Missouri Press, 2004, p. 81.

25 For example, Chrysippus: 'The universe itself is god and the universal outpouring of its soul,' quoted by Cicero in his *De Natura Deorum*, p. i.

26 Jaki, *Science and Creation*, p. 154.

27 See ibid., pp. 192–218 on the strengths and weaknesses of the Arab contribution to science in the early medieval period.

28 Einstein's remark was quoted most recently in Hawking, *The Grand Design*, p. 87. Jaki, *Science and Creation*, pp. 276–305.

'universal definitions, brief and exact statements that fitted every case of courage and, at the same time, fitted nothing except courage ... ' He'd made the discovery – although its beginnings can be found in the earlier medical treatises of Hippocrates – 'that a good definition ... had to apply to every instance of the defined and to no instance of something else'.[29]

Lonergan's *Insight* explores the richness of definition in modern science, including not only the kind of definition employed in classic Newtonian physics, but the later development of the science of probability. Statistical method deals not with the nature of an 'x' but how often that 'x' occurs, and its expansion within quantum mechanics. He further widens the notion of definition to include living things whose definition necessarily includes the facts of development, and – in an extension to the human sciences – articulates a scientific understanding of individual, social and historical breakdown. So definition can include classical, statistical, developmental and dialectical methods.[30]

However, just as the potential meaningfulness of the natural world ontologically has an origin outside itself, the natural scientific definitions of things don't exhaust the meaning of the realities they define. When we define what a star, an atom, a bacterium, a plant, an animal, or a human being is, there always remains the further metaphysical question about their existence. And this further question remains even when the 'nature' being defined is at a much higher level of explanation, as for example, overarching physical or astronomical theories, or the various theories of evolution connecting all living things into one overall explanatory context. As Voegelin puts it in his essay 'What is Nature?', 'there are no things that are merely immanent'.[31]

Echoing this, David Walsh writes, 'The reality of nature is contained not within itself, but within its tension toward being as such.'[32] This in no way means that philosophy can ever make up for the observation and experimentation that constitutes the methodology of the natural sciences – for example, only years of research in botany can yield the range of insights into the growth cycle of Californian redwoods, the difference between the coastal and High Sierra species, their ecosystem so complex that they

---

29 Bernard Lonergan, 'Dimensions of Meaning', in *Collection*, New York: Herder & Herder, 1967, pp. 256–7.

30 See Lonergan, *Insight*, chapters I–VIII.

31 Eric Voegelin, 'What is Nature?' in *Anamnesis: On the Theory of History and Politics*, ed. David Walsh, Columbia: University of Missouri Press, 2002, pp.157–74, at p. 164.

32 David Walsh, *The Modern Philosophical Revolution: The Luminosity of Existence*, New York: Cambridge University Press, 2008, p. 12.

cannot be reproductively grown anywhere else, and so on. But even when, in some botanical future, all such questions are finally answered, there still remains the questions Leibniz as a philosopher would ask: why have they the nature that botany shows them to have? Or, as we've seen, Hawking's assertion: 'Because there is a law like gravity, the universe can and will create itself from nothing ... '[33] doesn't make it unreasonable to ask the further question: why is there a law like gravity?

(c) **The world as contingent:** Thirdly, at the level of judgement, or the Is-Question, there's the notion of contingent being. Jaki writes of the Hellenistic attitude towards nature, as something 'one could speculate about in order to understand it, but one was not suppose to supplement his speculations ... by submitting them to tests consisting in changes imposed systematically on nature. This entailed the barring of repeated experiments' since nature was determined to repeat itself according to necessary laws.[34] He notes the 'inhibitory influence of the belief in eternal recurrences' on Greek science and how that was historically overcome by the Christian refusal to accept either the divinity of the heavens or the myth of necessarily recurring cycles, both because of belief in a divinity transcending the cosmos and that the world had a beginning in time.[35]

The point is that only if the natural world isn't necessary can we arrive at concrete judgments which verify or falsify our hypotheses or theories about this or that aspect of it. At least in this we can agree with the positivists of the Vienna School and Karl Popper's variation of it, that all our scientific insights have to be tested in the material under investigation and judged true or false on the basis of that testing. And again, that verification requires the background context of the radically different approach to reality in Judeo-Christian culture that can't be found either in the great Oriental religions or even in classic Greece. These other cultures did not develop the notion of the natural world as inherently contingent, and not necessary, which might explain the emergence of the natural sciences in the West, at least from the time of Galileo onwards.[36]

---

33 Hawking, *The Grand Design*, p. 180.

34 Jaki, *Science and Creation*, p. 130.

35 Stanley Jaki, *The Origin of Science and the Science of its Origin*, Edinburgh: Scottish Academic Press, 1978, pp. 70–1.

36 Aquinas developed the ontological tools in his reflection on inherently contingent created reality in his early monograph, *De ente et essentia*; Lonergan has fully explored Aquinas' parallel development of the epistemological tools for making judgements about contingent reality in his *Verbum: Word and Idea in Aquinas*, Notre Dame: Notre Dame University Press, 1967.

Again, our third factor of contingency is no more an ultimate than are the earlier two factors of possible meaningfulness or definition. As David Walsh has written, 'Contingency is not itself contingent. Once we realise that what characterises the flow of things does not necessarily, and cannot necessarily, be extended to the whole itself, we are no longer so lost in the cosmos.'[37] In the Judeo-Christian experience there was a strong awareness of the world's createdness. So the world did not necessarily exist, but as a matter of fact, had come into existence. And there could be no natural science without that awareness of a contingent world. It's a contingent world whose laws – unlike those of mathematics or logic, which are necessary and universal – are not necessary, yet when they're discovered they're found to be universal, Still, as Walsh has noted, contingency itself can only be understood in terms of what is not contingent, or it is itself without meaning.

Having discussed the epistemological, ontological and historical background for the natural sciences, let's have a quick look at an overall framework or heuristic for investigating the entire material world. This will help us interconnect the full range of natural sciences with one another and show their correspondence to the dynamic unity of the material world.

2. World process and the sequence of sciences that map it

2.1 World process in terms of the anthropic principle
We're all familiar with the outlines of the cosmos story narrated by the natural sciences, even if the details undergo constant modification by new discoveries and theoretical revisions. Edmund Hubble's and George-Henri Lemaître's discovery of the expansion of the universe at a constant rate in the 1920s and early thirties, the later development of the expansion theory as inflation theory by Alan Guth and others, and George Smoot's discovery in April 1992 of the variation in the density of matter at 300,000 years after the first instant of the existence of the cosmos, led to a renewed attempt to understand the origins and nature of the cosmos as a whole.[38]

Hugh Ross, in his *Why the Universe is the Way It is*, gives an excellent summary of up-to-date scientific conclusions regarding the series of improbable events that make the emergence of life, and later of human life, possible.[39] He begins with our galaxy, the Milky Way, and points out how its

---

37 David Walsh, 'The Turn Toward Existence and Existence in the Turn', in *Philosophy, Literature and Politics: Essays Honoring Ellis Sandoz*, eds. Charles R. Embry and Barry Cooper, Columbia: University of Missouri Press, 2005, pp. 3–27, at p. 24.

38 George Smoot and Keay Davidson, *Wrinkles in Time*, New York: Morrow, 1993.

39 Hugh Ross, *Why the Universe is the Way It is*, Grand Rapids, MI: Baker Books, 2008.

age and its position in a medium-sized system of galaxies known as the Local Group is just right as the star-based context within which life could emerge. The Milky Way itself emerged at the right time, since if it had belonged to the earlier galaxies, it wouldn't have been able to emit the metals required for the formation of the terrestrial planets needed for most higher forms of life.[40]

Then there's the wonderful positioning of our Solar System on a partial spiral of the Milky Way, which again falls within the requirements for a habitable zone. Our own Sun is at just the right age, neither too young – when it would be too bright – nor too old – when it would be too hot – for life to emerge. Then there is the position of the Earth within the Solar System, where the much larger gas planets, especially Jupiter and Saturn, largely shield it from the continual and life-threatening assaults of space-debris like comets and meteorites. The Moon's gravitational pull slowed the Earth's day from a two- to three-hour length – which would not have been the balanced twenty-four hour period of day and night that plants and animals which came later require.

This unfolding sequence of events exhibits a series where the earlier levels can function without the later ones, but the later ones depend on the earlier. As we know, the elements necessary for life could only come into existence through the process of nucleosynthesis. The only place hot enough to 'cook' the light element helium into the heavier element carbon, apparently, is the heart of a dying star. Some 10 to 5 billion years ago, the first generation of stars, when their hydrogen cores burnt up at a heat of $100m°K$, an incredibly finely tuned process, released carbon and the other heavier elements into the universe.[41]

It is up to astrophysics and biochemistry to understand the process by which, say, the heavier elements of carbon, nitrogen and oxygen, along with hydrogen, in the extremely apt compounds of amino acids, are swept up into at least one hundred proteins arranged in highly-ordered three-dimensional shapes, which constitute a living cell with its unique property of reproducing itself every twenty minutes.

The first signs of life on earth, the bacterial cells (that is, cells without a nucleus) of fossilised stromatolites – mat-like layers of cells – have been calculated at 3.7 billion years ago, along with the archaea (single-celled organisms living near high temperature vents in the ocean or at hot springs

40 We're not going into the question of whether there are forms of life unlike the prevailing carbon-based forms we know on Earth – it's more than enough here to deal with the only form we know.

41 See Barrow and Tipler, *The Anthropic Cosmological Principle*, p. 252f.

or salt lakes; more recently they've also been discovered in soil, marshland, and plankton) which were only discovered as late as 1977 by Carl Woese and George Fox. And the first complex eukaryotic cells (cells with nuclei) in algae date from 1.5 billion years ago.[42]

Towards the end of Smoot and Davidson's *Wrinkles in Time* they remark: 'We can see how very complex the universe is now, and we are part of that complexity.'[43] The universe is not simply one layer of existence heaped on top of another, like a gigantic world-burger. What makes the narration a story, as distinct from the discrete set of facts we have just given, is the dynamic interconnection between the different levels of being in the cosmos – physical, chemical, biological, botanical, zoological and human.

There are several frameworks which have tried to articulate the link between these various levels of existence. Two of the most common ones are what cosmologist Brandon Carter and later Barrow and Tipler called 'the anthropic principle', and the theory of biological evolution. We'll be discussing evolution in our next chapter, so we'll just say a few words about why the anthropic principle was developed here.

For example, we're familiar with the vital role played by the earliest life forms on earth, prokaryotic algae. These algae turn water, carbon dioxide and sunlight into their food, with oxygen as a very important by-product, which, from 2.7 billion years to 2.2 billion years ago, changed the Earth's atmosphere from lacking oxygen to containing almost 20 per cent oxygen. The careful survey in Barrow and Tipler's study dedicates chapters to the physical, quantum mechanical and biochemical examples of the so-called 'Goldilocks Principle' – which finds again and again that the natural order shows an amazing tilt towards the exact balance of neither too much nor too little needed for the emergence of life.[44]

They discuss the importance of water, the significance of carbon, carbon dioxide and carbonic acid, of nitrogen, and so on, without which life could not have emerged, or at least been maintained. While algae may be considered as plant life, still, since they are only single-celled, we may prefer to see plants in terms of the more complex forms of land plants, as late as 450 million years ago. The first multicellular animal life appears

---

42 Richard Dawkins, *The Ancestor's Tale: A Pilgrimage to the Dawn of Life*, London: Weidenfeld & Nicolson, 2004, p. 379.

43 Smoot and Davidson, *Wrinkles in Time*, p. 290.

44 John D. Barrow and Frank J. Tipler, *The Anthropic Cosmological Principle*, Oxford: Oxford University Press, 1986; see also Paul Davies, *The Goldilocks Enigma: Why is the Universe Just Right for Life?* Boston: Houghton Mifflin, 2008.

from around 550 million years back, with Australian Ediacaran and Canadian Burgess Shale fauna.[45] Later we'll be discussing the evidence for the earliest undeniably human beings perhaps as early as 150,000 years ago.

For Barrow and Tipler, it looks as if the universe did know we were coming, as theoretical physicist Freeman Dyson put it.[46] There are various versions of the anthropic principle, all asking the underlying question – how is it that a series of improbable events have made life, and then human life, possible? The 'weak' version simply holds that, as a matter of fact, life wouldn't be possible without that sequence of improbable events. The 'strong' version goes so far as to say that that sequence occurred in order that we should be here. However, the 'strong' version doesn't seem to belong to natural science, but to the area covered by philosophy or theology, and has been rejected by most scientists as scientifically untestable, and therefore unprovable. It might just be a playful metaphor, ascribing to the universe a capital letter and the power of thinking. But from a philosophical or theological perspective, it's a bit unadventurous – it avoids the further question as to why such a universe should be the case, and even more, whether it was created and by whom. The formulation of the strong anthropic principle seems due to the blurring of the two types of question we've spoken of, so that they think that 'how' questions somehow do away with the need for 'why' questions.

2.2 World process in terms of Aristotle's understanding of matter and form

Before saying a few words about Lonergan's approach to understanding cosmic process, I'd like to consider Aristotle for a moment. Aristotle developed a way for understanding the relationship between different levels of being particularly in his treatise called *De Anima*, or *On The Soul* – which is an investigation of vegetative, animal and human life. He spoke of

---

45 Martin F. Glaessner, *The Dawn of Animal Life*, Cambridge: Cambridge University Press, 1984; Simon Conway Morris, *The Crucible of Creation: The Burgess Shale and the Rise of Animals*, Oxford: Oxford University Press, 1998; Stephen Jay Gould, *Wonderful Life: The Burgess Shale and the Nature of History*, London: Hutchinson Radius, 1990.There has also been the recent discovery in the Draa valley or Fezouata formation in the Moroccan desert of a range of Burgess-like fauna from the Early Ordovician period, from 488 million years to 471 million. See Nicola Jones, 'Weird wonders lived past the Cambrian: Moroccan fossils show that strange early animals were no flash in the pan'. *Nature News*, 12 May 2010, http://www.nature.com/news/2010/100512/full/news.2010.234.html.

46 The full quotation is: 'As we look out into the Universe and identify the many accidents of physics and astronomy that have worked together to our benefit, it almost seems as if the Universe must in some sense have known that we were coming.' Freeman Dyson, quoted in Barrow & Tipler, *The Anthropic Cosmological Principle*, p. 318.

that heuristic, or intellectual context in terms of the relationship between matter and form. Eric Voegelin has a useful modern restatement of this:

These levels of the hierarchy of being [Voegelin had already mentioned them as human-psychic, animal, vegetative and inanimate being] are related to each other in (a) the grounding of the higher on the lower ones and (b) the organisation of the lower by the higher ones. These relationships are not reversible. On the one hand, there is no *eu zen*, no good life [that is, the full actualisation of the human level in its ethical realisation] in Aristotle's sense, without the foundation of *zen* [that is, the biological level of life]; on the other hand, the order of the good life does not emerge from the corporeal foundation but comes into being only when the entire existence is ordered by the centre of the existential tension [towards the Good].[47]

2.3 World process in terms of emergent probability

But is there an intellectual framework for understanding a world which is a lot more dynamic and interrelated than Aristotle's world? About twenty years before the anthropic principle was formulated, in a profound upgrade of the Aristotelian articulation of the relation between matter and form, Lonergan remarked in *Insight* that 'concrete extensions [spaces] and concrete durations [times] are the field or matter or potency in which emergent probability is the immanent form or intelligibility' (325). What Lonergan offers in *Insight* is a generalised framework for the entire dynamic sequence of interrelationships between the levels of reality from physics up to anthropology.

He writes: 'Let us say that the schemes P, Q, R … form a conditioned series, if all prior members of the series must be functioning actually for any later member to become a concrete possibility.' Then P (say, the physical and chemical levels of existence) can function without Q (say, the biological level of existence) or R (say, the zoological level of existence); Q can function without R; but Q can't function without P, nor can R function without P and Q (*Insight*, 118–19).

Emergent probability for Lonergan 'results from the combination of the conditioned series of schemes with their respective probabilities of emergence and survival'. He outlines the application of this insight in terms of its capacity to make sense in world process of its (i) spatial distribution,

---

47 Voegelin, *Anamnesis: On the Theory of History and Politics*, p. 407.

(ii) large numbers, (iii) long intervals of time, (iv) selection, (v) stability, and (vi) development (*Insight*, 122).

Attempting to summarise his explanation of these factors we can say (i) that the later and more advanced schemes, since they depend on the greatest number of conditions being fulfilled, 'will be limited to a relatively small number of places.' (ii) Large numbers are required, since 'the lower the probability of the last schemes of the conditioned series, the greater must be the initial absolute numbers in which elementary schemes can be realised. In brief, the size of a universe is inversely proportionate to the probability of its ultimate schemes of recurrence.' (iii) While 'the initial benefit of large numbers is lost by the successive narrowing of the basis for further developments', long intervals of time greatly increase the probability of more developments. (iv) There's 'a selective significance attached to the distinction between probabilities of emergence and probabilities of survival ... If both are high, the occurrences will be both common and enduring. If the probability of emergence is low and that of survival is high, the scheme is expected to be rare but enduring.' (v) 'The line of maximum stability would be of common and enduring schemes while the line of minimum stability would be of rare and fleeting schemes.' (vi) Lonergan notes that stability and development can conflict, since schemes 'with high probabilities of survival tend to imprison materials in their own routines', providing a stable basis for later schemes but tending 'to prevent later schemes from emerging'.

The best solution 'would be for the earlier conditioning schemes to have a high probability of emergence but a low probability of survival', forming a 'floating population, on which later schemes could successively depend'. Their low probability of survival 'would readily surrender materials to give later schemes the opportunity to emerge' (*Insight*, 122–4). Taken together, these factors help to make sense of the enormous size and age of our universe, and the small likelihood and incredible scarcity of life.

What Lonergan opens up, I think, is the possibility of a radically non-deductivist philosophical formulation of a cosmological-anthropological view of the world.[48] There, each level can be seen as providing the materials

---

48 William Stoeger speaks of different orders of emergence which are 'radically new and irreducible to causal influences at lower levels of organisation. They emerge as matter becomes organised in more and more complex ways. For instance, goals develop within systems which are not in any way determined by what occurs at lower levels of organisation.' Yet while 'we will probably never know exactly how these [key transitions between inanimate and animate ... organisms] actually happened, it is becoming clear that the laws of nature at the proper level are capable of explaining these emergent phenomena ... there are strong theological reasons for not making God just another secondary cause (instead of the primary cause) in the universe' ('Reduction and Emergence ... ' p. 242).

required for the next highest level. As he writes, 'World process is open. It is a succession of probable realisations of possibilities. Hence it does not run along the iron rails laid down by determinists nor, on the other hand, is it a non-intelligible morass of merely chance events.' This openness admits breakdowns and blind alleys, since schemes have no more than a probability of survival, and successful schemes can 'bind within their routines the materials for the possibility of later schemes and so ... block the way to a full development' (*Insight*, 126, 127). These remarks will be worth keeping in mind when we consider several blind alleys in hominid development, from *Australopithecus robustus* to the Neanderthals, where their greater physical strength may have blocked off opportunities for further development.

Lonergan notes that his heuristic for development is to be understood within the limits of empirical science, focusing only on what Aristotle would call material and formal causes: 'As empirical science it prescinds from efficient, instrumental, and final causes, which refer to distinct types of intelligibility and lie beyond the qualifications of empirical method either to affirm or to deny' (*Insight*, 260). By (a) efficient, (b) instrumental and (c) final causes, Lonergan means here: (a) the primary causation from non-existence into existence, (b) discussion of created or secondary causation in its relation to primary causation, and (c) the overall aim of the created universe.[49]

The openness of emergent probability is due to its radically non-deductive nature, accepting as a matter of fact that lower aggregates of existence make materially possible the emergence of the next level, but neither explain nor necessitate it. As a heuristic framework, it is not a hypothesis to be verified or falsified within any of the natural sciences, but a heuristic assumption that can only be empirically tested through specific determinations and applications (*Insight*, 261). For our purposes, its primary function is to provide an intellectual context within which the various findings of the natural sciences can be drawn together. Swiss philosopher of science Arthur Pap wrote of how such heuristic contexts could be verified in terms of what he called 'the contextual confirmation of

---

49 This meets the complaint Dennett makes about 'skyhooks' in *Darwin's Dangerous Idea* – a complaint which is justifiable insofar as extrinsic causes can be wrongly invoked within the domain of the natural sciences as such, which deal with intrinsic formal causes. I'd suggest that Dennett's complaint goes back to Darwin and his problems with the same issue – which we'll be discussing in the next chapter. But those who make extra-scientific claims for their preferred natural science often provoke equally unjustified counter-claims by others who also import non-scientific considerations into the domain of the natural sciences.

theoretical postulates'.[50] In other words, such general theories can only be found to be true or false in terms of how well they explain the wide ranges of material they purport to make sense of.

We can say that the series of six interconnected levels, from physical to human, in Lonergan's terminology is 'a linked sequence of dynamic and increasingly higher integrations' (*Insight*, 115f., 454f.). And since such sets of dynamic interactions between levels are recurrent, from plants through lower to higher animals, including the hominids, up to man, it's possible to form a viewpoint of the entire sequence, with lower levels providing the materials for the next highest level. That overall insight is into 'the immanent design or order' of the universe (*Insight*, 116).

2.4 Sequence of natural sciences correlative to sequence of levels of reality

Lonergan spells out the hierarchy of levels in being to which the different natural sciences correspond:

> The laws of physics hold for subatomic elements; the laws of physics and chemistry hold for chemical elements and compounds; the laws of physics, chemistry, and biology hold for plants; the laws of physics, chemistry, biology, and sensitive psychology hold for animals; the laws of physics, chemistry, biology, sensitive psychology, and rational psychology hold for men. As one moves from one genus [here meaning level of being] to the next, there is added a new set of laws which defines its own basic terms by its own empirically established correlations. (*Insight*, 255)

Against the view holding that all the higher sciences can ultimately be reduced to the lower sciences, of physics, chemistry and biochemistry, Lonergan finds the need to proceed to a higher science when it confronts data which can't be understood in terms of the lower sciences:

> ... if the laws of subatomic elements have to regard the regular behaviour of atoms as mere patterns of happy coincidences, then there is an autonomous science of chemistry. If the laws of chemistry have to regard the metabolism and division of cells as mere patterns of happy coincidences, then there is an autonomous science of biology.

---

50 Arthur Pap, *An Introduction to the Philosophy of Science*, London: Eyre & Spottiswoode, 1963, p. 351.

If the laws of biology have to regard the behaviour of animals as mere patterns of happy coincidences, then there is an autonomous science of sensitive psychology. If the laws of sensitive psychology have to regard the operations of mathematicians and scientists as mere patterns of happy coincidences, then there is an autonomous science of rational psychology [what we'll be calling philosophical anthropology].

The higher sciences don't take away the need for the lower ones, which must do their own explaining on their own terms. What the higher sciences do is to explain only what the lower sciences leave unexplained:

Nor does the introduction of the higher autonomous science interfere with the autonomy of the lower; for the higher enters into the field of the lower only in so far as it makes systematic on the lower level what otherwise would be merely coincidental. (*Insight*, 256)

What Lonergan is saying here is that corresponding to the various levels of reality – physical, chemical, biological, botanical, zoological, human – is the sequence of sciences, which function as a series of higher viewpoints.[51] Each higher viewpoint arises from a new set of questions the phenomena pose to the scientist, questions which can't be answered in terms of the lower science. Corresponding to the successive levels of reality, there will be distinct and autonomous empirical sciences. These distinct and autonomous sciences 'will be related as successive higher viewpoints' (*Insight*, 438–9).

A simple example for the need to move from a lower to a higher viewpoint would be trying to arrive at a scientific understanding of a field of buttercups. Let's say the buttercups show slight species variation depending on their position in wetter or drier parts of the field. However exhaustively the biochemical changes in the buttercups were registered, no such account would yield the specifically botanical insight into the kind of things buttercups are.[52] Nor are the millions of cells in each buttercup separate 'things', since intrinsic to the constitution of each cell is that they

---

51 As an example of a higher viewpoint, Lonergan spells out the 'complex shift in the whole structure of insights, definitions, postulates, deductions, and applications' that takes place in the move from school arithmetic to the much more generalised operations of elementary algebra (*Insight*, pp. 13–19).

52 I owe this example to Philip McShane's *Randomness, Statistics and Emergence* (pp. 71–6), and his discussion of the specific difference between botany and biochemistry in his *Plants and Pianos: Two Essays in Advanced Methodology*, Dublin: Milltown Institute, 1971.

are buttercup cells. The point is that when you ask questions as to why a whole range of data that's making some sort of sense can't be explained at a certain level, you may then have to move to another level of science, in this case from biology to botany.

We'll come back to the question of higher viewpoints when we discuss biology and evolution and especially when we're discussing the relative status of hominid studies and philosophical anthropology.

3. How science can sometimes lose its way
While we can look at science in terms of the scientist as knowing subject and of the object it studies, both of these aspects can get seriously distorted. Scientific inquiry gets derailed by the ideology of what's called 'scientism', and the objects of scientific inquiry find themselves downgraded through the corresponding blind spot of 'reductionism'. Lonergan has developed the correlative terms of 'scotosis' – the non-occurrence of relevant insights for whatever reason, and 'scotoma' – the reality eclipsed because not questioned. Thus, we can see scientism as the scotosis whose resulting scotoma is reductionism (*Insight*, 191–203).

Why these derailments? The comparatively late emergence of the experimental natural sciences in Western Europe from the 1300s on, with its great sequence from Copernicus, Kepler and Galileo to Newton, coincided with the epoch when the intellectual and cultural significance both of Judeo-Christian revelation and of classic Greek philosophy was breaking down in the West. Possibly to substitute for the loss of these sources of Western order, the natural sciences acquired an unquestioned authority, setting them over against both revelation and classic philosophy as inherently superior to them by reason of their experimental methods. However, many practitioners of the newly developing natural sciences failed to understand the specificity of the methodologies they were developing to the fields of data they were studying, and mistakenly assumed that their new methodologies were equally applicable in the areas covered by classic philosophy and Judeo-Christian revelation.

So we've arrived at the situation Neil Postman described in his essay, 'Science and the Story That We Need'. For Postman, the contemporary need for a narrative that will answer our quest for meaning occurs at a time when a series of attempted narratives have ceased speaking to anybody. The narrative of National Socialism died in the ruins of 1945 Berlin, Marx's narrative ended most dramatically in the rubble of the wall dividing that same city forty-four years later, and Freud's petered out perhaps in a Woody Allen spoof. Postman asks, 'Is there no secular god left to believe in?' and answers: 'There is of course the great narrative known as inductive science.' Certainly those Postman lists as its first storytellers – Descartes, Bacon, Galileo, Kepler and Newton – 'did not think of their story as a replacement for the great Judeo-Christian narrative but as an extension of it.'[53] Nonetheless, that is what it has come to be in Western society, in what has been called scientism rather than science. What do we mean by scientism?

3.1 Scientism

If natural science claims to be the total explanation of everything, it becomes what I believe Austrian economist von Hayek was the first to call 'scientism': 'natural science' as an ideology claiming to be the only valid science.[54] One of the sources of that cultural success has been the obvious achievement of physics and chemistry, leading to a privileging of the type of understanding employed in those natural sciences – as early as the 1550s, Rabelais felt the need to satirise this:

> Others were carefully measuring flea-hops in a long garden. This practice, they assured me, was more than necessary for the government of kingdoms, the conduct of wars, and the administration of republics.[55]

It does no harm to remind ourselves that scientism hasn't been arrived at by any inquiry by the natural sciences.

When a Richard Dawkins insists that unless an issue is decided on the basis of evidence, his presumption is that the only kind of evidence is that required by, say physics or biology. But, as Voegelin writes:

> ... the popular assumption that mathematical natural science is the model of science par excellence, and that an operation not using its methods cannot be characterised as scientific, is neither a proposition of mathematical science, nor of any science whatsoever, but merely an ideological dogma thriving in the sphere of scientism.[56]

---

53 Neil Postman, 'Science and the Story That We Need' (*First Things*, 69, January 1997), pp. 29–32, at p. 29, p. 30.

54 Friedrich von Hayek, 'Scientism and the Study of Society,' *Economica,* Vol. IX, 35, August 1942, pp. 267–91.

55 François Rabelais, *Gargantua and Pantagruel*, tr. John M. Cohen, London: Penguin, 1983, V, §22. Peter Gay in his *The Enlightenment*, Vol 2. *The Science of Freedom*, New York: Norton, 1977, has a section on eighteenth-century intellectuals who – generally untroubled by any scientific expertise – wanted to be considered 'Newtons of the Mind' (pp. 174–86).

56 Voegelin, *Anamnesis: On the Theory of History and Politics*, p. 376.

In his essay on 'The Origins of Scientism', Voegelin notes that along with scientism's 'assumption that the mathematised science of natural phenomena is a model science to which all other sciences ought to conform', what follows is 'that all realms of being are accessible to the methods of the sciences of phenomena', and 'that all reality that is not accessible to sciences of phenomena is either irrelevant or, in the more radical form of the dogma, illusionary'.[57] His critique of scientism, then, is part of a more general diagnosis of ideological thinking in general, a closure to rational inquiry characterised by its routine 'prohibition of questioning'.[58]

Up to his death in 2002, Stephen Jay Gould was probably the US's best-known evolutionary biologist. Still, he took Richard Dawkins and Daniel Dennett to task in a famous article called 'Darwinian Fundamentalism'.[59] While, as P. G. Wodehouse's Bertie Wooster would have said, 'and he meant it to sting', the title performs the useful service of reminding us that 'fundamentalism' isn't limited to narrow-minded religious attitudes.

What aroused Gould's ire was that Dawkins and Dennett were stepping outside their area of biological expertise and pronouncing on matters their science didn't deal with – an approach common to all those called fundamentalists and which I'll call the 'fallacy of answering the unasked question'. If I claim that the Bible answers questions in geology or paleontology that it doesn't ask, or that a theory in astronomy or biology fully accounts for the mystery of existence, including human existence, or that a Marxist or positivist philosophy rules out any possibility of divine revelation, then I think there's been an attempt to provide answers to questions which don't arise within their methodologies. In the natural sciences, that kind of intellectual closure is what we're calling scientism.[60] But there's a serious consequence of scientism we must now refer to.

---

57 Eric Voegelin, 'The Origins of Scientism' [1948], in *Published Essays 1940–1952*, ed. Ellis Sandoz (Columbia, MO: University of Missouri Press, 2000), pp. 168–96, at pp. 168–9.

58 Eric Voegelin 'Science, Politics and Gnosticism' in *Modernity Without Restraint*, ed. Manfred Henningsen (Columbia, MO: University of Missouri Press, 2000), p. 261.

59 Stephen Jay Gould, 'Darwinian Fundamentalism', *New York Review of Books*, June 12, 1997, pp. 34–7.

60 Sergio Rondinara's *Interpretazione del reale tra scienza e teologia* lists Steven Weinberg and Frank Tipler (to which we can surely add Stephen Hawking) in cosmology, Edward O. Wilson's sociobiology, and Francis Crick, Jacques Monod and Richard Dawkins in biology, as scientists respected in their own fields whose prestige wins publicity for their extra-scientific views (pp. 57–8).

3.2 Reductionism

In direct contrast with what Lonergan said about data requiring that the scientist move to a higher level, it's all too easy to find statements insisting that the lower level of, as here, genetics, determines 'who we are and what we do as humans':

> In *The Blind Watchmaker*, Dawkins ... writes that 'living organisms exist for the benefit of DNA rather than the other way round. In a similar way, Wilson proposes that genes play a pre-eminent role, even in the development of human behaviour and culture. He argues that the environment is important in the selection of genetic variants and their expression. In the end, however, it is the gene and its information that determines who we are and what we do as humans ... Even though allowances are made for some higher-level patternings, these are really epiphenomena of the structures that make up the whole.[61]

Reductionism is the name given to the claim to reduce all of reality to the areas dealt with by the natural sciences, often, as here, privileging physics and chemistry:

> Right up to the middle of the twentieth century, life was thought to be qualitatively beyond physics and chemistry. No longer. The difference between life and non-life is a matter not of substance but of *information* ... Most of the information is digitally coded in DNA, and there is also a substantial quantity coded in other ways ... [62]

As his encyclopedic *Ancestor's Tale* and *The Greatest Show on Earth* abundantly show – each full to the gills with ranges of biological, botanical and zoological data – Dawkins has made it his life's work to make accessible to the public Darwin's understanding of the interrelation of all life's phenomena, which was not in terms of physics or chemistry, but biology.[63] Dawkins' reductionist belief that physics, chemistry and

---

61 Martinez J. Hewlett, 'True to Life? Biological Models of Origin and Evolution', in Murphy and Stoeger, *Evolution and Emergence*, pp. 158–72, at p. 164.

62 Richard Dawkins, *The Greatest Show on Earth*, London: Bantam, 2009, pp. 403–4.

63 'Natural selection ... systematically seizes the minority of random changes that have what it takes to survive, and accumulates them, step by tiny step over unimaginable timescales, until evolution eventually climbs mountains of improbability and diversity ... ' (*The Greatest Show on Earth*, p. 416). Would natural selection of the more successful strategies of living species as understood by Dawkins fall under the sciences of physics or chemistry? Where does a notion like 'survival' fit into, say, astrophysics?

molecular biology will provide an adequate explanation for the living realities Darwin studied may stem from his failure to reflect on the methodological and ontological issues posed by his own scientific study of biology, botany and zoology. In Lonergan's language, from the viewpoint of the lower sciences all zoological behaviour is a 'mere pattern of happy coincidences'. As we've noted, the reason the higher science goes beyond the lower one is because it's required to make systematic what's merely coincidental from the viewpoint of the lower science.

Just as scientism can't be proved by the methods of the natural sciences, so reductionism is an ideological opinion or belief rather than a valid conclusion of any of the natural sciences, since it's not within their scope to make general statements about the nature of reality – for example, to declare that all of reality is material and only material. Reductionism's contention 'that things are all of one kind has rested, not on concrete evidence, but on mechanist assumption' (*Insight*, 257), and, as Rondinara writes, is 'normally due to a monistic conception of the real'.[64]

One way of understanding reductionism is in terms of its inability to see the whole for the part, an approach Lonergan discusses in a section in *Insight* on 'things within things' (258–9). While the laws of physics and chemistry hold for biological or zoological or anthropological reality, that does not mean that things of the lower order exist in things of the higher order. Laws express relations, but the fact there are relations of a lower order which are verified in something of a higher order doesn't mean that things of that lower order exist in the higher order reality:

> … it is one thing to prove that [lawful relations] of the lower order survive within the higher genus; it is quite another to prove that things defined solely by the lower correlations also survive. To arrive at correlations, abstractive procedures are normal; one considers events under some aspects and disregards other aspects of the same events. But to arrive at a thing, one must consider all data within a totality, and one must take into account all their aspects. (*Insight*, 258)

If I play the piano, the movements of my fingers may be partly explained by physics and chemistry, biochemistry and anatomy, but the thing that

---

64 Rondinara, *Interpretazione del reale tra scienza e teologia*, p. 56.

is taking place – for example, playing Beethoven's 'Moonlight Sonata' – would be missed by a description detailing these partial though true accounts of events on the lower levels. I'm more than my fingers and what I'm doing is more than the physics, chemistry, biochemistry and anatomy. This is the exact opposite to the reductionism of Richard Dawkins' *The Selfish Gene* whose blurb accurately summarises his argument: 'Our genes made us. We animals exist for their preservation and are nothing more than their throwaway survival machines.'[65]

To try to understand simply in terms of chemistry the blur of chemical reactions involved in, say, the photosynthetic action around that field of buttercups we mentioned would be to not understand why the plants engage in energy transfer from sunlight in order to stay alive. This would mean ignoring the aspect of the reality that can't be explained in terms of the lower viewpoint and that 'justifies the introduction of the higher viewpoint' and the higher level of botany that corresponds to it. So, 'if there is evidence for the existence of the higher genus, there cannot be evidence for things of lower genera in the same data' (*Insight*, 258).

Voegelin puts the non-reducibility of a plant to 'things' within it very concretely:

A plant is a plant. You see it. You don't see its physical-chemical processes, and nothing about the plant changes if you know that physical-chemical processes are going on inside. How these processes will result in what you experience immediately as a plant (a rose or an oak tree), you don't know anyway. So if you know these substructures in the lower levels of the ontic hierarchy (beyond the plant which is organism) and go into the physical, chemical, molecular and atomic structures, ever farther down, the greater becomes the miracle how all that thing is a plant. Nothing is explained. If you try to explain it in terms of some mechanism, you have committed the fallacy of reduction.[66]

Underlying this whole discussion has been the often uneasy relationship not only between the natural sciences themselves, but between them and philosophy, since the problems of scientism and reductionism are fundamentally what Rondinara calls 'metascientific, or if you wish,

---

65 Richard Dawkins, *The Selfish Gene*, Oxford: Oxford University Press, 1989.

66 Eric Voegelin, 'Conversations with Eric Voegelin,' in *The Drama of Humanity and Other Miscellaneous Papers* 1939–1985, pp. 290–1.

philosophical'.[67] Our final section here will at least point in the direction of a resolution of the issue.

4. Towards a complementarity of natural science and philosophy

So that the natural sciences don't derail into scientism or reductionism, reflection on their methodology and on their understanding of reality should include an understanding of their historic and cultural context, the theory of knowledge implicit in their practice, and the ontological presuppositions about 'the world', since all these factors underpin them as a human undertaking and achievement. A simple way of keeping in mind the relationship between biology and philosophy would be to compare it with the relationship between cookery and farming (including market gardening). Cookery presumes that its materials will be supplied by farmers and market gardeners, much in the same way as biology presumes the existence of living realities. No more than the busy cook has time to ask just how this or that piece of steak or turnip was produced, does the biologist have time to deal with the quite different questions regarding the existence of the material universe or of the huge range of living things. Both cook and biologist presume the existence of the materials they're dealing with.

To resolve the conflict between Newtonian and quantum physics, Niels Bohr introduced the notion of complementarity between the two apparently contradictory approaches. This is a complementarity between branches of the same natural science. But we can go further and suggest that the natural sciences can best operate as complementary to other sources of truth – for everyone, that should include philosophy, and for believers, revelation too. It's when complementarity breaks down that the limits of each area, revelation, philosophy and natural science, become most clearly exposed. If a believer, philosopher or natural scientist makes assertions which do not fall within their competence, we've spoken of their slipping, perhaps inadvertently, into what we've called the 'fallacy of answering the unasked question' – when they claim to answer a question that can neither be raised nor answered within their area of experience or discipline.

Instead of conflicting with one another, why can't natural science, philosophy and revelation each preserve their autonomy, purify one another whenever they go beyond their original premises, while in complementarity work at the common quest for an understanding of our universe and our own place within it? In this way, we can arrive at a more satisfactory account

---

67 Rondinara, *Interpretazione del reale tra scienza e teologia*, p. 56.

of the various levels of existence – the natural sciences, by presenting us with the latest insights regarding these levels and their contents; philosophy, in taking up the boundary issues that are sometimes raised by these levels in terms of primary causation.

Rondinara quotes from Pope John Paul II's 1991 'Message to the Director of the Vatican Observatory' on precisely this complementarity, where he focuses on the science/religion debate – I would add of course, the science/philosophy debate:

> Science can purify religion from error and superstition; religion can purify science from idolatry and from false absolutes. Each can help the other to enter into a more complete world, where both can prosper.

He speaks of 'a progress towards mutual understanding and a gradual discovery of shared interests', noting that today 'we have an unprecedented opportunity to establish a common interactive relationship where every discipline maintains its own integrity while remaining radically open to the discoveries and intuitions of the other'.[68]

Rondinara goes on to point out how such complementarity enriches not only philosophy and the natural sciences. As persons, scientists, philosophers and theologians involved in the different areas can become more human since science, philosophic understanding and faith enrich different aspects of the same person. Such a unification of knowledge in the first place occurs within the inquiring subject. He speaks of the need for those involved in the dialogue to undergo a certain loss of self in order to receive the gift of the other partners in dialogue. Drawing on Plato's famous Seventh Letter and the Fourth Gospel, he suggests making a gift of our intellectuality to the other, so that, while remaining faithful to the requirements of our own discipline, we transcend it in 'a new dimension of intellectuality capable of understanding and welcoming the differing intellectuality of every man and woman'.[69]

Obviously, this need for mediation between different modes of inquiry isn't only an individual matter. C. P. Snow's famous notion of 'the two cultures' – human and natural scientific studies – and the need for continual dialogue between them, has enormous social and political implications. While Snow was criticising the lack of scientific knowledge in educated

---

68 Rondinara, *Interpretazione del reale tra scienza e teologia*, pp. 79–80, pp. 82–3.

69 Ibid., pp. 82–7.

circles in Britain in the 1950s and sixties, perhaps C. S. Lewis was more perceptive of the imbalance in the other direction – of the stifling of the humanities in a culture where technology had achieved dominance over human values.[70] At any rate, the need for open and ongoing dialogue between the sciences and the humanities (including philosophy and theology) is a key imperative in Western society today.

Our next chapters will look first at the question of life and its explosion into millions of different forms, since it's from this matrix that we in part originate – although just what kind of emergence that is will remain to be seen. Our perspective is what we've just been discussing: while it's clear that the natural sciences have played a huge role in exploring these issues, we'll try to bring them into dialogue with philosophy – specifically, in terms of what German-American philosopher Hans Jonas called a philosophical biology.

---

70 See C. S. Lewis's related explorations of the issue in his 1943 essay on *The Abolition of Man* (London: Collins, 1981) and his 1945 novel *That Hideous Strength* (London: Pan Books, 1963).

Chapter Four: Darwin and the evolution of evolution

Having looked at some of the problems associated with the natural sciences, we'll now see how Darwin resolved some but not all of them. His partial failure to clarify the difference between scientific and theological issues has given rise to many of the extra-scientific issues biting at evolution's heels in the English-speaking world, particularly in the US.[71] Exaggerations by various of 'Darwin's bulldogs' (this was Thomas Huxley's *nom de guerre* as Darwin's most public and resourceful defender) – who claimed that Darwin's biological theory resolved issues far beyond biology – has a lot to do with negative reactions to Darwin. And as Richard Dawkins, among others today, has continued and expanded Huxley's war, so he's been awarded a similar *nom de grrr*. The negative reactions were mainly on the part of some Christians who felt their beliefs – particularly in a literal interpretation of the book of Genesis – were under attack.

In the meantime, the Darwinian paradigm has moved on, with key developments that modify the theory enormously, so that a new synthesis (way beyond what was called, in the 1930s and forties, the neo-Darwinian or modern synthesis, between Darwin's evolutionary theory and the genetics originally discovered by the Moravian monk, Gregor Mendel) may be in formation. Such a synthesis would include Niles Eldredge's and Steven Jay Gould's notion of punctuated equilibrium, the evolutionary-developmental theory known as evo-devo, Simon Conway Morris' notion of evolutionary convergences, and for some authors, the recognition of the role of animal consciousness in evolution. To help with a philosophical framework for evolutionary theory, we'll summarise what Lonergan has to say about biological development. And we'll apply what's been said towards the end of the previous chapter to suggest a complementarity between biology and philosophy. I've no intention of competing with highly technical surveys like *The Cambridge Companion to the Philosophy of Biology* – our aim here is simply to clear the way for our principal topic, the human mystery

---

71 Issues that were eminently resolvable: in a discussion with Richard Dawkins about his *Greatest Show on Earth* book on RTÉ's *Late Late Show* with Ryan Tubridy on 18 September 2009, I remarked that my mother, who'd left school at sixteen, used her time at the breakfast table to catch up on her education after she'd packed me and my brothers off to school. She saw no contradiction as an ordinary practicing Catholic in ploughing through *The Origin of Species* over one year, and then making her way for the first time through the whole Bible for another year or so.

considered in the light of evolution and creation – and I'll be focusing on some philosophical implications of the theory only.

1. Darwin's mixed legacy

1.1 Darwin's scientific strength

We'll start with the source of Darwin's scientific greatness: his break with mechanism and his development of an explanatory evolutionary biology. The neo-Kantian philosopher of science and of culture, Ernst Cassirer and the philosopher and theologian Bernard Lonergan, from somewhat different perspectives, acknowledge Darwin's theoretical greatness as consisting in his going beyond the synchronic (that is, at just one time) biology of classification of genera and species to the development of a diachronic (that is, over a period of time) context for biology – even if that diachronic context for Darwin sometimes tended towards dissolving the earlier synchronic one:

> One of its [Darwinism's] most noted achievements from an epistemological point of view is that it opened to natural science a new dimension of thought ... by showing that scientific [let's say, 'synchronic'] and historical [let's say, 'diachronic'] concepts are far from opposed but rather mutually supplement and need one another.[72]

The key insight into any development, whether of plants, animals or humans, has to do with the source of the difference between a less and a more developed stage. So the heuristic or guiding investigative context for understanding any developmental sequence is not the question, what is the nature of any X, but what is the operator or dynamic cause of the development from X_1 to X_2 (see *Insight*, 465ff.). Darwin then fully deserves the credit, half a century before Einstein made an equivalent shift from classical physics, for leaving aside a mechanist type of explanation in favour of a developmental one. For Lonergan, the *Origin of Species* 'presents the outstanding instance of the employment of probability as a principle of explanation ... As chance variation is an instance of probability of emergence, so natural selection is an instance of probability of survival' (*Insight*, 132).

Despite the various developments of evolutionary theory after Darwin, the basic questions raised by classical Darwinism are still discussed by

---

72 Ernst Cassirer, *The Problem of Knowledge: Philosophy, Science and History since Hegel*, New Haven: Yale University Press, 1969, p, 172.

Darwinians today, so we can be content with the theory's earlier format. The key point of that earlier statement of the theory is that nature selects the most successful living things in a way analogous to the way breeders select the best greyhounds or horses or pigeons.[73] As Darwin put it:

> I have called this principle, by which each slight variation, if useful, is preserved, by the term Natural Selection, in order to mark its relation to man's power of selection. That is to say, the selective breeding of domestic animals. But the expression often used by Mr Herbert Spencer of the Survival of the Fittest is more accurate, and is sometimes equally convenient.[74]

1.2 Darwin's persistent failure to distinguish between natural science and natural theology

In his own personal journey, Darwin moved from a rather narrow, literalist reading of the Bible to a sharp rejection of that view. At the same time, his notion of what constituted an intellectual defence of Christian revelation seems to have been chiefly formed by William Paley's *Evidences for Christian Belief*. Augros and Stanciu quote a letter of Darwin to Thomas Huxley:

> The old argument from design in nature, as given by Paley, which formerly seemed to me so conclusive, fails, now that the law of natural selection has been discovered. We can no longer argue that, for instance, the beautiful hinge of a bivalve shell must have been made by an intelligent being, like the hinge of a door by man. There seems to be no more design in the variability of organic beings and in the action of natural selection, than the course in which the wind blows. Everything in nature is the result of fixed laws.[75]

Neal Gillespie's *Charles Darwin and the Problem of Creation* brings out well Darwin's unresolved tension between a rather positivistic natural science and theology, as well as the difficulties Darwin experienced in defending scientific observation from what he saw as the interferences of a kind of

---

73 From a philosophical perspective, 'nature' doesn't 'select' anything, and what survives aren't the better bred or the selected, but the survivors. Once we realise such expressions are merely picture thinking, it's alright to use them, but they can mislead if taken literally.

74 Charles Darwin, *The Origin of Species by Means of Natural Selection or the Preservation of Favoured Races in the Struggle for Life*, London: John Murray, 1902, pp. 76-7.

75 See Robert Augros and George Stanciu, *The New Biology: Discovering the Wisdom in Nature*, Boston: New Science Library, 1987, pp. 228.

religious doctrine (what's now often called 'creationism' – which is not at all the same as a religious or philosophical understanding of creation) that would seem to make biological research unnecessary. He reminds us that Darwin at Cambridge found Paley 'one of the few authors worth reading', and notes that:

> It has been generally agreed (then and since) that Darwin's doctrine of natural selection effectively demolished William Paley's classical design argument for the existence of God. By showing how blind and gradual adaptation could counterfeit the apparently purposeful design that Paley, the Bridgewater writers, and others had seen in the contrivances of nature, Darwin deprived their argument of the analogical inference that the evident purpose to be seen in the contrivances by which means and ends were related in nature was necessarily a function of mind. This inference, in which human and divine purpose were identified, had been its whole strength as a proof. In natural selection Darwin substituted an alternative hypothesis that was both logically adequate to account for the forms of organisms and philosophically more appealing to the positive outlook.

Gillespie points out in the Preface that his book is not about Darwin's discovery of evolution by natural selection or an assessment of evidence for or against that view. While reading *Origins*, he 'became curious about why Darwin spent so much time attacking the idea of divine creation', and noted that 'the book had a surprising amount of positive theological content ... Further study seemed to show that he was quite seriously (if not profoundly) concerned with religious questions, and that his concern was involved ... in his idea of good science'.

Darwin thought *Origins* was good science: 'Yet behind the arguments of that volume lay prior beliefs about knowledge – particularly scientific knowledge – about nature and even about God.' Gillespie asks if these ideas reflected 'a basic antagonism within the natural history of his time [rather] than the famous conflict over evolution. In what way was creation a problem for Darwin?'[76]

Darwin saw science as endangered by theology – which is certainly the case in certain fundamentalist groups' anti-intellectual attitude to science

---

76 Neal C. Gillespie, *Charles Darwin and the Problem of Creation*, Chicago: University of Chicago Press, 1979, p. 86; pp. 83–4; p. xi; p. xii.

– in the sense that it seems to be claiming to explain the origin of species: and so, to protect science's own right to existence, he feels he has to get rid of theology. Typical are his remarks in the *Origin of Species*:

> In considering the *Origin of Species*, it is quite conceivable that a naturalist, reflecting on the mutual affinities of organic beings, on their embryological relations, their geographical distribution, geological succession ... might come to the conclusion that species had not been independently created, but had descended, like varieties, from other species.

> Although much remains obscure ... I can entertain no doubt ... that the view which most naturalists until recently entertained, and which I formerly entertained – namely that each species has been independently created – is erroneous.[77]

But, as John Haught points out, in rejecting special creation – a notion that would only make sense within theology if explained within the context of one single divine act of creation – Darwin is leaving his area of biological expertise to make comments that require a background in the discipline of natural theology:

> The narrow idea of 'special creation' is hard to reconcile with Darwin's theory as long as it is taken to be the answer to a purely scientific question about how to explain adaptive design. Science looks for physical causes and so appealing to the idea of God in any form cannot be part of scientific method. As a scientist, Darwin had every reason to reject special creation as do biologists today. But in the *Origin of Species* ... Darwin was not always thinking and writing in a purely scientific way.[78]

Victorian England's most prominent Catholic intellectual, John Henry Newman, was educated in a somewhat similar Anglican background to Darwin. His 1855 lecture on 'Christianity and Physical Science' – four years before *The Origin of Species* – noted how Paley's version of 'natural

---

77 Darwin, *Origin of Species*, p. 3, p. 6.

78 John F. Haught, *Making Sense of Evolution: Darwin, God, and the Drama of Life*, Louisville, KY: Westminster John Knox Press, 2010, p. 26.

theology' 'has almost been used as an instrument against Christianity'. He went on to say that 'the God of Physical Theology may very easily become a mere idol ... Indeed, a being of Power, Wisdom, and Goodness, and nothing else, is not very different from the God of the Pantheist.'[79]

Paley's basic error was to mix up two kinds of causation, the physical or secondary causation studied by the natural sciences and the ontological or primary causation of *Metaphysics* – what we earlier called the how question and the why question. Instead of simply accepting that he did not then have the means to explain what he called the gaps in the fossil record, it seems as if Darwin plugged those gaps by the simple assertion of what could be called the Great Wall of Gradualism.

Darwin in chapter 10 of *Origin*, entitled 'On the Imperfection of the Geological Record', shows his awareness that there are awkward breaches in that wall, and speaks of a principal objection to his theory as:

> ... the distinctness of specific forms, and their not being blended together by innumerable transitional links, is a very obvious difficulty ... Geology assuredly does not reveal any such finely graduated organic chain; and this, perhaps, is the most obvious and serious objection which can be urged against the theory. The explanation lies, as I believe, in the extreme imperfection of the geological record.[80]

Thomas Huxley warned Darwin of this problem: 'You have loaded yourself with an unnecessary difficulty in adopting *natura non facit saltum* [nature does not make jumps] so unreservedly.'[81] Helpfully, Richard Dawkins underlines precisely why gradualism was so important to Darwin:

---

79 Partly quoted in Haught, *Making Sense of Evolution*, p. 64, to whom I owe the reference. I've also drawn on John Henry Newman, *The Idea of a University: The Integral Text*, ed. Teresa Iglesias, Dublin: Ashfield Press, 2009, p. 451, p. 454. An indication of how a philosophically competent Victorian viewed Darwin's theory is a comment of Newman's some years later: 'I do not fear the theory, I do not see that the accidental evolution of organic beings is inconsistent with divine design – It is accidental to us, not to God.' See *The Letters and Diaries of John Henry Newman*, ed. Charles Stephen Dessain et al., Vol. XXIV, Oxford: Clarendon Press, 1973, p. 77. Ian Ker, in his *John Henry Newman: A Biography* (Oxford: Oxford University Press, 1990), quotes another passage from the same letter: 'It does not seem to me to follow that creation is denied because the Creator, millions of years ago, gave laws to matter' (p. 624). And to complete Newman's thoughts on the matter, Stanley Jaki in his *Science and Creation* (Lanham MD: University Press of America, 1990, p. 366) writes of the 'devastating simplicity' of his remark – again from *The Idea of a University* – that 'There is but one thought greater than that of the universe, and that is the thought of its Maker.'

80 Darwin, *Origin of Species*, pp. 412–13.

81 Phillip Johnson, *Darwin on Trial*, Downers Grove, IL: InterVarsity Press, 1993, p. 33.

In Darwin's view, the whole *point* of the theory of evolution by natural selection was that it provided a *non*-miraculous account of the existence of complex adaptations ... For Darwin, any evolution that had to be helped over the jumps by God was not evolution at all. It made a nonsense of the central point of evolution. In the light of this, it is easy to see why Darwin constantly reiterated the *gradualness* of evolution. It is easy to see why he wrote:

> If it could be demonstrated that any complex organ existed, which could not possibly have been formed by numerous, successive, slight modifications, my theory would absolutely break down.[82]

It very much looks as if an aspect of the theory, gradualism, is being introduced not because of observed biological or zoological data, but for the non-scientific or ideological reason of preventing the intrusion of a Paley-esque divinity-within-the-process. Apart from that distorting factor, there is also a lack of understanding of scientific understanding which would have allowed Darwin to accept that the relationship between different developmental or evolutionary stages isn't something that would ever be visible – that it's not a question of finding missing links or making up for the incompletion of the fossil record. He has done more than enough to communicate his profound interrelational understanding of all living animal species, which continues to function as a heuristic for further generations of biologists to fill in over the centuries. And he doesn't neatly fit into the pure scientific biologist he's sometimes presented as today. In fact, he has intimations about the overall plan of reality that go beyond those of a natural scientist, but of course not beyond those of a human being for whom wider questions are still questions.

1.3 Darwin's own awareness of ontological order

Gillespie writes about a tendency to turn Darwin into a late twentieth-century secularist 'by treating his vision of nature as thoroughly naturalistic and the man as completely secular – the first point is understandable and unhistorical, though what Darwin gave to the world was a naturalistic or positivistic theory; nor should the theological writing be dismissed as merely poetical or rhetorical or as some sort of elaborate deception.'[83]

---

82 Richard Dawkins, *The Blind Watchmaker*, London: Penguin, 1991, p. 249. The US edition has the informative subtitle, *Why the Evidence of Evolution Reveals a Universe Without Design*.

83 Neal C. Gillespie, *Charles Darwin and the Problem of Creation*, Chicago: University of Chicago Press, 1979, pp. xi–xii.

Although, as we'll see, evolutionary biologists themselves have added many qualifications to his theory, whether or not Darwin adequately specified the dynamic cause behind biological/botanical/zoological evolution is less important than that he asked the right kind of question for understanding any development. Darwin's often quoted closing words in the *Origin* are still worth repeating:

> There is grandeur in this view of life, with its several powers, having been originally breathed by the Creator [Darwin added 'by the Creator' to the second, and retained it right up to the sixth and last edition of *Origin of Species*] into a few forms or into one; and that, whilst this planet has gone cycling on according to the fixed law of gravity, from so simple a beginning endless forms most beautiful and most wonderful have been, and are being, evolved.[84]

Unlike some tendentious presentations of evolution today, Darwin was quite aware of the problems posed by organs of 'extreme perfection' – famously, the eye – but felt they could be overcome. Still, in 1881 he acknowledged to Lord Farrer 'that he was reluctant ... to extend to the universe itself the creative role of random chance that he saw operating without restraint or intelligent direction in the origination of species'. Quoting Darwin, Gillespie continues:

> 'The birth of the species and of the individual,' he wrote in *The Descent of Man*, 'are equally parts of that grand sequence of events, which our minds refuse to accept as the result of blind chance. The understanding revolts at such a conclusion, whether or not we are able to believe that every slight variation of structure, – the union of each pair in marriage, – the dissemination of each seed, – and other such events, have all been ordained for some special purpose.'[85]

Though Darwin distrusted design thinking, he confessed to Gray what he later told Lord Farrer: 'I grieve to say that I cannot honestly go as far as you do about Design. I am conscious that I am in an utterly hopeless muddle. I cannot think that the world, as we see it, is the result of chance; and yet I cannot look at each separate thing as the result of Design.'

---

84 Darwin, *Origin of Species*, p. 670. Richard Dawkins' strenuous attempt in his *Greatest Show on Earth*, London: Bantam, 2009, p. 403f., to explain away this addition seems to protest too much.

85 Gillespie, *Darwin and the Problem of Creation*, pp. 86–7.

Still, while never closing off the explicitly metaphysical questions of origin (or ontological causation) for Darwin, there was also the need to fight for biology's independence. So, Gillespie can note that: 'With some insight, he [the Duke of Argyll in his *The Reign of Law*] insisted that Darwinists preferred their doctrine of "fortuity" because it enabled them to exclude "mind or conscious direction" from nature.'

Yet Darwin writes to Hooker in 1870: 'I cannot look at the universe as the result of blind chance.'[86] And Gillespie notes that in 1881:

> Darwin read William Graham's *The Creed of Science* (1881), which defended evolution and theism together. 'It is a very long time,' he wrote to the author, 'since any book has interested me so much.' While disagreeing with Graham on some points (that the laws of nature imply design and his attempts to limit the role of natural selection), Darwin assured Graham that his book 'expressed my inward conviction, though far more vividly and clearly than I could have done, that the Universe is not the result of chance.'[87]

Gillespie remarks of Darwin that: 'for him, the rationality and moral probity of God underlay the rationality and meaningfulness of science: it was a metaphysical basis, a remnant of natural theology, a survival of the old *episteme* [knowledge], that Darwin required but acknowledged only by implication'.[88] I think it's fair to say that Darwin lacked the intellectual tools to spell out the implications of that 'remnant of natural theology' which would have enabled him to differentiate the different and complementary roles of natural science, philosophy and revelation.

2. Evolutionism as a 'secular religion'[89]

In fact, Darwinian evolution functions in our society as what Michael Denton once called 'the great cosmogenic myth of the twentieth century,' perhaps even more than as a theoretical framework within the science of biology.[90]

---

86 Ibid., p. 142.

87 Ibid., pp. 142–3.

88 Ibid., p. 102.

89 I came across Conor Cunningham's outstanding *Darwin's Pious Idea: Why the Ultra-Darwinists and Creationists Both Get It Wrong* (Grand Rapids, MI: Eerdmans, 2010) too late to draw on it for this discussion, but its treatment of the 'science versus religion' issues arising out of Darwinian evolutionary theory is the best I've read.

90 Michael Denton, *Evolution: A Theory in Crisis*, London: Burnett, 1985, p. 358.

It has the appeal of an attempt to explain the origin and unity of all living things, with the undeniable aura of science as the virtually uncriticisable narrative form in English-speaking culture. As John Haught puts it:

> Whether Darwin intended it or not, the shape and style of his long argument has often been interpreted in such a way that it fails to prevent a scientifically illuminating idea – that of evolution – from becoming the basis of a whole new belief system ... By giving this impression, and without meaning to be controversial, Darwin fired a shot that has provoked a century and a half of unnecessary 'warfare' between evolutionists and religious believers ... Whenever scientists put forth a new discovery or theory as an *improvement* on religious or theological accounts, they are still assuming that science and theology are both in the same business, that of answering ultimate theological questions ... implicitly turning science into something comparable to theology.[91]

We've already spoken of scientism as the claim by the natural sciences to provide the complete answer to the human quest for ultimate meaning. Kurt Vonnegut offers a light satire of this attitude in *Cat's Cradle*:

> '[Dr Hoenikker] was supposed to be our commencement speaker,' said Sandra ... 'He didn't show up.' 'So you didn't get a commencement address?' 'Oh, we got one. Dr Breed ... showed up, all out of breath, and he gave some kind of talk.' 'What did he say?' 'He said he hoped a lot of us would have careers in science,' she said. 'He said, the trouble with the world was ... that people were still superstitious instead of scientific. He said if everybody would study science more, there wouldn't be all the trouble there was ... He said science was going to discover the basic secret of life some day.' The bartender ... scratched his head and frowned. 'Didn't I read in the paper the other day where they'd finally found out what it was?' 'I saw that,' said Sandra. 'About two days ago.' 'That's right,' said the bartender. 'What *is* the secret of life?' I asked. 'I forget,' said Sandra. 'Protein,' the bartender declared. 'They found out something about protein.' 'Yeah,' said Sandra, 'that's it.'[92]

---

91 John Haught, *Making Sense of Evolution*, pp. 34–5.

92 Kurt Vonnegut, *Cat's Cradle*, London: Penguin, 1973, pp. 20–1.

Yet, rather than being treated by its practitioners as the sciences of physics and chemistry, that is as being open to permanent revision, why has Darwinian theory been defended as if it were basically unrevisable? Why was it possible for philosopher Mary Midgley to speak of it, along with Marxism, as 'one of the two great secular faiths of our day', displaying 'religious-looking features'.[93] Its status as a creed-movement is where the problems, apparently impervious to rational argument, occur. Some of these problems are caused, as we've suggested earlier, by Darwin's failure to make important differentiations between the methods of natural science and of metaphysics. Had he done so, he wouldn't have tried to deal with the question of existence – by ruling out creation – as if it were an issue in biology. For questions of existence are best dealt with in terms of what we mentioned in the previous chapter as 'why questions' regarding primary causation (efficient and final causation), while the methods of natural science focuses on 'what questions' regarding secondary causation.

In his short piece, 'Oppressed by Evolution', anthropologist Matt Cartmill criticises the pretensions, not of evolution, but of the attitude of those promoting evolutionism:

Science has nothing to tell us about moral values or the purpose of existence or the realm of the supernatural. That doesn't mean there is nothing to be said about these things. It just means that scientists don't have any expert opinions ... science's necessary silence on these questions doesn't prove that there isn't any infinite cause – or that right or wrong are arbitrary conventions, or that there is no plan or purpose behind the world ... The broad outlines of the story of human evolution are known beyond a reasonable doubt. However, science hasn't yet found satisfying, law-based natural explanations for most of the details of that story. All that we can do as scientists is admit our ignorance and keep looking. Our ignorance doesn't prove anything one way or the other about divine plans or purposes behind the flow of history. Anybody who says it does is pushing a religious doctrine. Both the religious creationists on the right and the secular creationists of the left object and say that a lot of evolutionists are doing just that in the name of science – and to this extent they are unfortunately right.[94]

---

93 Mary Midgley, *Evolution As a Religion: Strange Hopes and Stranger Fears*, London: Methuen, 1985, p. 15.

94 Matt Cartmill, 'Oppressed by Evolution', *Discovery*, March 1998, pp. 78–83.

Not at all unlike Cartmill's views are those of geneticist Jonathan Marks, who writes that 'the extraordinary thing is why the reductive scientific attitude overvalues itself and laments everyone else's shortsightedness'. He warns that it is 'the exaggerated claims of scientists, and their often arrogant misunderstandings of human behaviour and society, and of the domain of science itself, that are the problem.' He later notes: 'That is not science – that is scientism, an uncritical faith in science and scientists.'

He cites Richard Dawkins in *River Out of Eden*, who's said that 'The universe we observe has precisely the properties we should expect if there is, at bottom, no design, no purpose, no evil and no good, nothing but blind, pitiless indifference ... DNA neither knows nor cares. DNA just is. And we dance to its music.' Marks comments:

> Dawkins's interpretation of the universe *might* be true, but again, since there is no positive knowledge we can acquire, no controlled set of data we can collect that would indicate whether it is in fact *likely* to be true, we are obliged to identify the statement as nonscience ... The scientist says: 'Science has explained many things about the universe. Your life has no meaning. Have a nice day.' And then he is surprised and appalled at the public rejection of that philosophy.[95]

So, these scientists themselves are aware of the problem of scientism, particularly in its biological version of evolutionism. Michael Ruse, a philosopher of biology who has dedicated his working life to the study of evolution, with which he is in complete agreement, has some critical words for claims he considers go beyond the proper limits of the natural sciences:

> Biological progress per se is not the real issue here, however. The real issue is whether some evolutionists today use the supposed progressiveness of evolutionary theory to promote social and ethical programs. And indeed they do ... They shifted from a scientific theory of evolution to a quasi-religious commitment to evolutionism ... In this sense, evolutionary biology – Darwinian evolutionary biology – continues to function as a kind of secular religion.[96]

---

95 Jonathan Marks, *What It Means to Be 98% Chimpanzee: Apes, People, and Their Genes*, Berkeley: University of California Press, 2002, p. 275, p. 276, p. 279, p. 282, p. 283.

96 Michael Ruse, *The Evolution-Creation Struggle*, Cambridge, MA: Harvard University Press, 2005, pp. 212–13.

3. Creationism and intelligent design

Even if evolutionism has a lot to answer for, only a heart of stone would not feel sympathy for its proponents' attempt to defend the integrity of the empirical sciences against the anti-intellectualist claims of defenders of a literalist reading of the book of Genesis.[97] What's going on here is a row between two different approaches that seem to have got their lines hopelessly entangled. It seems to me primarily an English-language problem – since no equivalent major conflict has arisen in the continental European cultures, where there's perhaps a better awareness of the difference between inquiry in the natural sciences and in philosophy or revelation.

Darwin's theory of evolution was often presented rather aggressively as part of a scientistic (rather than scientific) attack on Christian beliefs, particularly in the US, and recently with redoubled energy in England, in full battle array against those who hold for a literal reading of the book of Genesis (a literalism never adhered to by Catholic, Orthodox, or many Protestant churches). This provoked the reaction known as creationism.[98] The whole issue of closure to scientific inquiry in the name of a literalising reading of Scripture makes one sympathetic to writers like Dennett's and Dawkins' exasperated desire to fend them off, however polemically, while the overbearingness and philosophical innocence of some defenders of evolutionism can make one sympathetic to the creationists.

Yet, as then director of the Vatican Observatory, Fr George Coyne said, 'It is unfortunate that, especially here in America, creationism has come to mean some fundamentalistic, literal, scientific interpretation of Genesis. Judaic-Christian faith is radically creationist, but in a totally different sense. It is rooted in a belief that everything depends upon God, or better, all is a gift from God.' And he goes on to add, thus finding both the creationists (who are emphatically not to be equated with the view he calls 'radically creationist', a view which can be defended philosophically as well as being the view of many believers) and those proposing evolutionism as an ideology equally misguided: 'The universe

---

97 We've already mentioned Stanley Jaki's and Joseph Ratzinger's realistic yet non-literalistic reading of Genesis in Chapter 3, and we'll see Aquinas's similar approach – for philosophical reasons – at the end of this chapter.

98 Robert T. Pennock, *Tower of Babel: The Evidence Against the New Creationism*, Cambridge, MA: MIT, 1999.

is not God and it cannot exist independently of God. Neither pantheism nor naturalism is true.'[99]

Towards the end of the twentieth century, an intellectually articulate attack on Darwinian evolution was developed by biologists like Michael Behe and mathematicians like William Dembski, who defended the notion of Intelligent Design (ID) in nature. Dembski gives a summary of what's meant by intelligent design:

> Within biology, intelligent design is a theory of biological origins and development. Its fundamental claim is that intelligent causes are necessary to explain the complex, information-rich structures of biology and that these causes are empirically detectable. To say intelligent causes are empirically detectable is to say there exist well-defined methods that on the basis of observational features of the world are capable of reliably distinguishing intelligent causes from undirected natural causes. Many special sciences have already developed such methods for drawing this distinction – notably forensic science, artificial intelligence (cf. the Turing test), cryptography, archaeology, and the search for extra-terrestrial intelligence ... Intelligent design is ... not the study of intelligent causes *per se* but of informational pathways induced by intelligent causes ... It detects intelligence without speculating about the nature of the intelligence.'[100]

I would see two weaknesses in this argument: (i) its moving from a natural scientific investigation dealing with secondary causation to an inquiry into primary causation without changing gears; and (ii) its notion of an intelligent designer 'without speculation about the nature of the intelligence'.

(i) The sciences Dembski compares the ID approach with are all human sciences, sciences dealing with the products of human intelligence. Lonergan makes a useful distinction between what is merely intelligible – the grasp of meaningful patterns in physics, chemistry, biology and

---

99 George V. Coyne, SJ, 'Science Does Not Need God. Or Does It? A Catholic Scientist Looks at Evolution', *Catholic Online*, 30 January, 2006 p. 3. Or, as my philosopher friend, Dr Joseph McCarroll, deeply involved in educational matters, put it, 'Evolution should be taught in science class, creation should be taught in religion class [I'd add, 'and in philosophy of God classes'], and evolutionism and creationism should be taught in the history of cultural ideas and ideologies class.'

100 William Dembski, *Intelligent Design: The Bridge between Science and Theology*, Downers Grove, IL: InterVarsity Press, 1999, pp. 106–7.

zoology – and the intelligibility that's also intelligent: 'The advance of technology, the formation of capital, the development of the economy, the evolution of the state are not only intelligible but also intelligent' (*Insight*, 210). So by the merely intelligible he means the meaning that we can grasp in reality which itself is not produced by human intelligence, while by the intelligibility that's also intelligent he means the meaning we can grasp in reality that itself has been produced by human intelligence. In terms of this distinction, it makes sense to look for the intelligent (human) designer of the products of human intelligence, since intrinsic to understanding the meaning of cultural, economic, political, or, using Dembski's own example, forensic or archaeological data, is that they are all the products of human intelligence.

But how can the science of biology speak about anything other than the data of biology? The ID scientists seem to proceed to an intelligent cause completely on the basis of biological explanation, while their evolutionist objectors deny a First Cause completely on the basis of biological explanation. But ontological issues can only be dealt with within an ontological context.

(ii) I've had to use the phrase 'intelligent cause' rather than First Cause to be fair to proponents of ID, since like Dembski or Stephen Meyer, they don't specify what this intelligent cause is.[101] Yet I don't find their placing a designing mind at the head of the chain of secondary causation makes sense, since no intelligence that wasn't divine could create or originate from nothing. In which case, why not leave considerations regarding the overall cause of existence to the philosophers?

Michael Ruse criticises evolutionists such as Richard Dawkins and Edward O. Wilson for an atheism which is 'smuggled in [to Darwinian theory] and then given an evolutionary gloss'.[102] A similar criticism of the intelligent design argument could be made, that it is an unwitting attempt to 'smuggle in' what amounts to deism of the type represented by William Paley into biology, which as a natural science has to hold off making judgements regarding either atheism, deism – or for that matter, theism.

---

101 For example, in his *Signature in the Cell: DNA and the Evidence for Intelligent Design* (New York: HarperCollins, 2010), Stephen C. Meyer writes: 'If intelligent design is true, it follows that a designing intelligence with some of the attributes typically associated with God acted to bring the first living cells into existence. The evidence of intelligent design in biology does not prove that God exists ... since it is at least logically possible that an immanent (within the universe) intelligence rather than a transcendent intelligence might have designed life' (p. 443).

102 Michael Ruse, *Can a Darwinian be a Christian? The Relationship Between Science and Religion*, Cambridge: Cambridge University Press, 2001, p. 128.

At the same time, what I find fully justified in the ID movement is their criticism both of Darwinian gradualism, and of Darwinian randomness (not necessarily in Darwin himself, but in some popular presentations). Mathematician David Berlinski's essay on the misuse of the notion of randomness includes a cheerful critique of Dawkins' notion that a monkey, given long enough, could correctly type the twenty-eight letters and spaces of Shakespeare's phrase, 'Methinks it is like a weasel':

> The probability that a monkey will strike a given letter is 1 in 26. But a letter is not a word. Should Dawkins demand that the monkey get 2 letters right, the odds against success rise to 1 in 676. [Shakespeare's sentence] occupies an isolated point in a space of 10,000 million, million, million, million, million, million possibilities. These are very long odds. And a 6-word sentence consisting of twenty-eight letters is a very short, very simple English sentence. The problem confronting the monkeys is, of course, a double one: they must find the right letters, but they cannot lose the right letters once they have found them.

To prevent this loss of the 'right' letters, in Dawkins' experiment, a computer checks the results of the monkey's typing. Berlinski instead promotes a Head Monkey to scrutinise and conserve the various results closest to the target phrase. The problem is that once such conservation in the light of the target phrase is admitted, any notion of conservation by chance seems to disappear. So Berlinski asks:

> A *target* phrase? Iterations that *most resemble* the target? A Head Monkey that *measures* the distance between failure and success? The mechanism of deliberate design, purged by Darwinian theory on the level of the organism, has reappeared in the description of natural selection itself, a vivid example of what Freud meant by the return of the repressed.[103]

With no connection to the ID proponents whatsoever, Russian-born US-based biologist Eugene Koonin criticises the presumption of gradualism in evolution. He makes a case for a sequence of what he calls BBBs, or Biological Big Bangs, including 'archaea and bacteria, and the principal lineages within each of these prokaryotic domains; eukaryotic supergroups;

---

103 David Berlinsky, 'The Deniable Darwin', *Commentary*, June 1996, pp. 19–29, at p. 27.

and animal phyla'. Koonin's opening remarks in the abstract of his long essay are worth reporting:

> Major transitions in biological evolution show the same pattern of sudden emergence of diverse forms at a new level of complexity. The relationships between major groups within an emergent new class of biological entities are hard to decipher and do not seem to fit the tree pattern that, following Darwin's original proposal, remains the dominant description of biological evolution. The cases in point include the origin of complex RNA molecules and protein folds; major groups of viruses; archaea and bacteria, and the principal lineages within each of these prokaryotic domains; eukaryotic supergroups; and animal phyla. In each of these pivotal nexuses in life's history, the principal 'types' seem to appear rapidly and fully equipped with the signature features of the respective new level of biological organisation. No intermediate 'grades' or intermediate forms between different types are detectable ...

Included in the abstract is his summary conclusion:

> A Biological Big Bang (BBB) model is proposed for the major transitions in life's evolution. According to this model, each transition is a BBB such that new classes of biological entities emerge at the end of a rapid phase of evolution (inflation) that is characterised by extensive exchange of genetic information which takes distinct forms for different BBBs. The major types of new forms emerge independently, via a sampling process, from the pool of recombining entities of the preceding generation. This process is envisaged as being qualitatively different from tree-pattern cladogenesis.[104]

---

104 Eugene V. Koonin, 'The Biological Big Bang model for the major transitions in evolution', *Biology Direct*, 20 August 2007, p. 2. One of the respondents to his paper quoted Koonin's remark that 'In each major class of biological objects, the principal types emerge "ready-made", and intermediate grades cannot be identified.' And added: 'Ouch, that will be up on ID websites faster than one can bat an eye.' To which Koonin replied: 'Here I do not really understand the concern. I changed "ready-made" to "abruptly", to avoid any ID allusions and added clarifications but, beyond that, there is little I can do because this is an important sentence that accurately and clearly portrays a crucial and, to the very best of my understanding, real feature of evolutionary transitions. Will this be used by the ID camp? Perhaps – if they read that far into the paper. However, I am afraid that, if our goal as evolutionary biologists is to avoid providing any grist for the ID mill, we should simply claim that Darwin, "in principle", solved all the problems of the origin of biological complexity in his eye story, and only minor details remain to be filled in. Actually, I think the position of some ultra-Darwinists is pretty close to that. However, I believe that this is totally counter-productive and such a notion is outright false ... '

Rather than discredit Darwinian theory, I'd suggest that these objections to gradualism – objections echoed by paleontologists like Nile Eldredge and ID-oriented biologists like Michael Behe and science-writer Stephen Meyer – qualify it.[105] They indicate what Edward Oakes has called the heuristic nature of the Darwinian hypothesis.[106] It provides a working framework for all biology, zoology, and to an extent, anthropology, without in itself yet being able to explain how we move across these major transitions, from non-living to living, and from the less complex to the more complex forms of life. Even though the mechanisms for these transitions are at present beyond the reach of biology, there's no need to presume they will forever remain so. But that should be a matter for biologists to decide. As Lonergan remarked more than half a century ago, while discussing the investigation of the intelligibility immanent in the universe of data:

> ... things are to be grasped in data; their numbers and differentiation, their distribution and concentrations, their emergence and survival, give rise to questions that require an answer. One does not escape that requirement by appealing to divine wisdom and divine providence, for that appeal reinforces the rejection of obscurantism and provides another argument for affirming an intelligible order immanent in the visible universe. (*Insight*, 261)

4. The evolution of evolutionary theory

In public debate, Darwinian evolution, not to mention evolutionism, is often presented as a theory which has undergone few major modifications since the Modern Synthesis of Darwin's theory with Mendelian genetics. But the major evolutions that evolutionary theory has undergone since then have in fact profoundly qualified how we think of the interconnected tree of life. Just four of these will be mentioned, always from the viewpoint of a layman whose focus is primarily philosophic, and in view of a more adequate consideration of human origins later.

---

105 Augros and Stanciu quote Niles Eldredge on what paleontologists felt constrained to say: 'We have proffered a collective tacit acceptance of the story of gradual adaptive change, a story that strengthened and became even more entrenched as the [neo-Darwinian] synthesis took hold. We palaeontologists have said that the history of life supports this interpretation, all the while really knowing that it does not.' Augros and Stanciu add that 'Something is gravely wrong with a theory that forces us to deny or ignore the data of an entire science'. *The New Biology*, p. 175.

106 See 'Edward T. Oakes replies' in *First Things*, 112, April 2001, pp. 5–13.

4.1 Eldredge-Gould: Punctuated Equilibrium

It's no secret that many of the gaps in the fossil record Darwin presumed would soon be filled have remained. But it was a methodological mistake on his part to have bothered about those 'gaps' for the reasons we've given: that science doesn't offer a picture of development, but grasps relationships between data, which his theory had done. Also, neither philosophy nor a properly understood revelation interfere with natural science, so he shouldn't have tried to cover up those 'gaps' at all costs. In 1972, Niles Eldredge and Stephen Jay Gould proposed what they saw was an important modification to gradualist Darwinian evolution, in their ground-breaking article, 'Punctuated Equilibria: An alternative to Phyletic Gradualism'.[107]

Succinctly, Eldredge explains:

If evolutionary change doesn't simply accumulate over the course of time, the question becomes, When and under what conditions does evolutionary change occur? ... new species ... tend to show up abruptly in the fossil record as the overwhelming rule ... Punctuated equilibria is a combination of empirical pattern (stasis interrupted by brief bursts of evolutionary change) coupled with preexisting biological theory.[108]

The supporters of classical Darwinism, represented most vocally by Dawkins in England and Dennett in America, regarded punctuated equilibrium less as a revision than a heretical betrayal of Darwin. Eldredge and Gould were subjected to vitriolic attack, even though Dawkins was quite aware that they consider themselves to be Darwinian biologists.[109]

4.2 Evolutionary-Developmental (evo-devo) Theory

The more recent breakthrough in the early nineties, called 'evolutionary-developmental' or 'evo-devo', seems in many ways to correspond at the

---

107 Reprinted in Niles Eldredge, *Time Frames: The Rethinking of Darwinian Evolution and the Theory of Punctuated Equilibria*, London, Heinemann, 1986, pp. 193–223.

108 Niles Eldredge, *Reinventing Darwin: The Great Evolutionary Debate*, London: Phoenix, 1995, p. 94, p. 104.

109 Martinez J. Hewlett, in his 'Biological Models of Origin and Evolution', includes Gould and Lewontin's 1979 notion of 'exaptation' in his reflection on punctuated equilibrium. The basic idea is that structures that were developed for certain purposes can be co-opted or 'exapted' for use in the context of later evolutionary developments. See Nancey Murphy and William R. Stoeger, eds., *Evolution and Emergence: Systems, Organisms, Persons* (Oxford: Oxford University Press, 2007), pp. 158–72, at pp. 166–7.

molecular level to Eldredge and Gould's punctuated equilibrium hypothesis. That is to say, that the relatively sudden appearance of new species could be due to underlying changes at the genetic level, causing a variation in that species' body-plan. Gould's last major work, *The Structure of Evolutionary Theory*, is a massive attempt to marry his revisionary Darwinism with evo-devo.[110] However, the impact on standard Darwinian theory shouldn't be underestimated – evo-devo involves a shift from an over-reliance on the species' adaptation to the environment to the internal developmental changes caused by gene-regulation. As E. H. Davidson puts it:

> The most important consequence is that contrary to classical evolution theory, the processes that drive the small changes observed as species diverge cannot be taken as models for the evolution of the body plans of animals ... that is why it is necessary to apply new principles that derive from the structure/function relations of gene regulatory networks to approach the mechanisms of body plan evolution.[111]

The basic discovery was that the sudden emergence of the thirty-five phyla or major zoological groups (chordates, crustaceans, mollusks, and so on), around 550 million years ago showed a common deep genetic structure. Each phylum had the same genetic instructions for its top/bottom axis, front/back polarity, head, and sensory organs. To get some of the flavour of what evo-devo involves, I'll quote from Rudolf Raff's *The Shape of Life*:

> Higher taxonomic groups, most notably phyla, possess suites [groups] of anatomical features that distinguish them from other groups. Such an underlying anatomical arrangement is called a body plan ... no new phyla appear to have originated since the Cambrian [the geological period around 550 million years ago when animal life first appears] ... [112]

Wallace Arthur gives his opinion that:

---

110 Stephen Jay Gould, *The Structure of Evolutionary Theory*, Cambridge, MA: Harvard University Press, 2002.

111 Quoted in Jerry Fodor and Massimo Piatelli-Palmarini, *What Darwin Got Wrong*, London: Profile Books, 2010, p. 41. The authors comment further: 'The double-edged ... character of developmental modules consists in their relative context insensitivity to external factors and their relative context sensitivity to some internal substitutions of subcomponents' (p. 46).

112 Rudolf A. Raff, *The Shape of Life: Genes, Development, and the Evolution of Animal Form*, Chicago: University of Chicago Press, 1996, p. xiv.

... there was no multicellular animal life prior to 600 [million years] ago; there was an explosion of body plans in Ediacaran times [a little earlier than the Cambrian period, called after a mountain range in South Australia], with many becoming extinct, and a second body-plan explosion in the early Cambrian; evolution in Vendian and Cambrian times was much more 'experimental' than it is now; and internal factors such as developmental constraint (or early lack of it) are important in evolution as well as considerations about niche space and external adaptation.[113]

The best known of expressions to date of what's been called the Cambrian Explosion are the Burgess Shale in Alberta (510 million years ago), along with the related Ediacaran in South Australia (545 million years ago) and the more recently discovered Chengjian fauna in China (520 million years ago), all discussed in chapter six of Sean Carroll's *Endless Forms Most Beautiful*. He calls this Cambrian event 'The Big Bang of Animal Evolution', and asks, 'What Ignited the Explosion? Why did large and complex animals first appear at this time? Why did these particular forms succeed?'[114] Davidson notes that evo-devo understands animal development as 'entirely unidirectional and internally controlled. It does not change direction, oscillate, or alter course depending on environmental factors'.[115] So perhaps a partial answer to the sudden emergence of life forms can be found in evo-devo, which is less focused on adaptation to the environment and more on internal genetic organisation.

4.3 Evo-devo and biological constancy at level of animal body plans
Neil Shubin writes of the 'common architecture' which constitutes the foundation for all animal body plans: 'Looking at embryos, it almost seems that the differences among mammals, birds, amphibians, and fish simply pale in comparison with their fundamental similarities.' Earlier, he had said that 'When you see these deep similarities among different organs and bodies, you begin to recognise that the diverse inhabitants of our

113 Wallace Arthur, *The Origin of Animal Body Plans: A Study in Evolutionary Developmental Biology*, Cambridge: Cambridge University Press, 2000, p. 81.

114 Sean Carroll, *Endless Forms Most Beautiful: The New Science of Evo-devo and the Making of the Animal Kingdom*, New York: Norton, 2005, p. 138. There's also been the huge haul of Burgess Shale types of marine animals recently discovered in the Draa Valley, Morocco, dating from 488 million years ago.

115 Eric H. Davidson, *The Regulatory Genome: Gene Regulatory Networks in Development and Evolution*, Burlington, MA: Academic Press, 2006, p. 88.

world are just variations on a theme.' What are these 'deep similarities'? Shubin's book details some of these: limbs, and the various senses of smell, sight and hearing. For example:

> Every limbed animal has the *Sonic hedgehog* gene ... We now know that *Sonic hedgehog* is one of dozens of genes that act to sculpt our limbs from shoulder to fingertip by turning on and off at the right time. Remarkably, work on chickens, frogs, and mice was telling us the same thing. The DNA recipe to build upper arms, forearms, wrists, and digits is virtually identical in every creature that has limbs.[116]

Probably one of the most impressive examples of how the evo-devo approach works is the way it illuminates the origin of the various kinds of eye emerging across the animal kingdom. Carroll lists the various kinds of eye:

> We and other vertebrates have camera-type eyes with a single lens. Crabs and other arthropods [lobsters, spiders, insects] have compound eyes in which many independent unit eyes gather visual information. Even though they are not close relatives to us, octopi and squids also have camera-type eyes, while their clam and scallop relatives have among them three types: the camera-type eye with a single lens, a mirror eye with a lens and a reflecting mirror, and compound eyes made up of from ten to eighty unit eyes.

In 1994, a common eye-gene underlying all the different types of eyes, called *Pax-6*, was discovered. Carroll writes: 'The new picture of eye evolution reveals different kinds of eyes as products of different evolutionary journeys that began at similar starting points.' Towards the end of his discussion of eye-evolution, Carroll remarks that:

> Discoveries in evo-devo have also revealed that common genetic tools are used to build the very different hearts, digestive tracts, muscles, nervous systems, and limbs of all sorts of animals.[117]

---

116 Neil Shubin, *Your Inner Fish: A Journey into the 3.5-Billion Year History of the Human Body*, New York: Pantheon Books, 2008, p. 99, p. 80, p. 53. Shubin, with Cliff Tabin and Sean Carroll, speak of these similarities as 'deep homology', used to explain the common origin of the genetic regulatory mechanism that gives rise to quite different animal features. See their 'Deep homology and the origins of evolutionary novelty', *Nature* , 457, 11 February 2009, pp. 818–23.

117 Sean Carroll, *The Making of the Fittest: DNA and the Ultimate Forensic Record of Evolution*, New York: Norton, 2006, p. 194, p. 199, p. 202.

For Raff, 'Darwinian selection is firmly established, and the internal architecture of animal genomes and ontogenies probably also plays a role'. He doesn't see the value of opposing these views. Rather, 'Internal rules should not be expected to supersede Darwinian selection, but rather, to complement it in predicting the behaviour of evolving ontogenies.'[118] It's not surprising that supporters of punctuated equilibrium, which up to then had been merely recording a perceived pattern of stasis followed by relatively sudden change, have welcomed evo-devo as a possible explanation of those sudden changes. A primary factor in those changes would be what Davidson and others speak of as 'regulatory genes', which are high-level command genes that can cause an organism to switch direction.[119]

4.4 Conway Morris on convergence

And what would cause such switching? That's a further question, which may find an answer at a level of organisation higher than the genetic or molecular: Simon Conway Morris quotes Michael Denton and Craig Marshall: 'underlying all the diversity of life is a finite set of natural forms that will recur over and over again anywhere in the cosmos where there is carbon-based life.'[120] In other words, there is a limited number of possibilities for the expression of the shared body-plans of all animals in wide ranges of behaviour, such as vocalisation, toolmaking, social play and cooperative hunting – all of which 'have evolved in the birds, and so quite independently of the mammals ... ' As a result, for Conway Morris, 'evolution may be considerably less random than is often supposed'.[121]

---

118 Raff, *The Shape of Life*, p. 324.

119 Sean Carroll notes that only 2 per cent or 3 per cent of an animal's genes (which he calls 'genetic switches') control major changes in animal bodies. He compares their activities to global positioning system (GPS) devices: 'Just as a GPS locator in a boat, car, or plane gets a positional fix by integrating multiple inputs, [genetic] switches integrate positional information in the embryo with respect to longitude, latitude, altitude, and depth, and then dictate the places where genes are turned on and off.' *Endless Forms Most Beautiful*, p. 112, p. 114.

120 Simon Conway Morris, *Life's Solution: Inevitable Humans in a Lonely Universe*, Cambridge: Cambridge University Press, 2003, p. 11. Raff has anticipated this notion of convergence at the level of genetics: 'In contemplating the rapid radiation of animal body plans during the Cambrian and their subsequent stability, both Gould and Jacobs have suggested that a form of internal genetic constraint may act as a brake on body plan evolution. They argue that an originally flexible developmental regulatory system allowed experimentation with very basic patterns of development. Once patterns were established, genetic regulatory system became rigidly fixed. After that, a powerful genetic constraint limited evolution to changes within existing body plans.' *The Shape of Life*, p. 309.

121 Simon Conway Morris, 'Evolution and Convergence: Some Wider Considerations', in the volume he edited, *The Deep Structure of Biology: Is Convergence Sufficiently Ubiquitous to Give a*

For evidence, Conway Morris, in his *Life's Solution*, discusses how bottle-nosed dolphins have similar social organisation to that of chimps, and makes a similar point regarding sperm-whales and elephants. Despite their different morphology he has also spotted psychological similarities in the vision, hearing and smell capacities of moths and hummingbirds. Again, he is good on similarities in crabs, vertebrates and cephalopods (octopus, squid), going so far as to speak of a similar 'oculomotor system' in species of these different phyla (the highest grouping for differences among animals).[122]

What seems to be coming together here are various approaches to evolution: evo-devo as possibly explaining at the genetic level Eldredge and Gould's punctuated equilibrium. Further, possibly explaining commonalities at the level of animal form, or morphologically, would be Conway Morris's argument for the convergence of different but recognisably similar 'solutions' to the problem of living by different types of animals. This would include, for example, the range of mammal and marsupial animals that 'match' each other by occupying similar niches in, say, North America the various large carnivorous members of the cat species and the South American marsupial tiger-like animals called thylacosmilids.

In other words, accompanying the inner similarities genetically laid down across different animal families in body-plans, there are also similarities in external appearance and behaviour. A greatly revised theory of evolution, then, has profoundly 'regulatory' (evo-devo + convergence) as well as 'adaptive' (Darwinian gradual adaptation) factors. So that it's good to note that biological science itself is in a state of continual 'evolution'.[123]

4.5 Denton on the role of animal consciousness in evolution

Although evo-devo has put the emphasis on the 'devo' side of animal origins, there remains the fact that genetics doesn't give the key to animal existence, since animals have to be grasped at their own level, which is in terms of animal consciousness. We've already seen that Sean Carroll speaks of the Cambrian explosion as 'The Big Bang of Animal Evolution'. The excitement of the genetically based evo-devo theory has perhaps distracted from a focus on the centrality for animals of the psychic aspect

---

Directional Signal?, West Conshohocken, PA: Templeton Foundation Press, 2008, p. 48, p. 49.

122 Conway Morris, *Life's Solution*, pp. 249–50; p. 68 n. 171, p. 373 n. 7; p. 151, p. 153.

123 Interestingly, Richard Dawkins, who can come across as an enforcer of Darwinism of strict observance, approvingly cites Conway Morris in his own discussion of convergence in *The Ancestor's Tale*, pp. 492–3.

of their existence – their capacity for sensation: sight, touch, taste, hearing, smell; and at the higher level of organisation of sensations by memory and perception, and 'a factor variously named conation, interest, attention, purpose' (*Insight*, 182). From this viewpoint, the newly emerged and genetically programmed body plan is only the material basis for that psychic life, but isn't itself conscious.

The difference between animals and plants turns on animal cognition and desire, that is, it's primarily due to psychological, not organic (morphological) differences. So the differences between the various animal species should be decided not primarily on their (in Aristotelian terms, 'material') bodily structure but on (again in Aristotelian terms, 'formal') sensory-perceptual grounds. As Lonergan notes of that psychic activity, 'For elementary [animal sensation and perception] knowing vindicates its validity by the survival, not to mention the evolution, of animal species' (*Insight*, 252). And he goes on to make the Aristotelian point that:

> An explanatory account of animal species will differentiate animals not by their organic but by their psychic differences ... the animal pertains to an explanatory genus beyond that of the plant; that explanatory genus turns on sensibility; its specific differences are differences of sensibility; and it is in differences of sensibility that are to be found the basis for differences of organic structure, since that structure, as we have seen, possesses a degree of freedom that is limited but not controlled by underlying materials and outer circumstances. (*Insight*, 265–6)

And the massive qualification of Darwinian evolution by evo-devo in terms of new knowledge of regulatory genes doesn't in itself explain either the enormous diversity of the thirty-six huge groupings of animals known as phyla or the variety within each phylum. Michael Denton, in his *Nature's Destiny: How the Laws of Biology Reveal Purpose in the Universe* (1998), while fully aware of evo-devo, suggests that this diversity and variety should include reflection on the 'evo' aspect too, which Darwin had already focused on in terms of the adaptation of animal species to their environment. Unlike Darwin, however, Denton is not in the least intimidated by fears that admitting any kind of purposiveness in nature would tend to invalidate biological science (Denton is himself a senior research fellow in human molecular genetics). So he suggests that, in addition to the genetic development at the material level, there is a corresponding emergent purpose within the biological phenomena themselves, shaping the evolution of diversity and variety.

He gives as an example the adaptation in shape and activity of the various species of the weta, the New Zealand giant ground cricket, a species sometimes confined to tiny islands. For example, the males of one species have developed tusks in front of their jaws, to joust with rival males (like stags and seals), thus preventing other males' access to the females. Denton asks, 'How did such adaptations come about?':

> If neither natural selection nor any other sort of undirected evolutionary mechanism seems plausible, then could they conceivably have been the result of the activities of life itself operating via some as yet undefined type of inventiveness inherent in all life? Consideration of the many exotic and complex adaptations that grace the living world led many French biologists in the first half of this century, such as Lucien Cuénot, to propose that life must possess to some degree an autonomous creative ability. As he puts it: 'The terms finality, adaptation, organisation have only meaning within the world of living matter ... One cannot disregard the analogy between the tools or the artifacts of man ... and the tools or systems of organised beings: accordingly there must be an analogy between the intelligence and the reason of man ... and some property of living matter. I don't dare to call this intelligence or reason so I call it the inventive power.'

> The possibility that some degree of adaptive evolution may be the result of an inherent emergent inventive capacity possessed by all living things cannot be ruled out ... Certainly the phenomenon of emergence is itself encountered throughout the natural world. We cannot predict the properties of water, or the speed of nerve conduction, from quantum mechanics. Nor can we predict the social behaviour of bees, ants, or indeed any organism from observing the behaviour of an individual in isolation.[124]

If we put together Conway Morris' notion of convergence with the hints Denton makes here, we might arrive at a more comprehensive

---

124 Michael Denton, *Nature's Destiny: How the Laws of Biology Reveal Purpose in the Universe*, New York: Free Press, 1998, pp. 364–5.

group of factors effecting zoological evolution – not only the internal, genetic development of evo-devo, along with the external adaptation of standard Darwinian evolution, but a movement from above, in the sense that psychic factors could also drive morphological development in animals.[125] Lonergan remarks on the increasing degree of freedom from constraint by the lower level on the next higher level as you move up the scale from atoms to animals: 'Hence, while the chemical elements appear as dominated by the manifolds that they systematise, a multicellular structure is dominated by an idea that unfolds in the process of growth, and this idea can itself be subordinated to the higher idea of conscious stimulus and conscious response' (*Insight*, 264).

Within the sequence of natural sciences, it's precisely at this level of animal consciousness that we'd have to move up from the natural science of biology to zoology. But there's also the question at the level of existence (or, the ontological question): where does animal consciousness come from? We can agree with Aquinas that animal consciousness is material, not spiritual, but it's of such a different level of matter to, say, genetic material, that it's certainly more than a minor issue to wonder how it could emerge from non-conscious material. Raff reports on how Slack and his fellow geneticists have called a hypothetical Hox-gene-centered genetic body plan for most animal phyla the 'zootype' – that is to say, an original early animal form or 'living-type' that would include things like the jellyfish, which doesn't have the kind of body plan most other animals have, yet whose eye structure is genetically similar to eyes in the later animals.[126] Yet

---

125 Terrence Deacon in his *The Symbolic Species: The Co-evolution of Language and the Human Brain* (London: Allen Lane/Penguin Press, 1997) points out that 'Cross-linguistic comparison of aphasic patients is beginning to demonstrate that the same deep grammatical operation may recruit different cortical regions, depending on the way it is encoded syntactically. This is particularly evident when comparing languages [his example is English] which depend on word-order cues to those that depend on morphological and inflectional cues [his example is Italian] to express the same grammatical function ... when word order is more critical, damage to ventral frontal regions [Broca's area] produces greater grammatical impairment; when inflection and morphology are more critical, damage to temporal regions [Wernicke's area] produces greater grammatical impairment' (p. 308). While the notion that the neural material in the human brain could grow after young adulthood was resisted up to the 1980s, it is now accepted that brain morphology can be affected all through life by the kinds of learning and activity we undertake. It's obviously beyond my competence to do more than suggest that psychic factors can modify morphology in the non-human animals too, even if the range of divergent experience and activity is far narrower than in humans.

126 Wallace Arthur has an important correction to this statement, in his *The Origin of Animal Body Plans*: ' ... neither the "zootype" of Slack et al. (1993) nor any other pattern of gene activity represents a body plan; rather such patterns may form part of the explanation of body plans' (p. 28).

these considerations, again at the genetic level, don't really touch the kind of systematic exploration of animal consciousness we find for example in the three 1973 Nobel prize winners for physiology, Karl von Frisch, Niko Tinbergen (Richard Dawkins' doctoral supervisor), or Konrad Lorenz, whose life work was to understand animals on their own terms, not to mention the various and heroic investigators like Jane Goodall in the field of bonobos, chimps and gorillas.[127] We'll return to this question in our next chapter; however Lonergan's reflections on development may be useful at this point.

5. Lonergan on development

We can now graft on to what we wrote about emergent probability in chapter three. When discussing development – whether biological, zoological or human – Lonergan writes firstly, of the principle of **emergence**. What's emerging are what would be seen from the level of previous development as just 'coincidental manifolds' of physical and chemical activities – say of carbon dioxide, water, photons or light energy, sugar (carbohydrate) and oxygen. However, activities that would be merely coincidental from the viewpoint of chemistry would 'invite the higher integration' in terms of, say, the process of photosynthesis, by which some bacteria, along with plants and fungi transform sunlight into life-giving energy, where that activity occurs at the next level of development.

Secondly, there is the principle of **correspondence**: 'Significantly different underlying manifolds require different higher integrations'. For example, chemical elements differ by atomic numbers and atomic weights, 'and these differences are grounded in the underlying manifold' (*Insight*, 451).

'Thirdly, there is the principle of **finality**. The underlying manifold is an upwardly but indeterminately directed dynamism towards ever fuller realisation of being. Any actual realisation will pertain to some determinate genus and species, but this very indeterminacy is limitation, and every limitation is to finality a barrier to be transcended.' Since 'finality' has various meanings, Lonergan points out 'what we do not mean' by finality

---

127 Fodor and Piatelli-Palmarini devote a whole chapter in *What Darwin Got Wrong* to 'The Return of the Laws of Form', where they discuss topics like 'invariants of animal locomotion' or honeybees' 'optimal foraging strategies' – the bees choose 'the optimum of the curve of the possible ratios of proactive versus reactive foragers': proactive bees seek out food sources and reactive ones wait for this information (p. 85). The authors' point is that natural selection is inadequate to explain how the honeybees arrived at this: 'nobody today really has a clue to the solution of these problems' (p. 86). But the direction of inquiry has to lie in the discovery of how honeybees' problem-solving consciousness works.

in this particular discussion of development. He notes that his concern here is 'not with ... extrinsic causes but with the immanent constituents' of biological, zoological and human reality. He cites the Aristotelian parallel not in Aristotle's first mover nor in his notion of 'telos' or final end, but as principle of movement within the reality itself (*Insight*, 451).

He continues:

> Fourthly, there is the principle of development itself. It is the linked sequence of dynamic higher integrations ...
>
> Fifthly, the course of development is marked by an increasing explanatory differentiation ...
>
> Sixthly, the course of development is capable of minor flexibility inasmuch as it can pursue the same goal along different routes ...
>
> Seventhly, the course of development is capable of a major flexibility that consists in a shift or modification of the ultimate objective. In biology this is the familiar fact of adaptation.
>
> In the light of the foregoing considerations, a development may be defined as a flexible linked sequence of dynamic and increasing differentiated higher integrations that meet the tension of successively transformed underlying manifolds through successive applications of the principles of correspondence and emergence. (*Insight*, 452–4)

Since development can be at various levels of existence, he notes that 'In the plant there is the single development of the organism; in the animal there is the twofold development of the organism and the psyche; in man there is the threefold development of the organism, the psyche, and intelligence (*Insight*, 459).

In an earlier chapter where he's discussing 'Species as explanatory', he says: 'Accordingly, emergent probability has quite different implications from the gradual accumulation of small variations that is associated with the name of Darwin. The fundamental element in emergent probability is the conditioned series of things and schemes ... ' (*Insight*, 264–5). This would explain Darwin's methodological mistake in trying at all costs to plug the gaps in what he saw as 'the imperfection of the geological record'. It's why punctuated equilibrium was never an objection against evolution as such, rather a recognition that evolution is the insight into the conditioned series of species over the aeons as a series, whose verification comes precisely through making sense of that series. It's also why various creationist critiques of Darwin on the basis that he hasn't explained those gaps away are based on a similar misunderstanding of scientific method.

So, an adequate understanding of evolution will involve a heuristic or overall context for approaching the data of biology, botany, zoology and anthropology. This anticipative framework includes the four elements we've been speaking about:, internal-genetic (evo-devo), external-adaptational (Darwinian evolution), the grasping of the constraints on these interactive factors called convergence (Simon Conway Morris), and as a possible explanation of convergence in the behaviour of rather different animals, Denton's and Lonergan's notion of the role of psychological factors. Each level, biological, botanical, zoological and anthropological, constitutes a 'correspondence' or 'form' to an 'emergence' or 'matter' provided by the level immediately below it. Then the upward dynamism Lonergan calls 'finality' can be understood as underlying the entire 'flexible linked sequence'. And grasping that is something that can be done by natural scientists who find the sequence to be a meaningful one.

Of course, as Pope Benedict XVI recently noted in a philosophic discussion, the sequence can give rise to a further question:

> It seems to me that the process, too, as a whole, has a rationality about it. Despite its false starts and meanderings through the narrow corridor, the process as such is something rational in its selection of the few positive mutations and its exploitation of the minute probabilities. This ... rationality, which in turn corresponds to our human reason, unavoidably leads to a question that goes beyond science yet is a reasonable question. Where does this rationality originate?[128]

And because of this and other further questions, we can continue the dialogue we've seen advocated by Sergio Rondinara in the previous chapter.

6. Complementarity of scientific, religious and philosophical modes of inquiry

Our discussion of complementarity between the natural sciences, philosophy and revelation at the end of chapter three can be expanded by

---

128 In Stefan Otto Horn and Siegfried Wiedenhofer, eds., *Creation and Evolution: A Conference with Pope Benedict XVI at Castelgandolfo*, tr. Michael J. Miller, San Francisco: Ignatius Press, 2008, p. 164.

a few comments on the relationship between biology and philosophy. It is interesting that discussion of the other factors in evolution – punctuated equilibrium, evo-devo, convergence and animal consciousness – doesn't give rise to the kind of philosophical or theological quarrels that seem endemic to Darwinian evolution as such. We've suggested that Darwin's own lack of clarity in this area must take much of the blame for these quarrels. Still, the conflicts show no signs of abating, so we'll conclude with a comment on how at least some evolutionists have resolved them. Our focus is on the philosophical rather than the religious aspect of the unnecessary strife. But before approaching it directly, maybe it's easier to understand the problem of differing but related areas of inquiry in terms of an ethical example.

J. Robert Oppenheimer was the nuclear physicist in charge of the Manhattan project for producing an atomic bomb during the Second World War. He always had ethical reservations about this work. Werner Heisenberg possibly had similar misgivings regarding the National Socialist atomic bomb project, and it could be that he deliberately tried to undermine it.[129] While the US project succeeded, and the German one failed, neither Oppenheimer nor Heisenberg thought the ethical questions about what they were doing could be decided by the science of nuclear physics they were expert in. Whether something is good for a human being involves the kind of considerations to be found, for example, in Plato's Gorgias or Aristotle's *Nicomachean Ethics* or the Decalogue, because ethical issues, like metaphysical ones, can't be resolved by explanation at the level of nuclear physics, or for that matter, of biology.

6.1 Stephen Jay Gould's 'Principle of Non-Overlapping Magisteria'

Both Stephen Jay Gould's *Rocks of Ages* and Michael Ruse's *Can a Darwinian Be a Christian?* show an openness to accepting types of investigation which are fundamentally different rather than opposed. Typically, these types of investigation are natural-scientific and religious – surprisingly, philosophic investigation never seems to be given the same attention. Still, however limited this breakthrough is, I feel it is of some cultural importance.

Brooklyn-born Gould (1941–2002) grew up with a secular Jewish, even Marxist, background. But his later writings showed him open to religion, even if he considers himself an agnostic. The central idea in his *Rocks of Ages* is that:

---

129 See, for example, Thomas Powers' *Heisenberg's War: The Secret History of the German Bomb*, London: Penguin, 1993.

Science tries to document the factual character of the natural world. Religion operates in the equally important, but utterly different, realm of human purposes, meanings and values. I propose that we encapsulate this central principle of respectful non-interference – accompanied by intense dialogue between the two distinct subjects – by enunciating the principle of NOMA, or Non-Overlapping Magisteria.

Later, Gould justifies NOMA as:

... a simple, humane, rational, and altogether conventional argument for mutual respect, based on non-overlapping subject matter, between two components of wisdom in a full human life: our drive to understand the factual character of nature (the magisterium of science), and our need to define meaning in our lives and a moral basis for our actions (the magisterium of religion).[130]

But in his 2005 Robert Boyle lecture, 'Darwin's Compass: How Evolution Discovers the Song of Creation', Conway Morris remarked:

I hope nobody here has fallen for Stephen Jay Gould's reckless canard of science and religion defining independent magisteria of influence (and ... should they toy with this superficially appealing idea be warned they face logical incoherence) – but far more importantly how science reveals unexpected depths to Creation while religion informs us what on earth (literally) we are going to do about it.[131]

However, whatever reservations Gould had about religion, and despite Conway Morris's accurate critique of NOMA, it would be churlish not to welcome, from a lifelong Darwinian, at least a recognition that there were quests other than the natural scientific that have validity.

And Michael Ruse, at least until recently himself a religious sceptic, is able to give an affirmative answer to the question he uses for a book title, *Can a Darwinian Be a Christian?* There, in apparent agreement, he summarises Ernan McMullin's view that: 'God is not simply forecasting

---

130 Stephen Jay Gould, *Rocks of Ages: Science and Religion in the Fullness of Life*, London: Jonathan Cape, 2001, pp. 4–5, p. 175.

131 My quotation is from p. 3 of the downloaded version, easily available on the Internet. Conway Morris used the same title for his as yet unpublished 2007 Gifford Lectures.

on the basis of what will happen. There is an act of creation which unfurls through time for us, but which is outside time for God and hence for which beginning, middle and end are all as one.' And he quotes McMullin's assertion that 'the contingency or otherwise of the evolutionary sequence does not bear on whether the created universe embodies purpose or not. Asserting the reality of cosmic purpose in this context takes for granted that the universe depends for its existence on an omniscient Creator.'[132]

6.2 Aquinas on the complementarity between philosophy, revelation and natural science

Awareness of the complementarity of different types of quests for truth isn't anything new. Eric Voegelin, in his study of the medieval period, remarked about an earlier achievement of cooperation between the areas of philosophy and revelation:

> It is no exaggeration to say that the authority of Thomas and his superb personal skill in achieving the harmonisation [between the spheres of reason and of faith] for his time have decisively influenced the fate of scholarship in the Western World. He has shown in practice that philosophy can function in the Christian system and that revealed truth is compatible with philosophy; and he has formulated the principle that gives philosophy its legitimate status in Christianity.[133]

In fact, Aquinas himself has in some ways anticipated how we can see an interaction between philosophy and biology, in the light of his understanding of the relation between creator and creation. Darwin's famous closing comment in *The Origin of Species*, 'There is grandeur in this view of life ... ' would easily harmonise with Aquinas' understanding of created process:

> Nor is it superfluous, even if God can by himself produce all natural effects, for them to be produced by certain natural causes. For this is not a result of the inadequacy of divine power, but of the immensity

---

132 Michael Ruse, *Can a Darwinian Be a Christian? The Relationship Between Science and Religion*, Cambridge: Cambridge University Press, 2001, pp. 87–8.

133 Eric Voegelin, *History of Political Ideas, Vol. II: The Middle Ages to Aquinas*, ed. Peter von Sivers, Columbia, MO: University of Missouri Press, 1997, pp. 209–10.

of his goodness, whereby he also willed to communicate his likeness to things, not only (1) so that they might exist, but also (2) that they might be causes for other things. Indeed all creatures generally attain the divine likeness in these two ways ... By this, in fact, the beauty of order in created things is evident. (*Summa Contra Gentiles* III, 70)[134]

Bernard Lonergan, as a contemporary Thomist, makes the same point in terms of the divine master-plan of creation, where the Creator shares his existence and creativity with his created, secondary causes:

God not only gives being to, and conserves in being, every created cause, but also he uses the universe of causes as his instruments in applying each cause to its operation and so is the principal cause of each and every event as event. Man [and we could add here with Darwin, nature] proposes, but God disposes.[135]

The differentiation of the natural sciences from myth and magic, from philosophical cosmology, and from revelation, is part of the cultural history of the second millennium. Just as physics needs philosophy to remind it of its limits, thus preventing pseudo- and dilettantish speculation, so also biology needs a strong philosophical awareness to keep natural scientific investigations clearly separated from metaphysical or theological reflection.

Obviously we can only point in the direction of a fuller investigation, like the one Norman Kretzmann carries out in his critical reading of Aquinas' *Summa Contra Gentiles* on creation.[136] But at least we can expand the discussion in the previous chapter on primary and secondary causation by mentioning Aquinas' philosophical approach towards creation, and his surprising modernity in insisting that reason and revelation, while mutually enriching one another, must be kept separated as different types of knowledge – even leaving room for natural scientific investigation before it had occurred!

Following Kretzmann, we can begin by saying what creation meant for Aquinas, 'God is for all things the cause of being' – which was his title

134 Quoted in Augros and Stanciu, *The New Biology*, p. 229.

135 Bernard Lonergan, *Collection*, New York: Herder & Herder, 1967, p. 58.

136 Norman Kretzmann, *The Metaphysics of Creation: Aquinas' Natural Theology in* Summa Contra Gentiles II, New York: Oxford University Press, 1999.

for chapter 15 of Book II of his *Contra Gentiles*. Or as he puts it in the following chapter, 'God has produced things as regard their being out of no pre-existing [subject], as out of matter' (*CG* II, 16). What Thomas means here, Kretzmann comments, is 'out of nothing', so that 'God is for any created thing considered ... the ultimate cause of its being *at all*'. And at the end of *CG* II, 16, Aquinas expands a classic philosophical principle. He's commenting on how the classic philosophers:

> ... observed that there is always something antecedent to action where the actions of particular agents are concerned. From that observation they derived the opinion, common to all, that nothing is made or comes about out of nothing (*ex nihilo nihil fit*). As regards *particular* agents that is of course *true*. But they had not yet arrived at a cognition of the *universal* agent, which is productive (*activum*) of the whole of being, [the agent] for whose action it is necessary to presuppose *nothing*.

In one of his earlier works, Kretzmann recalls, Aquinas had already seen how in the case of anything created, not-being is '*naturally* prior' to being – any created thing 'has being only from the influence of a higher cause' and 'if left to itself' reverts to not being. But what's of interest to us here in terms of how Aquinas sees reason and revelation as complementary rather than substituting for one another, is his clarification that 'not being' is not only naturally but also, as Kretzmann puts it, *temporally* prior to being. As Aquinas had written in the earlier work referred to above, 'in *that* way creation cannot be demonstrated, nor is it granted to philosophers. It is, however, supposed through faith'.

Thus, on the basis of divine revelation, and in common with all the medieval theologians, Aquinas accepted that the world had a beginning in time. But he disagreed with those who maintained Aristotle had not meant what he said when he wrote that the world had no beginning. He also disagreed with the majority of philosopher-theologians who held – with Bonaventure as the most prominent among them – they had proved by reason that it was impossible for the world not to have a beginning in time.

However, Aquinas denies that the world *must* have existed forever, which for him hasn't been demonstrated by anyone, including Aristotle. Still – and this is why he doesn't agree with the majority – for him, being created does not necessarily imply having a beginning. So, surprising as it may seem, Aquinas wouldn't disagree on principle with those astrophysicists who advance a theory of the universe as in a process of continued expansion, contraction and re-expansion. The beginninglessness of the world wasn't the key point for Aquinas. That key point was 'the very dependence of created being on the source by which it is established' (*CG* II, 18). Elsewhere, Kretzmann quotes him as writing: 'having been made and existing for ever are *not* incompatible considered in themselves'. And Kretzmann comments:

> He has thus already suggested ... that the *essential* relation of the created world to the omnipotent, beginningless creator is that of total existential dependence, not that of having been brought into existence for the first time, even if the created world was in fact brought into existence for the first time a finite number of years ago.

Yet, Kretzmann concludes, 'having undermined all those attempts to *demonstrate* the proposition he accepts on Scriptural authority', he still argues that it's more likely the created world began to exist, since their having a beginning in time would more clearly show their total dependence in existence from the creator (*CG* II, 38).

Not only does Aquinas show the non-interfering complementarity of reason and revelation by defending reason's own integrity in the case of Aristotle, he similarly does so in the case of the book of Genesis. He indicated by reason that there can be no temporal succession in the act of creation – since the creator isn't acting in time but creates time: 'For successiveness is proper to movement. But creating is not movement, nor is it the terminus of movement, like a change. Therefore there is no successiveness involved in it' (*CG* II, 19).

As a result, 'it seems to be that Aquinas's considered view that the work of the six days, as revealed in Genesis, is *not* creation, strictly speaking.' And Kretzmann continues by referring to the ten questions in the *Summa Theologica* (*ST* Ia. 67–74), sometimes called 'The Treatise on the Work of the Six Days'. There Aquinas makes the 'fundamental division between instantaneous creating to begin with, and successive distinguishing and furnishing thereafter ... ' He further quotes Aquinas from the same 'Treatise': 'Therefore, in order to show that *all* bodies were created by God *immediately*, Moses said, "In the beginning God created *the heaven and the earth*"' (*ST* Ia.65.3c).[137] So Aquinas, following Augustine's non-literal

---

137 Ibid., p. 71, pp. 74–6, p. 85, p. 91, pp. 94–6, pp. 145–8, p. 150, p. 182. All the emphases in texts of Aquinas are Kretzmann's.

reading of Genesis, once again is carefully interpreting revelation in a way that fully respects reason. I think both of these issues, vis-à-vis Aristotle and Genesis, indicate an attitude that's generously open to different and non-interfering (rather than non-overlapping) approaches towards truth.

Having, I hope, at least touched on some of the key issues in the debate between the natural sciences, including biology, and philosophy, let's move on to hominid evolution and see what questions it poses to a philosophy of science.

Part Three: How we belong and yet – because of the 'human revolution' – don't fully belong to the hominid sequence

Chapter Five: Hanging by our ancestors' tails?

We needed to sort out the evolutionary context, at least a little, because our origins have their roots there, even if only partly so. As G. K. Chesterton's piece of doggerel (dashed off in 1925, probably prompted by the Scopes Trial) implies, we belong, yet, as 'Firmanentalists' don't belong completely to the evolutionary sequence:

> **RACE MEMORY** (by a dazed Darwinian)
> I remember, I remember,
>   Long before I was born,
> The tree-tops where my racial self
>   Went dancing round at morn ...
>
> In that green-turreted Monkeyville
>   (So I have often heard)
> It seemed as if a Blue Baboon
>   Might soar like a Blue Bird.
>
> Low-crawling Fundamentalists
>   Glared up through the green mist,
> I hung upon my tail in heaven
>   A Firmamentalist.
>
> ... The past was bestial ignorance:
>   But I feel a little funky,
> To think I'm further off from heaven
>   Than when I was a monkey.[1]

It's fascinating to think of the sensitivity we'd have had to show to the Flores hominids (popularly, 'Hobbits'), whose remains were discovered on the Indonesian island of Flores in 2003, if they'd survived beyond the 12,000 years ago they died out. Since our focus is on the specific question of human origins, and there already exist excellent accounts of the sequence of hominids leading up to ourselves, we'll limit ourselves

---

1 G. K. Chesterton, *Collected Poetry, Part I*, San Francisco: Ignatius Press, 1994, p. 515.

here to a brief summary of that hominid sequence.[2] Then we'll have a look at what's probably been the most intensely studied hominid other than ourselves, the Neanderthals. We'll conclude with an attempt to place the hominids within the evolutionary framework we've just sketched out, and ask whether hominid study requires us to go beyond the kind of science already required in zoological or comparative primate studies.

I'll be suggesting later that the use in paleontology of the word 'human' – especially in its Latin form, *Homo* – is philosophically inaccurate. Still, the titles of books on the hominid sequence, technical as much as popular, acknowledge that the enormous interest in hominid studies is because they're seen as an integral part of the inquiry into human origins.[3]

1. The hominid sequence

In each great region of the world the living mammals are closely related to the extinct species of the same region. It is therefore probable that Africa was formerly inhabited by extinct apes closely allied to the gorilla and chimpanzee; and as these two species are now man's nearest allies, it is somewhat more probable that our early progenitors lived on the African continent than elsewhere.[4]

One of Darwin's many flashes of brilliance was to see that what he called 'the descent of man' would most likely originate in Africa. And whatever the various hypotheses are about when the break occurred between the specifically hominid or bidpedalline from what used to be called the pongids (including gorillas, chimpanzees and orang-utans), there seems

2 For accounts of the sequence of hominids leading up to ourselves see, for example, Matt Cartmill and Fred H. Smith, *The Human Lineage*, Hoboken, NJ: Wiley-Blackwell, 2009; Glenn Conroy, *Reconstructing Human Origins: A Modern Synthesis*, New York: Norton, 1997; Richard G. Klein, *The Human Career: Human Biological and Cultural Origins*, Chicago: University of Chicago Press, 1999; Roger Lewin, *Principles of Human Evolution*, Oxford: Blackwell, 1998; Stephen Jones, Robert D. Martin and David R. Pilbeam, eds., *The Cambridge Encyclopedia of Human Evolution*, Cambridge: Cambridge University Press, 1994.

3 For example, Patricia J. Ash and David J. Robinson, *The Emergence of Humans: An Exploration of the Evolutionary Timeline*, Chichester, West Sussex: Wiley-Blackwell, 2010; Rob de Salle and Ian Tattersall, *Human Origins: What Bones and Genomes Tell Us About Ourselves*, College Station, TX: Texas A & M University Press, 2008; Juan Luis Arsuaga and Ignacio Martínez, *The Chosen Species: The Long March of Human Evolution*, Oxford: Blackwell, 2006; Richard G. Klein with Blake Edgar, *The Dawn of Human Culture: A Bold New Theory on What Sparked the 'Big Bang' of Human Consciousness*, New York: Wiley, 2002; Chris Stringer and Robin McKie, *African Exodus: The Origins of Modern Humanity*, London: Pimlico, 1997; Richard Leakey and Roger Lewin, *Origins Reconsidered: In Search of What Makes Us Human*, New York: Anchor Books, 1993.

4 Charles Darwin, *The Descent of Man and Selection in Relation to Sex*, Vol. I, London: John Murray, 1871, p. 199.

a clear enough sequence from earlier loris or lemur types through to these two larger pongid and hominid groups, which may have split about 7 million years ago.[5] I'll give my own very summary list of four groupings of hominids currently known – it's a list that's constantly added to. As Schwartz and his co-editors point out in their huge four-volume survey, *The Human Fossil Record*, more hominid fossils have been discovered since 1980 than before then, and the overall hominid picture can change with each new find.[6] While there's no generally agreed definition of a hominid, it'll be enough here to see them as bipedal (walking on two feet) ancestors to human beings.

(i) A first group we can non-technically name pre-australopithecines, a grab-bag title for the various discoveries – all made in the last twenty years – predating the australopithecines. We begin with *Sahelanthropus tchadensis*, dated about 6.5 million years, discovered in Chad, central Africa, which would make it the earliest hominid. While quite apelike, it appears to have walked on two feet. Then there is *Orrorin tugensis*, 6 million years, from Kenya, followed in time by *Ardipithecus kadabba*, 5.8–5.6 million years, and *Ardipithecus ramidus*, 4.4 million years, both from Ethiopia. Schwartz and Tattersall have reservations about the hominid status both of *Sahelanthropus* and *Ardipithecus ramidus* on the basis that it's not clear that the relationship between their head and their trunk clearly implies a bipedal rather than apelike stance.[7]

(ii) A second group of hominids are the australopithecines (literally, 'southern apes', though they're neither confined to Southern Africa, nor are they apes). They've been classified into some six species mostly located in Eastern and Southern Africa. They all walk on two feet, their brain sizes range from 300cc–530cc, roughly three to four times the average for mammals of their size, and span a period from 4.5–1.25 million years ago.[8] A recent discovery associates the *Australopithecus afarensis* nicknamed 'Lucy' with tool use, since near where she was found in 1976,

---

5 'In recent years, in the absence of any workable morphological definition of the [hominid] family, the inferred behavioural attribute of bipedality has become the touchstone for hominid status.' *The Human Fossil Record, Vol. 4: Craniodental Morphology of Early Hominids and Overview*, eds. Jeffrey H. Schwartz and Ian Tattersall, Hoboken, NJ: Wiley-Liss, 2005, p. 469.

6 See the four volumes of *The Human Fossil Record*, ed. Jeffrey H Schwartz et al., Hoboken, NJ: Wiley-Liss, 2002–5.

7 Schwartz and Tattersall, *The Human Fossil Record*, Vol. 4, pp. 469–71.

8 There's a measure called the 'encephalisation quotient', or EQ, based on the ratio of the brain to body weight of all mammals, giving a rough notion of the animal's cognitive capacity. For example, a mouse has an EQ of 0.5, a cat's EQ is 1, an elephant's 5.25, a dolphin's 5.31.

the team led by Dr Zeresenay Alemseged from the California Academy of Sciences discovered two fossil animal bones dating back to 3.4 million years which gave evidence of being cut and having their marrow extracted with a stone tool.[9]

Another australopithecine species, *Africanus*, also appears to have used, but not made tools. *Africanus* is lightly built, or gracile, and generally considered to be ancestral to our species, while the heavier built or *Australopithecus robustus* (or *Paranthropus*) is considered an evolutionary cul-de-sac. The controversial East African species, *Homo habilis*, with a brain size of about 700cc, 4.2 times the mammal average, lived from 2–1.5 million years ago and also used tools. It was for a time considered to belong to the first group of hominids classified as *Homo*, but is now regarded as belonging to the australopithecine group.[10]

(iii) A third group of hominids (with early and later varieties) includes the longest-surviving hominid, *Homo erectus* (literally, 'erect human', though the australopithecines also walked on two feet), or erectines, which spread from Africa to Asia and Europe from 1.8 million–200,000 years ago. *Homo ergaster* regarded as an earlier African version, existed 2.5–1.7 million years ago, while *Homo heidelbergensis* (c. 650,000–400,000 years), a much later erectine, radiated out of Africa into Europe. Earlier erectines have a brain of about 1000cc, some 6.5 times the mammal average, and not only used, but made tools, with earlier claims that they used fire now strongly questioned. *Homo heidelbergensis* brains ranged from 1100–1400 cc, overlapping our brain size.

Homo neanderthalensis, perhaps the most complicated of all the hominid species, with a range of classic and derived types, is found in Europe, the Middle East and Central Asia, from some 400,000–30,000 years ago. Neanderthal brain size is c.1500cc, eight times the mammal average.[11] They made a wider range of tools than erectines, used fire for heat – although

---

9 Richard Alleyne, 'Hail Lucy! – the new Queen of the Stone Age: An archeological find has added a new chapter to the history of humans and could shift the Stone Age back almost one million years', *Daily Telegraph*, 12 August 2010.

10 Schwartz and Tattersall, *The Human Fossil Record*, Vol. 4, p. 487.

11 Just a sample of the enormous literature on Neanderthals: Paul Mellars, *The Neanderthal Legacy: An Archaeological Perspective from Western Europe*, Princeton, NJ: Princeton University Press, 1996; Steven Mithen, *The Singing Neanderthals: The Origins of Music, Language, Mind and Body*, London: Weidenfeld & Nicolson, 2005; Christopher Stringer and Clive Gamble, *In Search of Neanderthals: Solving the Puzzle of Human Origins*, London: Thames & Hudson, 1993; Ian Tattersall, *The Last Neanderthal: The Rise, Success, and Mysterious Extinction of Our Closest Human Relatives*, Boulder, CO: Westview Press, 1999.

apparently not for cooking – and left what seems to be some evidence of burying their dead.

Neanderthals are regarded as another evolutionary cul-de-sac, while it's from the wide range of hominids considered to have emerged from the erectines, including *Homo heidelbergensis*, that species with names like 'archaic *Homo sapiens*' and 'early modern human' are considered to have derived.

(iv) The fourth and final hominid group contains only one species – though I don't think that's the right word for it – *Homo sapiens*. It will be my contention later on that humans, while morphologically belonging to the hominid family, are immeasurably more distant from the previous hominid group than that group is from the australopithecines. While that diversity is not primarily morphological, it's still interesting that Schwartz and Tattersall note towards the end of the *Homo sapiens* section of their overview:

> At the beginning of this study we had expected to find that hominid fossils would sort into distinct clades [a technical animal grouping], within one of which *H. sapiens* could be accommodated. In the event, this has not turned out to be the case. Instead, *H. sapiens* appears in many ways to be an outlier among all of the hominid forms we have examined.[12]

Before asking how these various members of the hominid sequence may be interrelated, we'll stop to examine the Neanderthals, which Schwarz and Tattersall consider to be 'simply the best-known and latest-surviving member' of the hominid forms that included *Homo heidelbergensis*.[13] As a result, it's the hominid perhaps best placed for us to be able to ask whether its study requires a movement beyond the zoological to the specifically human.

2. Neanderthals: continuity with earlier hominids, discontinuity with us?

Even though it's generally agreed that the classic Neanderthals are not ancestral to modern humans, we have more information on them than on the many other hominid species just preceding humans. They are said to

---

12 Schwartz and Tattersall, *The Human Fossil Record*, Vol. 4, p. 510.

13 Ibid., p. 506.

have originated about 400,000 years ago, and co-existed with modern humans in parts of southwestern Europe from about 40,000 years ago, with the last known Neanderthal survivors in Portuguese cave sites, 28,000 years ago. Almost half a million years was certainly not a bad run. To help us form a picture of what exactly they are, we'll have a look at Neanderthal DNA, brain size, toolmaking, burials and the question of grave goods, and finally, symbolisation and language.

2.1 Neanderthal DNA

Paleontologist Paul Mellars wrote that:

> The recent publication of surprisingly well preserved mitochondrial DNA from the original Neanderthal type-specimen from Neanderthal itself leaves little doubt that in at least most areas of Europe, the Neanderthals became extinct without, apparently, leaving any genetically detectable descendants in later populations.

With regard to the possible new DNA evidence, Mellars adds:

> One could also argue that the survival of the Aurignacian [modern human] and Châtelperronian [Neanderthal] industries as clearly identifiable and sharply separated technological traditions over a period of several thousand years must imply some fundamental barrier to communication and interbreeding between the two groups, which prevented their total assimilation and integration over this span of time.[14]

Ian Tattersall discusses DNA from the first Neanderthal, discovered in the Neander Valley or Thal, which has also been recently dated to 40,000 years ago. For him, 'that Neanderthal DNA is well outside the range of variation defined by all modern human samples'.[15] There have been recent claims that there's a 1–4 per cent trace of Neanderthal DNA indicating interbreeding in the Middle East with humans on their way out of Africa.

---

14 Paul Mellars, 'The Archaeological Records of the Neanderthal-Modern Human Transition in France', in Ofer Bar-Josef and David Pilbeam, eds., *The Geography of Neanderthals and Modern Humans in Europe and the Greater Mediterranean*, Cambridge, MA: Peabody Museum of Archaeology and Ethnology, Harvard University, 2000, pp. 35–47, at p. 35 and p. 44.

15 Ian Tattersall, 'The Place of the Neanderthals in Human Evolution and the Origin of *Homo sapiens*,' in Donald C. Johanson and Giancarlo Ligabue, eds., *Ecce Homo: Writings in Honour of Third-Millennium Man*, Milan: Electra, 1999, pp. 157–75, at p. 161.

Still, paleoanthropologists of the stature of Ian Tattersall and Richard Klein have cautioned against going ahead of current paleontological and archaeological evidence on the basis of the little-understood mathematical interpretation of Neanderthal DNA.[16]

2.2 Neanderthal brain size

While speaking of Neanderthal behaviour as 'purposeful and intelligent', Paul Mellars asks how Neanderthal behaviour differed from that of humans.[17] The first point he mentions is that there are brain differences: there's a slightly higher neocortex ratio in humans than Neanderthals, given that Neanderthal brains are of similar volume, or sometimes of slightly greater volume, than humans.[18] At the same time, since Neanderthal brain size can be larger than humans, we should at least expect a higher level of perceptual experience and sophisticated behaviour than in earlier hominids, going far beyond, say, chimpanzee toolmaking and usage.

Richard W. Byrne challenges certain assumptions regarding Neanderthal brain size because the relation between 'cranial capacity and the skull's outside dimensions is not close'. Byrne gives the example of humans suffering from hydroencephaly:

> Hydroencephalics include intelligent and efficient people, whose brain matter is nevertheless reduced to a thin 'rind' around a massive, water-filled cranial cavity ... often the cranium is enlarged, accommodating the excessive water, so some hydroencephalics may well have a normal number of cerebral neurons.[19]

Cartmill and Smith make the important point that 'Similarity in size does not guarantee similarity in structure. The Neandertal brain was somewhat different in proportions from the brains of modern humans.'[20] With which

---

16 See Richard E. Green et al. 'A Draft Sequence of the Neanderthal Genome', *Science*, 7 May 2010: Vol. 328. No. 5979, pp. 710–22; Nicholas Wade, 'Signs of Neanderthals Mating With Humans', *New York Times*, 6 May 2010.

17 Paul Mellars, 'The Neanderthal Problem Continued', *Current Anthropology*, 40.3 (June 1999), pp. 341–64.

18 The neocortex is the six-layered outer layer, the evolutionarily latest part of the brain in all mammals.

19 Richard W. Byrne, 'Relating Brain Sizes to Intelligence in Primates', in Paul Mellars and Kathleen Gibson, eds., *Modelling the Early Human Mind*, McDonald Institute Monographs: Cambridge, 1996, pp. 49–56, at p. 49 and p. 50.

20 Cartmill and Smith, *The Human Lineage*, p. 361.

Byrne is in agreement, maintaining, rather than bigger is better, that 'relative size is what matters'. This works fine in the 'allometric scaling against body size', for example comparing the thickness of elephants' legs for a mammal of the same weight as an elephant's weight.

He finds that Robin Dunbar's calculation of the ratio for the volume of primate neocortex to that of the rest of the brain – the 'neocortical ratio' (which makes the assumption that cognitive function is both localised and cortical in most mammals) – is validated by its correlations and the indices of complexity in behaviour:

> Absolute brain size, or relative neocortical size, give more proper estimates of potential intelligence. Such estimates do correlate with social group size, and with tactical deception frequency, in haplorhine primates [southeast Asian tarsiers, considered closely related to the Old World and New World monkeys, primates and hominids] … The key to this increased intelligence is likely to be increased learning speed, allowing a richer social data base and acquisition of subtle tactics in only a few trials. Great apes' more insightful representational intelligence may not be based on brain expansion but on brain re-organisation.[21]

Also with regard to brain organisation rather than size, Cartmill and Smith point out that the larger development in the occipital or back portion of the Neanderthal brain could mean they may have possessed 'enhanced visual and spatial abilities'.[22]

2.3 Neanderthal toolmaking

Mark Lake notes with regard to creativity in stone tool manufacture that animals other than hominids *use* stone tools, but 'none spontaneously *make* stone tools'. Wild chimps use unmodified stones both as hammers and anvils; but only in captivity, when encouraged, do they make stone tools. But they routinely make other tools: for example Lake notes 'the deliberate and careful manufacture of termite fishing wands [from wooden branches]'. He considers that with regard to creativity, one individual chimp may have shown it by embracing stone as a workable raw material. For the most, there's the diminished creativity of those

---

21 Byrne, 'Relating Brain Sizes to Intelligence in Primates', p. 52, p. 49.

22 Cartmill and Smith, *The Human Lineage*, p. 361.

simply following that lead.[23] But are hominids, including Neanderthals, creative in the sense we associate with human beings? Well, according to Kirkpatrick Sale, Neanderthals didn't develop any specialised tools at all.[24]

Still, because modern humans and Neanderthals were living at the same time and in approximately the same places for several thousand years in France and Northern Spain, Mellars speaks of the possibility that 'the appearance of a range of distinctively "modern" behavioural features among the late Neanderthal populations of western Europe ... was the product of some form of contact and interaction between the two populations ... ' He notes 'a range of around ten or a dozen behavioural innovations, including increased blade technology ... several forms of bone or ivory points, regularly notched bones, several forms of perforated or grooved pendants ... bone tubes, ivory rings, and liberal use of powdered red ochre scattered across living areas.'[25]

At the same time, regarding the copying or replication of tools by Neanderthals from humans living at the same time, he writes: 'In my earlier comments I noted that the replication of aeroplane forms in the New Guinea cargo cults [after World War II] hardly implied an understanding of aeronautics or international travel ... [or that] if a child puts on a string of pearls she is possibly doing this to imitate her mother, not to symbolise her wealth, emphasise her social status, or attract the opposite sex.'[26]

So, despite the variety of Neanderthal tools, and their capacity to copy human toolmaking and usage, Steven Kuhn and Marcy Stiner write that:

> The Mousterian of Eurasia, the cultural period associated with the Neanderthals, is conspicuously bereft of evidence for artistic or aesthetic expression. Moreover, compared to later time periods, both artefacts and technology are remarkably uniform across space and stable over time [that is, from c. 250,000–33,000 – more than 200,000 years] during the Mousterian.[27]

---

23 Mark Lake, '"*Homo*": The Creative Genius', in Steven Mithen, ed., *Creativity in Human Evolution and Prehistory*, London: Routledge, 1998, pp. 125–42, at p. 136.

24 Kirkpatrick Sale, *After Eden: The Evolution of Human Domination*, Durham, NC: Duke University Press, 2006, p. 23, p. 39.

25 Mellars, 'The Archaeological Records of the Neandertal-Modern Human Transition in France', p. 44.

26 Paul Mellars, 'The Neanderthal Problem Continued', *Current Anthropology*, 40.3 (June 1999), pp. 341–64, at p. 350.

27 Steven L. Kuhn and Marcy C. Stiner, 'Middle Palaeolithic "Creativity": Reflections on an oxymoron?' in Mithen, *Creativity in Human Evolution and Prehistory*, pp. 143–64, at p. 143.

Mellars disagrees with an earlier article of Francesco d'Errico, which maintained there wasn't co-existence of late Neanderthals and early anatomically modern populations in Western Europe, and 'acculturation' between the two groups. [28] Mellars regards his argument proved by the discovery of a 'classic' Neanderthal skull in apparently direct association with Châtelperronian artifacts at Saint-Césaire in 1979. He also notes the 'Proto-Aurignacian' or typically Aurignacian [modern human] industry produced at several sites in Northern Spain, from about 40,000 years ago – when Neanderthals were also around, even though the earliest Aurignacian or human presence in the 'classic' region of South West France is no earlier than 36,000 years ago–5,000 years later. [29]

On Neanderthals' simpler toolmaking capacities, Roebroeks and Verpoorte write: 'Neanderthals carved their predatory niche with a small range of simple hunting weapons, including wooden thrusting and/or throwing spears ... ' While they may have 'tipped their spears with stone points', they find the archaeological record suggesting 'cutting tools rather than projectile weapons'. [30]

2.4 Neanderthal burials yes, grave goods no?

Robert Gargett investigated the sites most frequently claimed to contain Neanderthal 'burials'. For example, in Teshik-Tash, Uzbekistan, he finds no evidence of grave-cult, and thinks that the so-called 'ritual' assemblage of goat horns could be result of predator activity. 'Goat remains make up roughly 85 per cent of the faunal [animal remains] assemblage at Teshik-Tash, and, since horn is the most likely skeletal part to survive, the probability of six horns' being preserved in this area of the site by chance is high.'

At Shanidar, Iraq, he notes it was seven years after its investigation that the conclusion was drawn that the Neanderthal remains in Shanidar 4 were buried with flowers. Earlier, the investigator had considered that those whose remains were found in the various Shanidar sites, 4, 6, 8, and 93, had been killed by rockfalls. Gargett holds that: 'No clear evidence for purposeful burial exists in the Shanidar deposits. There are no grave pits, no non-naturally occurring protective strata.' He considers that because the investigators were inclined to believe that purposeful

---

28 Francesco d'Errico et al., *Current Anthropology*, 39 (June 1998, Supplement), S1–S44.

29 Paul Mellars, 'The Neanderthal Problem Continued', p. 342, p. 347, p. 348.

30 Wil Roebroeks and Alexander Verpoorte, 'A "language-free" explanation for differences between the European Middle and Upper Paleolithic Record', in Rudolf Botha and Chris Knight, eds., *The Cradle of Language*, Oxford: Oxford University Press, 2009, pp. 150–66, at pp. 154–5.

burial was a possibility, they thought the presence of an unusually high number of pollen grains indicated that flowers were buried with the dead. He suggests they were blown in by the wind. And there seems doubt as to at which level the pollen were found. He concludes that 'the removal of mortuary ritual from the behavioural repertoire of Neanderthals may make the observed discontinuity in material culture at the Middle/Upper Palaeolithic [Neanderthal/human] boundary a little easier to understand'.[31]

Paul Mellars, while broadly accepting Gargett's demolition of many Neanderthal 'burials', still agrees with Erik Trinkaus that so many Neanderthal remains have been found that 'the case for deliberate interment of most of these skeletons [where there are large numbers, seven at La Ferrassie, nine at Shanidar, many including the very delicate bones of very young children] appears virtually beyond dispute'. But he holds that arguments for deliberate grave offerings are much weaker. Kirkpatrick Sale would agree. He distinguishes Neanderthal 'interments' – practical disposal to prevent scavengers – from later ritualistic 'burials' by and of humans.[32]

There are 'only two convincing examples of intentional and potentially symbolic grave offerings recorded from well documented Middle Paleolithic contexts – the large fallow-deer antlers and the complete boar's jaw, associated respectively with the Middle Paleolithic burials in the Qafzeh and Skhul in Israel'. Mellars notes that these are associated with what he calls anatomically modern skeletons. He asks if the mere act of burial is symbolic, and says that deliberate burial implies at the least, 'some kind of strong social or emotional bonds within Neanderthal societies'. But 'In the absence of either clear ritual or unambiguous grave offerings associated with the documented range of Neanderthal burials in Europe, it must be concluded that the case for a symbolic component in burial practices remains at best unproven.'[33] This lack of grave goods in what may be conceded as Neanderthal burials seems closely connected to the following considerations regarding the lack of Neanderthal symbolisation and language.

2.5 Lack of Neanderthal symbolisation
Our basis for comparison is with the symbol-making capacities of early humans, for example the magnificent and detailed Hohe Fels and Vogelherd sculptures of a flying bird, a mammoth, of a woman with

31 Robert H. Gargett, 'Grave Shortcomings: The Evidence for Neanderthal Burial', *Current Anthropology*, 30.2 (1989), pp. 157–90, at pp. 168–9 and pp. 174–7.

32 Kirkpatrick Sale, *After Eden*, p. 51.

33 Paul Mellars, *The Neanderthal Legacy*, pp. 379–81.

exaggerated features linked to her generative power, a half-man, half-lion statuette, and so on, frequently accompanied by non-representational symbols such as crosses, all from around 35,000 years ago.[34] So Tattersall speaks of one of these Vogelherd sculptures as conveying the 'abstract essence of horse', in sharp contrast with the 'essentially symbol-free traces left by Neanderthals'.[35] Despite arguments by some paleontologists supporting Neanderthal symbolic activity, for Mellars, 'these specimens are very rare. The fact that alleged Mousterian [Neanderthal] symbolic objects tend to be unique casts further doubt on their actual symbolic content, for they provide no evidence for a shared system of meaning.' Still, 'Compared with the first million years or so of the Lower Palaeolithic, the Mousterian can seem like a veritable Renaissance.' And he adds that 'although the persistence of Middle Palaeolithic artefact forms is striking, it is not without precedent: relative technological stasis has been the rule in human [this should be hominid, as we'll be arguing in later chapters] evolution for 2 million years or more.'[36]

While, as we'll see later, the date of the earliest human symbolic activity has dramatically moved back to over 150,000 years ago, paleontologist Steven Mithen notes that the art of Chauvet (a French cave discovered in 1994, with a huge range of paintings dated back to 34,000BP) or of Cosquer (an underwater cave near Marseille, whose 27,000–19,000 year old art was discovered in 1991) 'broadly coincides with a host of other new types of behaviour': body adornment, new technology, and the colonisation of arid areas by the first humans. For Mithen, this only strengthens 'our belief that they [cave paintings] do signify a major transition in the nature of human thought and behaviour at this very late stage of human evolution'.[37] Jean Clottes, probably the most important contemporary expert on French cave art,

---

34 See Nicolas J. Conard, 'Palaeolithic ivory sculptures from southwestern Germany and the origins of figurative art', *Nature*, 426, 2003, pp. 830-832; 'A female figurine from the basal Aurignacian deposits of Hohle Fels Cave in southwestern Germany', *Nature*, 459, 2009, p. 248; also, Bruce Bower, 'Stone Age figurine has contentious origins: ivory female carving may be at least 35,000 years old, alter views of how Stone Age art developed', *Science News*, Vol. 175.13 (20 Jun 2009).

35 Ian Tattersall, *The World from Beginnings to 4000BCE*, New York: Oxford University Press, 2008, p. 99.

36 Ibid., p. 146, p. 147, p. 152.

37 Steven Mithen, 'A Creative Explosion? Theory of mind, language and the disembodied mind of the Upper Palaeolithic', in *Creativity in Human Evolution and Prehistory*, ed. Steven Mithen, London: Routledge, 1998, pp. 165–191, at p. 165, p. 167, p. 168.

notes that even when conditions for cave painting are perfect in a cave that Neanderthals clearly used, the lack of wall painting is conclusive proof that they didn't engage in such activity.[38] In his *Cave Art*, while conceding that 'Neanderthals must have learned a lot' from their thousands of years co-existence with *Homo sapiens*, Clottes says that 'we have no evidence' either of Neanderthal cave-painting or portable art.[39]

There have been claims by archaeologists like Robert Bednarik and Alexander Marshack for Neanderthal symbolisation, with a 230,000-year-old 'figurine' or carved female figure from the Israeli site of Berekhat Ram as a prominent example.[40] Still, Steven Kuhn and Marcy Stiner point out that 'The Mousterian of Eurasia, the cultural period associated with the Neanderthals, is conspicuously bereft of evidence for artistic or aesthetic expression. Moreover, compared to later time periods, both artefacts and technology are remarkably uniform across space and stable over time during the Mousterian.' For them, specimens such as Berekhat Ram 'are very rare. The fact that alleged Mousterian symbolic objects tend to be unique casts further doubt on their actual symbolic content, for they provide no evidence for a shared system of meaning.'[41] Similarly critical are William Noble and Iain Davidson: 'there is no evidence that the Berekhat Ram object was formed by human agency rather than by natural forces ... hence we cannot say that it was a thing *made* to resemble anything'.[42] As with views regarding Neanderthal grave goods and language, tantalisingly close to the human horizon, there will always be a possible case made for Neanderthal symbolisation. But, as Randall White asks, 'If the predecessors of the Aurignacian [that is, the species who existed before *Homo sapiens*] were capable of graphic representation of a symbolic nature in durable materials, why did such behaviour occur at such a low frequency?[43]

---

38 Quoted in Mithen, *The Singing Neanderthals*, pp. 242–3.

39 Jean Clottes, *Cave Art*, London: Phaidon Press, 2010, p. 12.

40 Alexander Marshack, 'The Berekhat Ram figurine: A late Acheulian carving from the Middle East', *Antiquity*, 71 (1997), pp. 327–37.

41 Steven L. Kuhn and Marcy C. Stiner, 'Middle Palaeolithic "Creativity": Reflections on an oxymoron?' in *Creativity in Human Evolution and Prehistory*, ed. Steven Mithen, London: Routledge, 1998, pp. 143–164, at p. 143 and p. 147.

42 William Noble and Iain Davidson, *Human Evolution, Language and Mind: A Psychological and Archaeological Inquiry*, Cambridge, Cambridge University Press, 1996, p. 75.

43 Randall White, 'Reply to Robert G. Bednarik's "Concept-Mediated Marking in the Lower Paleolithic"',*Current Anthropology*, 36.4 (Aug – Oct 1995), pp. 605–34, at p. 625.

2.6 Neanderthal language?

Mithen considers that brain size as large as modern humans could have arisen between 600,000 and 500,000 years ago, with late erectines, and later with Neanderthals, yet archaeological records show 'no trace of language-mediated behaviour until very late in human evolution'. Mithen feels that it would be unlikely that Neanderthals would have had a capacity for using the audible symbols of language while not showing evidence of using another kind of symbol, that is visual symbols: 'it may seem unlikely, to say the least, that symbolic capacities might exist in one medium but not the other'.[44] Paul Mellars notes that at the archaeological level there's 'the virtual lack of convincing evidence for symbolic behaviour or expression in Neanderthal contexts'. Whatever is made of this, no one would question 'that elaborate symbolic thought and expression is one of the defining hallmarks of all fully developed languages'.[45] So, the non-existence of symbolism in Neanderthal contexts is at least consistent with the lack of a highly developed Neanderthal language, even if not concrete proof of this.

At the physiological level, Philip Lieberman pointed out that Neanderthals don't have a human-type vocal tract:

> The problem arises because the length of the Neanderthal mouth is outside the range of modern human beings ... Neanderthal speech anatomy was more advanced than that of *Homo erectus* or human newborns but still incapable of producing the full range of human speech sounds with the stability and formant frequency structure of sounds like the supervowel 'i'.

He notes that Neanderthal retention of the primitive face extended prominently about the mouth, also typical of earlier hominids, where the lower face is positioned in front of the brain, 'clearly indicates less efficient speech communication. They represent an intermediate stage in the evolution of human speech. Although their brain was as large as our own, the neural substrate that regulates speech production may also have been less developed.' So he concludes that 'Neanderthals were inherently unable to produce human speech ... [46]

---

44 Mithen, 'A Creative Explosion', pp. 165–6.

45 Mellars, 'The Neanderthal Problem Continued', p. 389.

46 Philip Lieberman, *Eve Spoke: Human Language and Human Evolution*, New York: W. W.

Michael Corballis is in agreement with Philip Lieberman, drawing on D. E. Lieberman's comparison of Neanderthal and human facial structure, who argues that the shortening of the human sphenoid bone (the central bone at the base of the skull) from which the face grows forward, results in a flattened face. This could be an adaptation for speech, 'contributing to the unique proportions of the human vocal tract, in which the horizontal and vertical proportions are roughly equal in length, improving the ability to produce distinct speech sounds such as the "i" vowel' – this structure is not found in Neanderthals. Further, Corballis points out that the distinct roundness of the vault in the human skull favours an increase in the relative size of the brain's temporal and/or the frontal lobes, which could result in 'more refined control of articulation and also, perhaps, more accurate perceptual discrimination of articulated sounds'.[47]

Regarding such perceptual discrimination of speech, Cartmill and Smith in *The Human Lineage* point out that human ear structure is larger than Neanderthal. Still, they also note that the discovery that Neanderthals have the FOXp gene (which we'll discuss in the next chapter) indicates that they may also have had a shared 'capacity' for language with humans.[48] In fact, their chapter seven is entitled 'Talking Apes: The Neanderthals'!

Other paleontologists have suggested that the mental templates underlying Neanderthal tools are less defined than those of later, human tools, and particularly Lewis Binford has suggested that long-range planning for hunting activities and its associated socio-economic organisation would demand the existence of a relatively structured language. Similarly, the increased ability to share information about the distribution of economic resources, and the coordination of activities necessary to survive in the more extremely cold environments of central and eastern Europe first occupied during the specifically human period, would also require language.[49]

Norton: 1998, p. 93, p. 95, p. 97. But W. Tecumseh Fitch rules out the use of various factors in Philip Lieberman's discussion, for example the angle of the bone at the skull's base, along with the hyoid bone, since Fitch holds they can't be used for reconstructing the phonetic abilities of fossil hominids. 'No confident assertions can be made about hominid speech anatomy and/or motor control.' See his 'Fossil cues to the evolution of speech', in Botha and Knight, *The Cradle of Language*, pp. 112–34, pp. 122–5, p. 133.

47 Michael C. Corballis, 'Did language evolve before speech?' in Richard K. Larson, Viviane Déprez, and Hiroko Yamakido, eds., *The Evolution of Human Language: Biolinguistic Perspectives*, Cambridge: Cambridge University Press, 2010, pp. 115–23, at p. 118.

48 Cartmill and Smith, *The Human Lineage*, p. 160, p. 188.

49 Lewis R. Binford, 'Isolating the transition to cultural adaptations: an organisational approach', in Erik Trinkaus, ed., *The Emergence of Modern Humans: Biocultural Adaptation in the Later Pleistocene*, Cambridge: Cambridge University Press, 1989, pp. 18–34.

Additionally, linguists of sometimes opposing views, like Noam Chomsky, Derek Bickerton and Steven Pinker, hold that the emergence of essentially modern language must have been a sudden or catastrophic rather than a gradual process of mental and linguistic evolution. If so, we should expect to find 'a fairly dramatic reflection of this transition in the available behavioural records of human development' across the whole spectrum from technology through subsistence and social patterns to the more overtly symbolic patterns of the human group. Paul Mellars concludes his article on 'The Neanderthal Problem': 'The question is where, in the available archaeological records of Europe, might we identify such a watershed, if not over the period of the Middle-to-Upper Palaeolithic transition?'[50]

3. Where's the hominid sequence going – what 'breathes fire into the equations'?

What was the hominid sequence for? Hans Urs von Balthasar comments on the Book of Daniel's 'Praise the Lord, you sea monsters and all deeps, fire and hail, snow and clouds', and remarks: 'When Paul refers to an indefinite and tense straining of all of nature (*apokaradokia* [Rom 8:19; AV, "earnest expectation"]), it means in the first place that nature unconsciously strives towards mankind.'[51] Certainly, for this insight von Balthasar is going beyond the perspective of the natural science and beyond philosophy to revelation. But we can ask Stephen Hawking's wonderful question of natural scientists, including paleoanthropologists:

What is it that breathes fire into the equations and makes a universe for them to describe? The usual approach of science of constructing a mathematical model cannot answer the questions of why there should be a universe for the model to describe. Why does the universe go to all the bother of existing?[52]

---

50 Mellars, 'The Neanderthal Problem Continued', p. 391.

51 Hans Urs von Balthasar, *You Have Words of Eternal Life: Scripture Meditations*, San Francisco: Ignatius Press, 1991, p. 221.

52 Stephen Hawking, *A Brief History of Time*, London: Bantam Press, 1998, p. 190. Regarding this quotation, Joseph McCarroll notes that 'the word Hawking avoids is "being". What is added to the mathematics that makes sense of the data about the development of the physical universe as we find it is the actual existence of that universe with just these characteristics. If X is the unknown that gives all things their existence or being, then that X is the Giver-of-being-and-existence-to-all-things, which is/has to be outside the universe of things that elicit that question. So it doesn't and can't have anything in it that elicits that question (which most folks call God).'

We've already mentioned how most books about the hominid sequence use the word 'human' in their titles, which I think is a fair indication that what in fact breathes fire into all their incredibly painstaking analysis of hominid fossils is their presupposition that one way or another, all of them lead towards an understanding of human emergence. Without necessarily spelling it out, what they see in that valley of dry bones is a movement that 'unconsciously strives towards mankind'. And even though Darwin had jotted down as a stern reminder to himself the note 'never use the word higher or lower', he still wrote his own book on human origins, *The Descent of Man*, whose very focus seemed to imply evolution had some kind of direction towards the human.[53] The point is that all inquirers into the hominid sequence are themselves human and they just can't keep their humanity in brackets, that humanity G. K. Chesterton memorably addressed in the opening words of *The Napoleon of Notting Hill* as 'The human race, to which so many of my readers belong … '

Of course Darwin has to be given the credit for anticipating what is probably the best documented case of an evolutionary sequence there is, since the hominids belong to a large family which includes lemurs, lorises and tarsiers, the smaller African, Asian and the separate group of Central and South American monkeys, the lesser apes (gibbons) and the primates – chimpanzees and bonobos, gorillas and orang-utans. As we've said, it's generally considered that the hominids broke away from the primate line about seven million years ago, though the recent hominid discovery in Chad, if it really is hominid, might push that date further back.

To finish our brief consideration of the hominid sequence, drawing on topics discussed in the previous two chapters, we'll see how punctuated equilibrium and evo-devo, along with Denton's remarks on psychological factors in evolution, may help towards understanding the direction the sequence seems to be taking. We'll also use Lonergan's notion of emergent probability to help give a heuristic context to these various ways for understanding the hominid sequence. Then we can conclude with one of our basic questions – do we need to move to a level of scientific inquiry at a generically different level from zoology to grasp the hominids, particularly the latest pre-human ones?

---

53 Stanley Jaki gives the reference in his *The Origin of Science and the Science of its Origin*, Edinburgh: Scottish Academic Press, 1978, p. 144 n. 66.

3.1 How can the hominid sequence be explained?

Given that a Darwinian interpretation of the hominid sequence will surely tell part of the story, so that the shift from an earlier to a later hominid form can be partly explained by adaptation to changing environmental challenges, let's presume we can also suggest the evo-devo insight of genetic switches, those regulatory genes which can cause an organism to switch direction.

But genetic switches alone won't explain the hominid sequence. What marks off the lemurs, lorises and tarsiers, the Old and New world monkeys, along with the gibbons and primates, from other mammals, is their greater reliance on sight (including heightened three-dimensional visual capacities) over smell. Accompanying their greater visual capacity, there's an improvement in grasping and manipulative abilities, through their powerful hands and feet, with nails rather than the more specialised claws of the physically stronger large carnivorous animals, not to mention the opposable thumbs in old-world monkeys, gibbons and primates. Paleoanthropologist Wilfrid Le Gros Clark notes that 'the evolutionary progress of Primates, as Simpson (1950) has well said, has been in the direction of greater adaptability rather than of greater adaptation'.[54]

So that monkeys, gibbons and primates have the advantage of greater sensori-motor and perceptual capacities (also indicated by their greater average brain size, with proportionately larger areas dealing with sight over smell, and increasing overlapping/interconnection between different parts of the brain). This would mean that apart from the hominids they are perceptually the most advanced animals, with a flexibility far beyond the kind of 'Innate Releasing Mechanisms' (IRMs) studied by zoologists like Niko Tinbergen and Konrad Lorenz. IRMs are highly specific triggering mechanisms, where, for example, a hen feeds its young if their plumage has head markings eliciting 'species-specific instinctive patterns of parental care'. Otherwise, the hen may kill the chicks.[55]

The hominids, at least from *Homo erectus* on, have an even greater proportionate brain size and can be presumed to have been perceptually more advanced than earlier hominids. We have to be careful of exaggeration here, because West African chimpanzees have been observed using stones to break up nuts, with the mother chimps handing on this skill by teaching

54 Wilfrid Le Gros Clark, *The Fossil Evidence for Human Evolution*, Chicago: Chicago University Press, 1978, p. 13.

55 Konrad Lorenz (tr. Robert D. Martin), *Studies in Animal and Human Behaviour*, Vol. 1, London: Methuen, 1970, p. 169; Nikolaas Tinbergen, *The Study of Instinct*, Oxford: Clarendon Press, 1951.

their young to imitate them. And this level of tool use has been compared to at least some australopithecine tool-using behaviour. At the same time, the recent discovery of early australopithecine tool-usage with its evidence that the stones were used to extract marrow from animal bones, seems to indicate some of the earlier hominids already going beyond primate tool use.

Frédéric Joulian compares chimpanzee tools to those of both gracile and robust australopithecines, and *Homo habilis*, particularly the nut-cracking activities of Ivory Coast chimps. What he observed were identical hammers and anvils to those found in early hominid sites at Olduvai Gorge or Melka Konturé, but now being used by modern Ivory Coast chimps. He notes that 'gestures involved in cracking nuts are related in many ways (notably to the motor control of movement) to the percussion gesture involved in knapping stone'. The chimps are hitting nuts and the pre-erectine hominids we've just mentioned are removing matter, that is, reducing stone. Joulian doesn't feel that these are essentially different: 'It seems to me that there are no major differences in qualitative terms between what the chimpanzee do when they crack nuts and what pre-Acheulean [that is, australopithecines and *Homo habilis*] hominids did when they knapped a chopper or produced a flake.' Joulian has pointed out that the chimps prefer stone to wooden tools, and harder stones to less hard ones – granite or gneiss rather than quartzite, quartzite rather than laterite. So, on a behavioural level, it's possible that there's no essential difference between australopithecine and *Homo habilis* species and chimpanzees, which isn't too surprising, given their almost identical brain-ratio sizes of three times the normal for mammals.[56]

Then of course there's the wonderful haul of tools for the later hominids including the Neanderthals, which, while often showing stasis over long periods, still indicates a capacity to manipulate their environment by showing greater adaptability in toolmaking than their primate cousins. Later again, as we've noted, there's the interesting phenomenon of Neanderthal copying or (somewhat less likely) initiating toolmaking of a more advanced standard, where what they may have been copying were tools used by their human neighbours.

This is where the kind of point Michael Denton was suggesting for some animals – that the psychological level of their existence may have had an effect on their morphology – may also be considered. Just as the individual

---

56 Frédéric Joulian, 'Comparing Chimpanzee and Early Hominid Techniques: Some Contributions to Cultural and Cognitive Questions', in Mellars and Gibson, eds., *Modelling the Early Human Mind*, pp. 173–89, at p. 179, pp. 182–4, p. 187.

human brain can be stimulated to grow by our learning activities, could it be possible that the struggle for survival by meat-eating australopithecines may have stimulated the underlying brain development needed to support more flexible hands – and by extension – toolmaking and use?

What of hominid toolmaking? Mark Lake says with regard to the archaeological evidence for the behaviour of early *Homo*, that it 'essentially comprises scatters of flaked tools and fossilised animal bones' in locations along the African Rift Valley. It used to be thought their activities were as complex as those of modern hunter-gatherers, but now, they're seen neither as merely marginal scavengers nor exclusively as hunters. Their strategy is that of opportunistic meat acquisition, 'which does not necessary imply creative thought, merely flexibility'.[57] So, while we'll suggest that hominids may use lower-level cognitive strategies within slightly higher sensori-motor and perceptual contexts, they never proceed to the level of abstraction we associate with human creativity.

In his introduction to *Creativity in Human Evolution and Prehistory*, Mithen refers to Thomas Wynn as 'attempting to infer the levels of intelligence of human ancestors from the form of early prehistoric stone tools by adopting a recapitulationist position and using the developmental stages proposed by Piaget as models for stages of cognitive evolution',[58] This would imply that sensori-motor and perceptual capacities developed by earlier hominid species were the emerging cognitive abilities that gave rise to the corresponding further cognitive developments of the somewhat more advanced later hominids.

Still, in comparison to later human tools – and in spite of Neanderthal and late erectine developed toolmaking skills – Mithen notes 'the range of tool types appears remarkably narrow, and to have made a limited contribution to coping with the glaciated landscapes ... Neanderthals lacked the highly-specialised tools, dedicated to specific tasks, which have characterised modern humans when exploiting open environments'. He also compares the Upper Paleolithic (that is, from after 45,000 years ago) 'use of facilities such as fish-traps, drive lines and portable fences. These influence the behaviour of game, effectively structuring their mobility patterns to allow effective slaughter ... The best preserved archaeological examples are fish traps from the Mesolithic [after 10,000 years ago].'

---

57 Mark Lake, '"*Homo*": The Creative Genius', in Steven Mithen, ed., *Creativity in Human Evolution and Prehistory*, London: Routledge,1998, pp. 125–42, at pp. 130–3.

58 Mithen, 'Introduction', *Creativity in Human Evolution and Prehistory*, p. 10.

There's sparse direct archaeological, but some circumstantial evidence from the Upper Paleolithic (*Homo sapiens* period) for mass kills. Also there's the development, with great variation, of 'projectile point technology' during the Upper Paleolithic, whereas Middle Paleolithic points don't vary. This later development derives from the capacity 'to integrate understanding of animal behaviour and the possibilities of technology in a fashion that appears to have been absent from Neanderthal minds'.

Regarding late hominid cognition, Mithen points out that while Wynn had suggested 'a Piagetian framework' to understand the evolution of intelligence since 'handaxes indicate that an operational level [that is, above the sensori-motor level] of intelligence has been attained, i.e. one that is essentially the same as modern humans':

> In his later work, Wynn has been more cautious, adapting a domain-specific approach, and suggesting that handaxes imply a high degree of spatial thought the relationship of which to other aspects of the [Neanderthal] mind remain unclear ... Neanderthals were able to develop very high levels of technical intelligence. It appears just as complex to manufacture a handaxe or a Levallois core, as to make the blade cores that dominate the stone tool technology of modern humans during the Upper Paleolithic. In this regard, as with social intelligence, Neanderthals appear to have possessed equivalent levels of technical intelligence to modern humans.[59]

While we're certainly not suggesting that Neanderthals actually used language, what Cartmill and Smith referred to – that the FOXP2 gene regarded as a possible neural basis for human language can be found in Neanderthal DNA – certainly could indicate at least the rudiments of the neural basis for language.[60] And while not for language, the larger back portion of the brain characteristic of Neanderthals can be presumed to have permitted visual and perceptual capacities greater than those of earlier erectine brains.

---

59 Steven Mithen, 'Domain-Specific Intelligence and the Neanderthal Mind', in *Modelling the Early Human Mind*, eds. Paul Mellars and Kathleen Gibson, pp. 217–29, at p. 221, p. 222, p. 225.

60 Recent research indicates this important regulatory gene occurs not only in chimpanzees, but according to one report, in all animals, so this finding is perhaps less indicative of proto-linguistic capacities than Cartmill and Smith thought. See Kerri Smith, 'Evolution of a single gene linked to language: Mutations in the FOXP2 gene could help explain why humans can speak but chimps can't', *Nature News*, 11 November 2009; Nicholas Wade, 'Speech Gene Shows Its Bossy Nature', *New York Times*, 11 November 2009.

We've already mentioned Lonergan's treatment of development in terms of 'a flexible linked sequence of dynamic and increasing differentiated higher integrations that meet the tension of successively transformed underlying manifolds through successive applications of the principles of correspondence and emergence'. If we focus on the increasing cognitive and related toolmaking skills from australopithecines to Neanderthals and late erectines, the 'emergence' after millennia of stasis would presumably be the higher neural organisation of the hominids which we can presume included greater imaginative, mnemonic and communicative capacities. And the principle of 'correspondence' would be the new higher perceptual and motor skill 'exapting' or co-opting the lower level of cognitive-motor skill within the somewhat more enriched world of the next level of hominid existence.

As Lonergan noted, not all changes would be developments from lower to higher cognitive levels. Various hominid species, including the robust australopithecines and the Neanderthals are regarded by paleontologists as evolutionary dead ends, since the greater reliance of the robust australopithecines on powerful chewing mechanisms or of the Neanderthals on physical strength wasn't accompanied by greater cognitive capacities.[61]

Still, at the material level, neurally and physiologically there isn't an enormous difference between the latest hominids and human beings. In relation to what looks like a fairly obvious sequence from the earliest hominid to ourselves, the question is: what were all the previous hominid developments for? Tattersall and Schwartz speak of 'experimentation':

> ... our pattern has essentially been one of business as usual for the natural world: a story of repeated evolutionary experimentation, diversification, and, ultimately, extinction. And it was clearly in the context of such experimentation rather than out of constant fine tuning by natural selection over the eons, that our own amazing species appeared on Earth.[62]

We've already mentioned Lonergan's consideration of a situation where earlier sets of conditions could facilitate species with a high probability of emergence but a low probability of survival, forming a 'floating population, on which later schemes could successively depend'. Their low probability

---

61 Mithen, *The Singing Neanderthals*, p. 248.

62 Ian Tattersall and Geoffrey H. Schwartz, *Extinct Humans*, New York: Westview Press, 2000, p. 9.

of survival 'would readily surrender materials to give later schemes the opportunity to emerge' (*Insight*, 122–4). Perhaps this might explain the bewildering multiplicity of late hominid forms preceding the emergence of the human.

Could it be said then that all the lower levels of existence, from physical to zoological, but even more dramatically the sequence of hominids, materially enabled our coming into existence? Certainly it's that perspective more than anything else that 'breathes fire into the equations' in the sense that understanding the hominids is considered by most paleontologists as essential for understanding *Homo sapiens*. Yet, we still have to ask if the cognitive, toolmaking and hunting capacities of the later hominids require a higher viewpoint than zoology.

3.2 Are hominid studies a branch of zoology or anthropology?

Our final question here is whether the hominid sequence requires us to move to another scientific level, as zoology does from biology, or biology from chemistry. Can the pre-human hominids be understood within branches of zoology like comparative primatology, or another zoological subset like hominid science? Before trying to answer that question it does no harm to remember the struggle recent paleontologists have had to make to overcome an excessive gradualism in hominid studies.

Ian Tattersall and Geoffrey Schwartz give an excellent account of the original Neanderthal discovery, and how Thomas Huxley, while generally embracing saltationism (an earlier version of punctuated equilibrium), plumped for Neanderthals as part of the continuum of human evolution (although his seeing them as parallel to Australian aboriginals was hardly based on an appreciation of what is arguably the most profound mythologically articulated culture known). They note how in an 1864 paper to the British Association for the Advancement of Science, William King of the Queen's University Galway had the temerity to insist that Neanderthals were almost another genus. They go on to describe how the neo-Darwinian synthesis of Dobzhanzsky and Mayr (classic Darwinian evolutionists from the late thirties on), in slightly different ways, fitted humans into the standard Darwinian unilinear and gradually continuous paradigm of evolution, and ask:

> ... how could anyone, much less a bunch of paleoanthropologists who were not equipped with the supposedly more biologically informed backgrounds of Mayr and Dobzhansky, disagree with them? No one

could. At least, no one would who didn't want to be accused of being anti-evolutionary – or much worse, anti-Darwinian.

This bias towards developmental continuity led to less focus on diversity, as would have been normal with other species. In fact, the hominid record, like others, has many species coming into and going out of existence. The authors say that had Johann Friedrich Blumenbach's (1752–1840) approach been followed, it would have been a lot better for paleoanthropology – of which they consider Blumenbach the 'father'. They write that the 'intellectual stranglehold on our evolutionary notions, which 'portrays human history as a smoothly transforming continuum of change', is beginning to loosen. The discovery of 'such an unexpected array of early human species, with combinations of brain, jaw, tooth and limb that clearly cannot be accommodated by the traditional notion of a single evolving lineage [show] that it is impossible ... to avoid reality.' He provided a much better outline of distinguishing marks of the human than Linnaeus: bipedal posture and locomotion; a chin; feet unlike the hands; small upper and lower canines without gaps between them and neighbouring teeth; shapes and chewing surfaces of the cheek teeth; attributes of the brain, such as reason and the arbitrariness of language and invention. So they commend Blumenbach for 'presenting the first anatomically based definition of the genus *Homo*' while saying we have to go beyond both his, but also Mayr's and Dobzhansky's, 'constraints'.

They point out that Mayr and Dobzhansky provided paleontology with the Modern Synthesis as a framework, even though the fossil record wasn't replete with intermediate forms. So, 'we have to abandon the linear dictates of the Evolutionary Synthesis in favor of a recognition that every process is much more complex and many-layered than these dictates suppose'.

What the authors do is provide us with material for a possible understanding of the relation between pre-human hominids and humans in terms of emergent probability, with the lower levels providing the matter for the formally higher level: 'Any new structure must arise before it can assume a function.' And we note that pre-adaptation or exaptation – Stephen J. Gould's and Elisabeth S. Vrba's word for a lower function being lifted up into a higher context – is an instance of what philosophically used to be called matter suitable (or *materia apta*) for a higher form, as can be seen with the development of the vocal tract. They speak of the 'emergent quality', which fits in with their argument against the notion of natural selection as 'driving' evolution. And they point out that 'the prosaic phenomenon of exaptation was what set the stage for the emergence of the unprecedented human capacity'.[63]

So, while these and other paleontologists argue against an over-simplified evolutionary narrative for the hominids, as we'll see in the next chapter, they unhesitatingly regard our species as requiring quite different treatment to all the other hominids. We can ask if, for example, Neanderthal 'burials' and the occasional claims for Neanderthal 'symbols' require an explanation in terms of an order above zoological or animal. Since – unlike the 'Venus' female figurines focusing on fertility that can be found all across Upper Paleolithic Europe from the Pyrenees to Siberia, not to mention disputed 'Venus figurines' like Berekhat Ram in Israel or Tan-Tan in Morocco – there's no evidence these 'burials' or 'symbols' occur according to any regular pattern, nor does their interpretation seem to require an explanation in terms of intelligence. If the burials were ritual interments like, for example Sungir or Newgrange, or even those first known human burials at Lake Mungo, then there would be some recognisable indication of Neanderthal intent – for example an expression of hope to go beyond death, in van Gennep's phrase, to undertake a 'rite of passage'.

As we've said, hominids seem to have far more advanced toolmaking skills than any primate, or indeed any other animal. Still, we don't find among Neanderthal or other late hominids indications of self-awareness, or any of the other qualities we regard as central to adult human existence. Their greatly increased sensori-perceptual-mnemonic-motor capacities are shared with most other higher mammals, rather than manifesting something specifically new that would require us to move beyond the zoological level to anthropology, the study of the specifically human. No more than a chimpanzee or bonobo, could we have ever addressed a Neanderthal or other late hominid as a 'thou'.

But are we 'hanging from our [hominid] ancestors' tails?' Or will the tale Thomas Mann spoke of, telling of 'the beginnings of the human, its history, its culture', turn out to be 'completely beyond our grasp'? Did we gradually develop from the late hominids nearest to us (paleoanthropologists are agreed that Neanderthals were not our

---

63 Ibid., pp. 25–46, p. 50, pp. 242–6.

closest hominid relatives) or was there some sort of unbridgeable gap between ourselves and the most advanced hominids? The next chapter will discuss this question, which has come to be posed in terms of whether there was a 'human revolution' or not.

Chapter Six: On the threshold of the Human Mystery: was there a 'human revolution'?

Now that we've had a look at the hominid sequence, the obvious question to ask is, what makes us different from the hominids closest to us in time and in appearance? On the flattening out of this difference among their paleontological colleagues we've already quoted part of a criticism Tattersall and Schwartz make:

> ... our pattern has essentially been one of business as usual for the natural world: a story of repeated evolutionary experimentation, diversification, and, ultimately, extinction. And it was clearly in the context of such experimentation rather than out of constant fine tuning by natural selection over the eons, that our own amazing species appeared on Earth. Albeit, in the end, with a difference: for unlike even our closest relations, *Homo sapiens* is not simply an extrapolation or improvement of what went before it ... our species is an entirely unprecedented entity in the living world, however we may have come by our unusual attributes.[64]

And American novelist Walker Percy reflects on this 'entirely unprecedented entity' in his hilarious yet serious farrago, *Lost in the Cosmos*. One of his opening suggested subtitles for the book is: 'Why it is that of all the billions and billions of strange objects in the Cosmos – novas, quasars, pulsars, black holes – you are beyond doubt the strangest.'[65] In this chapter we'll have to have a shot at finding a way through the difficult maze of paleoanthropological discussion about what makes *Homo sapiens* different from the hominid species closest to us that aren't human. Then we'll see when the first humans show up in the paleontological or archaeological record, and consider the vexed question of what's become known as 'the human revolution'.[66] We'll ask what caused the human revolution, and finally, whether its study can be adequately undertaken by the natural sciences. Only then will we have cleared the way to the final part of our investigation into that strangest of realities, the human mystery.

---

64 Ian Tattersall and Geoffrey H, Schwartz, *Extinct Humans*, New York: Westview Press, 2000, p. 9.

65 Walker Percy, *Lost in the Cosmos: The Last Self-Help Book*, New York: Washington Square Press, 1984, p. 7.

66 Up-to-date details on these first humans and their places of discovery are easily available both in the surveys already mentioned and online.

1. Paleoanthropology on defining 'human'

Although we've already discussed the 'barcode for humanity' in chapter one, paleoanthropologists have their own way of defining what it is to be human.[67] Perhaps indicating their awareness that the answer doesn't fully lie within their own disciplines, De Salle and Tattersall make a rueful comment at the start of their inquiry into human origins: 'When we began our careers as scientists, we never realised that philosophy would be such a huge part of our everyday work.'[68] And in another study, Schwartz and Tattersall repeat a criticism they'd made earlier. They note that Carl Linnaeus 'was content to skip over the diagnosis of the genus *Homo* with the comment '*nosce te ipsum*' ('know yourself'), and further complain that paleoanthropologists have 'been comfortable with describing fossil specimens as hominid in the absence of an effective morphological notion of the family'.[69] Or as Chris Stringer puts it, 'One of the most serious remaining areas of uncertainty and confusion in studies of modern human origins is the question of species recognition.'[70]

It's this lack of clarity at the paleontological level that leads to so many claims that this or that species is human. Still, Linnaeus can take at least some of the blame. In his great work of classification, *Systema Naturae* (1735–1758) he used the word *Homo* to name a genus or generic biological classification for 'human', and filled in the one existing 'species' then known, namely ourselves, as *Homo sapiens*. (Maybe so we wouldn't be lonely, he added another 'species', *Homo troglodytes*, cave-dwelling human, whose description matched an orang-utan.) Once the various hominid species were discovered, the later ones like erectines and Neanderthals were also classified under *Homo*. This presupposed that human beings belonged to just another species along with these later hominids, which I'll be questioning in these chapters. Italian philosopher Giorgio Agamben, in a short chapter on Linnaeus, notes

---

67 I'm writing as a philosopher, not a biologist or paleoanthropologist, so won't be entering into the technical discussion about categorisation that can be found for example in the first chapter of Richard G. Klein's *The Human Career: Human Biological and Cultural Origins* (Chicago: University of Chicago Press, 1999).

68 Rob DeSalle and Ian Tattersall, *Human Origins: What Bones and Genomes Tell Us About Ourselves*, College Station, TX: Texas A & M University Press, 2008, p. 11, p. 45.

69 *The Human Fossil Record, Vol. 4: Craniodental Morphology of Early Hominids and Overview*, eds. Jeffrey H. Schwartz and Ian Tattersall, Hoboken, NJ: Wiley-Liss, 2005, p. 471.

70 C. B. Stringer, 'Modern Human Origins: Progress and Prospects', in Russell L. Chiocon and John G. Fleagle, eds., *The Human Evolution Source Book*, Upper Saddle River, NJ: Prentice Hall, 2006, pp. 512–28, at p. 522.

how fond of apes Linnaeus was, having seen various species of them in Amsterdam. Agamben writes:

> In a letter to a critic, Johann Georg Gmelin, who objected that in the *Systema* man seemed to have been created in the image of the ape, Linnaeus responds ... 'I ask you and the entire world to show me a generic difference between ape and man which is consistent with the principles of natural history. I most certainly do not know of any.'[71]

A summary of the ever increasing number of species variously named as 'human' or 'early modern human' or 'archaic *Homo sapiens*', would say that most fossils belonging to this group show a mosaic of characteristics, some closely approaching human, but often with larger teeth areas or brow ridges. Very rarely – we've already met this issue with claimed Neanderthal burials and the presence of red ochre, for the first humans a symbol of life due to its bloodlike colour – do they exhibit the characteristics of fully modern humans at the archaeological level. And of course, the Neanderthals and other late non-human hominids are always associated with fairly complex stone toolmaking. Yet, if we allow for the higher perceptual and motor skills we'd expect from proportionately larger brained hominids using their free hands, the very fact that such tools are only used in relation to survival skills, without indications of any other concerns, only strengthens the impression that hominids were, after all, the highest pre-human animal there was, but no more.

Some of the key sites for these 'early modern humans' or 'archaic *Homo sapiens*', are Ethiopia's Herto hominids, Israel's Jebel Qafzeh and Skhul sites, South Africa's Border Cave and Klasies River Mouth.[72] The problem

---

71 Giorgio Agamben, *The Open: Man and Animal*, tr. Kevin Atell, Stanford: Stanford University Press, 2003, p. 26.

72 T. D. White and others find the Herto hominids from 160,000 years ago to be intermediate between archaic and modern humans; see: 'Pleistocene Homo sapiens from Middle Awash, Ethiopia,' *Nature* 423 (2003), pp. 742–7. Chris Stringer disagrees and sees them as *Homo sapiens* in 'Out of Ethiopia,' *Nature* 423 (2003), pp. 692–4. Robin Dunbar notes that unlike the huge range of materials worked by the first humans, before they came on the scene, almost the only objects found by archaeology are stone tools. See his 'The social brain and the cultural explosion of the human revolution', in Paul Mellars, Katie Boyle, Ofer Bar-Yosef and Chris Stringer, eds., *Rethinking the Human Revolution*, Cambridge: Oxbow Books, 2007, pp. 91–8, at p. 92.

Stringer considers a range of fossils from Florisbad, Skhul and Qafzeh, all from around 100,000 years ago, as probably belonging to the overall *Homo sapiens* group, while not necessarily belonging to 'modern' humans; he notes, under the heading 'Problems with Concept of Modernity', that modern human skeletal variation is smaller than what's recognised for species considered as belonging to *Homo sapiens* in Skhul and Qafzeh, which are characterised by a

with some fossils regarded as modern humans is that their artefacts, for example those of Skhul and Jebel Qafzeh, fall more within the Neanderthal range. Particularly because of the mixed messages from the Skhul and Qafzeh sites, the question comes up of whether there can be morphological (skeletal) modernity before behavioural (archaeological evidence of human activity) modernity. Could there be human beings who leave no signs of specifically human activity, as several paleoanthropologists, including Chris Stringer, have asked?[73] Obviously the answer is yes – absence of evidence isn't evidence of absence – but the rush to media with the latest groundbreaking discovery of the earliest humans is a temptation to be resisted.

Rather than favouring morphological modernity as evolving before behavioural modernity, would it not be more consistent to control the application of the category of modern human? Kathy Schick and Nicholas Toth gave as one possible explanation for the apparent gap between the appearance of modern human morphology and what would be recognised as specifically human activity, that 'The early anatomically modern humans were not truly modern in their brain structure and neural organisation.'[74] And indeed Bernard Vandermeersch, the first to excavate the Qafzeh site, while holding that the fossils exhibit Cro-Magnon (or modern human) features, also finds erectine rather than Neanderthal features in the mosaic of similarities. And, while considering the most human of the Qafzeh fossil skulls, Qafzeh 9, 'for the most part identical to modern humans', he still lists four technical cranial features she shares with erectine skulls.[75]

Obviously, it can't be ruled out that humans existed who failed to leave any archaeological traces, but I think it's more useful to move on to what seems to be definite archaeological or paleontological evidence

---

mosaic of evolutionary patterns. Other fossils from Border Cave and Klasies River Mouth he finds not to be *Homo sapiens* at all. Not unlike Schwartz and Tattersall, he writes of the entirely unexpected morphological variety of these almost-human hominids, noting that the systematic framework underlying our notions of human evolution are entirely inadequate. See his 'Modern Human Origins: Progress and Prospects', in *Human Evolution Sourcebook*, p. 508, p. 511, p. 517, p. 523.

73 Chris Stringer, 'Modern *Human Origins*: Progress and Prospects,' in *Human Evolution Sourcebook*, while accepting that the Qafzeh and Skhul fossils are not necessarily modern humans, showing a mosaic evolutionary pattern, points out that their artefacts, along with those of Klasies River Mouth, are typical of the African Middle Stone age, that is, definitely pre-human (p. 524).

74 Kathy D. Schick and Nicholas Toth, *Making Stones Speak: Human Evolution and the Dawn of Technology*, New York: Simon and Schuster, 1993, p. 295.

75 Bernard Vandermeersch, *Les homes fossiles de Qafzeh (Israel)*, Paris: Editions du Centre National de Recherche Scientifique, 1981, p. 94.

for the very first humans – evidence that vastly predates the dating of more or less 100,000 years before our time generally given for the Qafzeh and Skhul remains. I'd suggest that the much earlier dating to 164,000 years ago at South Africa's Pinnacle Point – which we'll discuss later – makes it all the more likely that the other sites we've just mentioned in their earliest phases were not occupied by beings already capable of symbolic activity.

But how do paleoanthropologists actually define what makes us human? Colin Renfrew gives Paul Mellars' much quoted list of seven characteristics of the first humans: (i) the shift in stone tool production from flake technology to the more standardised blade manufacture; (ii) the increase in variety and complexity of these stone tools; (iii) the first elaborately shaped bone, antler and ivory artefacts; (iv) the increased tempo and regional diversification of technological change; (v) the first appearance of a wide range of beads, pendants and personal ornaments; (vi) significant change in economic and social organisation of human groups; and (vii) the first appearance of representational 'art' in small bone, antler or ivory carvings, along with the great series of cave paintings we find in Chauvet, Lascaux and Altamira.[76]

Another, much shorter list of specifically human capacities is given by Christopher Henshilwood, who sees modern human defined in terms of fully symbolic behaviour, and considers syntax as central to *Homo sapiens*' success. He considers the Herto hominids at 160,000 years ago to be carrying out the deliberate interment of the dead, but with a stone technology which is a mixture of Acheulian (from 2 million years ago) and Middle Stone Age (from 300,000 to 50,000 years ago), but certainly not modern human. He finds fully symbolic, therefore human, behaviour beginning 77,000 years ago (as we'll see, at Blombos, South Africa).[77]

We'll take a look at how paleoanthropologists deal with three issues here – their approaches to when and to how human beings first emerged, with a final question: whether that emergence can be fully explained by paleoanthropologists within the methods of paleontology and archaeology.

---

76 Colin Renfrew and Iain Morley, eds., *Becoming Human: Innovation in Prehistoric Material and Spiritual Culture*, New York: Cambridge University Press, 2009, pp. 77–8.

77 Christopher Henshilwood, 'Fully symbolic sapiens behaviour: Innovation in the Middle Stone Age at Blombos Cave, South Africa', in Paul Mellars et al., *Rethinking the Human Revolution*, pp. 123–32.

2. 'Multiregionalism' and 'Out of Africa': two approaches to human emergence

Up till about 2000 AD, paleoanthropologists held two competing theories about when modern humans first came into existence, one called 'Out of Africa', the other the theory of multiregional evolution.[78] Without going into the complicated details, the Out of Africa theory maintained that modern humans emerged once, in Africa, moving out to Asia and Europe after 50,000, in one or more waves, gradually replacing Neanderthals in Europe and erectines in Asia. Converse to this theory of relatively sudden and once-off emergence has been the multiregional theory (with the advantage of being more in tune with Darwinian gradualism), which holds that there were separate speciation events resulting in several different human emergences, most specifically from Asian as well as from African erectines.[79]

To complicate matters, again up to around the beginning of this century, not only did most paleoanthropologists agree with Out of Africa, but they also supported an interpretation that linked the first appearance of modern humans with the spectacular outburst of cave painting and brilliantly sculpted or carved ivory and other materials occurring in Europe from after 40,000 years ago, and given various names like 'the human revolution', or 'the creative explosion'.[80]

In 2000, paleoanthropologists Sally McBrearty and Allison Brooks published 'The revolution that wasn't: a new interpretation of the origin of modern human behaviour'. They carefully outlined an argument for a gradual emergence of humans in Africa in reaction to their perception of a bias towards linking the European 'creative explosion' of symbolic activity with the first appearance of *Homo sapiens*. So, they remark:

> ... if aspects of modern human culture in Africa were developed by hominids using existing cognitive capabilities and transmitted by cultural rather than by genetic processes, the most likely scenario

---

78 Richard G. Klein gives a magisterial summary of these theories in 'Behavioural and Biological Origins of Modern Humans', an undated lecture at Stanford University (probably from the late 1990s) easily available on the Internet.

79 See for example Milford Wolpoff's 'Multiregional Evolution: The Fossil Alternative to Eden', in Paul Mellars and Christopher Stringer, eds., *The Human Revolution: Behavioural and Biological Perspectives on the Origins of Modern Humans*, Edinburgh: Edinburgh University Press, 1989, pp. 62–108.

80 For this latter term, see John E. Pfeiffer, *The Creative Explosion: An Inquiry into the Origins of Art and Religion*, New York: Harper and Row, 1982.

would be an accretionary process, a gradual accumulation of modern behaviours in the African archaeological record.[81]

The authors cite both recent genetic and fossil discoveries clearly indicating the first humans were Africans – or as they put it, 'the earliest modern Europeans were Africans'.[82] And evidence has kept coming in over the last ten years pushing the date McBrearty and Brooks suggested for the first appearance of *Homo sapiens* further back. For example, Ben Smith discusses Richard Klein's 1999 view that modern humans were only able to expand out of Africa and occupy the world after about 50,000 years ago, given that, as a matter of fact, modern humans didn't do so, say 100,000 years ago.[83] However, 'the beads from Blombos [77,000 years ago], the marked ostrich eggshell from Diepkloof [60,000 years ago] and, if they are really that old, the harpoons from Katanda [90,000 years ago] are mortal blows to this picture of recent modern human behavioural origins'.[84] In their significantly titled *Rethinking the Human Revolution*, Mellars and Stringer note that at the Ethiopian Herto and Omo sites, the fossils have most features of characteristic modern anatomy, going back to at least 200–150 thousand years, so that they consider the multi-regional versus single culture models row to be almost irrelevant now.[85]

In fact, the view of the two principal defenders of multiregional origins, Milford Wolpoff and Alan Thorne – Thorne held that early Australians evolved from Indonesian *Homo erectus* – has been shaken by genetic analysis indicating that all humans including Chinese have instead descended from a single type originating in Africa between 35,000 and 89,000 years ago.[86]

81 Sally McBrearty and Alison S. Brooks, 'The revolution that wasn't: a new interpretation of the origin of modern human behaviour', *Journal of Human Evolution* 39 (2000), pp. 453–563, at p. 456.

82 Ibid. p. 455

83 Ben Smith, 'The Rock Arts of Southern Africa', in Geoffrey Blundell, ed., *Origins: The Story of the Emergence of Humans and Humanity in Africa*, Cape Town: Double Storey Books, 2006, pp. 97–117 at pp. 111–12. See the 1999 edition of Klein's *The Human Career*. The 50,000 years ago dating for what was called 'the human revolution' was shared by many contributors to Paul Mellars and Christopher Stringer, eds., *The Human Revolution: Behavioural and Biological Perspectives on the Origins of Modern Humans*, Edinburgh: Edinburgh University Press, 1989.

84 Ben Smith, 'The Rock Arts of Southern Africa', in Blundell, *Origins: The Story of the Emergence of Humans and Humanity in Africa*, p. 111.

85 Paul Mellars et al., *Rethinking the Human Revolution*, p. xix. Mellars also in the opening article, 'Rethinking the Human Revolution,' refers to symbolic-ritualistic treatment of skulls at Herto, 160,000 years ago, and grave offerings with the Skhul burials, though he still finds the Skhul technology belonging to an earlier, Middle Paleolithic, period. Ibid., p. 7.

86 Richard G. Klein, with Blake Edgar, *The Dawn of Human Culture: A Bold New Theory On What Sparked the 'Big Bang' of Human Consciousness*, New York: Wiley, 2002, p. 246, referring to Ann Gibbons, 'Modern Men Trace Ancestry to African Migrants', *Science* 292 (2001), pp. 1051–2.

While the Out of Africa theory is held by most paleoanthropologists today, we can ask if the widespread view up to 2000AD regarding a human revolution has been successfully challenged by opposing paleontological approaches such as that of McBrearty and Brooks, or by the multiregional theory? As we've seen, the dating has certainly had to be changed. And, as far as I can make out, paleoanthropologists have no problem with the array of facts from the African record that McBrearty and Brooks have assembled. It's how McBrearty and Brooks interpret them – their criterion for deciding what is modern human and what is not – that has been questioned by some. Ben Smith is critical of their much longer timescale for modern human origins, where they claim that certain sophisticated 'blades', 'points', 'pigment processing' and 'grindstones' all originated before 250,000 years ago. He notes that Middle Stone Age assemblages 'more than 120,000 years ago are very hard to find, so that any continuity has to be assumed, not demonstrated'. For Smith, there's also 'the problem of variable definitions ... Are the blades of 280,000 years ago really the blades of 20,000 years ago?' McBrearty's and Brooks' position seems to assume that the hominids of that much earlier period were doing the same things as much later hominids on the basis of 'occasional traces'.[87]

In fact, their figure 13 – 'Behavioural Innovations of the Middle Stone Age in Africa' – lists several hundred thousand years of archaeology to make their gradualist case for human emergence.[88] The figure categorises the achievements of various periods: images (40,000), beads (60,000), microliths (70,000), incised notational pieces, mining, barbed points, bone tools (all up to 100,000), fishing (110,000), long-distance exchange, shell-fishing, both (140,000); points (240,000), pigment processing, grindstones and blades (270,000). But while all these achievements can be arrayed in one diagram, they don't necessarily overcome the question of whether a sudden cultural change like a 'human revolution' has occurred or not.

Clive Gamble asks how McBrearty and Brooks recognise human behaviour as modern if they haven't specified what constitutes modern.[89]

---

87 Ben Smith, 'The Rock Arts of Southern Africa', p. 112.

88 McBrerty and Brooks, 'The revolution that wasn't', p. 530.

89 In fact, they are quite breezy about their use of criteria, saying that while they've adopted the usual European standards for human modernity, use of this 'inappropriate paradigm' will eventually be superseded, since '[t]he behaviours unique to *H. sapiens* are to be discovered, not prescribed'. As another indication of how easily they move from a category that could be described in terms of animal communication to human language, they say of Neanderthals that it would 'not be surprising if they are shown to have possessed language or rudimentary symbolising abilities, either inherited from a common ancestor, developed in parallel, or learned from *H. sapiens* through culture contact.' See 'The revolution that wasn't', p. 534, p. 533.

For him, they've addressed the timetable question but not the reason why the change to modern human occurred.[90] And Mellars' article, 'Rethinking the Human Revolution', defends the notion of a human revolution as entirely valid, while fully accepting that modern human origins are ultimately African. Still, he asks what happened in Africa? While conceding a certain amount of gradualism, Mellars finds the African emergence of modern humans not to be continuous. The 'rethinking' of the human revolution in the light of recent African discoveries has required the date of human emergence to be pushed back. But for Mellars, the question of what initiated that revolution is still the central issue in the current debate about modern human origins. For him (making what I would see as a very solid Aristotelian point), a capacity for specifically human activity must be there before its expression.[91]

To sum up, we could say the multiregional theory and McBrearty and Brooks' theory of gradualism both dissolve the question of specifically human emergence by collapsing the notion of the human into the group of pre-human hominids, so that they can see humans emerging with the more advanced erectines anytime from 300,000 years ago. The Out of Africa theory on the other hand seems to focus better on the specifically human. Having revised its proposed dating of the human revolution backwards in time, it accepts the evidence of intentional symbolic activity, currently dated to 164,000 years ago at Pinnacle Point as the present earliest indication of the existence of *Homo sapiens*.

3. What caused the human revolution?

Our earlier discussion of Darwinian evolution and the various qualifications that have evolved has prepared us for the differing approaches to the emergence of modern humans. The enduring criticism of *The Origin of Species* – that it concentrates on the development of one species from another rather than on species themselves – returns here with a vengeance. In the sense that while the species problem may be passed over when dealing with processes of multi-million-year duration, when the species is our own, the issue of sharp definition can hardly be avoided. And this is why, I would suggest, a heuristic based on standard Darwinian gradualism of the sort to be found both in the multiregional theory and in McBrearty and Brooks, runs into such difficulties.

---

90 Clive Gamble, *Origins and Revolutions: Human Identity in Earliest Prehistory*, New York: Cambridge University Press, 2007, p. 47.

91 Paul Mellars, 'Rethinking the Human Revolution', in: Mellers, *Rethinking the Human Revolution*, pp. 3–8.

As a result, Daniel Lieberman and Ofer Bar-Yosef affirm that human emergence is a 'speciation event' whose occurrence can be explained in terms of punctuated equilibrium.[92] N. J. Conard opposes this view, because Neanderthals made bone tools and archaic humans have undertaken big-game hunting, and use materials from distant locations. However, while ascribing deliberate burials to pre-human hominids, he notes that they use no grave goods, and though finding perforated shells in the Middle Stone Age, he finds that pigment use is 'likely, but difficult to archeologically demonstrate'. He also writes that there is no evidence for figurative representations or music before the Upper Paleolithic (the period associated with modern humans).[93] This effectively concedes that the very characteristics claimed to be unique to humans by those advocating a human revolution don't show up in the hundreds of thousands of years of late non-human hominid existence.

Ian Tattersall also regards human emergence as a punctuated equilibrium rather than gradual event. He contrasts 'phyletic gradualism, whereby one species gradually transforms over time into another under the guiding hand of natural selection' with 'the notion of punctuated equilibria' which sees changes 'as episodic; species are essentially stable entities that give rise to new species in relatively short-term events'. He speaks of the Blombos symbols as exhibiting a 'new behavioural potential', and considers that there is 'no deeper mystery than how we came to acquire our distinctive mental qualities'. For Tattersall, *Homo sapiens* is 'a totally unprecedented kind of being ... something entirely new', with a 'difference not just in degree but in kind'.[94]

If we apply to human emergence the same heuristic we suggested for biological emergences, I'd suggest we can draw on all the various factors focused on there, taking a both/and rather than an either/or approach. So standard Darwinian adaptive gradualism, governed by natural selection, surely has a huge part to play in the emergence of *Homo sapiens* within the

---

92 Daniel E. Lieberman and Ofer Bar-Yosef, 'Apples and Oranges: Morphological Versus Behavioural Transitions in the Pleistocene' in Daniel E. Lieberman, Richard J. Smith and Jay Kelley, eds., *Interpreting the Past: Essays on Human, Primate, and Mammal Evolution in Honor of David Pilbeam*, Boston: Brill, 2005, pp. 275–96, at p. 289.

93 N. J. Conard, 'An overview of the patterns of behavioural change in Africa and Eurasia during the Middle and Late Pleistocene' in *From Tools to Symbols: Early Hominids to Modern Humans*, Francesco d'Errico and Lucinda Backwell, eds., Johannesburg: Witwatersrand University Press, 2005, pp. 295–332, at p. 296, pp. 304–18.

94 Ian Tattersall, *The World from Beginnings to 4000BCE*, New York: Oxford University Press, 2008, pp. 6–9, pp. 100–2.

hominid sequence. Without accepting multiregionalism, McBrearty and Brooks' gradualist thesis for human emergence within an African matrix still stands. But, as evo-devo complemented the standard Darwinist explanation, so here too, various paleoanthropologists have suggested regulatory genes as at least a complementary aspect of a full understanding of human origins.

For example, Klein and Edgar write of how White and Bar-Yosef note the new ways of food production, larger population and higher levels of social and economic organisation characterising *Homo sapiens*. Yet, they don't think White and Bar-Yosef have explained why such sudden technological or social change takes place. 'In our view, the simplest and most economic explanation for the "dawn" is that it stemmed from a fortuitous mutation that promoted the fully modern human brain.' They give three reasons: (i) natural selection that would have selected the more effective brains that largely drove the earlier stages of the human revolution; (ii) Increased brain size accompanying earlier technological shifts, like the initial appearance of stone artefacts from around 2.6–2.5 million years ago, followed by later events like movement to open treeless environments from 1.8–1.6 million years ago, to the improved hand axes and first permanent occupation of Europe from 600,000 years ago; and (iii):

> ... the relationship between anatomical and behavioural change shifted abruptly about 50,000 years ago. Before this time, anatomy and behaviour appear to have evolved more or less in tandem, very slowly, but after this time anatomy remained relatively stable while behavioural (cultural) change accelerated rapidly. What could explain this better than a neural change that promoted the extraordinary modern human ability to innovate? ... Arguably the last key neural change promoted the modern capacity for rapidly spoken phonemic language ... [95]

This is closer to an evo-devo approach, and Tattersall also suggests regulatory genes rather than hominid evolution, a sudden event and not a slow stately progression from archaic humans to modern human body structure.[96] Lieberman and Bar-Yosef agree. They note a poor correspondence between toolmaking techniques (archaeology) and fossil

---

95 Klein and Edgar, *The Dawn of Human Culture*, pp. 268–71.
96 Tattersall, *The World from Beginnings to 4000BCE*, pp. 14–15.

species (paleontology). So they regard the huge flowering of specifically human artistic and technological activites in the Upper Paleolithic not as representing a speciation event but as a technological revolution post-dating others of our species, analogous to the agricultural revolution occurring much later. That is to say, that the actual speciation event could have occurred before the Upper Paleolithic evidence. Allowing for these differences of interpretation of when it occurred, for these paleoanthropologists, the actual shift to *Homo sapiens* was a punctuated speciation event involving a profound reorganisation of the skull as a whole.[97]

As well as drawing on a complementary internal evo-devo and external adaptationist approach, can an understanding of human origins be further clarified in terms of emergent probability? Ian Tattersall remarks that 'it is not at all clear what that final physical innovation [to the human brain] might have been that made our immediate precursor at least potentially capable of symbolic thought. But it is fairly evident that we will never be able to illuminate that final leap without evoking the phenomena of exaptation and emergence.'[98] And Sue Parker and Karin Jaffe refer to Mithen's notion of 'the Big Bang of the Upper Paleolithic culture', and to his adoption of a Piagetian approach towards mental evolution.[99] Let's suggest that the 7-million-year-long hominid sequence has provided the principle of emergence of what we've seen Tattersall call a 'new behavioural potential'. Then the principle of correspondence, or exaptation, would refer to what he's spoken of as not an extrapolation from earlier hominids but 'something entirely new', with a 'difference not just in degree but in kind'.

---

97 Lieberman and Bar-Yosef, 'Apples and Oranges: Morphological Versus Behavioural Transitions in the Pleistocene', p. 275, p. 289.

98 Tattersall, *The World from Beginnings to 4000BCE*, p. 102.

99 Sue T. Parker and Karin E. Jaffe, *Darwin's Legacy: Scenarios in Human Evolution*, Lanham, MD: AltaMira Press, 2008, p. 171, p. 182. On that Piagetian parallel, suggesting how the perceptual levels of late hominid cognition can be taken up within a higher intellectual level, here's a summary of Piaget's work I attempted many years ago: 'Intelligence for Piaget is an organ whose function is intrinsically structure-free and explanatory, a pure constructivity articulated in a triple group of cognitive operations [what Piaget refers to as (i) sensori-motor – so the perceptual level we share with animals including hominids; (ii) the level of (ii) concrete, and (iii) of formal, or abstract intellectual operations] and controlled by the immanent norms of attention to data, of coherence and of truth. Unlike biological, neural and sensitive higher integrations, intelligence conserves the lower manifolds it synthesises. Corresponding to this progressively widening understanding there is the noematic [what is understood] pole of an unlimited field of reality.' See Brendan Purcell, *Aspects of Method in Human Psychology*, unpublished Master's thesis, University College Dublin, 1969, p. 143.

4. Is human emergence fully explicable by paleontology and archaeology?

Although subsequent discoveries in Africa have in some ways confirmed McBrearty and Brooks' careful analysis and critique, it's just possible that extra-scientific prejudices might be detected in their work, as when they remark:

> We believe that by continuing to insist upon revolutions, researchers, perhaps unwittingly, create a gulf separating humans from the rest of the biological world. By stressing human uniqueness, proponents of the 'human revolution' effectively remove the origin of *H. sapiens* from the realm of normal scientific inquiry. (533)

McBrearty and Brooks here are unwittingly pre-empting a boundary or threshold question about human origins from being raised, simply because it doesn't fall within 'the realm of normal scientific inquiry'. But again, most prominently, a paleoanthropologist like Ian Tattersall would not agree. For example he has consistently affirmed that Cro-Magnons belong to an entirely new order of being, with how they emerged being 'the most baffling' question 'in all biology'.[100] More recently, with Rob DeSalle, he has written that 'We are separated from the rest of Nature by a profound cognitive chasm.'[101] We'll come across similar remarks when we discuss the origins of language, which at least suggest that paleoanthropology as a science may well need to consider the kind of complementary inquiry with philosophy that astrophysics has sometimes been prepared to undertake.

Now that we've reached what I believe is the real threshold marking off the difference between ourselves and all other living things on the planet, let's explore the factors that constitute that difference.

---

100 Ian Tattersall, *The Monkey in the Mirror: Essays on the Science of What Makes Us Human*, New York: Harcourt, 2002, p. 141.

101 DeSalle and Tattersall, *Human Origins: What Bones and Genomes Tell Us About Ourselves*, p. 191.

Part Four: The seven grace notes in the 'Sonata for a Good Man'

Chapter Seven: The first three grace notes in the human sonata:[1] [1] the genetic 'African Eve & Adam', [2] our culture-oriented body plan, and [3] our meaning-oriented brain and vocal tract

In Florian Henckel von Donnersmarck's film, *The Lives of Others*, based in East Berlin in 1984, a Stasi agent, Captain Gerd Wiesler, is spying on an artistic couple (Dreyman, a playwright, and Christa-Maria, his actress girlfriend). Gradually Wiesler is attracted by the beauty, meaning and love present in their life but absent from his own. Various scenes show Wiesler's gradual transformation from remorseless defender of the German Democratic Republic to one who's prepared to risk his life for those he's spying on. One day he eavesdrops on Dreyman playing a piano piece, 'Sonata for a Good Man'. After the Berlin Wall comes down in 1989, Dreyman discovers how Wiesler protected him, and writes a novel with the same title as the piece of music. Wiesler, now unemployed, opens the novel in the Karl Marx Bookshop in East Berlin, and discovers it's dedicated to what was his official Stasi codename, HGW XX/7. The shop assistant asks, 'Do you want it gift-wrapped?' 'No,' says Wiesler, 'es ist für mich' – 'it's for me'. As Sukhdev Sandhu, reviewing the film in the London *Daily Telegraph* wrote, the film 'demonstrates that the human soul is mysterious and hard to obliterate. Even the coldest heart can thaw. Even the most technocratic imagination can respond to a sudden whisper, an implicit grace note.'[2]

Having explored the views of paleoanthropologists on tackling human emergence, I'd like to suggest seven grace notes to listen out for which go a long way to explain why we're different from the latest pre-human hominids. The first trio of grace notes are amazing components of our humanness – firstly our specifically human genetic origins, secondly the cultural time-sequencing of our growth, and thirdly, in what's often been described as the most complicated piece of matter in the entire universe,

---

1 I can feel my fingers being rapped by Miss Bergin, my first and rather strict piano teacher, for misusing 'grace notes' here – in music they're non-essential ornamentations. But I'd like to give them quite another meaning: here they'll refer to the essential components of our being human, with the 'grace' a reminder that they're all gifts to us along with our existence.

2 Sukhdev Sandhu, 'Magnificent Tribute to the Human Soul', review of *The Lives of Others*, *Daily Telegraph* (13 April 2007).

our brain and vocal tract. We'll speak of these as our trio of preconscious characteristics because they provide the material foundations for human consciousness. Chapters seven to ten will play the rest of the human sonata, the quartet of characteristically human conscious aspects: our capacity for language and symbolisation, understanding and freedom, and their intrinsic transfinite orientation. Underlying that sonata, there's the 'good man', the fully actualised good person – the origins for whom our final chapter will try to find the words.

1. Human genetics

1.1 Aren't we 98% chimpanzee?

Before exploring an important matter of our genetic heritage, there's a problem that keeps coming up, well caught in the title of geneticist Jonathan Marks' book *What It Means to Be 98% Chimpanzee: Apes, People, and Their Genes*. How often have you been told how slight the human biochemical difference is from chimpanzees? Marks writes that 'The first topic this book addresses is: What does the genetic similarity of humans to apes mean?' He goes on to note that 'the very structure of DNA compels it to be no more than 75% different, no matter how diverse the species being compared are. Yet the fact that our DNA is more than 25% similar to a dandelion's does not imply that we are over one quarter dandelion ...' He further notes that in fact humans are about 35% genetically similar to daffodils, in which context, 'the 99.44% similarity of the DNA of human to chimp doesn't seem so remarkable'. And he goes on to say that 'The paradox is not that we are so genetically similar to the chimpanzee; the paradox is why we now find the genetic similarity to be so much more striking than the anatomical similarity.'

While the closeness of humans to apes has always been recognised, what he calls 'The Central Fallacy of Molecular Anthropology' had to wait for 'the molecularisation of biology in the 1960s'. He continues: 'Ultimately, the fallacy is not a genetic but a cultural one – our reduction of the important things in life to genetics.'

Marks tells how, in the 1960s, biochemist Emile Zuckerkandl, on the basis of almost similar haemoglobin in humans and gorillas, could write that 'from the point of view of haemoglobin structure, it appears that the gorilla is just an abnormal human, or man an abnormal gorilla, and the two species form actually one continuous population'. And he gives eminent US evolutionist George Gaylord Simpson's response: a gorilla is not an abnormal man, it's a gorilla. A man is not an abnormal gorilla, he's a man. Gorillas and humans don't form a single population, any more than gorillas and daffodils do.[3]

It's not just humans and chimps who are biologically close: there are strong genetic similarities between quite different species. For example there's the even closer (99%) DNA similarity between dolphins and whales, between camels and South American alpacas, along with the slightly less (97%) DNA similarity between whales and hippopotami.[4] But the genetic closeness of, for example, hippos to whales doesn't translate into what they look like or act like – in other words, as with the 98% similarity between ourselves and chimps, genetic similarity on its own doesn't tell us very much. There are far more interesting dissimilarities at the genetic and other levels that begin to indicate just how strange we are compared to all other living species on this earth. Let's begin then with some key genetic details regarding the human family.

What's been discovered in the late 1980s about our human genetic origins goes a long way towards undermining any attempt at a scientific backing for any human race being superior to any other, although Africans must take a bow for being the first humans. What these discoveries show is that all of us belong genetically to the same human family, with two interesting sets of genetic clues leading through the female and the male lineages towards a single human species emerging very recently in biological terms – in Africa around 150,000 years ago.

1.2 Mitochondrial DNA (mtDNA) and the children of Eve

Mitochondria are substructures within the cell with their own genetic machinery, information and rate of change in a given species. Unlike ordinary, or nuclear DNA, inherited from both parents, in all species studied, nonhuman as well as human, mitochondrial DNA (or mtDNA) is inherited only from the mother.

Because mtDNA inheritance seems to imply a single mother, paleoanthropologists Rebecca Cann, Chris Stringer and others support what has been called the 'Noah's Ark' theory – the emergence of the human race from a single maternal origin, which Pamela Willoughby, among others, refers to as 'an African "mitochondrial Eve" population'.[5] When Cann and

3 Jonathan Marks, *What It Means to Be 98% Chimpanzee: Apes, People, and Their Genes*, Berkeley: University of California Press, 2002, p. 5, p. 29, p. 31, pp. 42–3.

4 Daniel J. Fairbanks, *Relics of Eden: The Powerful Evidence of Evolution in Human DNA*, New York: Prometheus Books, 2007, pp. 126–7.

5 Pamela Willoughby, *Evolution of Modern Humans in Africa: A Comprehensive Guide*, Lanham, MD: Altamura Press, 2007, p. 145. From the viewpoint of biology, this doesn't amount to saying there was only one human female at that time.

her associates at the Department of Human Biology at Berkeley studied the mtDNA variation in different species, they discovered a 5% variation between the two slightly different orang-utan species in Borneo and Sumatra, a 0.6% variation among gorillas, and an amazingly low 0.3% variation among humans of all races. Stringer remarks:

> It is not the gorilla, nor the chimpanzee, nor the orang-utan, that is unusual ... Each enjoys a normal spectrum of biological variability. It is the human race that is odd. We display remarkable geographical diversity, and yet astonishing genetic unity ... The realisation that humans are biologically highly homogeneous has one straightforward implication: that mankind has only recently evolved from one tight little group of ancestors ... We are all members of a very young species, and our genes betray this secret.[6]

The first researchers based themselves on a hypothetical rate of change or 'molecular clock' for mtDNA, and suggested 200,000 years ago as an approximate benchmark for the first humans. Neither paleontologists nor archaeologists were impressed, since at that time there was no evidence on the ground for such an early human origin. But the recent archaeological discoveries at Pinnacle Peak and Blombos would seem to support the earlier hypothetical biological clock – that the first humans originated in Africa at least some time before 150,000 years.

The Swedish researcher Ulf Gyllensten and others suggested in 2000 that the divergence between the first humans, who had originated in Africa and those who had left Africa, occurred between 52,000 and 28,000 years ago and was followed shortly afterwards by a population explosion outside the continent.[7] The approximately 25,000 years difference is the time it is reckoned by the newly recalibrated molecular clock it would have taken for the greater diversity to develop in African mtDNA compared to all the rest.

Daniel Fairbanks tells how the Russian botanist Nicolai Vavilov was the first to suggest that 'the greatest genetic diversity of a species is found in the region where it originated'. This helps to explain why human geneticists found 'the highest degree of diversity in people indigenous to sub-Saharan Africa ... *twice* as high as the rest of the world combined!

---

6 Chris Stringer, and Robin McKie, *African Exodus: The Origins of Modern Humanity*, London: Pimlico, 1997, p. 113.

7 U. Gyllensten, M. Ingman, H. Kaessman, S. Pääbo, 'Mitochondrial genome variation and the origin of modern humans', *Nature*, 408, 7 December 2000, pp. 708–13.

According to analysis of mitochondrial diversity in light of Vavilov's principle, modern humans – *Homo sapiens* – originated in sub-Saharan Africa.' The same holds for distribution of human blood types (A, B, AB, O). 'The most diverse groups were the Africans and Europeans. The least diverse were people native to North and South America, and they were most similar to Asians.'[8]

Willoughby reports Ingman et al. as carrying out the first sequencing of the entire mitochondrial genome, producing:

> ... a tree where the three deepest [earliest] branches were exclusively sub-Saharan Africans, while the fourth was the first to link Africans and non-Africans. Their estimated date for the most recent common ancestor for all living people averaged at 171,500 ± 50,000 years ago. The youngest branch with both Africans and non-Africans began about 52,000 ± 27,000 years ago; shortly afterward there was a population expansion in non-Africans. The Out of Africa expansion began around 38,500 years ago, which overlaps with the onset of the Eurasian Upper Paleolithic.[9]

As we've mentioned, the multiregional school of paleontology held that humans evolved in the different regions where *Homo erectus* was distributed.[10] The reason they objected to what amounts to a punctuationist approach to human origins is that, for example, Milford Wolpoff sees it as 'anti-Darwinian' because of its conflict with gradualism.[11] However, the biological riposte is that: 'It is not biologically feasible to have multiple lines of descent without a common ancestor.'[12] Or, as a newspaper article put this, in more popular language: 'DNA survey finds all humans are 99.9pc the same':

> Whether you hail from Surbiton, Ulan Bator or Nairobi, your genetic make-up is strikingly similar to that of every other person on

---

8 Daniel J. Fairbanks, *Relics of Eden: The Powerful Evidence of Evolution in Human DNA*, New York: Prometheus Books, 2007, p. 108, p. 109, p. 113.

9 Willoughby, *The Evolution of Modern Humans in Africa*, p. 143.

10 See Wolfpoff's 'Multiregional Evolution: The Fossil Alternative to Eden' in Paul Mellars and Christopher Stringer, eds., *The Human Revolution: Behavioural and Biological Perspectives on the Origins of Modern Humans*, Edinburgh: Edinburgh University Press, 1989, pp. 62–108.

11 Stringer, *African Exodus*, p. 81.

12 Mark Stoneking and Rebecca Cann, 'African Origin of Human Mitochondrial DNA' in *The Human Revolution*, Mellars and Stringer, pp. 17–30, at p. 17.

Earth, an analysis concludes today. Although scientists have long recognised that, despite physical differences, all human populations are genetically similar, the new work concludes that populations from different parts of the world share even more genetic similarities than previously assumed. All humans are 99.9% identical and, of that tiny 0.1% difference, 94% of the variation is among individuals from the same populations and only 6% between individuals from different populations.[13]

The acceptance by many paleoanthropologists of a single human race is of more interest for our investigation than the as yet not fully resolved issue of mtDNA dating and rate of change. They note that the various racially different modern human populations 'show a fundamental similarity in anatomy, and it is difficult to believe that such a large number of characters in common could have evolved independently ... in various parts of the world'.[14] Given the biological definition of species as 'communities of reproductively interacting organisms', this single origin or Out of Africa hypothesis provides a strong indication of the biological uniqueness of the human race.[15] So Willoughby can quote geneticist Svante Pääbo: 'from a genomic perspective, we are all Africans, either living in Africa or in quite recent exile outside Africa'.[16]

1.3 The human Y-chromosome and an African Adam
What makes the genetic tracing of human origins so like a detective story is that along with these clues to a single maternal source of the human race, there are parallel clues leading to a single paternal source too. Tattersall and Schwartz remark that 'Recent comparative studies of the human Y chromosome (uniquely passed along by men, presumably from an "African Adam") suggest a pattern similar to that suggested by the maternally derived mtDNA'.[17]

And Stephen Oppenheimer in his book dedicated to the topic, *Out of Eden: The Peopling of the World*, writes:

---

13 Roger Highfield, 'DNA survey finds all humans are 99.9pc the same', *Daily Telegraph*, 20 December 2002.

14 Christopher Stringer, 'Homo sapiens', in *Encyclopedia of Human Evolution and Prehistory*, Ian Tattersall, E. Delson and J. Van Couvering, eds., New York: Garland, 1988, pp. 267–74, at p. 270.

15 Niles Eldredge, 'Species', in *Encyclopedia of Human Evolution and Prehistory*, pp. 537–9, at p. 538.

16 Willoughby, *Evolution of Modern Humans in Africa*, p. 160.

17 Tattersall and Schwarz, *Extinct Humans*, New York: Westview Press, 2000, p. 230.

Analogous to the maternally transmitted mtDNA residing outside our cell nuclei, there is a set of genes packaged within the nucleus that is only passed down the male line. This is the Y chromosome, the defining chromosome for maleness ... Like mtDNA, the non-recombining part of the Y chromosome remains uncorrupted with each generation, and can be traced back in an unbroken line to our original male ancestor ... Y chromosomes have already helped to chart a genetic trail parallel to the mtDNA trail. At the major geographical branch points they support the story told by mtDNA: They point to a shared ancestor in Africa for all modern humans, and a more recent ancestor in Asia for all non-Africans.[18]

What's also very interesting is that both theories now suggest that humans began to leave Africa about 50,000 years ago, gradually spreading to Asia, Europe, Australia, and much later, to the Americas. But to get two supporting theories – which will surely undergo modification as time goes on – both yielding an unambiguous indication of the biological unity of the human family has important implications for how we relate to one another in the first place as brothers and sisters in the same human family rather than as members of this or that nationality or racial group.

2. Human culture is built into our body plan
One of the biggest surprises I got when I began this inquiry was when I found out that our physical growth patterns are closely bound up with how we learn our culture and our first language. So that our bodies are programmed for the slow accumulation of learning how to be with other humans as humans. Unlike animals who are fairly well provided for by instinct (though of course they learn too), the most important things we need for existing as humans take a long time to learn. So we have both a long childhood and a long period of post-reproductive survival, ageing processes which have no counterpart either among apes, or, according to new techniques for dating the age at death of fossil remains, among hominids – including Neanderthals or what are called 'archaic sapiens' populations.[19] Mithen notes that studies of tooth growth indicate that 'Neanderthal children grew up at a faster rate than those of modern humans. Hence they had a relatively shorter time

---

18 Stephen Oppenheimer, *Out of Eden: The Peopling of the World*, London: Constable, 2003, p. 41.

19 Christopher Stringer, 'Homo sapiens', in *Encyclopedia of Human Evolution and Prehistory*, p. 269.

in which to acquire their communication system ... '[20] Cartmill and Smith confirm this in their recent study: 'More rapid maturation in Neanderthals may also have been associated with a shorter lifespan. Few Neanderthals seem to have survived beyond their peak reproductive years. Trinkaus concludes that disproportionate numbers of Neanderthals died before reaching the age of 40.'[21]

The Swiss human biologist Adolf Portmann contrasted the highly specialised young animal's body structure with the extremely unspecialised human infant body. But it's this very lack of specialisation that allows the human infant unlimited adaptability in relation to what Portmann calls the 'social womb' of its human environment, including the language it's wrapped in.[22]

At the other end of our lives, we've a long ageing period which ensures that the accumulated and radically non-instinctual experience and tradition of the human community is passed on by the older to the younger generation. What is of interest in both of these growth patterns is that they do not confer a biological advantage, but are meaningful primarily in terms of the human intellectual and spiritual culture they are aimed at serving.

Richard Alexander makes an interesting point regarding the menopause in human females:

> ... in no monkey species are females known to undergo an evolved menopause. Sometimes very old females in zoo animals or domestic species become incapable of becoming pregnant a few years before they die, but this is not the same as a complex programmed cessation of ovulation in approximately the middle of the maximum lifetime, as happens in human females.[23]

He notes that in a few other species, such as elephants and pilot whales, some females seem to live several years beyond their last offspring, so,

---

20 Steven Mithen, *The Singing Neanderthals: The Origins of Music, Language, Mind and Body*, London: Weidenfeld and Nicolson, 2005, p. 241. Sean Carroll extends this remark on enamel formation to include 'australopiths and early members of the genus *Homo*' in his 'Genetics and the Making of *Homo sapiens*,' in Russell L Chiocon and John G. Fleagle, eds., *The Human Evolution Source Book: Second Edition*, Upper Saddle River, NJ: Pearson/Prentice-Hall, 2006, p. 630.

21 Matt Cartmill and Fred H. Smith, *The Human Lineage*, Hoboken, NJ: Wiley-Blackwell, 2009, p. 384.

22 Adolf Portmann, 'Anthropologische Deutung der Menschlichen Entwicklungsperiode', in his *Vom Lebendigen*, Frankfurt: Suhrkamp, 1979, pp. 75–92.

23 Richard D. Alexander, *How did Humans Evolve?* Ann Arbor Museum of Zoology, University of Michigan, Special Publication No.1, 1990, p. 12.

in this matter seem to be closer to humans.[24] Richard Dawkins makes the same point:

> ... menopause is a system whereby the human female turns her effort from adding new objects of maternal care to teaching those she has already produced ... In addition ... post-menopausal women may be even dramatically more capable at contributing to the success of their offspring and other kin than younger women, simply because success in social and political matters is to a large extent a consequence of gradually acquired knowledge, wisdom, and power.[25]

So it could be suggested that women have written into their genes not only the possibility of childbearing but also of long-term cultural nurturing when they can no longer bear children.

3. Our brain and vocal tract as material basis of language, understanding and freedom

3.1 The human brain

What's the material basis for the difference between our brains and those of primates? According to Robin Dunbar, the neocortex occupies 10–40% of non-primate brains, 50–80% of primate brain, and 80%, or 4/5 of the human brain. So he states:

> In other words, when we ask what has driven primate brain evolution, what we are really asking is what has driven primate neocortical evolution. However, since the neocortex is also the locus for most of the more sophisticated aspects of human cognition, it is perhaps significant that it is this component of the brain that has expanded out of all proportion.[26]

The parts of the brain dealing with sensation and movement occupy only about a quarter of the neocortex so three quarters of it have to do

---

24 This point is supported by Simon Conway Morris, who suggests a continuum in the emergence of cultural capabilities, while not denying that 'humans have gone further; they have what has been termed a "hyperculture"', Still, without specifying which (possibly referring to whales and elephants), he writes of post-reproductive females in species other than human in *Life's Solution: Inevitable Humans in a Lonely Universe*, Cambridge: Cambridge University Press, 2003, p. 259.

25 Richard Dawkins, *The Selfish Gene*, Oxford: Oxford University Press, 1989, p. 13.

26 Robin I. M. Dunbar, 'The Social Brain and the Cultural Expansion of the Human Revolution', in Paul Mellars, Katie Boyle, Ofer Bar-Yosef and Chris Stringer, eds., *Rethinking the Human Revolution*, Cambridge: Oxbow Books, 2007, pp. 91–8, at p. 91.

with activities that are specifically human – the ones we'll be mentioning in the next chapter.[27] Because one of the most amazing things about our brains is that though they're obviously material, important parts of them make sense only in terms of activities that transcend matter, like seeking the truth and choosing what's good in itself. I remember a comment made by the great Russian neurologist Alexander Romanovich Luria during a clinical demonstration in Leuven in the early 1970s. He remarked that 'the brain is dumb', that, considered on its own, without the conscious activities of the patient, no merely physical examination of the human brain would ever tell us what some of its most important properties were.

That's why, to understand our brains, we have to work back from what we know about human knowledge and freedom: only then can we grasp how the brain is the launching pad from which our most human activities take off. You'd need a similar approach to understand the human vocal tract (the human larynx, pharynx, tongue, high palate, shape of our teeth) – if we couldn't speak it would make no sense, physiologically. And we can't ignore the mystery of how both our vocal tract and those functions of our brains dedicated to speech are united in a single symphonic interaction all at the service of spoken and heard language.

And this amazing symphonic interaction of brain and vocal tract is itself linked to what we've noted about the intrinsic cultural orientation of the human body plan, in that it's precisely timed with human infancy and early childhood growth within a learning context. For example, Derek Bickerton, who specialises in the origins of language, discusses the 'language' of 'Genie'. 'Genie' was a thirteen-year-old Californian girl, who was found in 1970, having been isolated from all human communication by her mentally disabled parents. Bickerton notes that her acquisition of 'language' after she was rescued was rather the acquisition of what he calls protolanguage – which, 'despite its richer content and greater cognitive sophistication, is formally no more developed than that of apes or children under two'.[28] The case of 'Genie' seems to show that there is a definite cutting off period – Lenneberg's 'critical period hypothesis' – in terms of which, if children don't

---

27 As Rob De Salle and Ian Tattersall point out in *Human Origins: What Bones and Genomes Tell Us About Ourselves* (College Station, TX: Texas A & M University Press, 2008), our brains (along with those of the latest non-human hominids) 'are seven times or more larger than what we'd expect to find in an average mammal of our size' (p. 192).

28 Derek Bickerton, *Language and Species*, Chicago: University of Chicago Press, 1990, p. 118.

grow up among other people already using language, they themselves will never subsequently be able to acquire it.[29]

Since our brains aren't much different in size to Neanderthals (a recent comparison puts Neanderthals at 1412cc with fossil humans at 1487cc), its relatively large size compared to primates and hominids can't be the decisive issue. And human brains can vary from 1100cc–2100cc with no noticeable difference in intelligence. However, comparative measurements of Neanderthal and human infant skulls by Philipp Günz and others at the Max Planck Institute for Evolutionary Anthropology in Leipzig have discovered that the brains of newborn Neanderthals and humans are very similar at birth. But human brain development in the first year of life results in the uniquely globular shape of the human brain case as distinct from the elongated shape of the Neanderthal brain case. Günz is quoted as saying:

The development of cognitive abilities during individual growth is linked to the maturation of the underlying wiring pattern of the brain; around the time of birth, the neural circuitry is sparse in humans, and clinical studies have linked even subtle alterations in early brain development to changes in the neural wiring patterns that affect behaviour and cognition. The connections between diverse brain regions that are established during this period in modern humans are important for higher-order social, emotional, and communication functions. It is therefore unlikely that Neanderthals saw the world as we do.[30]

29 In his *Biological Foundations of Language* (New York: Wiley, 1967), Eric H. Lenneberg popularised a theory first advanced by neurologists Wilder Penfield and Lamar Roberts in 1959. Although the exact window of neurological opportunity varies, Lenneberg's suggested 4–10 years in the child still seems more or less accurate. This may be due to the delay in development of the child's prefrontal cortex, which is unique to humans compared to other mammals, including primates. It's been suggested that, due to that late development of the part of the human brain most associated with cognitive control, human infants focus on the conventions of human language rather than idiosyncratic variations, enormously facilitating their language learning. Which looks like a specifically human instance of Le Gros Clark's notion of adaptability rather than adaptation. See Melody Dye, 'The Advantages of Being Helpless: Human brains are slow to develop – a secret, perhaps, of our success', in *Scientific American*, 9 February 2010; Dye refers to Simon Thompson-Schill, Michael Ramscar, Evangelia Chrysikou (2009), 'Cognition without control: When a little frontal lobe goes a long way' in *Current Directions in Psychological Science* 8.5, pp. 259–63; and to Carla L. Hudson Kam and Elissa L. Newport, 'Getting it right by getting it wrong: When learners change languages' in *Cognitive Psychology*, Vol. 59.1 (August 2009), pp. 30–66.

30 'The brains of Neanderthals and modern humans developed differently', 8 November 2010, *Max Planck Society News* B/2010 (p. 247); Philipp Günz, Simon Neubauer, Bruno Maureille and Jean-Jacques Hublin, 'Brain development after birth differs between Neanderthals and modern humans', *Current Biology*, 9 November 2010; 'Babies' brains resemble those of Neanderthals: New-born humans' brains are about the same size and of similar appearance to those of Neanderthals, but alter in the first year of life, a new scientific study suggested', *Daily Telegraph*, 9 November 2010.

The most striking characteristics of the human brain, then, are its qualitative structure, with the most distinctive features being the frontal lobes and those parts of the brain dealing with the reception and the production of speech.

The frontal area of the brain is where development between australopithecines and erectines is most noticeable. In humans, we know that it provides the material basis for decision making and future planning, since when it's seriously injured, time-related human action is also seriously impaired. In one of the demonstrations I remember Luria giving, for example, he examined a patient, and asked him to sing part of a song – the fact that he could do so indicated the patient wasn't injured in the frontal area that had to do with time-sequences, since to sing even a few bars of music means we can structure it in terms of which notes come first, in the middle, and at the end.

In smaller monkeys, the frontal area occupies 11% of the total neocortex (the topmost part of the brain with its six layers), in chimpanzees, 17%, and in humans 29% – that is, almost a third. The function of the frontal area in integrating all the other parts is clear even at the neurological level, since it has two-way connections with almost all other areas of the brain.

What seems to make the human frontal area unique is its connection with Wernicke's area (for speech-reception, Luria's 'impressive speech') and Broca's area (for speech production, Luria's 'expressive speech') – since all our decision-making and specifically human action involves internal as well as external verbal communication.[31]

Wernicke's area, close to our left ear, analyses heard speech (linguistic input), identifying its significant elements and integrating them into a meaningful sequence. John Eccles points out that the area corresponding to it is proportionately very small in the orang-utan brain, for example, while area 37, adjoining Wernicke's area and regarded as instrumental in understanding language, seems to have no equivalent, for example, in macaque or orang-utan brains.[32] Broca's area deals with the synthesis of individual sounds into complex, successive units. The area is in direct contact with the lower parts of area 6, which control the movements of lips, tongue and larynx, that are essential for articulation.

Again Broca's area is far less well-developed in smaller monkey and ape brains. There is evidence for a well-developed Broca's area in a *Homo habilis* skull, ER 1470, and in erectine and later hominid skulls. But Ralph

31 Alexander Romanovich Luria, *The Working Brain*, Harmondsworth: Penguin, 1973, 306.

32 John Eccles, *The Human Mystery*, Berlin: Springer, 1979, pp. 88–93.

Holloway, an expert in the examination of endocasts (plaster casts) from these skulls, remarks that:

> Unfortunately, the posterior portion of the endocast, which contains Wernicke's region ... seldom if ever shows convolutional details that would permit one to conclude that these hominids possessed language.[33]

Still, Sean Carroll notes that indications of Broca's and Wernicke's area can be found in primates and in early erectines at 2.5 million years ago.[34] And Philip Lieberman criticises the 'Broca-Wernicke model' since patients 'having extensive damage to Broca's or Wernicke's areas' generally do not suffer permanent loss of language 'unless subcortical damage also occurs'. However, even if Broca-Wernicke doesn't have as dominant a role in our linguistic abilities as was once thought, he still reports that all the members of the KE family who suffer from an anomaly in a gene affecting their linguistic ability show abnormalities in their Broca's area.[35]

The challenge is to identify more subtle differences unique to human brains, for example, quantitative changes in specialised areas.[36] Investigation of a gene underlying both brain function and vocal tract function was spurred on by the famous case of about half the members of the family referred to as the KEs, whose difficulties with grammar were discovered in 2001 to be due to the malfunctioning of a gene known as FOXP2.[37] Mithen notes that it's not unique to humans:

> ... it is found in an almost identical form among a great many species. Indeed, there are only three differences between the seven hundred amino acids that form the FOXP2 gene in mice and in humans. Those three differences appear to be vital, because the KE family shows us that when the human version of the FOXP2 gene malfunctions, significant language deficits arise.

---

33 Ralph Holloway, in *Encyclopedia of Human Evolution and Prehistory*, pp. 98–105, at p. 99.

34 Sean Carroll, 'Genetics and the Making of *Homo sapiens*' in Russell L. Chiocon and John G. Fleagle, eds., *The Human Evolution Source Book*, Second Edition, Upper Saddle River, NJ: Pearson/Prentice-Hall, 2006, pp. 628–9.

35 Philip Lieberman, 'The creative capacity of language, in what manner is it unique, and who had it?' in Richard K. Larson, Vivane Déprez and Hiroko Yamakido, eds., *The Evolution of Human Language: Biolinguistic Perspectives*, Cambridge: Cambridge University Press, 2010, pp. 163–77, at p. 166, p. 171.

36 Sean Carroll, 'Genetics and the Making of *Homo sapiens*', p. 629.

37 Fifteen individuals across three generations according to J. A. Hurst et al., 'An extended family with a dominantly inherited speech disorder', *Dev. Med. Child Neurol.* 32.4 (1990), pp. 352–5.

He reports how Wolfgang Enard's team at Leipzig's Institute for Evolutionary Anthropology found that chimpanzee, gorilla and monkey versions of FOXP2 were 'only two amino acids different from our own. They proposed that the two amino acid changes that led to the *Homo sapiens* version of the gene were critical to both speech and language.'[38]

There's more interesting recent genetic research underlying our speech capacities. Daniel Fairbanks reports the 2006 discovery at the University of California at Santa Cruz of 'dramatically accelerated change' in a recently discovered gene now named HAR1F. The human version of this gene 'is highly different from the chimpanzee version', where that difference is 15.3%, compared to a mere 2% difference between the various primate versions of the gene, with eighteen mutations specific to the human version of HAR1F. Fairbanks notes that we don't yet know how 'this small but uniquely human gene' can 'explain the substantially different advanced brain development in humans', but it's an interesting indication of a genetic underpinning to the obvious morphological and performative difference between human and primate brains.[39]

We'll conclude our few thoughts on the specific difference of the human brain with neurologist Richard Passingham's own conclusion to his *What is Special About the Human Brain?*, where he lists 'ten suggestions as to how one can account for the mental gap between humans and our nearest animal relatives', some of the most interesting of which are:

(i) The vast gap opened up by the difference in brain size between humans and chimpanzees ... there has been a tendency to downplay its effect. The difference in relative size between the human and chimpanzee brain is larger than the difference between the brains of the chimpanzee and shrew.

(ii) The expansion of the human prefrontal cortex correlates with an increase in the peak branching complexity and number of spines on pyramidal cells. This has important consequences for the integration of information.

(iii) The human brain has specialisations for speech and language ... Just as some birds are specialised as song learners, so humans are specialised as primates that speak.

(iv) Communication by speech depends on the ability to understand the effect of what one says on the thoughts of others ... The ability to do this depends on the ability to reflect on one's own thoughts ...

38 Mithen, *The Singing Neanderthals*, pp. 249–50.
39 Daniel J. Fairbanks, *Relics of Eden*, pp. 99–100.

(v) As the result of the development of language, the human neocortex has been fundamentally reorganised. In other primates, the two hemispheres duplicate functions ... In the human brain, the development of language has led to left-hemisphere specialisation for phonological, semantic and grammatical processing, and right-hemisphere specialisation for visuo-spatial processing. There is less duplication of function, and thus an increase of efficiency.[40]

3.2 Our vocal tract

Along with the inbuilt psycho-cultural time factor of the human body, there is, uniquely in humans, a vocal tract capable of producing the rapid, articulated sounds essential to speech. The vocal tract includes the larynx, which produces the sounds in its vocal folds or cords; the pharynx above it, where the sounds receive major modification; along with these are the wide throat, tongue, high palate and smaller tooth area, which are all unique to humans. Some paleontologists consider that the crania of late *Homo erectus* and archaic *Homo sapiens* indicate that they had a vocal tract similar to our own.[41] And Ian Tattersall, seeing language as emergent a quality as water is in relation to hydrogen and oxygen, suggests that the vocal tract developed long before it was used for modern speech.[42]

In all other animals, the larynx is positioned very high in the neck, severely limiting their sound repertoire – as is the case with the human infant until about eighteen months. Australopithecine crania, at the base of the skull, seem to indicate a larynx position similar to apes, while Philip Lieberman maintains that Neanderthals have a high larynx and would have been incapable of articulate speech, since they lacked the supralaryngeal vocal tract (SVT): 'The key is the length of the fossil's neck, which can in some cases be accurately estimated from preserved cervical vertebrae.' He continues:

Surprisingly, neck lengths that would support a fully human SVT are not apparent in the fossil record until ... some 50,000 years ago, when a blossoming of complex tools and art appears in the archaeological

---

40 Richard Passingham, *What is Special About the Human Brain?*, Oxford: Oxford University Press, 2008, pp. 203–4. Numeration added.

41 See J. T. Laitmann, 'Speech (Origins Of)', in *Encyclopedia of Human Evolution and Prehistory*, pp. 539–40.

42 Ian Tattersall, *The Monkey in the Mirror: Essays on the Science of What Makes Us Human*, New York: Harcourt, 2002, p. 164, p. 167.

record ... The presence of the human STV in the Upper Paleolithic supports this view.[43]

Cela-Conde and Ayala explain why the high larynx is required:

> The anatomical arrangement of the human supralaryngeal vocal tract allows a very particular modulation of air flowing out. Through the coordination of the tongue, palate, teeth, and lips, we are able to pronounce a multitude of vowels and consonants. But whereas vocalizing requires a larynx placed in a relatively low position, certain brain mechanisms are essential for sequencing the phonemes that make up words according to precise rules.[44]

Lieberman has noticed that human speech sounds require that the length of the kind of tube formed by the mouth be equivalent to that of the other tube descending behind the tongue. Thus only a relatively low larynx will allow human vocalisation.

Lieberman also links the FOXP2 gene with the vocal tract, noting that it's not a 'language' gene, but 'a regulatory gene that turns on other genes during embryonic development', involved in 'the development of lung tissue' and 'appears to have a role in facilitating learning and precise motor control in humans and other species'.[45]

In addition, the shape of human teeth, which with their great evenness in height and width are not comparable to ape or hominid teeth, means that they form 'an unbroken palisade around the oral cavity', a structural peculiarity essential for the production of spirant sounds such as f, v, s, sh, th, and others.[46]

Another hint about the unique requirements for human speech, this time however, in relation to hearing, emerges from a comment by Cartmill and Smith comparing the human to the Neanderthal ear:

43 Philip Lieberman, 'The creative capacity of language, in what manner is it unique, and who had it?', p. 162.

44 Camilo J. Cela-Conde and Francisco José Ayala, *Human Evolution: Trails From the Past*, New York: Oxford University Press, 2007, p. 345, p. 346.

45 Philip Lieberman, 'The creative capacity of language, in what manner is it unique, and who had it?', p. 171, p. 177; see also his *Uniquely Human: The Evolution of Speech, Thought, and Selfless Behaviour*, Cambridge, MA: Harvard University Press, 1991, pp. 63–9. However, Matt Cartmill and Fred H. Smith in *The Human Lineage* (Hoboken, NJ: Wiley-Blackwell, 2009, pp. 391–95), after a discussion of the literature, conclude that the fossil evidence claiming to rule out Neanderthal speech is inconclusive.

46 Eric Lenneberg, *Biological Foundations of Language*, New York: Wiley, 1967, p. 42.

The bony labyrinth of the Neandertal inner ear is also distinctive. The bony labyrinth comprises a system of cavities that enclose the semicircular canals and cochlea inside the petrosal (petrous) part of the temporal bone and provide a sort of loose-fitting external cast of those inner-ear structures ... High-resolution CT scans reveal that in Neanderthals the anterior and posterior semi-circular canals are relatively smaller than in modern humans ... these morphological differences appear early in ontogeny ... The labyrinth of the Erectines is more like that of moderns.[47]

Where does this range of preconscious factors fit into our general picture of emergent probability? Well, our genetic structure, particularly the hints we're getting of specific genes that are required for language, is linked with whatever grouping of brain functions (and by no means just a particular location in the brain) are required for what Luria called impressive and expressive speech; these are further linked with the vocal tract and auditory system. This would seem to amount to a flexible circle of recurring schemes that could be grouped under the principle of emergence. Rather clearly, none of these alone, nor all of them functioning together make sense without human language and symbolisation. So we'll be suggesting that it's precisely the functions of symbolisation and language (which can easily be seen as one) that are the principle of correspondence – what in Aristotelian language would be the form to the matter, the higher synthesis to the lower material manifold; a manifold, as we've said, that only makes sense insofar as it's the material basis of language, linguistic communication and symbolisation.

And the hints we've encountered regarding the erectine and Neanderthal brain and what look like the beginnings of that material basis for speech is a reminder of how this specifically human capacity fits into an evolutionary narrative. A fuller appreciation of unique human capacities would of course have to include human hands with their own uniquely flexible capacities and the human ear. But we can easily outline a flexible circle of capacities from australopithecines through early and late erectines, along with the Neanderthals and the closest pre-human hominids. This would include a multiple, interacting range of capacities: bipedalism, increased manual dexterity, higher sensory and perceptual skills, all correlating with larger

---

47 Cartmill and Smith, *The Human Lineage*, pp. 360–1.

brains and more efficient forms of communication, and widening areas of impact on the external world through improved toolmaking and basic hunting skills. Philip Lieberman puts it like this:

> Natural selection that retained small variations enhancing an individual's ability to execute the skilled manual maneuvers needed to make stone tools would place a higher adaptive value on variations that enhanced the brain-power necessary to coordinate one's hand, arm, and body, enabling one to strike a powerful, precise blow [in toolmaking]. It is impossible to state which came first, adaptations that enhanced brainpower or the finger anatomy, but the net process would characterise what engineers term 'positive feedback' – brain and body evolving together. However, we can infer the presence of the brain mechanisms that enabled these fossils to make stone tools from the fact that their anatomy is shaped to this end.[48]

But we must move on now to examine what these preconscious features are laying the foundations for, enabling the being Terrence Deacon calls 'the symbolic species' to cross the 'symbolic threshold' that only human beings have crossed.[49]

---

48 Philip Lieberman, *Eve Spoke: Human Language and Human Evolution*, New York: W. W. Norton, 1998, p. 76.

49 See the section 'The Symbolic Threshold' in Terrence Deacon, *The Symbolic Species: The Co-Evolution of Language and the Brain*, London: Allen Lane/Penguin Press, 1997, pp. 79–91.

Chapter Eight: Two more grace notes in the human sonata: (4) symbolisation and (5) language

Of course the three preconscious factors we've been discussing are by no means all of what constitutes human embodiedness, what Levinas calls our 'exteriority'. French paleoanthropologist André Leroi-Gourhan and others always emphasised the huge advance that bidepalism gave to all hominids, freeing their hands to make tools, and their mouths to communicate. So a careful consideration of the difference between human and, say, Neanderthal hands, would also be important. Still, the genetic basis of our belonging to a common human family, a body plan facilitating both the learning and teaching of human culture, and a brain and vocal tract enabling us both to listen to others speaking, and to speak ourselves, are surely among the most important material bases for our specific human existence.

We'll now touch on two of those four notes in the human sonata that are accepted by many anthropologists and philosophers as most clearly and consciously marking us out as human – we can think of them as chords rather than single notes, since of course they can only be 'heard' because of the earlier three notes playing in the background. These two new grace notes, not found in any pre-human hominid, are symbolisation and language.

We're obviously rooted in the material universe, from the Big Bang through the 'cooking' of the heavy elements essential to life in the incredible heat of dying stars, to the first bacteria on Earth with the DNA structure common to all living things – deep indeed is the well of the past. Yet the nearer we get to our specifically human capacities, the less they seem merely continuous with what's gone before. Charles Darwin said in his *Descent of Man* that 'every one who admits the general principle of evolution, must see that the general powers of the higher animals, which are the same in kind with those of mankind, though so different in degree, are capable of advancement'.[50] Not everyone would agree. For example, philosopher Anthony O'Hear summarises the argument of his book on the limits of the evolutionary paradigm:

> The aim of this book is to examine the extent to which evolutionary accounts of human experience are adequate. In examining this question,

---

50 Charles Darwin, *The Descent of Man and Selection in Relation to Sex*, Vol. II, London: John Murray, 1871, p. 390.

I focus on human knowledge, on morality, and on our sense of beauty. I suggest that our current activities in each area certainly derive in important ways from our biological nature, but that once having emerged they cannot usefully be analysed in biological or evolutionary terms.[51]

Or as Leroi-Gourhan put it, '*Homo sapiens* represents the last known stage of hominid evolution and also the first in which the constraints of zoological evolution had been overcome and left immeasurably far behind.'[52] Since paleoanthropologists generally accept that symbolisation is one of the strongest evidences for the first appearance of humans like ourselves, we'll discuss that evidence first, before touching on the debate about the origins of language.

1. Symbols

1.1 Their cognitive and ontological meaning

DeSalle and Tattersall speak of the 'profound cognitive chasm' that separates us from 'the rest of nature', and continue: 'Yet it was not that long ago, it seems, that our immediate ancestors were non-symbolic animals themselves.'[53] But what's so special about the use of symbols, and why are they so often taken by paleoanthropologists as indicating the emergence of something completely new in terms of evolution?[54] To answer that question as briefly as possible, I'll just draw on Lonergan and Jonas for the cognitive or epistemological aspect of symbols and Voegelin for what symbols are actually of, their ontological aspect – not that these aspects are separated by either Lonergan or Voegelin.

---

51 Anthony O'Hear, *Beyond Evolution: Human Nature and the Limits of Evolutionary Explanation*, Oxford: Oxford University Press, 1997, p. vii.

52 André Leroi-Gourhan, *Gesture and Speech*, tr. Anna Bostock-Berger, Cambridge, MA: MIT Press, 1993, p. 20.

53 Rob DeSalle and Ian Tattersall, *Human Origins: What Bones and Genomes Tell Us About Ourselves*, College Station, TX: Texas A & M University Press, 2008, p. 191.

54 There are various approaches to symbols, among them psychoanalytic (and Leroi-Gourhan and his student, Annette Laming-Emperaire, may have been influenced by Sigmund Freud in their gender-based interpretation of cave paintings). In fact, the various interpretations of symbols, Freudian, Marxist (especially Ernst Bloch's future-oriented interpretation of symbols in *Das Prinzip Hoffnung*), Claude Lévi-Strauss' structural, Gilbert Durand's physiological, David Lewis-Williams' neurological, Paul Ricoeur's cognitive and volitional, the history of religions approach of Mircea Eliade, and the cognitive, linguistic, mythic and artistic treatments by Ernst Cassirer and Susan K. Langer, surely all must be considered in an integral understanding of symbol. Bernard Lonergan has a brief discussion of symbols in his *Method in Theology*, London: Darton, Longman & Todd, 1972, pp. 64–73.

While Lonergan in *Method in Theology* speaks of symbol as 'a real or imaginary object that evokes a feeling or is evoked by a feeling', I'll use his wider notion of 'instrumental acts of meaning', which are expressions that 'externalize and exhibit for interpretation by others' a range of acts of affection, understanding, judgement and decision, that is, all 'acts of meaning of the subject'.[55] What Lonergan says about symbol in this wider sense is complemented by Jonas's meditation on the kind of representational visual symbols we know as cave paintings.

Jonas puts himself in the position of an explorer from another planet seeking evidence of a specifically human presence. He rules out tools, hearths and tombs, focusing on images. Entering a cave, he notices lines or shapes on its walls which must have been produced artificially and suggest a likeness to some living forms of types seen outside the cave. He takes these as sufficient evidence of man. Why? Because animal artefacts are directly connected with biological ends, such as nutrition, reproduction and hibernation, while a visual representation does not change the animal's condition and must have another purpose.

He points out that these paintings are intentionally produced likenesses, where the likeness is incomplete. The incompleteness involves selective omission and inclusion, focusing on two dimensions only, to the point of the symbols being positively different or the creation of shapes never actually seen. And this increasing freedom moves from representation of actually seen animals to symbols expressing greater and greater freedom from such representation in terms of imaginary beasts or abstract symbolisms. Jonas' discussion of what we could call the epistemology of these early symbols is surprisingly Aristotelian in flavour:

> The principle here involved on the part of the subject is the mental separation of form from matter. It is this that makes possible the vicarious presence of the physically absent at once with the self-effacement of the physically present. Here we have a specifically human fact, and the reason why we can expect neither making nor understanding of images from animals. The animal deals with the present object itself.[56]

---

55 Lonergan, *Method in Theology*, p. 64, pp. 74–5; see also his *Insight*, ch. XVII, §3.3 on 'Levels and Sequences of Expression.'

56 Hans Jonas, 'Image-Making and the Freedom of Man,' in his *The Phenomenon of Life: Towards a Philosophical Biology*, New York: Delta, 1968, pp. 157–82, at pp. 161–2, p. 167.

These remarks recall Tattersall's comment on the 'symbol-free traces left by the Neanderthals' in contrast with the Cro-Magnons who lived at the same time and in the same region as some Neanderthals, and what he's written about the 34,000-year-old horse figurine from Vogelherd, near Ulm: since it is unlike 'the chunky, pony-like horses' of the time, 'it is an elegant evocation of the abstract essence of the horse'. Central to the wider meaning of symbol is that such instrumental acts are available to the senses as 'manifestations of meaning through gestures, speech and writing'.[57] As instrumental expressions or carriers of meaning they cannot be understood except in terms of the experience of reality they intend to convey.

This understanding of symbols comes across in the title Voegelin gave to his 1965 Ingersoll Lecture at Harvard, 'Immortality: Experience and Symbol'. There he focused on experiences of transcendence whose symbolisation still occurs in space and time, so that both symbol and symboliser in some way participate in the transcendent reality experienced and symbolised:

> *Immortality* is one of the language symbols engendered by a class of experiences to which we refer as the varieties of religious experience ... The symbols in question intend to convey a truth experienced. Regarding this intent, however, they suffer from a peculiar disability. For, in the first place, the symbols are not concepts referring to objects existing in time and space but carriers of a truth about nonexistent reality.[58] Moreover, the mode of nonexistence pertains also to the experience itself, inasmuch as it is nothing but a consciousness of participation in nonexistent reality. As Heb 11:1 has it: 'Faith is the substance of things hoped for, and the evidence of things unseen.' And finally, the same mode also pertains to the meaning of the symbols, as they convey no other truth than that of the engendering consciousness.

The symbols are never to be separated from the experience of the reality they intend to symbolise, with a resulting requirement from whoever wishes to interpret them:

---

57 Ian Tattersall, *The World from Beginnings to 4000BCE* (New York: Oxford University Press, 2008), p. 98, p. 99.

58 Voegelin has probably taken 'nonexistent' from F. M. Cornford's translation of Plato's *Parmenides* (160e) in his *Plato and Parmenides* (London: Routledge, 1977), where Plato is trying to convey an existence that's not the same as perceptible existence but beyond it. Voegelin doesn't want to use the more obvious 'transcendent' since the lecture goes on to interpret ancient Egyptian texts belonging to an epoch where the later differentiation between what's within this world and what's beyond it hadn't yet been made.

We have spoken, therefore, of a truth experienced rather than of a truth attaching to the symbols. As a consequence, when the experience engendering the symbols ceases to be a presence located in the man who has it, the reality from which the symbols derive their meaning has disappeared. The symbols in the sense of a spoken or written word, it is true, are left as traces in the world of sense perception, but their meaning can be understood only if they evoke, and through evocation reconstitute, the engendering reality in the listener or reader. The symbols exist in the world, but their truth belongs to the nonexistent experience which by their means articulates itself.[59]

So, only if they evoke an equivalent experience in the interpreter can the symbols be adequately understood or 'reconstituted'.

1.2 The degradation of the symbol

Unfortunately, Voegelin went on, such meditative effort by the interpreter is highly demanding. And what Mircea Eliade called 'the degradation of the symbol', where its meaning is lost by its would-be interpreter, can afflict paleoanthropologists and archaeologists as much as anyone else. Barry Cooper quotes what seems a reductionist understanding of human symbolisation by anthropologist David Lewis-Williams:

By 2010, 'modern research on the ways in which the human brain functions to produce the complex experiences we call consciousness provides a foundation for an understanding of religion that unites its social, psychological and aetiological elements'. Various 'mental states', he said, are both physiological and neurological and 'as integral to the human body as, say, the digestive system'. Indeed, these 'mental states' are simply 'the product of the human brain'.[60]

---

59 Eric Voegelin, 'Immortality: Experience and Symbol' in *Published Essays 1966–1985*, Ellis Sandoz, ed., Baton Rouge: Louisiana State University Press, 1990, pp. 52–94, at p. 52. Marie König's, *Am Anfang der Kultur: Die Zeichensprache des frühen Menschen* (Berlin: Mann, 1972), along with Mircea Eliade's work on early human cultures, is perhaps the best extended reflection on paleoliothic experience of reality in terms of what Voegelin calls 'the truth of the cosmos'.

60 Barry Cooper, 'The First Mystics? Some Recent Accounts of Neolithic Shamanism' (Paper presented to the Eric Voegelin Society, APSA Annual Meeting, Washington, DC, September, 2010). Cooper is quoting David Lewis-Williams, *Conceiving God: The Cognitive Origin and Evolution of Religion*, London: Thames & Hudson, 2010, p. 137, p. 158. See also David Lewis-Williams, 'Neuropsychology and Upper Palaeolithic Art: Observations on the Progress of Altered States of Consciousness', *Cambridge Archaeological Journal* 14:1 (2004), pp. 107–11. (Both the Cooper and the Lewis-Williams articles are available on the Internet.) Cooper details the use of this neurological interpretation of ancient symbolisations in Lewis-Williams' *The Mind in the Cave: Consciousness and the Origins of Art* (London: Thames & Hudson, 2002, pp. 151–4) and his *Conceiving God*, pp. 144–8.

And Steven Mithen criticises the interpretation of prehistoric rock art in terms of neurologically caused images formed by people in altered states of consciousness to explain 'almost any occurrence of spirals, abstracts or imaginary beasts in Upper Paleolithic art and later prehistoric rock art'. To use this for an explanation 'for extremely complex designs in prehistoric art simply enables archaeologists to avoid asking questions about the human imagination, creative thought and the symbolism of prehistoric art'. He uses the term 'cognitive archaeology' for studies of past societies focusing on the 'processes of human thought and symbolic behaviour'.[61] When Mithen diagnoses some archaeologists as avoiding 'asking questions', he's not denying the relevance of neurological or psychological studies. It's just that they hardly touch on why in fact human beings, in Voegelin's phrase, 'engender' such symbols.

A current attempt at answering that 'why?' which Lewis-Williams shares with Jean Clottes is shamanism. While criticising the inadequacy of structuralist interpretations of Paleolithic symbols, Clottes goes on to say that:

> The hypothesis that best accounts for the facts … is that Paleolithic people had a shamanic religion and created their art within its framework. First suggested by Mircea Eliade … this hypothesis has been developed … by the work of David Lewis-Williams … The basic belief of shamanic religions is that certain persons, particularly the shamans, can send the souls out of their bodies in order to travel to another world where they directly communicate with the powerful supernatural forces that rule matters relating to everyday life, such as hunting, illness, weather and human relationships. They are then transformed into a spirit, often taking on the appearance of an animal. Shamans thus play the part of mediators between the world of the living and the world of the spirits.[62]

However, simply invoking shamanism doesn't get over the problem of evoking the experience that gives rise to the symbols, and in fact may distance the paleoanthropologist from the task of interpretation. There are two problems here: firstly, the methodological question of how one interprets an experience without having within oneself a experience

---

61 Steven Mithen, ed., *Creativity in Human Evolution and Prehistory*, London: Routledge, 1998, pp. 7–8.

62 Jean Clottes, *Cave Art*, London: Phaidon Press, 2010, pp. 24–5.

equivalent to, say, the Cro-Magnons' self-interpretation of their own quest for attunement with the ground of existence expressed by their 'art'.[63] Secondly, that specific methodologies have already been developed for interpreting archaic experiences, for example by Mircea Eliade, Henri Frankfort, Marie König and Eric Voegelin. As a result of what seems his inadvertence to both of these issues, even as fine a paleoanthropologist as Clottes can write that 'the geometric signs in the painted caves ... are devoid of any real meaning. Though their makers must have used them as symbols, the absence of any syntax means that these signs constituted neither a language nor a script. The ideas and perhaps the stories and religious practices behind them will always elude us.'[64]

1.3 Mircea Eliade and Marie König on Paleolithic symbols

But that would be like rejecting, say, a Constantin Brancusi sculpture or a Barnett Newman painting on the basis that it was non-representational, when in fact both artists were trying to convey the essence beyond the appearance. In earlier chapters we've mentioned the philosophic and revelational breakthroughs into the discovery of human nature and also some mythic and mytho-speculative approaches towards the natural world. In fact, the study of mythic experience is by no means concluded with Eliade's notion of shamanism – his wonderful *Patterns in Comparative Religion* is an enormously useful heuristic for approaching any archaic symbolisation, as I found out for myself when using it to try and decipher a range of Neolithic symbols at Newgrange and Knowth.[65] In that first

---

63 In the early nineteenth century, Friedrich Schlegel had already criticised the 'axiom of familiarity' – in our context here, that 'familiarity' would be in terms currently taken for granted in an academic culture which seems to avoid taking the issue of transcendent orientation personally. Lonergan calls it the 'principle of the empty head' – the presumption that the interpreter doesn't need such prior experience in order to understand equivalent experiences. The issue is discussed in Richard E. Palmer, *Hermeneutics: Interpretation Theory in Schleiermacher, Dilthey, Heidegger, and Gadamer*, Evanston, IL: Northwestern University Press, 1969. The key point is what Lonergan in *Method in Theology* calls 'the presence or absence of intellectual, of moral, of religious conversion' in interpreters, giving rise to 'opposed horizons', p. 247; see also Chapter 7 on 'Interpretation' in ibid., and *Insight*, pp. 562–94.

64 Clottes, *Cave Art*, p. 25.

65 Mircea Eliade, *Patterns in Comparative Religion*, London: Sheed & Ward, 1971. But see also his *Images et Symbols* (Paris: Gallimard,1952); *The Two and the One* (London, Harvill Press,1965); *Le sacre et le profane* (Paris: Gallimard,1965); *The Quest: History and Meaning in Religion* (Chicago: Chicago University Press, 1969); *Yoga: Immortality and Freedom* (Princeton: Princeton University Press, 1973; *A History of Religious Ideas, Vol. I: From the Stone Age to the Eleusinian Mysteries* (London: Collins,1979); *The Myth of the Eternal Return: Cosmos and History* (London: Arkana,1989); *Shamanism: Archaic Techniques of Ecstasy* (New York: Pantheon, 1964). Brendan Purcell, 'In Search of Newgrange: Long Night's Journey into Day' in *The Irish Mind: Exploring Intellectual Traditions*, Richard Kearney, ed., (Dublin: Wolfhound Press, 1985), pp. 39–55.

attempt at understanding the very kind of abstract and geometric signs Clottes regards as 'devoid of meaning', I also drew on Marie König's major interpretative work of interpretation of Paleolithic symbolisations, *At the Beginning of Culture: The Sign-Language of Early Humans*, along with her more popular *Our Past is Older*.[66]

No doubt there are limitations in both their interpretations, but Voegelin's remark regarding interpretation of Heraclitus' so-called 'fragments' seems apposite: 'As a matter of principle, whenever I must decide between two interpretations which both can be supported philologically I prefer the profounder to the flatter meaning.'[67] And it's this presumption that Paleolithic humans were no less human than ourselves that both Eliade and König fiercely defended. Cooper notes how 'König's 1954 book, *Das Weltbild des Eiszeitlichen Menschen*, examined the Lascaux images in terms of lunar symbols rather than hunting magic', and expanded this interpretation in her *Sign-Language of Early Humans*. He continues:

> Instead of considering the images as magic formulae or as expressions of totemic, primitive, or even shamanic experiences, König argued 'that the development of religion began with a primordial image of the world' and that these primordial images could be detected in these early 'documents'. That is, by looking at the cave images and rock-shelter petroglyphs in terms of the most basic orientation, one discovers in them the expression of the fundamental experiences of reality.[68]

1.4 Voegelin's 'depth grammar' of human symbolisation

However, along with Eliade's and König's detailed effort at interpreting Stone Age symbols, there's been Voegelin's attempt at developing a framework philosophically rich enough to envisage not only the later differentiated civilisations, but the earlier ones that understood themselves in terms of the myth of the cosmos. He defined myth simply as 'that body of symbols that had in fact been found adequate by the members of such civilisations for expressing their experiences of the cosmos in which they lived'.[69] The dynamic quest underlying all attempts at orienting ourselves in existence – mythic, philosophic, revelational,

---

66 Marie König, *Am Anfang der Kultur; Unsere Vergangenheit ist älter*, Frankfurt: Krüger, 1980. On Marie König, and her later collaboration with Eric Voegelin, see Cooper, 'The First Mystics?' pp. 11–20.

67 Eric Voegelin, *The World of the Polis*, Baton Rouge: Louisiana State University Press, 1964, p. 228n.

68 Cooper, 'The First Mystics?', pp. 12–13.

69 Eric Voegelin, *The Drama of Humanity and Other Miscellaneous Papers, 1939–1985*, William Petropulos and Gilbert Weiss, eds., Columbia: University of Missouri Press, 2004, p. 189.

mystical, ideological and contemporary – was formulated by Voegelin in the introduction to *Order and History*. Voegelin wrote to his editor that:

> I have hit on something like a theory of relativity for the field of symbolic forms, and the discovery of the theoretical formula that will cover all forms to whatever civilisation they belong has made possible an abbreviation of the whole presentation ...[70]

Although this was after he'd written the first three volumes of *Order and History*, he'd already arrived at a basis for a general understanding of humanity in the first volume in the series, *Israel and Revelation*, which I believe provides as useful a framework as is available for the interpretation of Paleolithic symbols. Here's a summary of what he wrote there:

(a) **The four basic partners in human existence:** Every human being experiences himself or herself in a world with others, so that some kind of human society is always a given. Of course we experience ourselves as in something like a natural world as well. Along with that are whatever words or symbols we use to convey our experience of what we consider to be the source or sources of our existence in society and nature – whether in terms of gods, or God. Voegelin sees these four areas – God and man, world and society – as constituting the basic community of being where all human beings live or have lived. We'll mention three of the factors that he suggests are typical features in the process of symbolisation.

(b) **Participation in existence:** Voegelin calls our sharing existence with the Earth, sun, moon and stars, with every human being, with God or the gods, 'participation'. In the myth, this participation is so strong that the differences in the partners – man and the gods, the world and society – are overwhelmed by the experience of belonging to the same reality. In philosophy and revelation, each of the partners becomes differentiated or symbolically and intellectually clarified, which was one of the huge advances made by what Bergson had called the 'opening of the soul'.

(c) **Lasting and passing:** In 1909 Arnold van Gennep wrote *The Rites of Passage*, and the title gives a clue to one of the most basic changes in existence that human beings undergo, from life to death, with many rituals celebrating the hope or belief that humans can arrive at a form of existence which is beyond death. I'm not presuming here that a differentiated notion of what it is to be human has been reached – as we've been saying, within

---

70 Quoted in 'Editors' Introduction' to Eric Voegelin, *What is History? and Other Late Unpublished Writings*, Paul Caringella and Thomas Hollweck, eds., Columbia: University of Missouri Press, 2000, p. xiii.

the experience of the myth, it hasn't. Yet humans have often experienced mere mortality as meaningless in itself. So how then can we somehow outlast the obvious passing away we must one day undergo? Within the experience of the myth, Voegelin writes that humans are conscious of being outlasted by the societies they belong to, that their society is outlasted by the natural world around it, and that the world is perhaps outlasted by the gods. It's something that seems to mark the emergence of human beings on this earth as distinct from animals: that human beings from their very beginning have refused to accept death as the last word.

Far from seeking to avoid the reality of death, our earliest human brothers and sisters sought to integrate its unavoidability within a deeper experience, which we'll now explore.

(d) **Attunement:** What were those early humans seeking with their elaborate burial rituals? I've said they didn't accept death as final, but what did they believe awaited them after death? For example, both the builders of Ireland's Newgrange mound 5200 years ago and the Romans several millennia later, believed in what the Romans called *sol invictus*, the unconquered sun. Those Irish Neolithic builders of 3200BC – and also, if recent reports that Stonehenge's focus was on the same midwinter solstice as Newgrange, Stonehenge's builders of 2200BC believed that they participated in the sun's own outlasting of its apparent death at the end of the solar year on 21 December. Mircea Eliade explains the importance of stone as the medium with which early humans wanted to be associated:

> ... the hardness, ruggedness and permanence of matter was in itself a hierophany [manifestation of the sacred] in the religious consciousness of the primitive. And nothing was more direct and autonomous in the completeness of its strength, nothing more noble or more awe-inspiring, than a majestic rock, or a boldly-standing block of granite. Above all, stone *is*. It always remains itself. Rock shows him something that transcends the precariousness of his humanity. Stone [at burial grounds] was a protection against animals and robbers; and, above all, against 'death,' for, as stone was incorruptible, the soul of the dead man must continue to exist as itself.[71]

Voegelin speaks of this dramatic attempt at sharing in the lastingness of the sun through and beyond its own passing, in terms of 'attunement',

---

71 Mircea Eliade, *Patterns in Comparative Religion*, London: Sheed & Ward, 1971, p. 216f.

with the use of stone as another expression of the longing for attunement to what seemed the more lasting elements than our own mortal remains. Long before the inner nature of what makes a human being human had been discovered, our earlier brothers and sisters could still desire – and undertake concrete action to fulfil that desire – to overcome death by being attuned to those realities they could see outlasted them: their society, the earth and the heavens, and the gods or God.

(e) **From compact to differentiated symbolisations:** Another feature is 'the attempt at making the essentially unknowable order of being intelligible as far as possible through the creation of symbols, which interpret the unknown by analogy with the really, or supposedly, known. The first period of human history – which we now know is by far the longer – is where human existence in society is symbolised 'as an analogue of the cosmos and its order.'[72] The *Tao Te Ching*, or *Book of the Way of Virtue*, offers us a good example of how the quest for attunement to the four more lasting components in being could be symbolised in an expansion of the basic symbol of the way or path of the sun – an equivalent play of symbols can be found in the two parts of Psalm 19. In this densely concise Chinese conception of a hierarchy of order, the lower participants achieve a greater lastingness by attuning themselves to the higher, moving upwards from the King (*Wang*) to the Earth (*Ti*) to the Heaven (*Tien*) and finally to the Way (*Tao*) of Heaven:

> Therefore,
> Tao is great,
> Heaven is great,
> Earth is great,
> And the King is also great.
> Within the borders [of the universe],
> Are four great things,
> And the King is one of them.
> The King takes for law the Earth,
> The Earth takes for law the Heaven,
> The Heaven takes for law the Tao,
> The Tao takes for law its own weave.[73]

---

72 Eric Voegelin, *Israel and Revelation*, Baton Rouge: Louisiana State University Press, 1964, pp. 1–5.

73 *Tao Te Ching*, XXV, following Peter-Joachim Opitz's translation in *Lao-tzu: Die Ordnungs-spekulation im Tao-tê-ching*, Munich: Paul List Verlag, 1967, pp. 115–16, and his argument for that translation, pp. 130–1. Opitz sees the Chinese experience as a unique form of 'theophysicism' that doesn't quite go beyond a divinised cosmic reality.

For Voegelin, 'the history of symbolisation is a progression from compact to differentiated experiences and symbols', where the more differentiated forms are to be found in the culture grounded in philosophy and revelation. In these later forms, 'the symbolisation of social order is by analogy with the order of a human existence that is well attuned to being'.[74] Our first chapter focused on some of the differentiated philosophical and revelational symbols of the human.

(f) **The constancy of human nature as quest for mystery:** We've already touched on this issue in chapter one, but it becomes sharper here. That is: how do we interpret anything as human without having a good idea of what being human involves? And how can there be any connection – which all paleoanthropologists without exception feel and write about – between those earliest symbolisers and ourselves unless we share not only in the similar brain-structure David Lewis-Williams' acknowledges, but in a similar experience of wondering exploration of reality? Further on in *Israel and Revelation*, Voegelin affirms that through the various forms in which human beings have experienced and expressed their existence – in terms of myth, philosophy, revelation, or the various post-ideological recoveries of the full range of human existence that had been eclipsed or obliterated by ideologies – human nature remains constant.[75]

Later, Voegelin drew on the more explicit formulations of philosophers who arrived long after the first humans, such as Aristotle's defining of human nature as a quest for truth. Voegelin suggested that every human being and society is faced with similar basic questions about existence, and he capitalised these questions as the Question in relation to Mystery.[76] For Voegelin, Aristotle grasped what was in common to the two cultural forms he was acquainted with, myth and philosophy – both being symbolisations of the quest for the ground.

This was the key principle of equivalence, that is to say, 'the recognisable identity of the reality experienced and symbolised on the various levels of differentiation'. Equivalence refers to the fact that in historical reality, each person and each society's quest for the ground is their exegesis of their experience of participation in that ground – whether in Paleolithic Europe or contemporary Western culture. However compactly and incompletely

---

74 Voegelin, *Israel and Revelation*, p. 5.

75 Ibid., p. 60.

76 See Eric Voegelin, 'Question and Mystery' in *The Ecumenic Age*, Baton Rouge: Louisiana University Press, 1974, pp. 316–30.

they may articulate that experience, and however much in need of further revision their experience and symbolisation of reality may be, it has its dignity as a real person's or society's image of the mystery of reality surrounding and embracing them. And it is because of this dignity that a fundamental interpretative principle for Voegelin could be stated like this:

> ... *the reality of experience is self-interpretive.* The men who have the experiences express themselves through symbols; and the symbols are the key to understanding the experience expressed.[77]

1.5 Lascaux as symbolising the drama of cosmic destruction and renewal

Without that constancy of a common human nature, there could not be a drama of humanity in history, nor, I suggest, would all those books with titles varying from *Human Origins* to *The Human Revolution* to *The Human Lineage* have been written. And that common humanity is always engaged in a search for what Voegelin calls the order of existence. We've already spoken of how humans have sought attunement to the realities greater than themselves. Voegelin uses the word 'order' to explain this:

> The reality of order is not my discovery. I am speaking of the order in reality discovered by mankind as far back as we have any written records, and now ever farther back as we become familiar with the symbols in monuments discovered by archaeologists as far back as the Paleolithicum. By order is meant the structure of reality as experienced as well as the attunement of man to an order that is not of his making – i.e., the cosmic order.[78]

How might we understand Lascaux in terms of a symbolisation of the Cro-Magnons' search for attunement to the everlasting order of the cosmos, so that they transformed the cave-system into a *cosmion*, or reflection of the unity of the cosmos in which they desired intensely to participate?

What we're trying to do in interpreting the 16,000-year-old symbols is to keep in mind Voegelin's admonition that 'their meaning can be understood only if they evoke, and through evocation reconstitute, the engendering reality in the listener or reader'. Take, for example, Norbert Aujoulat's

---

77 Eric Voegelin, *Autobiographical Reflections*, Ellis Sandoz, ed., Baton Rouge: Louisiana State University Press, 1989, p. 108, p. 80.

78 Ibid., p. 75.

comments on the underlying themes he's discovered in the cave-paintings. In his study, *Lascaux: Movement, Space and Time*, Aujoulat brings out how the original Cro-Magnons transformed the various branches of the cave into a splendid Paleolithic cathedral with 1,963 representations, including 915 animal figures and 434 abstract signs. This sacralised space has its own levels of mystery, with the relatively modest apse having 1,073 figures, so that it is 'a sanctuary at the heart of a sanctuary'.

There's also the sacralisation of time, with the various seasons represented by different animals – horses for spring, aurochs (the far larger ancestor of modern cattle) for summer, and stags for autumn – each are represented as they appear during those seasons, which also correspond to that species' mating season.[79] To complete Lascaux's attunement to the recurring order of the seasons, we can bring in Marie König's understanding of the grounding story of Lascaux, which is based on the winter season.[80]

The composition in the six-metres-deep shaft at Lascaux portrays a life and death struggle between two figures. On the right is a bison, whose head is turning back, either to attack with its horns, or to gaze at its terrible stomach wound, from which its entrails are hanging out. The wound seems to have been inflicted by a long spear lying across its body over the wound. Facing the bison on its left is a figure of what could be a man with a bird's head, a long narrow rectangle for a body, four fingers on each hand, and an erect phallus. Since the bison's horns are aimed menacingly in his direction, and the male figure is falling backwards, it looks as if he's been gored by the bison. Underneath the man is a complete painting of a bird, facing left, away from the scene of conflict. The bird is perched on a vertical line. What the bird is looking towards is the partly completed figure of a powerful rhinoceros, striding further leftwards. Three vertical sets of two dots are painted, in a horizontal direction, two sets under the rhinoceros' tail and one in the direction of the man.

Marie König has found bull, mammoth and other horns frequently used to represent moon-phases, and is inclined to see the dying bison as symbolising the waning moon. Since the earth is often represented by symbolisations of its four directions – four lines, squares, and so on – she interprets the rectangular-bodied male figure with its four-fingered hands as symbolising the dying earth. The long vertical line the bird is perched

79 Norbert Aujoulat, *Lascaux: Movement, Space and Time*, New York: Harry N. Abrams, 2005, p. 257, p. 262.

80 König, *Unsere Vergangenheit ist älter*, pp. 106–11.

on could represent the sun, moving in a line from east to west across the sky, while bird symbols often represent messengers from the heavens. The rhinoceros, the only one depicted in Lascaux, by contrast with the two dying figures, might represent vigorous new life, while the six dots could indicate the six moons/months of the New Year.

The choice of the natural shaft could indicate its functioning as a symbol of the underworld, contrasting with the painted cave ceilings possibly representing the heavens. Basically, if we combine Aujoulat's and König's interpretations, it's possible to understand Lascaux's attunement to the unchanging rhythms of the four seasons. The dramatic focus for this cosmic attunement – if we can take the shaft as the spiritual centre of the entire 'cathedral' complex – is on the cosmic struggle between death and life in the depths of winter, with the hope of cosmic rebirth symbolised by the rhinoceros closely linked to the six moons of the new year. Far from being meaningless, the close proximity of 'abstract' geometrical symbols with representational ones could imply a 'theological' explanation included with the representational symbols.

At the same time, care must be taken in ascribing the character of symbol. So when Francesco d'Errico et al. offer a 100,000-years-ago Blombos Cave 'engraving of parallel or joining lines' as an example of early symbolisation, the illustration seems not unlike the doodling of a pre-linguistic human infant, and far below the level of the hundreds of thousands of symbols from around 10,000 years ago scattered throughout the Valcamonica region in Northern Italy, or the some million images in, say, the Burrup rock inscriptions of Western Australia.[81] The fact that d'Errico et al. are prepared to accept the Berekhat Ram 'figurine' of some 230,000 years ago as a 'reliable example' of 'ancient ... symbolic expression' raises questions about their standards for what constitutes a symbol.[82]

1.6 Human burial rituals as expressing desire to overcome death in new life

Voegelin has written about the experienced tension between the lasting and the passing, and perhaps nothing more dramatically expresses the spiritual

---

81 See Emmanuel Anati, *I camuni: alle radici della civiltà europea* (Milan: Jaca book, 1982) and Mike Donaldson, *Burrup Rock Art: Ancient Aboriginal rock art of Burrup Peninsula and Dampier Archipelago* (Mount Lawley, WA: Wildrocks Publications, 2009).

82 Francesco d'Errico et al., 'From the origin of language to the diversification of languages: What can archaeology and palaeoanthropology say?' in Francesco d'Errico and Jean-Marie Hombert, eds., *Becoming Eloquent: Advances in the Emergence of Language, Human Cognition, and Modern Cultures*, Amsterdam: John Benjamins, 2009, pp. 13–68, at pp. 27–9.

calibre of the earliest humans than their refusal to accept that death is final. David Walsh makes two remarks that are helpful here regarding human burial:

> Heidegger shows that the teleological perspective that we apply to animals cannot be the perspective of the animals themselves for they do not 'adapt' to their environment but are rather captured by it.

> In a certain sense, Heidegger points out, only men can die for it is only they that can be aware of death as the end of their existence.[83]

What marks out archaic human burials as human is the occurrence of body-adornment or grave goods along with them, implying a burial ritual, sometimes providing the deceased with the means to negotiate the spirit world. Most paleoanthropologists contrast this practice with that of the non-human hominids, who in certain cases may inter their dead. But the lack of goods to accompany them for use in the next life is perhaps a sufficient indication of the difference between pre-*Homo sapiens* interments and human burials. We've already mentioned the Lake Mungo burials of around 41,000 years ago, known as such because of the ritual by which those bodies were committed to the earth. In 1956, nearly 200 kilometres north east of Moscow, an astonishingly rich burial dating back to 28,000-years-ago was discovered in Sungir. Tattersall's description is hard to improve on:

> The most striking example of Cro-Magnon burial comes from the twenty-eight-thousand-year-old site of Sungir, in Russia, where two young individuals and a sixty-year-old male (no previous kind of human had ever survived to such an age) were interred with an astonishing material richness. Each of the deceased was dressed in clothing onto which more than three thousand ivory beads had been sewn; and experiments have shown that each bead had taken an hour to make. They also wore carved pendants, bracelets, and shell necklaces. The juveniles, buried head to head, were flanked by two mammoth tusks over two yards long ...

And he appends an insightful interpretation of those burials:

---

83 David Walsh, *The Modern Philosophical Revolution: The Luminosity of Existence*, New York: Cambridge University Press, 2008, p. 261, p. 256.

These Cro-Magnon burials tell us a great deal about the people who carried them out ... In all human societies known to practice it, burial of the dead with grave goods (and the ritual invariably associated with placing such objects in the grave) indicates a belief in an afterlife: the goods are there because they will be useful to the deceased in the future ... The knowledge of inevitable death and spiritual awareness are closely linked, and in Cro-Magnon burial there is abundant inferential evidence for both. It is here that we have the most ancient incontrovertible evidence for the existence of religious experience.[84]

1.7 Earliest human symbols

The earliest 'symbols' known at present are those at Pinnacle Point in South Africa from 164,000 years ago. They were developed by people who'd mastered the calendar so they could regularly harvest seasonally occurring seafood, and who left evidence of the use of ochre pigments to decorate themselves, implying symbolic behaviour.[85] However it's at Blombos Cave nearby, with archaeological remains dated about 75,000 years ago, where – along with 2,000 pieces of blood-red ochre brought there for body pigment, and shell beads showing evidence of ochre on the bodies of those who wore them – two engraved slabs of ochre were found. Christopher Henshilwood, who led the team, discovered two slabs of ochre there in 1999 and 2000 and describes them as having been 'repeatedly scraped or rubbed to form a flat facet'. Following which:

> ... an abstract design was ... deliberately engraved on that surface. On one piece the design consists of a serious of oblique lines in one direction and a lesser number of lines that cross over these ... On another piece a

84 Ian Tattersall, *Becoming Human: Evolution and Human Uniqueness*, New York: Harcourt Brace, 1998, pp. 10–11. (Pictures of the wonderful Sungir burials and artefacts are easily available on the Internet.) At least by Neolithic times, an entire culture would seem to have been centred on a necropolis – as in the Irish Boyne Valley complex of enormous passage graves, Newgrange, Knowth and Dowth, oriented to three, and perhaps even all four of the major solar positions at mid-winter, mid-summer, and the spring and autumn equinoxes. There's also the Sligo configuration of the megalithic triple necropolises of Carrowmore, Carrowkeel, both oriented towards the huge passage grave on top of Knocknarea, constituting an impressive landscape dominated by these memorials of death with their built-in positional attunements to hoped-for cosmic regeneration. See Stefan Bergh, *Landscape of the Monuments: A Study of the Passage Tombs in the Cúil Irra region, Co. Sligo, Ireland*, Stockholm: Riksantikvarieämbetet Arkeologiska Undersökningar, 1995; Eliade, *Patterns in Comparative Religion*, p. 414ff., and König, *Am Anfang der Kultur*, p. 38.

85 Curtis W. Marean et al. 'Early human use of marine resources and pigment in South Africa during the Middle Pleistocene', *Nature* 449, 18 October 2007, pp. 905–8; 'Earliest Evidence Of Modern Humans Detected', *Science Daily*, 17 October 2007.

distinct crosshatched pattern was engraved and, as if to emphasise the design, three further lines were engraved across the top, through the middle and at the bottom of the pattern ... These designs were engraved with deliberate symbolic intention and had meaning for the maker and very likely for a wider social grouping ... The Blombos ochre engravings are perhaps two of the earliest known examples of abstract designs that represent symbolic systems stored outside the human brain.[86]

In terms of later symbolisations, it's not too difficult to decipher a possible meaning for the two roughly rectangular-shaped ochre 'boxes' just a few centimetres long. The rectangular shape could stand for the world in its various dimensions. Marie König comments on cube-shaped stones from Mas d'Azil in the Pyrenees around 10,000 years ago as possibly symbolising the world too. The prominent lozenge-like shapes divided into triangles across the face of both pieces reminded me of the so-called 'false lintel' in the 5,200-year-old Newgrange mound in Co. Meath, Ireland, where that rectangular surface features eight such triangles within bisected lozenges. There, the four-sided figures may, following König, be interpreted as representing the world or the earth or space, with the triangles symbolising the three principal moon phases, and more generically the heavens or time. König speaks of seven as the building block of culture, in the sense that it brings together Earth and Heaven symbolisation.[87]

Whatever the meaning of those ochre blocks, we can presume they carried the myths of those who created them, where like every myth they're an expression of the human desire to understand our place within the cosmos. Mithen sees Blombos Cave as:

> ... the most important currently known archaeological site for understanding the origin of modern thought and behaviour – and, by implication, language ... The patterns ... are sufficiently ordered to rule out any risk that they arose by chance. Moreover, as the same design

---

86 Christopher Henshilwood, 'Modern humans and symbolic behaviour: Evidence from Blombos Cave, South Africa' in Geoffrey Blundell, ed., *Origins: The Story of the Emergence of Humans and Humanity in Africa,* Cape Town: Double Storey Books, 2006, pp. 78–85, at p. 82. (Again, there are excellent, fully illustrated Internet sites both on Pinnacle Point and Blombos.)

87 On the cube as a possible representation of the Whole, see König, *Am Anfang der Kultur,* pp. 143–5; on 4-symbols (Earth) + 3-symbols (Heavens) as the building block of culture, pp. 240–8. For Eliade on squares as Earth symbols, see his *Patterns in Comparative Religion,* p. 374.

is repeated on two separate artefacts, the impression is of a symbolic code.[88]

Colin Renfrew sees the blocks as marking 'the first step of what Merlin Donald has termed "external symbolic storage"', while Tattersall writes of the 'new behavioural potential' revealed by Blombos and other early symbolisations.[89] And it's precisely this 'new potential' in symbolisations from the Paleolithic to the Neolithic that poses, I'd suggest, an entirely new question to paleoanthropologists – not only of an unprecedented cognitive nature, but as evidence of an ontological participation in what Voegelin called 'non-existent reality', and which we can call transcendence.[90] We can now move on to the very specific kind of symbolisation Lonergan calls 'linguistic meaning'.[91]

2. Language

André Leroi-Gourhan doesn't sees the animal figures in Paleolithic cave paintings as merely representations – they're 'symbols, not copies'. And he supports the prevailing paleoanthropological presupposition that the use of geometrical symbols also implies linguistic capacity. For him, the 'best proof – were it still necessary to supply one – of the existence of language in the Upper Paleolithic, is precisely that words had to exist for the figures to be intelligible'.[92]

Language, as a form of symbolisation, isn't intrinsically related to any particular reality – it's the strange in-between means by which we have access to that reality underlying every other reality we call 'existence' or 'being'. Drawing on Heidegger, David Walsh writes of language and its intrinsic relationality towards being:

> It is for this reason that man plays a special role in relation to Being. He is the 'shepherd' or 'guardian' of Being because it is only in him

---

88 Steven Mithen, *The Singing Neanderthals: The Origins of Music, Language, Mind and Body*, London: Weidenfeld and Nicolson, 2005, pp. 250–1.

89 Colin Renfrew, 'Situating the creative explosion: universal or local?' in Colin Renfrew and Iain Morley, eds., *Becoming Human: Innovation in Prehistoric Material and Spiritual Culture*, New York: Cambridge University Press, 2009, pp. 74–92, at p. 77. Tattersall, *The World from Beginnings to 4000BCE*, p. 100.

90 See p. 210 n. 58 above for why he chose this word.

91 Lonergan, *Method in Theology*, p. 70.

92 Leroi-Gourhan, *Gesture and Speech*, p. 383.

that Being is disclosed and nowhere else in existence. All other beings provide a mute testament to Being, that by which they are disclosed, but only man can give voice to that awareness through language. This special relationship, however, is not made possible because man has the capacity for articulation, rather he has the capacity for speaking because of his relationship with Being.[93]

In other words, it's not 'language' we have to understand as something on its own, but rather as the means by which being, reality, reveals itself to us. So any attempt to reduce language to communication at an animal level would miss out on its primary task, which is to literally put words on our experience of being. We've already mentioned Parmenides, who gave us our earliest reflections on what he called *Is*. If you want to go further back, there's the Book of Exodus, where Moses experiences God's self-revelation through the words 'I am Who Am', signifying profoundly personal subsistent existence – an even greater shock to the system than Parmenides' experience of *Is*.

Heidegger speaks of language as 'the house of being', that is, that our experience of being somehow becomes present and remains present to us through language. This philosophical awareness, that our capacity for language derives from our relationship with Being, is the perspective we're taking here. And it's perhaps in implicit awareness of this that paleoanthropologists discussing the origins of language often arrive at the more general question of human origins too. So here we'll touch on some approaches to the origins of language, then have a look at language as a carrier of meaning, before getting to grips with the strange infinity that's central to language. We'll conclude with a few words on the difference between language and animal communication.

2.1 Theories about the origins of language
Perhaps Voegelin's comment on the impossibility of accounting completely for new emergences in reality is worth attending to here: 'the epiphany of structures in reality – be they atoms, molecules, genes, biological species, races, human consciousness, or language – is a mystery inaccessible to

---

93 David Walsh, 'The Turn toward Existence as Existence in the Turn', in *Philosophy, Literature and Politics: Essays Honoring Ellis Sandoz*, Charles R. Embry and Barry Cooper, eds., Colombia, MO: University of Missouri Press, 2006, p. 14. Walsh discusses this more fully in his chapter on Heidegger in *The Modern Philosophical Revolution: The Luminosity of Existence*, New York: Cambridge University Press, 2008.

explanation'.[94] What he's referring to is the ontological dimension of the emergence of language, which we'll see in our remaining chapters is tied up with the emergence of the human mystery itself. This in no way means that scientific inquiry into what led up to the origination of language is impossible. It's just that the 'that' of all emergences remains a philosophical rather than a natural scientific question.

However, it does no harm to remember that indications that brain areas like Broca and Wernicke, along with certain aspects of our vocal tract, are shared with, for example, primates or late hominids, only deepen the mystery of how human language actually occurs, since these other species clearly don't have language. Bingham notes that 'earlier theories of language evolution have been notably sterile', and refers to his discussion of 'elements in the evolutionary logic of animal and human communication and of its underlying neurobiology'. He continues:

These considerations plainly suggest that human language involves *no qualitatively new* elements or features … there is no reason whatever to suppose that any qualitatively new neural/cognitive capability was necessary to initiate the evolution of human language … [95]

Maybe the difference between Voegelin and Bingham isn't as enormous as it seems, since most attempts to account for the origin of language use a notion common to evolutionary discussions, that is, 'exaptation', or the taking up of an earlier capacity to be used in a later, differing context.[96] One approach has been to suggest that 'the rather late and

---

94 Eric Voegelin, *In Search of Order*, Baton Rouge: Louisiana State University Press, 1985, p. 17. Linguistic scholar Rudolf P. Botha quotes from a perhaps unlikely source which appears to back up Voegelin's agnosticism here: 'Stephen Jay Gould "evolved" from a scholar subscribing to a particular view of how language emerged … into one considering questions about the origins of language to be "intractable": " … we know that many kinds of evolutionary events leave no empirical record – and that we therefore cannot formulate scientific questions about them. (For example, I doubt that we will be able to resolve the origins of human language, unless written expressions occurred far earlier than current belief and evidence now indicate.)"' See Botha's *Unravelling the Evolution of Language*, Amsterdam: Elsevier, 2003, p. 203 n. 5.

95 Paul M. Bingham, 'On the evolution of language: implications of a new and general theory of human origins, properties, and history' in Richard K. Larson, Vivane Déprez and Hiroko Yamakido, eds., *The Evolution of Human Language: Biolinguistic Perspectives*, Cambridge: Cambridge University Press, 2010, pp. 211–24, at p. 223 (Bingham's emphasis).

96 Stephen Jay Gould uses it for 'structures coopted for utility from different sources of origin … and not directly built as adaptations for their current function', in his *The Structure of Evolutionary Theory* (Cambridge, MA: Harvard University Press, 2002), p. 43. Exaptation as used here only refers to the hypothetical use by our linguistic capacity of pre-linguistic capacities developed for non-linguistic purposes. However, exaptation is also used in linguistics for morphological shifts within specific languages.

rather rapid emergence of symbolic thought instead of the gradual long-term honing of the human capacity' could have been triggered by 'the invention of language, combined with a brain and vocal tract that were already enabled for it. Language, after all, is the ultimate symbolic activity … '[97]

But how did language come about? Philip Lieberman compares Jean Piaget's sensori-motor stage to the 'reptilian' motor basis of language in human beings, placing that development within the evolutionary history of the hominids. He points out that neurologist Karl Lashley had already observed what he's also proposing, 'that the neural mechanisms that confer human syntactic ability evolved from ones originally adapted for motor control'. Not unlike Luria, Lieberman acknowledges the importance of the Broca-Wernicke areas, including the modern left/right brain approaches, but also holds that while specific functions may be performed in particular parts of the brain, 'these operations must be integrated into a *network* … so a particular aspect of behaviour usually involves activity in neuroanatomical structures distributed throughout the brain'. He writes of 'motor equivalence, where we can achieve the same goal using different muscles or body parts: for example, writing your name with a pen between your teeth instead of your fingers'. For Lieberman, the production of human speech is a supreme example of motor equivalence.[98]

Another approach towards explaining the origin of language is that of Merlin Donald. He writes of three major cognitive transitions, each including a different system of memory representation: mimetic (or imitative) skill, language, and what he calls 'the externalisation of memory' through external symbols. In an approach not that different from Lieberman's, he writes of the relationship between primate motor-imitative capacities and the later human acquisition of language. For Donald, evolution requires that, while human language is unique, it can't be completely unique; rather, it must show some continuity with previous preadaptation: first, for what he calls protolanguage, and later, specifically human language. And his theory 'posits a series of radical evolutionary changes – the punctuations, as it were, in punctuated equilibrium – rather than a continuous or unitary process'.[99]

---

97 DeSalle and Tattersall, *Human Origins: What Bones and Genomes Tell Us About Ourselves*, p. 200.

98 Philip Lieberman, *Human Language and Our Reptilian Brain: The Subcortical Bases of Speech, Syntax and Thought*, Cambridge MA: Harvard University Press, 2000, p. 1, p. 4, p. 39.

99 Merlin Donald, 'Précis of Origins of the Modern Mind: Three stages in the evolution of culture and cognition', *Behaviour and Brain Sciences*, BABC, 16 (1993), pp. 737–91, at p. 737.

Steven Mithen in *The Singing Neanderthals: The Origins of Music, Language, Mind and Body* develops Robin Dunbar's notion that 'language went through a musical phase during the course of its evolution', along with Elizabeth Tolbert's view on 'the relationship of music to symbolism and bodily movement', where music 'must have coevolved with language'.[100]

Derek Bickerton's view of the origins of human language accepts that apes, pre-human hominids and human infants have what he calls 'protolanguage', a rudimentary use of occasional symbols, but without the syntax – or rules governing the formation of a grammatically correct sentence – essential to human language. He defends the original notion of a 'human revolution' against the gradualist critique of McBrearty and Brooks, in the sense of a rapid evolutionary development:

In the absence of any other convincing cause for this development, we may assume that it resulted from the emergence of syntax, an agency just as powerful in its manipulation of thought as in its manipulation of words. We may think of ourselves as 'the Symbolic Species' ... but 'the Syntactic Species' perhaps more accurately distinguishes us from all the species that preceded us.[101]

It can be that the gradualist approach conceals a desire to diminish the sheer uniqueness of an emergence. This seems to be the case with Steven Pinker's chapter, 'The Big Bang', in his *Language Instinct*, where he attempts to explain language in terms of standard Darwinian gradualism, asking:

... is [language] any more extraordinary than coral that build islands, earthworms that shape the landscape by building soil, or the photosynthesising bacteria that first released corrosive oxygen into the atmosphere ...? Why should talking humans be considered any weirder than elephants, penguins ... giant sequoias ...?[102]

100 Steven Mithen, *The Singing Neanderthals: The Origins of Music, Language, Mind and Body*, London: Weidenfeld & Nicolson, 2005, p. 5.

101 Derek Bickerton, 'Did Syntax Trigger the Human Revolution?' in Paul Mellars, Katie Boyle, Ofer Bar-Yosef and Chris Stringer, eds., *Rethinking the Human Revolution*, Cambridge: Short Run Press, 2007, pp. 99–105, at p. 104.

102 Steven Pinker, *The Language Instinct: The New Science of Language and Mind*, London: Penguin, 2000, p. 406

Pinker seems to be emptying human language of what makes it different from zoological adaptations. Chris Knight asks what Darwinian selection pressures could have given rise to the kind of mind human beings have, and queries the apparent simplification of the origin of language to something coming about incrementally:

> If these were easy questions, the origins of language – recently dubbed the 'hardest problem in science' – might long ago have been solved. Chomsky has condemned previous attempts to apply Darwinism as 'a complete waste of time, because language is based on an entirely different principle than any animal communication system.' The origin of language, insists Chomsky, was 'effectively instantaneous, in a single individual, who was instantly endowed with intellectual capacities far superior to those of others, transmitted to offspring and coming to predominate ... ' The new faculty was so 'perfect' as to suggest the work of a 'divine architect'.[103]

Tattersall has a similar view of language as an 'exaptation' or what Lonergan calls 'sublation' of the neural substrate which itself arose due to the physical reorganisation of the hominid body.[104] For him, language 'is virtually synonymous with our symbolic reasoning ability, 'invented by creatures that obviously *already* possessed the potential to acquire it'. He sees 'the acquisition of symbolic cognition' as an '*emergent*' ability, 'rather than a simple extrapolation of pre-existing trends – for although our vaunted mental capacities are clearly based on earlier historical acquisitions, they were not *predicted* by them'. So that the notion of 'the human capacity as an accretionary capability acquired in a series of sequential steps is misleading'.[105]

---

103 Chris Knight, 'Language, ochre, and the rule of law' in Rudolf Botha and Chris Knight, eds., *The Cradle of Language*, Oxford: Oxford University Press, 2009, pp. 281–303, at p. 282. Tattersall also stresses that language is a sudden emergence: see his 'Language and the Origin of Symbolic Thought' in Sophie De Beaune, Frederick L. Coolidge and Thomas Wynn, eds., *Cognitive Archaeology and Human Evolution,* New York: Cambridge University Press, 2009, pp. 114–15.

104 Lonergan uses the term 'sublation' to mean 'that what sublates goes beyond what is sublated, introduces something new and distinct ... yet far from interfering with the sublated or destroying it, on the contrary, needs it, includes it, preserves all its proper features and properties, and carries them forward to a fuller realisation within a richer context.' See his *Method in Theology*, p. 241. Sublation characterises the relationship between higher and lower levels in terms of correspondence and emergence.

105 Tattersall, 'Language and the Origin of Symbolic Thought', p. 115 (Tattersall's emphasis).

All that was said earlier about emergence and correspondence seems extremely well instantiated here. Whatever the hypothetical nature of the various neural, gestural-mimetic – and especially for Robin Dunbar – social presuppositions for language, they're as good an example as one could hope for of what the Scholastics called *materia apta* or a suitable material basis provided for the new 'form' of language which would sublate it. Massimo Piattelli-Palmarini has a fierce, and I think justified, criticism of any attempt at erecting the pre-linguistic material bases of language, whether Lieberman's motor-control, Bickerton's protolanguage, or Pinker's communicative-needs, into adequate explanations of language itself.[106]

And, incidentally, given the incredibly long time-scale in which hominids physically almost identical to ourselves finally emerged without any evidence of symbolic or linguistic capacities, the hope of inventing computers which can actually think – as distinct from perform calculations – on the basis of language, seems slight. At present it's not even remotely feasible to carry out the 'wet' or biological engineering that would result even in something like a bacterial cell. But to produce something of the complexity of a Neanderthal brain seems well beyond the bounds of possibility. Yet in all the nearly 400,000 years Neanderthals existed, even such a brain couldn't get as far as a two-and-a-half-year old human child who's made the breakthrough into language.

2.2 Language as carrier of meaning
Lonergan has developed the notion of language as an instrumental act of meaning. For him, the 'Sources of meaning are all conscious acts and all intended contents ... Instrumental acts of meaning are expressions' which 'externalise and exhibit for interpretation by others' the range of acts of meaning: experiences, understandings, judgements and decisions. It's precisely this aspect of language as a carrier of meaning which isn't always sufficiently adverted to in treatments of language and its origins. As such, language can only be understood in relation to the being that's intended in every act of meaning.[107] Probably the most graphic example of someone's coming to awareness of this remains Helen Keller, who had the

---

106 Massimo Piattelli-Palmarini, 'What is language, that it may have evolved, and what is evolution, that it may apply to language' in Larson et al., eds., *The Evolution of Human Language*, pp. 148–62.

107 Lonergan, *Method in Theology*, p. 73, p. 74. For his more detailed discussions, *Insight*, pp. 553–8 on 'Truth and Expression' and his essay, 'Dimensions of Meaning' in *Collection*, New York: Herder & Herder, 1967, pp. 252–67.

use of language as a young child, then lost it due to illness, rediscovering it again when she was about nine. She describes her moment of discovery:

> We [herself and her teacher, Anne Sullivan] walked down the path to the well-house … Someone was drawing water and my teacher placed my hand under the spout. As the cool stream gushed over one hand she spelled into the other the word water, first slowly, then rapidly. I stood still, my whole attention fixed on the motions of her fingers. Suddenly I felt a misty consciousness as of something forgotten – a thrill of returning thought; and somehow the mystery of language was revealed to me. I knew then that 'w-a-t-e-r' meant the wonderful cool something that was flowing over my hand. That living word awakened my soul, gave it light, hope, joy, set it free! … I left the well-house eager to learn. Everything had a name, and each name gave birth to a new thought.[108]

What Helen Keller's experience highlights is how our knowledge of the world depends on language and how our language shapes that knowledge. Taking it as an example, Lonergan discusses this intrinsic relationship between language and insight:

> In Helen Keller's emotion and interest one can surmise the reason why ancient civilisations prized names so highly … Prizing names is prizing the human achievement of bringing conscious intentionality into sharp focus and, thereby, setting about the double task of both ordering one's world and orientating oneself within it … So it is that conscious intentionality develops in and is moulded by its mother tongue … The action is reciprocal. Not only does language mould developing consciousness but also it structures the world about the subject. Spatial adverbs and adjectives relate places to the place of the speaker. The tenses of verbs relate times to his present. [Grammatical] Moods correspond to his intention to wish, or exhort, or command

---

108 Helen Keller, *The Story of My Life*, New York: Airmont Books, 1965, p. 21. St Petersburg linguist Vadim B. Kasevich speaks of how what he calls the 'Big Bang' in the child's linguistic development 'comes about with the child's discovery of the independence of the sign from the thing it stands for; at a still later stage, the child makes another important discovery, namely that the sound he or she utters to form the signs are also relatively independent.' See his 'On Universal Grammar and Cognitive Primitives' in Bernard H. Bichakjian, Tatiana Chernigovskaya, Adam Kendon, Anke Möller, eds., *Becoming Loquens: More Studies in Language Origins*, Peter Lang: Frankfurt am Main, 2000, pp. 273–92, at p. 289.

or declare. Voices make verbs now active and now passive and, at the same time, shift subjects to objects and objects to subjects.[109]

Elsewhere he discusses this intrinsic relationship between language and insight:

> ... coming to know is a process; it advances by stages in which inquiry yields insights only to give rise to further questions that lead to further insights and still further questions. At each stage of the process it is helpful to fix what has been reached and to formulate in some fashion what remains to be sought. So expression enters into the very process of learning and the attainment of knowledge tends to coincide with the attainment of the ability to express it. The interpenetration of knowledge and expression implies a solidarity, almost a fusion, of the development of knowledge and the development of language ... Were words only related to other words, their meaning would never be more than verbal. But the mere fact that a word can occur in a sentence that is affirmed endows it with a basic reference to the objective of intelligent and rational consciousness, to being. (*Insight*, 554–5)

We've already considered the trio of preconscious yet profoundly human characteristics. The language-oriented properties of the human brain (along with the whole vocal tract) underpin this capacity we have of recognising and assigning words (and other 'carriers of meaning' as Lonergan calls them) for various realities. Yet the material underpinning does not itself trigger the use of language – that requires human subjects operating in an interpersonal context. And we cited Bickerton's discussion of the 'language' of Genie, clearly indicating a definite cutting-off period for language acquisition, indicating a symphonic interaction between the child's neural-psychological readiness and his or her milieu of competent speakers.[110]

Australian paleoanthropologists Iain Davidson and William Noble are in agreement about the intrinsic relation between language, meaning, being, and the community of persons essential to its functioning. The authors equate human mindedness with language: 'This view of mind recognises its existence through its expression, and its inseparability from

---

109 Lonergan, *Method in Theology*, pp. 70–1.

110 Derek Bickerton, *Language and Species*, Chicago: University of Chicago Press, 1990, p. 118.

the embodied and contextualised agent of that expression.'[111] But they're emphatic that that mindedness must be a shared one. They write that 'Depiction, particularly in the making of images to resemble things, can only have emerged prehistorically in communities with shared systems of meanings ...' Regarding the imagery of the earliest humans, they agree that the knowledge encoded in cave art was not intrinsic to the object but part of a system of communication which included such objects.

For example, the Venus figurines, with no faces or feet, accompanied by no figures of males, distributed in a 3,000km-long area from the Atlantic to the Don in a swathe 500km wide, from 25,000–23,000 years ago, require 'a shared understanding across the region. We cannot detect any sort of convention, with or without exceptions, earlier than the Upper Palaeolithic'. The authors insist that it would be 'misleading to talk of culture for any hominids before fully modern humans'. For them, 'the late emergence of reflective language accounts for the nature of the break in the rate of change in artefact technology, ritual and burial, regional variation in style, social differentiation, the emergence of hunting and gathering and of agricultural systems, and the migratory capacity of humans in colonising Australia [where they had to build boats to cross at least 89kms of water] and the new world'.[112] Again, while the 'human revolution' has had to be backdated, the fact of that human revolution seems undeniable.

2.3 Language and infinity

Expanding what has become a celebrated paper he co-wrote with fellow linguists Noam Chomsky and Marc Hauser, W. Tecumseh Fitch develops their discussion of what's called 'recursion' in linguistics.[113] He notes that recursion is 'a core operation, appearing in many guises in syntax and semantics, for which there is little evidence in animal communication'. For example, to a sentence like 'John is angry' there can be added: 'Mary says that' and it will still make sense. A mathematical example of recursion would be the series of numbers, which can continue on to infinity. Fitch remarks:

---

111 Iain Davidson & William Noble, *Human Evolution, Language and Mind: A Psychological and Archaeological Inquiry*, Cambridge: Cambridge University Press, 1996, p. 226.

112 Iain Davidson and William Noble, 'The Archaeology of Perception: Traces of Depiction and Language', *Current Anthropology*, 30 (1989) 2, pp. 125–37, at p. 136, p. 137.

113 'The faculty of language: what it is, who has it, and how did it evolve', reprinted in Larson et al. *The Evolution of Human Language*, pp. 14–42. The book is based on a conference focusing on the original essay.

Recursive embedding of phrases within phrases is an important tool allowing language users to express *any* concept that can be conceived, to whatever degree of accuracy or abstraction is needed. The achievements of human science, philosophy, literature, law, and of culture in general depend, centrally, upon there being no limit to how specific (or how general) the referents of our linguistic utterances can be.

Linguistic recursion is how 'our finite brains achieve this unfettered potential', and Fitch regards it as 'at the heart of one of the characteristics that makes language so precious and irreplaceable for our species: what Humboldt aptly termed 'the infinite use of finite means'.[114] On the quasi-infinity of language, Chomsky goes so far as to remark that 'If a divine architect were faced with the problem of designing something to satisfy these conditions, would actual human language be one of the candidates, or close to it?'[115]

2.4 Animal communication yes, language no

If we can assert both that language is a capacity with an infinite possibility of expression and that this capacity requires a context of self-aware persons in relation, then we can see why non-human animals (including the pre-human hominids) could not speak.

Novelist and linguist Walker Percy's interest in the meaning of human language was sharpened because one of his children was born completely deaf, and his *Message in a Bottle* contains his attempts at developing a philosophy of language.[116] He calls human linguistic communication 'triadic', since in addition to the subject-object relationship that can be found in animal communication, human language is characterised by the intrinsic self-awareness of the speaker or listener. It's this third quality that lifts it above and beyond the non-self-conscious 'dyadic' interaction typical of animal communication. Here's a comment of his we've already cited:

Thus there is a sense in which it can be said that, given two mammals extraordinarily similar in organic structure and genetic code, and given

---

114 W. Tecumseh Fitch, 'Three meanings of "recursion": key distinctions for biolinguistics' in Larson et al., *The Evolution of Human Language*, pp. 73–90, at p. 74, pp. 89–90.

115 Noam Chomsky, *Powers and Prospects: Reflections on Human Nature and Social Order*, London: Pluto Press, 1996, pp. 29–30.

116 Walker Percy, *The Message in the Bottle*, New York: Farrar, Straus & Giroux, 1975.

that one species has made the breakthrough into triadic behavior and the other has not, there is, semiotically speaking, more difference between the two than there is between the dyadic animal and the planet Saturn.[117]

What Percy is saying is that, for example, a Sumatran orang-utan is closer to Saturn's beautiful rings than you or I am to an orang-utan, because the difference between what makes a human being human and the orang-utan is greater than the difference between the Sumatran animal and the physical being of Saturn. While these may seem to be fighting words, almost completely against the run of play in our culture, they wouldn't seem to be so for many linguists.

For example, Bickerton notes that 'naive continuists' had high hopes 'that a bridge between primate communication and human language might actually be forged'. Rather, the most striking difference between ape and human vocabularies is that no ape has acquired more than a few hundred elements, compared to the many thousands of words in the average human's vocabulary. With unimportant exceptions, apes never get beyond lexical items – no ape has acquired syntax, that is, has grasped the rules for constructing sentences in ordinary languages.

He gives samples of ape and under-two human 'language', suggesting that human under-twos don't need language-ability to imitate adults, but share a power of association with non-human species; similarly their verbal usage indicates they have semantics (that is they can respond to individual words) rather than syntax. One difference for Bickerton is that while apes 'talk' only about objects they want, or actions they want to do, young children enjoy 'categorisation for categorisation's sake'.[118]

Bickerton distinguishes language, which can store information and carry out thought processes, from communication – for him, animals have communication systems but not language. For example, body language can 'convey information about states, conditions, or feelings, but cannot convey much in the way of factual information about objective features of the world'. Similarly, animal 'languages' indicate how the animal feels, knows or wants within a narrow range of topics,

117 Walker Percy, *Lost in the Cosmos: The Last Self-Help Book*, New York: Washington Square Press, 1984, 97.

118 Derek Bickerton, *Language and Species*, Chicago: University of Chicago Press, 1990, p. 106, pp. 108–9, pp. 112–4.

to do with willingness to mate, to defend territory, aggression, or appeasement directed towards a conspecific, maintenance of contact with others in one's group, alarm calls to warn of approach of predators, and so on. This doesn't in any way take from the enormous complexity of field-specific information, like the bee dances which tell other bees in which direction nectar is to be found. But, Bickerton points out, 'language ... knows no limitations of space or time', unlike animal communication, which always has to do with localised states, particular feelings – what Dennett calls 'first order intentionality'.

For Bickerton, 'Language is an open system, while animal communication systems are closed.' Animals have only a small number of units in their communication systems. He cites a tabulation which shows fish ranging from 10–26; birds from 15–28; mammals from 16–37 units in their communication systems. Not only animals – Bickerton makes similar remarks of the pre-human hominids. He writes, for example, about the Chinese Zhoukoudian limestone caverns, occupied 500,000–200,000 years ago:

> Yet during that entire period, not a single structural improvement was made to those caves; the tiny handful of artifacts produced by its inhabitants underwent no change or improvement ... Instead of a steady ascent toward modern, complex culture, we find, for 95 percent of the period, a monotonous, almost flat line.

He goes on to say that 'there is no trace of *invention* by Neanderthals, and unlike modern humans they did not follow game herds out onto the steppes of southern Russia'.[119]

Dan Sperber and Gloria Origgi point out that 'animal communication codes ... are typically tiny, without syntax, and highly stable within a given species. The great majority of them involve no learning (and when learning is involved, as in the case of songbirds, it usually concerns only a single signal that serves to distinguish local populations of the same species ... '[120]

---

119 Derek Bickerton, *Language and Human Behaviour*, Seattle: University of Washington Press, 1996, p. 12, p. 16, p. 17, pp. 46–8 (Bickerton's emphasis).

120 Dan Sperber and Gloria Origgi, 'A pragmatic perspective on the evolution of language' in Larson et al., *The Evolution of Human Language*, pp. 124–31, at p. 128. See also the classic essay by H. S. Terrace, L. A. Petitto, R. J. Sanders, T. G. Berer, 'Can an Ape Create a Sentence?', *Science*, 23 November 1979, pp. 891–902; and Clive D. L. Wynne, *Do Animals Think?*, Princeton: Princeton University Press, 2004.

We can conclude this section with Vadim B. Kasevich on the closed nature of animal communication. He writes that the difference between animal and human communication systems is that the animal communication system 'is a closed set of tightly-knit monolith-like signals where any given signal ... is a manifestation of its unique meaning and vice versa, while the latter, that is, human language, is an open-ended system'.[121] However, this apparently negative characterisation of animal existence is in no way to deny the specific quality of animal psychology which has been touched on by texts like Huizinga's *Homo Ludens*, which discuss the superabundance of animal play. This goes far beyond Darwinian notions of mere survival, not to mention the sheer joy so many of us feel when observing animal behaviour or the huge following for animal programmes and films – animals both domestic and wild somehow give us contact with another Eden, another window into transcendence.

3. A modern reminder of the richness contained in symbol

Although the ancient cave paintings can't properly be described as art in the modern sense – where art is differentiated from economics, politics, religion, and so on – that didn't prevent paleoanthropologist Jean Clottes entitling his recent huge collection, *Cave Art*. Which makes all the more apposite these words by Solzhenitsyn, a writer for whom the word takes on the role of linguistic symbol, because analysis of symbol and language can easily lead us to forget their primary role, which is to lead us beyond ourselves. Here is what Solzhenitsyn has to say, in words that I think catch as well as any the sheer mysteriousness and non-graspability of symbol and language at their deepest:

Archaeologists have yet to discover an early stage of human existence when we possessed no art. In the twilight preceding the dawn of mankind we received it from hands which we did not have a chance to see clearly ... Not everything can be named. Some things draw us beyond words. Art can warm even a chilled and sunless soul to an exalted spiritual experience. Through art we occasionally receive – indistinctly, briefly – revelations the likes of which cannot be achieved by rational thought ...

---

121 Kasevich, 'On Universal Grammar and Cognitive Primitives' in Bichakjian et al, eds., *Becoming Loquens*, p. 289.

There is, however, a particular feature in the very essence of beauty – a characteristic trait of art itself: The persuasiveness of a true work of art is completely irrefutable; it prevails even over a resisting heart.

A true work of art carries its verification within itself: artificial and forced concepts do not survive their trial by images; both image and concept crumble and turn out feeble, pale, and unconvincing. However, works which have drawn on the truth and which have presented it to us in concentrated and vibrant form seize us, attract us to themselves powerfully, and no one ever – even centuries later – will step forward to deny them.

So perhaps the old trinity of Truth, Goodness and Beauty is not simply the decorous and antiquated formula it seemed to us at the time of our self-confident, materialistic youth. If the tops of these three trees do converge, as thinkers used to claim, and if the all too obvious and the overly straight sprouts of Truth and Goodness have been crushed, cut down, or not permitted to grow – then perhaps the whimsical, unpredictable, and ever surprising shoots of Beauty will force their way through and soar up *to that very spot*, thereby fulfilling the task of all three. And then no slip of the tongue but a prophecy would be contained in Dostoevsky's words: 'Beauty will save the world'.[122]

Obviously, as we've seen, this profound meaning for symbol isn't freighted with significance only for the individual, but for an entire group or people or culture as a representation 'in concentrated and vibrant form' of an entire *cosmion*, or indeed of 'the new heavens and the new earth' of Jewish and Christian hope.

In an earlier chapter, we spoke of having to move from a lower to a higher science when confronted with data that systematically diverged from the data of the lower science, in this case, either zoology, primatology, or the study of the pre-human hominids. It seems hard to avoid the conclusion on the basis of the data on human symbolisation and language, that we have phenomena here that many paleoanthropologists and linguists are clear can't be explained by those lower sciences. Now we'll turn to the final two factors we're considering, along with symbolisation and language, as constituting what makes us human: understanding and freedom.

---

122 Aleksandr Solzhenitsyn, 'Nobel Lecture', Alexis Klimoff, tr., in *The Solzhenitsyn Reader: New and Essential Writings*, Edward E. Ericson, Jr. and Daniel J. Mahoney, eds., Wilmington, DE: ISI Books, 2006, pp. 512–26, at p. 514.

Chapter Nine: The last chords in the human sonata: (6) understanding and (7) freedom

Arthur Sullivan's famous setting of 'The Lost Chord' has a certain resonance here: there's no shortage of paleoanthropological studies of symbolisation and language, but – apart from the recent topic of cognitive archaeology – there hasn't been anything like the same interest in what traditionally were regarded as the most human of characteristics, understanding and freedom. All the more reason for us to at least gently play these last grace notes in the human sonata now.

1. Understanding

> With me, the horrid doubt always arises whether the convictions of man's mind, which has been developed from the mind of the lower animals, are of any value or at all trustworthy. Would any one trust in the convictions of a monkey's mind, if there are any convictions in such a mind? (Charles Darwin, in a Letter to W. Graham, 3 July 1881)[123]

At least Darwin was aware of the problem: that if human knowledge is simply one among the many expressions of zoological evolution, it can hardly claim to be knowledge in any meaningful sense at all. We've suggested that symbolisation and language can themselves only be understood as the means by which we articulate our experience of reality. But it's only when we arrive at a discussion of the specific kind of knowing we call understanding that the relationship between understanding and the levels of our existence we share in some sense with animals becomes explicit. We'll begin this section by continuing the dialogue with paleoanthropologists we've been conducting in these final chapters, with a look at the criteria two cognitive archaeologists lay down for human knowing. Then we'll see if approaches presenting themselves as in continuity with Darwin's notion that our minds have 'developed from the mind of the lower animals' live up to the requirements of cognitive archaeology, and suggest that a classic philosophic approach towards understanding would measure up better. Our thoughts on understanding will conclude with its most important actualisation, in terms of our living the truth, and with an issue that can't easily be handled by a Darwinian approach to cognition, the problem of the lie in communication.

---

123 This much-quoted but irresistible comment is found in *The Life and Letters of Charles Darwin*, Francis Darwin, eds. New York: Basic Books, 1959, p. 285.

1.1 A 'strict standard for recognising human cognition in prehistory'

Having pointed out the need for a strict standard for recognising human cognition, Thomas Wynn and Frederick Coolidge suggest that paleoanthropologists must first know what features of cognitive archaeology are in fact modern.[124] Secondly they must identify acts and sets of acts which have been enabled by that ability, and thirdly, define a set of criteria or abilities by which those acts can be identified.[125] Such a strict standard will have two components: (i) cognitive validity – the evidence must require the abilities attributed to it, and (ii) archaeological validity – the archaeological evidence must itself be credible.

Regarding tools made by modern humans, they discuss the qualities they should exhibit. In terms of being maintainable, they should be relatively easily made and maintained; in terms of reliability, they should be designed to reduce the possibility of failure. Matching these requirements are traps, fish-weirs and barbed harpoons, all appearing in the late Upper Paleolithic, while they find wanting Middle Stone Age bone points.[126] Turning to 'foraging systems', they rule out all but 'managed foraging', which includes burning in Western Australia, movement of plants in Southern California, adjusting to drought, use of wild cereals, intercepting of herds, and use of corn in South Africa during the Late Stone Age.

When it comes to symbolisation, they only accept calculative symbolisation, for example the Ishango bone from Central Africa, where it's suggested the various markings refer to notations of lunar positions or the notched and engraved bones (such as the over 30,000-year-old

---

124 See Thomas Wynn and Frederick L. Coolidge, 'Implications of a strict standard for recognizing modern cognition in prehistory,' in Sophie De Beaune, Frederick L. Coolidge and Thomas Wynn, eds., *Cognitive Archaeology and Human Evolution*, New York: Cambridge University Press, 2009, pp. 117–28, at pp. 117–19, p. 122ff., p. 125.

125 For a technical discussion on the nature of this ability, see *Insight*, pp. 517–20, where Lonergan distinguishes the material from the spiritual, with human understanding and judgement not intrinsically conditioned by the material presentations they receive from sensation and imagination. He notes that unlike what's material, 'the spiritual is comprehensive; what can embrace the whole universe through knowledge, can provide the centre and ground of unity' in the material capacities of a single human being (p. 520).

126 In his chapter on 'Common Sense as Object', Lonergan focuses on the practical insights required for the advanced toolmaking discussed by Wynn and Coolidge: 'primitive hunters take time out from hunting to make spears, and primitive fishers take time out from fishing to make nets. Neither spears nor nets in themselves are objects of desire. Still, with notable ingenuity and effort, they are fashioned because, for practical intelligence, desires are recurrent, labour is recurrent, and the comparatively brief time spent making spears or nets is amply compensated by the greater ease with which more game or fish is taken on an indefinite series of occasions.' (*Insight*, pp. 207–8).

Lartet and Blanchard bones studied by Alexander Marshack.[127] The 28,000-year-old Hohlenstein-Stadel 'Lion-Man' statue qualifies since its composition combines very different figures (presumably they'd also accept the 35,000-year-old, wonderfully sculpted Vogelherd woolly mammoth and horse for the sheer quality of the workmanship, along with the Hohle Fels Venus from the same epoch.) The authors don't find the Blombos cross-hatching or large collection of worked ochre as sufficient expression of their standards for cognition.

In *Cognitive Archaeology's* concluding essay, Thomas Wynn notes that prehistoric actions had to be structured by prehistoric minds, and that we have limited access to those minds. The two modes of access for Wynn are firstly, evolutionary cognitive archaeology (ECA), whose goal is to find the products of such prehistoric minds by means of the 'mental template' underlying those products. Secondly, there has to be a focus on reconstructing the sequences of action: this is achieved by arriving at the sequence of decisions giving rise to a range of artefacts rather than to single artefacts.[128] Archeologists may well differ regarding Wynn and Coolidge's application of their 'strict standard for recognising modern human cognition in prehistory'. What strikes me as most important is that as paleoanthropologists they are aware of a new type of data – objects they claim are produced by human 'minds' and could not have been produced by animal or pre-human hominid activity.

The question I'll be asking of those who maintain that our capacity for understanding is only a somewhat more complex but continuous development from animal cognition, is whether that explanation comes up to Wynn and Coolidge's 'strict standard'.

1.2 Are 'memes' ideas?
One well-known attempt to deal with human knowing as, in Darwin's terms and sense, 'developed from the mind of the lower animals' is in terms of the notion of 'memes' – originally proposed by Richard Dawkins and enthusiastically championed by philosopher Daniel Dennett and linguist Steven Pinker. In *The Selfish Gene*, Dawkins introduces as a 'cultural replicator' the notion of a 'meme' (from the Greek *mimeme*, 'to

---

127 Alexander, Marshack, *The Roots of Civilization: The Cognitive Beginnings of Man's First Art, Symbol and Notation*, London: Weidenfeld & Nicolson, 1972.

128 Thomas Wynn, 'Whither evolutionary cognitive archaeology: Afterword' in De Beaune, Coolidge and Wynn, *Cognitive Archaeology and Human Evolution*, pp. 145–50, at p. 145, p. 147f.

imitate') to parallel the gene as a biological replicator.[129] Steven Pinker gives a descriptive account of memetic activity:

> Memes such as the theory of relativity are not the cumulative product of millions of random (undirected) mutations of some original idea, but each brain in the chain of production added huge dollops of value to the product in a nonrandom way. Indeed, the whole power of minds as meme nests comes from what a biologist would call *lineage-crossing* or *anastomosis* (the coming back together of separating gene-pools) ... When memes come into contact with each other in a mind, they have a marvellous capacity to become adjusted to each other, swiftly changing their phenotypic effects to fit the circumstances.[130]

The difficulty here seems to be in maintaining a consistently reductionist version of Darwinian evolution while at the same time dealing with what actually happens when we know something. Take a famous example from scientific knowing: When in 1911 he calculated that light from another star would be bent by the sun's gravity, Einstein moved from proposing as possibly true his theory of general relativity to suggesting how that possible truth might be verified (or falsified, as Karl Popper would put it later). Arthur Eddington's measurements on the West African island of Principe during the solar eclipse of 29 May 1919 confirmed Einstein's prediction of this gravitational deflection of starlight by the sun, a confirmation that has withstood objections in light of later observations. As a thought-experiment, just imagine how Einstein's theory, well understood by astrophysicist Eddington, could be a theory without both scientists' actually grasping its non-visible meaning, or how Eddington's complex observation could have been made without his awareness of the conditions required for verifying or falsifying that theory.

But what's the anthropology underlying the meme-theory of human cognition? Pinker called chapter seven of *The Blank Slate*, 'The Holy Trinity', which sets out three views on what it is to be human: (1) the 'Blank Slate' view (for Pinker, represented by Stephen Jay Gould and Richard Lewontin), where human beings construct their own nature from their experience of social interaction. So our nature is a blank slate to be written upon

---

129 Richard Dawkins, *The Selfish Gene*, Oxford: Oxford University Press, 1989, p. 192.

130 Quoted in Daniel Dennett, *Darwin's Dangerous Idea: Evolution and the Meanings of Life*, London: Penguin, 1995, p. 355.

by society; (2) the 'Noble Savage' view (also held by Gould), implying that humans are innately good, but inevitably corrupted by the social environment; (3) the 'Ghost in the Machine' view, held by those who maintain that the human mind is immaterial.[131]

I'd say that each of these views expresses a partial perspective on the human condition: (1) we're obviously affected by our social interactions, (2) we have a capacity for truth and good, and (3) there's something in us which even Pinker admits is a 'mystery'.[132] But instead of going beyond the partial nature of these views – about which there's nothing modern, they've been around at least since Descartes' time – Pinker offers his own view of the 'human nature' he claims they are denying, which amounts to little more than standard sociobiology.[133] He writes that:

> ... we are equipped with different kinds of intuitions and logics, each appropriate to one department of reality. These ways of knowing have been called systems ... faculties, mental organs ... reasoning engines. They emerge early in life ... and appear to be computed in partly distinct sets of networks in the brain. They may be installed by different combinations of genes, or they may emerge when brain tissue self-organises in response to different problems to be solved and different patterns in the sensory input. Most likely they develop by some combination of these forces.

> ... science is showing that what we call the soul – the locus of sentience, reason, and will – consists of the information-processing activity of the brain, an organ governed by the laws of biology.[134]

It is not possible here to enter into a fully-fledged discussion of a theory of human cognition based on the notion that it's merely an extension of

---

131 Steven Pinker, *The Blank Slate: The Modern Denial of Human Nature*, London: Allen Lane, 2002, p. 121.

132 ' ... our world might always contain a wisp of mystery, and our descendants might endlessly ponder the age-old conundrums of religion and philosophy, which ultimately hinge on concepts of matter and mind (Ibid., p. 240.)

133 'Sociobiology' has been popularised by Edward O. Wilson in his *Sociobiology: The New Synthesis*, Cambridge, MA: Harvard University Press, 1975. His original specialisation was in ants, but Dostoevsky's *Notes from Underground* anticipated the application of insights from ant society to humans in 1864. I'll use the term here as a shorthand for any kind of biological or zoological determinism.

134 Ibid., pp. 219–20, p. 224.

animal cognition – but what Dawkins, Dennett and Pinker are aiming at – a comprehensive and explanatory account of human knowing – is surely a worthwhile goal. A question I asked of Jean Piaget's excellent work on children's intelligence can be put to them as well: have they sufficiently 'adverted to the intrinsic differences between an organic structure, say an insect's tracheal system as a solution to the function of respiration, and an answer or a set of possibly correct answers as a solution to the function of explanation'?[135] Only close attention to the data of human knowing would make it possible to either affirm or deny a clear boundary between humans and animals. Can we understand the specifically human data of consciousness, symbolisation, language, understanding and freedom in biological or zoological terms (let's say, in terms of what is variously called evolutionary psychology or sociobiology), or does understanding have to be understood on its own terms?

Certainly the defenders of memes would put humans plainly in the zoological camp. As often, the disciples are stricter than the masters. The final paragraph of Susan Blackmore's *The Meme Machine*, with its unqualified biological determinism, has a refreshing clarity:

> Memetics thus brings us to a new vision of how we might live our lives. We can carry on our lives as most people do, under the illusion that there is a persistent conscious self inside who is in charge, who is responsible for my actions, and who makes me me. Or we can live as human beings, body, brain, and memes, living out our lives as a complex interplay of replicators and environment, in the knowledge that that is all there is … In this sense we can be truly free – not because we can rebel against the tyranny of the selfish replicators but because we know there is no one to rebel.[136]

The underlying problem – already there in Darwin's comment about 'convictions' – is that everyone makes truth claims about what they are saying. So if with Pinker I claim that everything I know is determined by brain processes, I make that claim as true, rather than mere opinion, certainly as more than mere neurological activity in my brain. Or if with Blackmore I sternly declare that my consciousness of myself is just a

---

135 Brendan Purcell, 'Aspects of Method in Human Psychology', unpublished MA thesis, University College Dublin, 1969, pp. 198–9.

136 Susan Blackmore, *The Meme Machine*, Oxford: Oxford University Press, 1999, p. 246.

delusion, at least I'm saying that that declaration is no mere delusion. Because if what I say is genetically determined, or a delusion, then we're back to Darwin's 'horrid doubt' whether such convictions 'are of any value or at all trustworthy' – they certainly can't claim to be true.[137] We so live within our awareness of truth, that even to deny truth, what Lonergan calls a performative contradiction, we have to affirm our denial to be true.

Returning to Wynn and Coolidge's 'strict standard for recognising human cognition in prehistory', the question is whether a sociobiological account in terms of 'memes' is going to be able to differentiate human from pre-human cognition and action. Sociobiology taken strictly would have to analyse both late hominid and *Homo sapiens* activity in terms of their struggle for physical survival and reproduction, whether in terms of memes or not.

1.3 Lonergan on understanding

What these authors haven't adverted to is the enormous breakthrough in the study of human understanding made by Bernard Lonergan, a study which, though intellectually indebted to Aristotle and Aquinas, is also fully cognisant of Kant and Hegel, and deeply enmeshed in a consideration of the kind of knowing found in mathematics, physics and the other natural sciences. Even more importantly, Lonergan presents the data in such a way that his approach can be empirically verified or falsified in that data, so that it goes beyond the descriptive analogies, however well developed, by those who have proposed memetics as a way forward.[138]

Just to convey the range of his inquiry, Lonergan often characterised what he was doing in terms of three questions: 'What am I doing when I am knowing? Why is that knowing? What do I know when I do that?' whose answers respectively occurred in cognitional psychology, epistemology and metaphysics. We needn't repeat our outline in chapter three of Lonergan's upgrading of Aristotle's and Aquinas' articulation of the structure of human knowing, but will focus on what's been called the 'hard problem' encountered by philosophers and cognitive scientists.

For us here, the 'hard problem' is our conscious experience, particularly at the underlying level of our awareness of ourselves, an awareness that's

---

137 Or, as Thomas Nagel put it in his *The Last Word* (New York: Oxford University Press, 1997), 'The judgment of relativity or conditionality cannot be applied to the judgment of relativity itself. To put it schematically, the claim "Everything is subjective" must be nonsense.' (14f)

138 For an illuminating recent study of Lonergan's *Insight* see William A. Mathews, *Lonergan's Quest: A Study of Desire in the Authoring of Insight*, Toronto: University of Toronto Press, 2005.

heightened in our acts of understanding and choosing.[139] Briefly, Lonergan speaks of the activities we called experience, understanding and judging as both intentional – in that they refer to objects, at the sense level of our senses, at the intellectual level of our questioning – and conscious, in that those activities are characterised by an awareness that is always immanent in them – when I understand something I am aware that I am understanding it:

> The operations then not only intend objects. There is to them a further psychological dimension. They occur consciously and by them the operating subject is conscious. Just as operations by their intentionality make objects present to the subject, so also by consciousness they make the operating subject present to himself.[140]

We have to widen the meaning of 'experience' beyond sensory and perceptual experience so that it refers to this internal experience of ourselves and of our actions. Then the 'hard problem', while certainly not becoming easy, at least can be clarified. You could say that the 'hard problem' is hard only from the viewpoint of a reductionism that just can't fit the fact of consciousness into its straitjacket of recognising the only reality as whatever's studied by the natural sciences.[141] But can that fact of specifically human rational and moral self-consciousness become the object of a scientific inquiry? In his essay 'Cognitional Structure', Lonergan gives a very short summary of the results of the over-700-page analysis of human understanding in its different modes presented in his magnum opus, *Insight*:

---

139 To get a flavour of a discussion of some of these problems by someone belonging to the English-language philosophical tradition known as analytic philosophy, David J. Chalmers' 'Facing Up to the Problem of Consciousness,' and 'Moving Forward on the Problem of Consciousness,' are easily available on the Internet, and were later published in Jonathan Shear, ed., *Explaining Consciousness: The 'Hard Problem'*, Cambridge, MA: MIT Press, 1997.

140 Bernard Lonergan, *Method in Theology*, London: Darton, Longman & Todd, 1972, p. 8. I'm not saying that the criterion for our being human is our being actually (as distinct from potentially) self-conscious, since obviously we're not so when we're in deep sleep, not to mention the whole discussion about the humanity of the unborn or of the irreversibly comatose – we'll discuss these issues in our final chapter.

141 The second chapter of Nagel's *The Last Word*, titled 'Why We Can't Understand Thought from the Outside', affirms this fact of human consciousness just as trenchantly as did his famous (and easily available on the Internet) 1974 essay on the fact of animal consciousness, 'What Is It Like to Be a Bat?'

> Where knowing is a structure, knowing knowing must be a reduplication of the structure ... If knowing is a conjunction of experience, understanding and judging, then knowing knowing has to be a conjunction of (1) experiencing experience, understanding and judging, (2) understanding one's experience of experience, understanding, and judging, and (3) judging one's understanding of experience, understanding, and judging to be correct.

> There follows ... a distinction between consciousness and self-knowledge. Self-knowledge is the reduplicated structure: it is experience, understanding and judging with respect to experience, understanding and judging. Consciousness, on the other hand, is not knowing knowing but merely experience of knowing, experience, that is, of experiencing, of understanding, and of judging.[142]

Clearly Lonergan's analysis offers us a new tool for approaching the whole question of the difference between animal and human cognition, in the light of which the picturing by Darwin, or latterly, writers like Dennett and Pinker, of human cognition as a higher development of animal cognition, appears merely descriptive in comparison to Lonergan's explanatory account.

I'd suggest that Wynn and Coolidge's question, even if formulated for working archaeologists rather than philosophers or cognitive scientists, is just another way of asking for specifically human activity to be explained as a generically different phenomenon from zoological-hominid activity. However, let's move from the psychology of our understanding of reality to the concrete task of living in the truth, which is where we get to see more clearly the enormous gulf between animal cognition and the human quest, not just for truth as known theoretically, but truth as lived.

1.4 Living in the truth
(a) **John Henry Newman:** Under the impact of Charles Kingsley's attack on his integrity, John Henry Newman formulated his attempt to live the truth in his 1864 *Apologia Pro Vita Sua*, which translated is entitled 'A defence of his life':

> My Accuser asks, *What, then, does Mr Newman mean?* ... I reflected, and I saw a way out of my perplexity. Yes, I said to myself, his very question

---

142 Lonergan, *Collection*, New York: Herder & Herder, 1967, p. 225.

is about my meaning; 'What does Mr Newman mean?' It pointed in the very same direction as that into which my musings had turned me already. He asks what I mean; not about my words, not about my arguments, not about my actions, as his ultimate point, but about that living intelligence, by which I write, and argue, and act ... I must, I said, give the true key to my whole life.[143]

Newman came close here to a concrete version of a classic definition of truth – that it's the conformity or correspondence of our affirmations or negations to what is or what is not (*Insight*, 552) – giving its most important instance: the conformity of who I affirm that I am to who I actually am. And since who I am is an intrinsically relational being, where the key relationships are both with those around me and with whatever is the ultimate origin of my existence, Kierkegaard's formulation of that struggle is also relevant here. He speaks of the self, which 'by relating itself to its own self and by willing to be itself the self is grounded transparently in the Power which posited it'.[144]

This struggle for self-transparency is especially clear in certain figures who've marked history by being prepared to set aside their biological survival in order to maintain their unswerving relationship to the truth they're living by. It's particularly obvious in those who are conscious of having a transfinite source that grounds their existence. There have been non-believers too, who have similarly opposed threats to individual autonomy, but common to all such profoundly courageous individuals has been their capacity, at critical and testing moments, to put their adherence to truth and freedom above the obvious biological and human desire we all have to survive.

Over the years, while teaching Plato's dialogue, the *Phaedo*, where he sets out a series of arguments for the soul's continued existence after death, it became obvious that the strongest case for this is Socrates' own attitude to his imminent execution for the sake of the truth he'd witnessed to all his life.[145] All we'll have time for here are for two more examples of living in the truth: Socrates and, closer to our own times, Sophie Scholl.

---

143 John Henry Newman, *Apologia Pro Vita Sua*, London: Longmans Green, 1905, p. xxiv.

144 Søren Kierkegaard, *The Sickness unto Death* [1849], Princeton: Princeton University Press, 1968, p. 147.

145 Since Socrates put such a priority on living that he never wrote anything down, we know of him mostly through Plato's dialogues, with a reasonable confidence that the *Apology* and the final scene of the *Phaedo* are accurate accounts, even if given a literary gloss. For our purposes, it's more than enough to work with Plato's version of Socrates.

(b) **Socrates' readiness to die as witness to truth:** There's a telling exchange between Socrates and the powerful and threatening Callicles in Plato's *Gorgias*. Gorgias is a famed media-expert equivalent to a donnish TV interviewer with the cultivated air of knowing everything. The dialogue opens with Socrates suggesting the one question he'll have difficulty answering: 'Ask him who he is' (447d). And the rest of the dialogue is an exploration of how various characters measure up to this question. In the most important clash, between Socrates and the powerful and threatening politician Callicles – who represents those who will vote for Socrates' execution – Socrates asks him: 'May not he who is truly a man cease to care about living a certain time? – he knows, as women say, that no man can escape fate, and therefore he is not fond of life; he leaves all that with God, and considers in what way he can best spend his appointed term' (512d–e). As Voegelin remarks, 'The sneers of Callicles can be effective only against men of his own ilk. They fall flat before a man who is ready to die.'[146]

How Socrates does spend his time is in openly seeking the truth and encouraging his fellow-citizens to do the same. In the *Apology* he reminds his fellow-Athenians that at the risk of his life he stayed at his post when doing military service. Should he do anything less, 'if ... when God appointed me, as I supposed and believed, to the duty of leading the philosophic life, examining myself and others, I were then through fear of death or of any other danger to desert my post?' (28e). Echoing this line and indicating the significance for humanity of all such dissidents against the lie of mere power without moral authority, is the Polish poet and philosopher, Stanisław Brzozowski (1878–1911): 'Our life, our self, is a sentry post; when we abandon it, the whole of humanity loses it forever.'[147]

And, in what's become probably Socrates' most quoted line, when he's invited to commit spiritual suicide by abandoning his quest for truth, he replies, 'life without this sort of examination is not worth living' (38a). Already living in the truth experienced within but extending beyond space and time, he can serenely bid farewell to those who've voted for his execution. Voegelin remarks of his last words:

The philosopher's life toward death and the judgement in eternity separates from the life of the dead souls. And then the pathos of the

---

146 Eric Voegelin, *Plato and Aristotle*, Baton Rouge: Louisiana State University Press, 1964, p. 37.

147 Quoted by Czesław Miłosz in his *Emperor of the Earth: Modes of Eccentric Vision*, Berkeley: University of California Press, 1981, p. 186.

moment is relieved by the last irony of Socratic ignorance: 'Who of us takes the better way, is hidden to all, except to the God.'[148]

(c) **The last days of Sophie Scholl:** A modern example of the growth of the soul under pressure to deny one's own convictions is Sophie Scholl, who, together with her brother Hans and their friend Christl Probst, was executed by the National Socialists in February 1943. Their crime was distributing leaflets protesting the regime at the University of Munich. Transcripts of the interrogations long held in the former German Democratic Republic became public over the last decade or so.[149] They revealed a young woman whose letters and diaries already indicate a profound quest for living in the truth – of which her taking part in the peaceful protest that led to her death was an expression.

Her interrogator, Robert Mohr, an unbeliever and convinced Nazi, was almost won over by the clarity and bravery of her answers. 'I tried with all the powers of persuasion I knew,' he later wrote, 'to explain to her that she was not ideologically in rapport with her brother, that she had relied on him and followed him without thinking of the consequences of her actions. Sophie Scholl saw right away what I was trying to do, and decisively rejected any such assertion. This would have been in fact the only way to save her life.'

She refused to grasp at a way that would have led to her physical survival by admitting it hadn't really been her idea, but that she'd been led by her brother, or by saying she hadn't realised the consequences of her acts. When Mohr tried to explain the National Socialist 'worldview' to her and show her what Adolf Hitler had accomplished, she replied, 'You're wrong; I would do it all over again – because I'm not wrong. You have the wrong worldview.' She told her cellmate, Else Gebel, of a dream she had on her last night on earth:

It was a sunny day. I was carrying a child in a long white dress to be baptised. The way to the church led up a steep slope, but I held the child in my arms firmly and without faltering. Then suddenly the footing gave way and there was a great crevice in a glacier. I had just time enough to set the child down on the other side before plunging into the abyss.

---

148 Voegelin, *Plato and Aristotle*, p. 10.

149 For many details regarding the historical documents on which a recent film, *Sophie Scholl: The Last Days*, was based, see *Sophie Scholl: Die letzten Tage*, Fred Breinersdorfer, ed., Frankfurt: Fischer Taschenbuch Verlag, 2005.

She explained to her fellow prisoners what the dream meant: 'The child is our idea. In spite of all obstacles, it will prevail. We were permitted to be pioneers, though we must die early for its sake.' When she was led out to the guillotine she'd left the sheet of paper with the indictment on it behind her, with the word 'Freedom' scribbled on the other side of the page. Sophie Scholl wasn't only being true to 'an idea' – she was living out the truth she'd achieved in her few years of adulthood before her arrest. During the show trial, she spoke up to contradict the notorious president of the People's Court, Roland Freisler: 'Somebody had to make a start,' she called out. 'What we said and wrote is what many people are thinking. They just don't dare to say it out loud!' Her commitment to truth even pierced through Freisler's normally terrifying harangue, so that many of the military in the rent-a-crowd audience found themselves on her side of the truth, as her Gestapo interrogator, Mohr, had earlier.

Sophie's sister describes the impact she and the others had on the prison staff:

The prison guards reported: 'They bore themselves with marvellous bravery. The whole prison was impressed by them. That is why we risked bringing the three of them together once more – at the last moment before the execution. If our action had become known, the consequences for us would have been serious. We wanted to let them have a cigarette together before the end. It was just a few minutes that they had, but I believe that it meant a great deal to them. "I didn't know that dying can be so easy," said Christl Probst, adding, "In a few minutes we will meet in eternity."

Then they were led off, the girl first. She went without the flicker of an eyelash. None of us understood how this was possible. The executioner said he had never seen anyone meet his end as she did.'

And her fellow prisoner Else Gebel in her signed deposition in 1947, testifying to the overwhelming effect of Sophie's lived truth on Robert Mohr, described how he came to herself and other prisoners at 4.30pm on the day of execution:

He is still in his hat and coat, white as chalk. I am the first to ask, 'Herr Mohr, is it really true that all three will die?' He only nods, himself still shaken by the experience. 'How did she take the sentence? Did you have a chance to talk to Sophie?' In a tired voice he answers, 'She was very brave; I talked with her in Stadelheim prison. And she was permitted to see her parents' ... He looks up at the clock on the wall and says softly, in a dull voice, 'Keep her in your thoughts during the next half hour. By that time she will have come to the end of her suffering' ... Finally it is five o'clock ... [150]

To complete our reflections on the human capacity for truth as something that can't be understood at the level of zoology or hominid psychology, we can touch on how we can deliberately fail to actualise that capacity.

1.5 The problem of the lie: living in untruth

The many studies of what's sometimes called intentional deception between animals have to do with activities like making false calls to distract competitors from food resources or to fool rivals and gain access to mates, and the huge range of camouflage and subterfuge to 'deceive' predators. These are linked to basic survival and reproduction needs, and so may be accommodated within our understanding of instinctual or learned behaviour at the level of perception and animal (mis-)communication.

A different explanation is clearly needed to account adequately for the commonplace human range of experiences of aversion from truth, from evasiveness, distortion and denial to impromptu or systematic rationalisation and the prevention of insight Lonergan termed 'scotosis'. There's nothing new, of course, in the reductionist account that sees human knowing as completely determined by materially based sensation. Plato addressed this materialist approach in the *Phaedo*, asking, how, if our knowledge is conditioned by matter, it can ever be involved in evil (93a–94b).

We've already suggested that we're so possessed by truth that even its denial involves us in a performative contradiction. Yet we can choose not to live in the light. It is precisely this willed oblivion that Voegelin, in his diagnosis of the collusion by the elites in National Socialism, explores in his 'Hitler and the Germans' lectures. Let's start with his discussion of Robert Musil's account of the different kinds of stupidity – where it's clearly a somewhat ironic way of dealing with deliberate self-delusion.

---

150 See Annette Dumbach and Jud Newborn, *Sophie Scholl and the White Rose*, Oxford: Oneworld, 2006, p. 151; Inge Scholl, *The White Rose: Munich 1942–1943*, Wesleyan University Press: Middletown, CT, 1983, p. 58, p. 138, pp. 146–7.

In his 1937 Vienna lecture, 'On Stupidity', Musil distinguished the ordinary meaning of stupidity – which as Lonergan puts it occurs in the individual in whom insight happens less frequently – from the higher stupidity by which the educated elites choose not to understand the horror of oncoming Nazism unfolding about them:[151]

> This higher stupidity is the real disease of culture (but to forestall misunderstanding: it is a sign of nonculture, of misculture, of culture that has come about in the wrong way, of disproportion between the material and the energy of culture) [*So, all these negations of genuine education.*] and to describe it is an almost infinite task. It reaches into the highest intellectual sphere. Years ago I wrote about this form of stupidity that 'there is absolutely no significant idea that stupidity would not know how to apply; stupidity is active in every direction, and can dress up in all the clothes of truth. Truth, on the other hand, has for every occasion only one dress and one path, and is always at a disadvantage' [*as opposed to this intellectual stupidity, of which the ideologies are the most flagrant examples*]. The stupidity this addresses is no mental illness [*he says once again*], yet it is most lethal; a dangerous disease of the mind that endangers life itself.'[152]

We've mentioned von Doderer's notion of *Apperzeptionsverweigerung*, or the refusal to perceive reality. A character in his 1956 *The Demons* – again in reference to the National Socialist period and of the type of person who made it possible, says that: 'A person who has been unable to endure himself becomes a revolutionary, then it is others who have to endure him. The abandoned, highly concrete task of his own life ... has of course to be consigned to oblivion, and along with it the capacity for remembering in general.'[153]

And, not to limit our examples to the attitude of willed oblivion that facilitated Nazism, Hungarian writer Sándor Márai describes how in 1948,

---

151 Echoed by George Orwell's well-known and strikingly similar remark: 'One has to belong to the intelligentsia to believe things like that: no ordinary man could be such a fool.' (See his May 1945 criticism of leftist intellectuals in 'Notes on Nationalism)'.

152 Eric Voegelin, *Hitler and the Germans*, Detlev Clemens and Brendan Purcell, trs. and eds., Columbia: University of Missouri Press, 1999, p. 102. (The remarks in square brackets are Voegelin's comments on Musil's text.)

153 Quoted, ibid., p. 256.

not long before he was able to leave Hungary, it didn't matter which way he went in Budapest, or whom he spoke to, a closure equivalent to Musil's 'higher stupidity' reigned:

> An acquaintance passing by on the street might speak to me, but while we exchanged words, I would suspect that he wasn't saying anything he wanted to but reeling off something warily and then looking around because, for all we knew, what he was saying confidentially could be overheard. I could go right or left in a city whose inner and outer map I knew tolerably well, but now a shadow enveloped everything familiar to me in the city.

> It took me aback because for the first time since I returned home from the West, a suspicion dawned in me which had not occurred to me before. I began to suspect that what surrounded me was something worse than the brute force present ... not just organised terror but an enemy more dangerous than anything else, an enemy against which there is no defense: stupidity ... I was living among individuals who learned by rote and parroted breathlessly that the One Idea is eternal, and indivisible ... But no one dared to speak about this. The hidebound, grinning, stubborn orthodoxy ... transplanted 'Marxism' into the changed present: that raging and idiotic egoism which wanted to force a society, a people, to live in a way contrary to human nature ... I walked along the sun-drenched street in Pest, and following me came the suspicion that no matter which direction I took, the shadow of a great danger crept after me. Stupidity was the danger that cast a shadow on every step I took.[154]

The reflective analyses by Musil, Buber, Márai, Voegelin and Lonergan of the phenomenon Voegelin calls 'the eclipse of reality', a widespread shared false understanding of reality, lay bare its grounding in a shared willed avoidance of self-awareness, a deliberate choice not to know.[155]

---

154 Sándor Márai, *Memoir of Hungary 1944–1948*, Albert Tezla, tr., Budapest: Corvina, 1996, pp. 386-8.

155 See Martin Buber, *Good and Evil: Two Interpretations*, New York: Scribners, 1953. The opening chapter has a brilliant analysis of this issue in his commentary on Psalm 12, 'Against the Generation of the Lie' (pp. 7–10). Eric Voegelin, 'The Eclipse of Reality,' in *What is History? and Other Late Unpublished Writings*, Thomas Hollweck and Paul Caringella, eds., Baton Rouge: Louisiana State University Press, 1990, pp. 111–62.

The critical fulcrum of these analyses is the performative contradiction involved in having to be somehow aware of the truth one wishes to deny, distort or conceal, in order to be able to do so. I'm unaware of any serious attempt from a Darwinist, sociobiological or memeticist perspective to account for this complex but important phenomenon. We don't have time here for a longer diagnosis of the human desire not only to avoid the truth, but to manufacture a counter-truth or lie. Pascal has already provided the bare bones of such a diagnosis:

> We are not satisfied with the life we have in ourselves and our own being. We want to live an imaginary life in the eyes of others, and so we try to make an impression. We strive constantly to embellish and preserve our imaginary being, and neglect the real one.

What he calls 'aversion from the truth', easily slides from self-deception into hatred of truth, whether that truth originates in self or others:

> It conceives a deadly hatred for the truth which rebukes it and convicts it of its faults. It would like to do away with this truth, but not being able to destroy it as such, it destroys it, as best it can, in the consciousness of itself and others; that is, it takes every care to hide its faults both from itself and others, and cannot bear to have them pointed out or noticed.[156]

It is only when we move to the specifically human level of explanation that we encounter not only the question of self-consciousness and the quest for truth, but also the mystery of evil at the level of the choice of the lie.

2. Freedom

Among scientists, the prevailing winds of thought, at least in English-speaking countries, has tended to vote against human freedom, opting instead for a determinism of human choice and action by the underlying material, genetic, biochemical and neurological manifolds, and relegating our experience of being free in our significant moral choices to the realm of illusion, useful or otherwise. At the same time, the scientists who hold this view are, after all, human beings. While denying what I'd see

---

156 Pascal, *Pensées*, Harmondsworth: Penguin, 1983, p. 270, p. 348, p. 349.

as the core of their humanity, they almost invariably manage to bring freedom – without its scientific passport – back in through the side door. So, we'll first see how three fairly representative public figures who hold deterministic views of freedom – Richard Dawkins, Daniel Dennett and Stephen Hawking – being human, also argue for non-determinist views of freedom. Then we'll briefly explore what human freedom involves, and why our capacity for freedom and, even more, our life of freedom, clearly separates us from everything else originating in this universe.

2.1 Two scientists' and a philosopher's case for our unfreedom

We've already mentioned the blurb for Richard Dawkins' *The Selfish Gene*, summarising his argument: 'Our genes made us. We animals exist for their preservation and are nothing more than their throwaway survival machines.' In the book he writes of what he calls our 'replicators':

> They are in you and in me; they created us, body and mind; and their preservation is the ultimate rationale for our existence. They have come a long way, those replicators. Now they go by the name of genes, and we are their survival machines.[157]

Daniel Dennett's book, *Freedom Evolves*, gives a comprehensive range of constraints on freedom – neural, psychological, sociological, and so on – presented as a form of unavoidable determinism. For him, human freedom is evolving, 'like every other feature of the biosphere ... Our brains have been designed by natural selection, and all the products of our brains have likewise been designed ... by physical processes in which no exemption from causality can be discerned.'[158] He makes much of Benjamin Libet's much-quoted experiments – which purport to show we're not really free because our brains can indicate movements (for example, raising a finger) before we have actually decided to make them – in a long section, not unlike a similar example Stephen Hawking will give.[159]

Dennett has an ability to raise the key questions (sometimes leaving that to a fictional character 'Conrad' in the text) without answering them. So when 'Conrad' asks how mere brain-processes can be the same as his consciousness of himself, Dennett writes that the question betrays

---

157 Dawkins, *The Selfish Gene*, p. 20.

158 Daniel Dennett, *Freedom Evolves*, London: Allen Lane, 2003, p. 305.

159 Ibid., pp. 227–43.

confusion, 'for it presupposes that what *you* are is something *else* ... in addition to all this brain-and-body activity. What you are, Conrad, just is this organisation of all the competitive activity between a host of competences that your body has developed'.[160]

Stephen Hawking asks:

> Do people have free will? ... . Though we feel we can choose what we do, our understanding of the molecular basis of biology shows that biological processes are governed by the laws of physics and chemistry and therefore are as determined as the orbits of the planets. Recent experiments in neuroscience support the view that it is our physical brain, following the known laws of science, that determines our actions, and not some agency that exists outside these laws.

And the example from neuroscience he gives is of patients undergoing awake brain surgery, where by electrically stimulating the brain in certain regions, the patient wanted to move 'the hand, arm or foot, or to move the lips and talk'. He goes on to say that it's 'hard to imagine how free will can operate if our behaviour is determined by physical law, so it seems that we are no more than biological machines and that free will is just an illusion'.[161]

It is interesting that cognitive neuroscientist Richard Passingham is critical of claims made for the Libet experiment Dennett uses as part of his case against freedom as ordinarily understood. Passingham notes that 'the movements chosen in these experiments are simple and semi-automatic, and thus the Libet task requires subjects to pay attention to something of which we do not normally need to be aware'.[162] The real test of freedom has always been understood to be where human beings show their readiness to lose their lives for the sake of a good which is greater than mere survival – protagonists like Socrates, Thomas More or Sophie Scholl, whose choices can hardly be said to conform to a morality based on biological survival at all costs.

And biologist H. Allen Orr points out that the evolution of morality in Dennett's *Darwin's Dangerous Idea* in terms of natural selection is merely

---

160 Ibid., p. 254.

161 Stephen Hawking and Leonard Mlodinow, *The Grand Design*, London: Bantam Press, 2010, pp. 31–2.

162 Passingham, *What is Special About the Human Brain?*, Oxford: Oxford University Press, 2008, p. 148.

unproven assertion – comments which I believe are also relevant to the merely asserted claims of Dawkins and Hawking:

'[Natural] Selection may explain the spread of ethical codes among humans. But at each milepost the sceptical reader grumbles, 'But maybe not'. After all, the evidence for each claim is non-existent (alternative universes, origin of morality) to negative (Darwinian evolution of memes).[163]

2.2 But they also say we can rebel against our genes

Given Richard Dawkins' unflinching support for the completely genetic basis of human existence, 'body and mind', his equally strong defence of human freedom, is hardly coherent with the selling point of the book:

It is possible that yet another unique quality of man is a capacity for genuine, disinterested, true altruism ... Even if we look on the dark side and assume that individual man is fundamentally selfish, our conscious foresight – our capacity to simulate the future in imagination – could save us from the worst selfish excesses of the blind replicators. We have at least the mental equipment to foster our long-term selfish interests rather than merely our short-term selfish interests ... We have the power to defy the selfish genes of our birth and, if necessary, the selfish memes of our indoctrination. We can even discuss ways of deliberately cultivating and nurturing pure, disinterested altruism – something that has no place in nature ... We are built as gene machines and cultured as meme machines, but we have the power to turn against our creators. We, alone on earth, can rebel against the tyranny of the selfish replicators.[164]

It is hard not to get the impression here that Dawkins is trying to have his determinist cake and then eat it without telling us. If the preservation of our genes 'is the ultimate rationale for our existence', if we are their survival machines, then going against our genes is simply impossible. Simon Conway Morris, in his *Life's Solution*, has noted that 'ultra-Darwinists attempt to smuggle back the moral principle through the agency of the gene', and in such passages, Dawkins' consciousness of his own freedom seems to be getting the better of himself, despite his theory.[165]

---

163 Quoted in Rudolf P. Botha, *Unravelling the Evolution of Language*, Amsterdam: Elsevier, 2003, p. 215 n. 9.

164 Dawkins, *The Selfish Gene*, p. 20, pp. 200–1.

165 Simon Conway Morris, *Life's Solution: Inevitable Humans in a Lonely Universe*, Cambridge: Cambridge University Press, 2003, p. 325.

Similarly, Daniel Dennett doesn't consider he's replaced ethics although he states that he's placed it on a 'foundation' that 'does not require any human "exceptionalism"' – presumably from animals. Yet, he concludes that 'We can understand how our freedom is greater than that of other creatures, and see how this heightened capacity carries moral implications: *noblesse oblige.*'

What this *noblesse* amounts to can be found earlier, where he writes of the evolutionary development of cooperative behaviour, which is 'broadly moral'. He proposes ethics as 'benselfish', which is his expression for far-sighted self-interest, amounting to a standard utilitarian morality. Yet in his chapter on 'Benselfishness' he still reminds us that 'organisms can come to be *designed* by evolution to cooperate, or more precisely to behave in such a way as to prefer the long-term welfare of the group to their immediate individual welfare'.[166]

Despite approvingly quoting Cato's preference to be rather than seem good, he speaks of the 'advantages' of being known as a cooperator – one who will work together with others for a goal, as if Dostoevsky's *Underground Man* hadn't already had an ironic description of the pseudo-morality of 'advantage'.[167] For example, for Dennett, the only reason we don't commit perjury is our fear of being found out, since morality is a question of what's acceptable to people, not what's intrinsically right or wrong.

To defend his notion of a 'freedom' which is still determined, he tries to show how it derives in an evolutionary way 'from blind selfishness through pseudo-altruism to quasi-altruism (benselfishness) to something that may be quite good enough for all of us'. Candidly, Dennett admits that he's adding nothing to ethical theory since his aim is to arrive at what everyone would acknowledge as being a responsible moral agent within a survival-based Darwinian framework. To square this circle of freedom within an intrinsically animal context, he proposes 'luck, environmental

---

166 Dennett, *Freedom Evolves*, p. 197.

167 'After all, gentlemen, as far as I know, you deduce the whole range of human satisfactions as averages from statistical figures and scientifico-economic formulas ... But there is one very puzzling thing: how does it come about that all the statisticians and experts and lovers of humanity, when they enumerate the good things of life, always omit one particular one? ... One's own free and unfettered volition, one's own caprice, however wild, one's own fancy, inflamed sometimes to the point of madness – that is the one best and greatest good which is never taken into consideration because it will not fit into any classification, and omission of which always sends all systems and theories to the devil ... "Ha, ha ha! But, you know, as a matter of fact volition doesn't exist!" you interrupt me with a laugh. "Science has already got so far in its anatomisation of man that we know that so-called free will is nothing more than ..."' Fyodor Dostoevsky, *Notes from Underground* and The Double, Jessie Coulson, tr., London: Penguin, 2003, p. 30, pp. 33–4.

scaffolding, and gradualism', somewhat ruefully noting that 'Like everything else evolution has created, we're a somewhat opportunistically contrived bag of tricks, and our morality should be based on that realisation'.[168]

Unlike Dawkins and Dennett, Stephen Hawking is less inclined to draw on biological determinism, and tries to rescue the freedom he's resolutely denied simply by saying what we do is mathematically unpredictable. 'We cannot even solve exactly the equation for three or more particles interacting with one another.' Earlier he's spoken of an 'effective theory', which allows physicists and chemists to provide, say, 'an adequate explanation of how atoms and molecules behave in chemical reactions without accounting for every detail of the interactions'. Since human beings contain 'about a thousand trillion trillion particles' it couldn't be predicted what those particles would do. 'We would therefore have to say that any complex being has free will – not as a fundamental feature, but as an effective theory, an admission of our inability to do the calculations that would enable us to predict its actions.[169]

Hawking wants to allow us some kind of free will, although inclined to deny its possibility because it is subject to the laws of physics and chemistry. But all he concedes is that what he considers our freedom is free because it participates in the unpredictability of the kind of non-systematic existence found in, say, subatomic particles.

In fact, we're aware in at least some instances of hard choices, when we've reached the moral judgement and we say to ourselves: 'I know I have to do this here and now to honour those goods lying within my field of action.' Even at that moment the 'have to' doesn't automatically or necessarily flow into actually doing it. Far from it. I still have to choose to do it. The drama of each serious moment of moral choice isn't exhausted

---

168 Dennett, *Freedom Evolves*, pp. 307–8, p. 201, p. 194, p. 203, p. 205, p. 217, p. 268, p. 273, p. 280.

169 Hawking and Mlodinow, *The Grand Design*, p. 33, p. 178. Hawking is referring to the famous three-body problem, going back to Newton. Newton was able to solve the equations for the motion of two bodies like the sun and the earth as they interact through gravity. But when a third body, like the moon, is added, he couldn't solve the equations for all three bodies, nor, as a result, predict their movements. An obituary for the Russian mathematician, Vladimir Arnold, who'd worked on this problem, notes that Arnold applied his discovery 'that small changes had an immense impact on outcomes' to weather systems, which 'explained why long range forecasting was effectively impossible because small events could have dramatic, unforeseen, consequences'. (*Daily Telegraph*, 12 July 2010). Hawking's 'effective theory' identifies freedom with mathematical unpredictability. Just how empty a freedom that is becomes clear when you realise that on the same basis, our weather systems would have free will because they're unpredictable in Arnold's sense.

until the resolution of that tension happens. What makes it happen is not more deliberation but me freely choosing and doing the action. The word 'freely' catches the characteristic self-awareness immanent in the choice, the consciousness that even though I know I ought to, should, must, have to, do X, still: I mightn't do X. I don't have to follow that self-direction of conscience, I'm free either to follow it or not to follow it. So we might allow a merely verbal agreement with Hawking by saying that in such a moment I experience that purely psychological 'unstable ion' on which the weight of the word indeterminacy rests.

2.3 Lonergan on human freedom

Lonergan's analysis of the meaning and foundation of human freedom proposes a different kind of contingency to Hawking's:

> Freedom ... is a special kind of contingence. It is contingence that arises, not from the empirical residue that grounds materiality and the non-systematic, but in the order of spirit, of intelligent grasp, rational reflection, and morally guided will ... Freedom possesses not only the negative aspect of excluding necessity but also the positive aspect of responsibility. (*Insight*, 619)

We've already outlined Lonergan's treatment of human cognitional structure in terms of experience, understanding and judgement. To those three levels of consciousness, decision adds a fourth level, where, as Lonergan puts it, consciousness becomes conscience. As he wrote some ten years after he'd written *Insight*:

> Though being and the good are coextensive, the subject moves to a further dimension of consciousness as his concern shifts from knowing being to realising the good. Now there emerge freedom and responsibility, encounter and trust, communication and belief, choice and promise and fidelity. On this level subjects both constitute themselves and make their world. On this level men are responsible, individually for the lives they lead and, collectively, for the world in which they lead them ...

And he argues that our choices, while often apparently focused on the objective world outside ourselves, have even more consequence for ourselves; in making those choices, we're also making ourselves:

What is revealed? It is an original creation. Freely the subject makes himself what he is; never in this life is the making finished; always it is still in process, always it is a precarious achievement that can slip and fall and shatter ... [170]

Dawkins, Dennett and Pinker support the view that human beings are basically material, and oppose what Pinker characterises as a dualism where humans are an uneasy combination of the material and the spiritual, a view he summarises using Gilbert Ryle's notion of 'the Ghost in the Machine'.[171] They don't consider the radically non-materialist and non-dualist understanding of the human by Aristotle and Aquinas. For Aristotle, Aquinas and Lonergan, rather, we're a psychophysical composite. That classical philosophical tradition fully accepts that our freedom is limited by our bodies, yet not intrinsically determined by those limitations.

For example, Lonergan's updated version of Aquinas' discussion of freedom deals with the emotional and cognitive factors preceding a decision: at the sensory level, what he calls 'the underlying sensitive flow'; then, corresponding to the acts of understanding and judgement, he discusses 'practical insight', and the process of 'practical reflection'.[172] He employs Aristotle's categories of act, habit and capacity or potency, to note the difference between our acts of willing, our gradually acquired habits of willingness and our underlying capacity of will. He makes the crucial distinction between our essential freedom – the capacity of will that all humans have – and our effective freedom, which is the actual exercise of will that we attain. That attainment is a real conquest of freedom, since it is far from being automatic.

So he lists four conditions for effective freedom, all of which limit the exercise of our freedom: external circumstances, the actual development of our sensitivity, our intelligence, and the willingnesses we have already developed. I can be essentially free to give up smoking, yet not effectively free to do so, if I haven't got round to persuading the various habits at the sensory level to cooperate with my desire to give up the habit.

---

170 Lonergan, in *Collection*, p. 237, p. 238.

171 For example, while denying that genes influence on human behaviour means that 'we are cuckoo clocks or player pianos, mindlessly executing the dictates of DNA', Pinker asserts that 'higher faculties, including learning, reason, and choice, are products of a nonrandom organisation of the brain ... ' (*The Blank Slate*, p. 243).

172 In what follows on Lonergan's view of freedom, I'm drawing from sections 2 and 3 of Chapter XVIII in *Insight* where he discusses 'The Notion of Freedom' and 'The Problem of Liberation'.

2.4 The priority of freedom over its denial or its evasion

What of freedom itself? There are two key aspects, a negative and a positive one. On the negative side, every attempt to water down our experience of freedom, to say that we only think we're free, runs up against the objection: how do you know that this experience we have doesn't in fact refer to our freedom? Because to have a criterion, even a negative one, regarding free will, parallels the sceptic's problem: to deny that affirmations of truth are true, the sceptic claims to know at least one truth, that there are no truths. But it gets worse: if I deny freedom, including of course my own freedom, then I have no choice in denying freedom. For my denial of freedom to be convincing, there must be at least one exception: I at least must be freely denying freedom, or why should anyone take me seriously?

In fact, I can only deny the truth of the experience of freedom on the basis of a deeper experience of freedom as the criterion for declaring what is or isn't freedom. Dawkins, Dennett, Hawking and Pinker all seem to run into the same problem. That, as Thomas Nagel puts it, 'One cannot just exit from the domain of moral reflection: It is simply there.'[173] And it's this overwhelmingly given experience of freedom that I believe is why the thinkers we've referred to, while denying freedom in any meaningful sense, still feel driven to make a case for freedom, however inadequate that case may be. What's strange is how some scientists or philosophers can pronounce on freedom without examining the data on freedom – sometimes denigrated as 'folk psychology' – data available to anyone who rises to the level of responsible, unselfish action.

A concrete example of this negative aspect of freedom doesn't come from various illustrious thinkers, but from ourselves. Because we can find out just how free we are even when we fail to actualise our capacity for freedom. We may have won over our feelings, have had the practical insight and made the moral judgement on what's to be done. Yet we don't do it, we delay, we avoid self-consciousness of our responsibility, we do anything but make a decision – what Lonergan calls 'the common experience of a divergence between what one does and what one knows one ought to do'. It's hard to see how this specifically human experience could ever be primarily determined by our genes or brains or a desire for the survival of the fittest, since even when we're presented with what we should do, we still don't do it.

---

173 Nagel, *The Last Word*, p. 21.

2.5 Freedom as lived unselfishness

The key positive aspect can, I think, best be grasped in David Walsh's remarks about Kierkegaard:

> Kierkegaard utterly eliminates the notion of arbitrariness that has afflicted the notion of freedom by locating it squarely at the core of human existence. It cannot be exercised arbitrarily because it cannot be exercised with anything less than the whole of our being. The significance of the ethical is not that it is a choice but that it is the meaning of choice. We do not therefore choose between good and evil – this is not our 'either/or' – but more fundamentally we choose to choose. Then the choice is disclosed.[174]

It's this core reality of human freedom – that 'we choose to choose' – that can't be reduced to anything other than itself, nor can be explained away by any causation outside itself, such as the range of causes given by the thinkers we have mentioned, fairly representative as they are of majority consensus in English-speaking scientific academe. Since our freedom is only fully disclosed in our actual choices, it can only be discovered through how we live. Kierkegaard discussed this concrete instantiation of freedom in his *Journals*:

> There are many differences – and eternity can surely remove every other difference: but one difference between man and man it cannot remove, the difference of eternity between whether you lived in such a way that there was truth in you, that something higher existed for which you really suffered, or whether you lived in such a way that everything turned upon your own profit.[175]

I remember when I first came across this statement while working on my doctoral thesis on interpersonal relations. More than anything I'd read in the wonderfully well-stocked Katholieke Universiteit Leuven psychology library, where there were many texts on topics like personality differences, Kierkegaard's remark seemed to get to the heart of the only difference that really counted. And that difference turned on how a person lived in

---

174 David Walsh, *The Modern Philosophical Revolution: The Luminosity of Existence*, New York: Cambridge University Press, 2008, p. 411.

175 Søren Kierkegaard, *Journals 1853–1855*, Ronald Gregor Smith, tr., London: Fontana, 1968, p. 248.

terms of their effective freedom to love. Which brings us to our final topic in these thoughts on freedom.

2.6 The mystery of evil

Just how could a diagnosis of the horrors of recent human history be carried out with the tools of sociobiology or the various other explanations of freedom that only explain it away? David Walsh notes that 'failure to acknowledge that holocausts are not primarily external phenomena, but first exist as a possibility within each of us, has been the principal reason why we have still not been able to clarify the enormity of our recent modern past'.[176] And that possibility becomes an actuality – in the case of the Holocaust and similar events of genocidal mass murder – when individuals refuse to choose what's good, and prefer to allow their passionate wilfulness to substitute for their lack of responsible willingness.

It'll have to be enough here to simply give two examples of evil, and ask the reader to see whether they can be explained outside an understanding of human freedom and its catastrophic refusal to achieve responsible action. In 1933, with the National Socialist government in power for less than a year, Viennese satirist Karl Kraus reported on what Hannah Arendt would later call 'the banality of evil' – definitely evil, though nothing approaching the scale of what was to follow. But the ugly face of human evil is clearly displayed in the deliberate sadism of the punishment meted out to a German woman seen in public in the company of a Jewish man:

> They should <u>not be surprised</u> – says the race warden – if one day they get <u>a thrashing</u>. But who would still be surprised at anything? Everywhere the one who administers the beating is precisely the one who deserves it. In the satrapy of that Streicher [the local governor of Franconia] from whose brain the thought of a more comprehensive boycott arose, a barrier was broken, and a girl with shaven head was led by six uniformed men through the bars, so that she could be spat at by the public. Someone, who on Sunday August 13 saw it, reported it, and *The Times* also reported that a board had been hung around her neck with her plaits, which had been cut off fastened to it, and these words could be read:
>
> I offered myself to a Jew.
> Storm-troopers surrounded her from time to time on the stage of the cheap music-hall and, with abuse, roared out the text into the hall.

---

176 Walsh, *The Modern Philosophical Revolution*, p. 463.

The girl, 'slim, fragile and in spite of her shorn head, exceptionally pretty', was led along the block of international hotels.

She tripped a few times and then was brought to her feet again by the men, sometimes lifted up high so that the onlookers further away could see her. On this occasion she was roared at by the public, ridiculed and for a joke invited to give a speech.

The children of the American consul saw it. Europe heard it. Never before was anything like it experienced in a nightmare. Some days later it was reported that she had gone mad. If all the revenge of a dishonored mankind was paralysed at the sight of the spectre of blood that besieged it – this act and this fate will one day kindle it into flame![177]

A second example is linked with one of Solzhenitsyn's towering expressions of moral judgement, where he quotes a New York State Supreme Court judge in *Life* magazine, who having visited the Gulag said: 'what an intelligent, farsighted, humane administration from top to bottom. In serving out his term of punishment the prisoner retains a feeling of dignity.' Solzhenitsyn adds: 'Oh, fortunate New York State, to have such a perspicacious jackass for a judge!' And follows with an account of a young woman prisoner whose moans he himself had heard from his relatively comfortable prison in Marfino, Moscow. For some minor infringement she is made to stand out all night in the freezing wind, every now and then begging, 'Citizen Chief! Forgive me! Please forgive me! I won't do it again!' Solzhenitsyn continues: 'To you girl, I promise: the whole wide world will read about you.'[178]

However, lest we're ever so unaware of ourselves as to imagine we're not touched by the possibility of a slide away from freedom into unfreedom, Solzhenitsyn has also given us the classic warning:

If only it were so simple! If only there were evil people somewhere insidiously committing evil deeds, and it were necessary only to separate them from the rest of us and destroy them. But the line

---

177 Quoted by Eric Voegelin in his *Hitler and the Germans*, Detlev Clemens and Brendan Purcell, trs. and eds., Columbia: University of Missouri Press, 1999, pp. 131–2. The underlined parts of the quotation are from a current German newspaper report on the event, the rest is Kraus's commentary.

178 Aleksandr Solzhenitsyn, *The Gulag Archipelago 2: 1918–1956*, Parts III and IV, London: Collins, 1976, pp. 134–5.

dividing good and evil cuts through the heart of every human being. And who is willing to destroy a piece of his own heart? During the life of any heart this line keeps changing places. Socrates taught us: Know thyself![179]

So, it's in the light of all these data – archaeological, paleontological, neural – and on symbolisation, language, understanding and freedom, that we have the answer our question: to understand human existence do we need to move to a level beyond that of biology and zoology? The very haplessness of reductionists' attempts to explain language, understanding and freedom in any terms other than specifically human ones, I believe, is an indication that we need to go beyond the zoological. However, before directly considering the human person underlying these seven 'grace notes', I'd like to reconsider the conscious ones as occurring within, yet transcending space-time constraints. This is because it is precisely our being 'lost in the cosmos' – in the sense that we don't belong only to it – that's denied, at least on principle, by attempts to explain the human in less than human terms.

---

179 Ibid., Parts I and II, p. 168.

Chapter Ten: The human person's limitless orientation to horizons of beauty, meaning, truth and goodness[180]

Sean Carroll points out that 'the history of our species represents just 3% of the time span of hominin evolution', and that 'many characteristics are present not only in humans, but also in apes'. This suggests 'that modification of existing structures and developmental pathways, rather than invention of new features, underlies much of human evolution'.[181] If so, then the specific human qualities we discussed in the previous few chapters are all the more amazing, making it less of a stretch to expect that some factor, radically more than the biological, physiological and neurological ones considered in an evolutionary context, have had a big part to play in who we are. Right through the book, we've been asking, do we need to move to another scientific level when we're confronted with the data on humanity? Are we broadly continuous with the hominids and higher primates, as Darwin considered we were in his *The Descent of Man*? Or is there such a discontinuity that we need to shift to a quite different level of scientific consideration?

Many paleoanthropologists, writing simply in terms of the data, don't seem so sure of the continuity thesis. We've already quoted Ian Tattersall, who's written that 'in the behavioural realm *Homo sapiens* as we know it today is a totally unprecedented kind of being':

> Clearly, the acquisition of what has been termed 'the human capacity' cannot have been a matter of fine-tuning over the eons by inexorable natural selection. Instead, this capacity was something entirely new – and not simply an extrapolation of trends that had preceded it in hominid history.

As we have seen, he continues by saying that the difference in *Homo sapiens*' cognitive capacity 'and even its closest extinct relatives is a huge

---

180 Some philosophers distinguish 'human being' from 'human person', linking person with consciousness, and morally prioritising the actually self-conscious person over the not yet self-conscious human being. I'll be using both terms interchangeably, since I'd consider self-consciousness to be the actualisation of an innate capacity of the same human being.

181 Sean B. Carroll, 'Genetics and the Making of *Homo sapiens*,' in Russell L. Chiocon and John G. Fleagle, eds., *The Human Evolution Source Book: Second Edition*, Upper Saddle River, NJ: Pearson/Prentice-Hall, 2006, pp. 626–37, at p. 630.

one. And it is not just a difference of degree. It is a difference in kind.'[182] We've already touched on the specifically different human capacities for language and symbolisation, for understanding and for freedom. But we've still to arrive at the unique and concrete reality of the one who has these capacities, the human person. Only if we know who or what a human person is can we assess whether it's enough to treat us as on a continuum with what we now call hominids, or whether we need to move to a quite different level of science.

To help us finally answer the question of our difference from all other living beings on this earth, we'll begin our penultimate chapter with a re-assessment of the four conscious grace notes of the human person to see how each of those notes, while embodied in time, can only make sense as oriented towards the timeless. We spoke of those notes as from 'a sonata for a good human person' and the more resonance we can discern in those notes, the more we'll appreciate what Heraclitus meant when he wrote 'The invisible harmony is more powerful than the visible' (B54).[183]

1. Our orientations towards beauty, meaning, truth and goodness

We could start with what we already referred to as an understanding of the human: 'in some way, horizon and frontier of the bodily and non-embodied, insofar as it is a non-embodied substance, while still being the form of the body'.[184] The horizon is a good symbol of our dimensions of openness or unfinishedness because as we know, a horizon isn't the absolute end but the limit of what's visible from here. It's also known to extend beyond what we can see to an unending more. In this way it reminds us that any present limit of beauty, understanding, truth, goodness and communion may be shifted 'outwards' by taking just one step further. That's why 'horizon' keeps us on our toes, trying to peer beyond it.

---

182 Ian Tattersall, *The World from Beginnings to 4000BCE*, New York: Oxford University Press, 2008, pp. 100–1.

183 I'm reminded here of Ralph Ellison's masterpiece, *Invisible Man*, with its famous opening meditation on identity and its interpersonal vicissitudes: 'I am an Invisible Man. No, I am not a spook like those who haunted Edgar Allan Poe ... I am a man of substance, of flesh and bone, fibre and liquids – and I might even be said to possess a mind. I am invisible, understand, simply because people refuse to see me ... When they approach me they see only my surroundings, themselves, or figments of their imagination – indeed anything and everything except me.' New York: Vintage, 1995, p. 3. Because he was African-American, he was aware of people not seeing him but only his outer skin.

184 *Summa Contra Gentiles, II*, 50.

In Part 1, chapter 5 of Dostoevsky's *The Idiot*, Prince Myshkin says of himself, 'I kept fancying that if I walked straight on, far, far away, and reached that line where sky and earth meet, there I should find the key to the mystery'. Maybe if we take those further steps towards the unbounded that's aimed at by our symbolisation and language, understanding and freedom, we'll find their horizons merge into the unbounded interpersonal horizons of the human person. David Walsh has explored this issue in contemporary philosophy and politics, and I'll draw on his interpretation of these issues in his *Guarded by Mystery*.[185]

The range of our feeling and imagination, of our understanding and our effective freedom, while still rooted in incarnate finitude, opens out to a transfinite horizon of beauty, truth and goodness. Our laying out of the seven 'grace notes' in the 'sonata of a good man' was to an extent patterned by the discussion with the paleoanthropologists. But if I may revert to a more directly philosophic mode, I'll speak in this chapter of four basic orientations not quite corresponding to the four conscious characteristics of the human, though very close to them. I'll let 'symbolisation' refer to our orientation, in mythic and artistic experience, towards the horizon of beauty. Though it conveys all conscious levels, here I'll unite language with the first of Lonergan's two levels of intellectual activity, understanding, to denote our horizon of meaning. What Lonergan treats as the second stage in intellectual activity, judgement, will here refer to our horizon of truth. And Lonergan's fourth level of consciousness, decision, will here be seen in terms of our horizon of the good, concretely identified with our love towards other persons. The fact is, there are many ways of exploring our personal activities, and all we're aiming at here is to suggest ways of achieving a deeper awareness of our own personal substance.

To set up the contrast I'm making, I'd like to mention the German-Estonian zoologist Jakob von Uexküll (1864–1944). He wrote a famous comparative study of what he called *Pathways Through Animal and Human Worlds*. In contrast to the human world, the animal 'worlds' or *Umwelten* he explored are intrinsically bound cognitively by the animals' sensori-perceptual-motor capacities, and conatively by the animals' needs of survival

---

185 David Walsh, *Guarded by Mystery: Meaning in a Postmodern Age* (Washington DC: Catholic University of America Press, 1999), which I'll indicate in the text as *GBM* – we can expect a development of this in his forthcoming *The Politics of the Person*. I've also been inspired by Joseph McCarroll's *Journey to the Centre of the Person* (Dublin: Radix Press, 1986), which I used as a course text for years. So much of his text, however inadequately absorbed, remains in my mental DNA that I won't bother trying to unravel its influence here.

and reproduction. In his *The Open: Man and Animal*, Giorgio Agamben writes about Uexküll's masterly description of the non-communicating worlds of different animals and on Heidegger's contrasting of these limited animal worlds with human openness to the world of reality.[186]

Lonergan has also discussed our unlimitedness in terms of openness by distinguishing between 'openness as fact' (each human being's desire to know and love) from 'openness as achievement' (the various actualisations of that desire). He adds a third kind, 'openness as gift'.[187] In light of Lonergan's later writings, this third kind of openness might also be included in terms of the mutual gift persons can be to one another. As we'll be suggesting, the reason I need to be open to others is that if, on principle, I exclude any you from my I, I am excluding myself from full participation in the 'we' of the family of humanity. I need your emotional, intellectual, moral and spiritual help, but most of all, I need you. If I'm not open to your acknowledgment of who I am, I may lose contact with my true self. As Buber has put it:

> The basis of man's life with man is twofold, and it is one – the wish of every man to be confirmed as what he is, even as what he can become, by men; and the innate capacity in man to confirm his fellowman in this way ... For the inmost growth of the self is not accomplished ... in man's relation to himself, but in the relation between the one and the other ... in the making present of another self and in the knowledge that one is made present in his own self by the other ... Man wishes to be confirmed in his being by man, and wishes to have a presence in the being of the other ... he watches for a Yes which allows him to be and which can come to him only from one human being to another.[188]

While this anticipates what we'll be saying in the following chapter, it is still important to remember that our orientations towards the horizons of beauty, meaning, truth and goodness primarily occur within an interpersonal setting. But as Lonergan's earlier two forms of openness bring out well, each orientation has a painful struggle to move from bare capacity to fully-fledged actualisation. Which is one of the reasons why the supporting presence of others is so necessary.

---

186 Giorgio Agamben, *The Open: Man and Animal*, Kevin Atell, tr., Palo Alto, CA: Stanford University Press, 2003, pp. 39–62.

187 Bernard Lonergan, 'Openness and Religious Experience' in *Collection*, New York: Herder & Herder, 1967, pp. 198–201, at p. 199, pp. 200–1.

188 Martin Buber, *The Knowledge of Man*, New York: Harper, 1965, p. 71.

1.1 Mythic and artistic symbolisation: expressing the inexpressible

(a) **Mythic symbolisation:** Both in ancient cave painting and modern art we can easily find symbolisations of experiences that reach beyond our needs for mere survival or mere utility, beyond our space-time universe. To deny on principle the truth of such experiences of transfinite reality requires first, a distinction between immanence and transcendence. But this needs a transfinite experience in terms of which we can discriminate between the two. Then – paradoxically – the basis on which the distinction is made has to be denied. Philosophically, not a pretty sight. And the affirmation has the backing of millennia of human experience from Chauvet to the Western European megalithic centres of attunement we know as Newgrange in Ireland, Maes Howe in the Orkneys, Stonehenge in England, through the late Roman and Gothic cathedrals of Europe, the temple complexes of Borobudur in Java and Angkor Wat in Cambodia, the constellation of mosques during the Islamic Golden Age from Cordoba to Samarkand, the Pueblo temple city in Chaco Canyon, New Mexico, not to mention the transformation of Uluru/Ayer's Rock into a ritual cathedral by the Anangu people.[189]

In fact, it is becoming normal now for paleoanthropologists to characterise the earliest cases of symbolisation as having religious significance, as have three well-known authors in the recent collection of essays, *Becoming Human*.

Merlin Donald writes that 'the word "religion" refers broadly to a subcategory of high culture that comprises the fundamental beliefs that encapsulate and support the worldview of a society.' These beliefs are conveyed by myths and mythologies, which 'are collectively remembered stories that tell people by example who they are, how to live and what to value'. Donald observes that in archaic societies, 'the uses and themes of art tend to be dominated by religion', which particularly includes the most important French and Spanish Paleolithic cave paintings, which he considers 'religious in motivation'. He regards it as 'a virtual certainty' that the cave art we've mentioned 'reflects the presence of an influential Animistic worldview that was widely disseminated'.[190]

---

189 For a more extended discussion of the notion that all such symbolisations are delusional, see my 'Dawkins' Fear of Reason' in Fran O'Rourke, ed., *Human Destinies: Philosophical Essays in Memory of Gerald Hanratty*, Notre Dame: Notre Dame University Press, 2011.

190 Merlin Donald, 'The roots of art and religion in ancient material culture' in Colin Renfrew and Iain Morley, eds., *Becoming Human: Innovation in Prehistoric Material and Spiritual Culture*, New York: Cambridge University Press, 2009, pp. 95–103, at p. 96 and p. 101.

Steven Mithen finds Neanderthals incapable of combining the 'ways of thinking and stores of knowledge from different cognitive domains/intelligences ... characteristic of *H. sapiens*. In other words, they lacked the ability for metaphor and had limited imagination.' For him, 'the mental conception of a supernatural being requires cognitively fluid thought – that which makes such connections between cognitive domains'. And language 'is the key to the transition from domain-specific thought to cognitive fluidity, which, in turn, is necessary for conceiving of supernatural beings'.[191]

Finally, in the same collection, Jean Clottes writes that one of 'the major clues to Paleolithic religious thinking is the art in the caves'. Entry into the caves wasn't casual; the Cro-Magnons didn't live there. 'The obvious reason for doing so was a desire to reach beyond the ordinary world, that of the living, to pierce the veil barely separating it from the supernatural forces literally at hand and to touch them either directly or by means of an offering, however symbolic it might be.' And the reason for the many objects stuck into cracks found in those caves, he suggests, is that they 'perhaps wanted to pierce the veil separating the world of the living from that of the spirits. It was not the object itself that was important ... but rather the gesture, the will to bridge the gap, and to contact the power hidden within the rock or the ground in that supernatural world of the dark ... '[192]

However, apart from Clottes, who draws on the parallel with Jewish petitions placed in the Western Wall at Jerusalem, or objects left by Catholics in the grotto at Lourdes, the way words like 'religion', 'Animism' or 'the supernatural' are used convey an enormous distance between the paleoanthropologists and the archaic symbolisers they're studying. Yet, despite that distance, these paleoanthropologists have no doubt that these first symbolisations convey what we've already discussed as experiences of attunement to the order of the cosmos. And they recognise that these early humans were trying to 'pierce the veil' to another level of reality. That meant that even in what was then their present existence, the Cro-Magnons experienced their participation in a reality transcending them.

As we've noted, one of the strongest indications of the specific difference of humanity from the pre-human hominids is the earliest humans' refusal to accept death as ultimate, as shown by their burial rituals. Their

---

191 Steven Mithen, 'Out of the mind: material culture and the supernatural' in ibid., pp. 124–34, at p. 126 and p. 127.

192 Jean Clottes, 'Sticking bones into cracks in the Upper Paleolithic' in ibid., pp. 195–211, at p. 195, pp. 208–9.

grasp of the non-ultimacy of their obvious contingency arises from an awareness that their human existence isn't exhaustively and exclusively contained within the limits of time. But that holds for contemporary culture too. Walsh, discussing 'The End of the Modern World' in the light of a critique of the radical inability of the modern age to resolve core human questions, notes that we're 'back at the original meaning of secular, that is, what can be separated from the spiritual. The deepest truth of our age is not that the modern world is over but that we have already passed into the transcendent perspective that enables us to view it as limited' (GBM, 121).[193]

(b) **Artistic symbolisation of beauty:** Nor is it surprising that 'so many of the dissidents of the twentieth century came from the world of art. Their own work puts them in touch with the unfathomable mystery of existence, and the contrast with the hollow instrumentalisation of ideology could not be greater' (GBM, 151). I'll just sample two of these more or less contemporary artists – none of them easily fitting into any religious category – whose symbolisations, equivalent to those of the earliest humans, lead them to experiences of the transfinite. An example is Georgia O'Keeffe's 1958 painting, Ladder to the Moon, of which she commented, 'Ladders are wonderful things – very important in the world' (they were needed in traditional Pueblo houses to reach the roof). Roxana Robinson comments on this painting:

> In this a luminous wooden ladder hangs magically in the evening sky, leaning lightly to one side, halfway between a high, half-visible moon and the low, noble black silhouette of the Pedernal. The images are all of transition: the ladder itself implies passage from one level to another; the moon is cut neatly in half by the bold slicing light, halfway between full and new; and the evening sky is in flux, still pale along the line of horizon, shading into deep azure night at the top of the canvas. It is not difficult to read this painting as a self-portrait: the light, hopeful form of the ladder, balanced, serene, and radiant, is poised between the vanishing glow of earthly day and the rich blue night of the heavens; O'Keeffe was seventy-one when she painted it.[194]

---

193 On this issue, in his *Anamnesis: On the Theory of History and Politics*, David Walsh, ed., (Columbia: University of Missouri Press, 2002), Voegelin notes that terms like 'immanent' and 'transcendent' only make sense in light of a prior experience that 'dissociates the cosmos into existing things and their divine ground of being ... they designate the relational order between the divine and nondivine realms of reality ... ' (pp. 374–5.)

194 Roxana Robinson, *Georgia O'Keeffe: A Life*, New York: Harper & Row, 1989, p. 415, p. 495.

From what seems a completely different perspective, Gerhard Richter paints and repaints his canvases, allowing the history of his work on the paintings to gleam through the various layers of colour. His destruction isn't negative but constructive: rather than becoming less beautiful, the repainting communicates an experience of the more beautiful. The repainting makes possible what's surprising, what's unplanned, what's uncategorisable. So Richter remarks, 'The paintings generally say nothing – never mind all the ideologies – and are always only attempts to arrive at the truth'.[195] And in his 'Notes 1988' he emphasises the deep relationship between art and the inexpressible mystery:

> Art is the pure realisation of religious feeling, capacity for faith, longing for God. All other realisations of these, the outstanding human qualities, abuse those qualities by exploiting them: that is, by serving an ideology. Even art becomes 'applied art' just as soon as it gives up its freedom from function and sets out to convey a message. Art is human only in the absolute refusal to make a statement. The ability to believe is our outstanding quality, and only art adequately translates it into reality. But when we assuage our need for faith with an ideology, we court disaster ... And so I hope that my 'incapacity' – the scepticism that stands in for capacity – may after all turn out to be an important 'modern' strategy for humankind.[196]

Michelangelo reminds us of the enormous suffering the achievement of such artistic openness can demand: '*Con tanta servitù, con tanto tedio/e con falsi concetti e gran periglio/dell'alma a scolpir qui cose divine*' – 'With such servitude, with so much tedium/and with false ideas and great danger/of soul, to sculpt here divine things.'[197]

1.2 Language and the lie, building and destroying relationship

I remember, in a talk at a conference on art in April 1999 at Castelgandolfo, Giuseppe Zanghí mentioning what the nineteenth-century Italian poet Giosuè Carducci said when asked what his favourite poem was: 'the one I haven't written yet'. For Zanghí, Carducci was expressing his unsatisfied

---

195 In Hans-Ulrich Obrist, ed., *Gerhard Richter: 100 Bilder*, Ostfildern-Ruit bei Stuttgart: Hatje-Canz Verlag, 1996, p. 154.

196 Gerhard Richter, *The Daily Practice of Painting*, London: Thames & Hudson, 1995, pp. 170–1.

197 Michelangelo, *Rime*, Milan: Rizzoli, 1954, p. 152.

thirst for what was still beyond him. Walker Percy has his own way of dealing with this incapacity to ever say completely what we have in us:

> If a novelist has a secret, it is not that he has a special something but that he has a special nothing. In this day and age, I think, a serious writer has to be an ex-suicide, a cipher, a naught, zero. Being a naught is the very condition of making anything. That's the secret. People don't know that writing well is simply a matter of giving up, of surrendering, of letting go. You say, 'All is lost. The jig is up. I surrender. I'll never write another word again. I admit total defeat. I'm washed up.' What I'm telling you is, I don't know anything. It's a question of being so pitiful God takes pity on you, looks down and says, 'He's done for. Let's let him have a couple of good sentences.'[198]

And the title of Giorgio Agamben's recent book, *The Sacrament of Language: An Archaeology of the Oath*, conveys this participation of language in the mystery of human existence.[199] Rather than follow him in that inquiry, I'd like to take an example of how our language goes beyond the sayable, not only in the 'space' beyond space of our present relationships with other persons, but also beyond the 'time' that's both within time and yet binds us beyond time. Gabriel Marcel explores what's involved in our making a promise to another person – his example is a promise he made to visit a dying friend:

> To make it a point of honour to fulfil a commitment – what else is this but putting the accent on the supra-temporal identity of the subject who contracts it and carries it out? And so I am brought to think that this identity has a validity of itself, whatever the content of my promise may be ... However overwhelmingly men of sense object, however often my friends remonstrate, I shall take no notice: I have promised and will keep my word.[200]

Having often witnessed couples making their wedding vows, I sometimes mention that the original meaning of 'to pledge one's troth' – the word 'troth' meant 'truth' – was, essentially, 'to be true (to)' the other person.

---

198 Walker Percy 'Writing in the Ruins.' Interview with Robert Cubbage, *Notre Dame Magazine*, Autumn 1987, pp. 29–31, at p. 31.

199 Giorgio Agamben, *The Sacrament of Language: An Archaeology of the Oath*, Adam Kotsko, tr., Palo Alto, CA: Stanford University Press, 2010.

200 Gabriel Marcel, *Being and Having*, London: Fontana, 1965, p. 60.

Again Marcel reflects on what underlies our pledge to be true, where lived faithfulness is an always partial fulfilment and renewal of an unconditional promise to another person, carried in English in two simple words, 'I do':

> The faithful soul is destined to experience darkness and ... it must even be familiar with the temptation to let itself be inwardly blinded by the night through which it has to pass ... Fidelity is not a preliminary datum, it is revealed and established as fidelity by this very crossing of the darkness, by this trial combined with everyday life, the experience of 'day after day' ... there is room for every sort of error, false move and deception on the side of the subject. It is through these errors and vicissitudes that we are allowed to behold the intermittent gleaming of the indefectible fire.[201]

So we can agree with Agamben's title, that language at its deepest level is indeed a 'sacrament', at the very least in the sense of Andy Warhol's painting camouflage colours over his *Last Self-Portrait* and his *Camouflage Last Supper* in 1986, during the last year of his life. The colouring expressed, behind the camouflaged face and the lithograph copy of Leonardo's *Last Supper*, a hidden depth, since the function of camouflage is to conceal and to protect from harm. For Warhol, the second meaning of sacrament was also there – to signify a hidden reality.[202] Obviously not all language has that high significance, but I'd suggest, all language depends on that high significance for its task of communicating and binding us together in truth. All language presupposes that we will be true to our word. Again, there's that awareness of the painful and interpersonal task of achieving integrity of meaning.

Similarly, the significance of the lie isn't merely verbal – a section of Voegelin's *Hitler and the Germans* is headed 'Criminal stupidity and loss of experience of reality in a disordered society', where he describes the political phenomenon of the systematic lying required to ensure that ideological or second reality will overcome the truth or first reality. It's what Karl Kraus in 1922 called *Untergang der Welt durch schwarze Magie* (*The End of the World Through Black Magic* [Kraus's term for the print media]). On this soul-and community-destructive activity of lying, Voegelin writes:

---

201 Gabriel Marcel, *Homo Viator*, New York: Harper, 1962, p. 151.

202 For a fuller exploration of this theme in Warhol, see Jane Dillenberger, *The Religious Art of Andy Warhol*, New York: Continuum, 1998.

In practice, the consequence of the conflict between second and first reality is, not the intellectual swindle, but the lie. The lie becomes the indispensable method because the second reality claims to be true, and since it constantly comes into conflict with the first reality, it is necessary to lie constantly: for example, one holds that the first reality is quite a different one from what it actually is, or that the second reality is most horribly misunderstood. The result of this conflict of the lie in the practical sphere is the phenomenon of compact honesty at an intellectually less differentiated level.

An example of this 'compact honesty' has been given some pages earlier in a quotation from Kraus's biting satire, *Dritte Walpurgisnacht* (*Third Witches' Sabbath*), written in 1933, where Kraus has already diagnosed how the National Socialist party functionary maintains an easy conscience by tricks enabling him to bypass self-awareness:

> That the comrade (*Volksgenosse*) does not believe the things he maybe just hears about, may still be explained through the barrier that has proved necessary in the vicissitudes of life's circumstances. However, that he also does not believe the things which he sees, indeed not even the things he does: that he does not know what he does and therefore immediately forgives himself, that testifies to a soul without falsity, which those differently constituted should well avoid but not mistrust. For his was the gift of not being able to lie, and because it would still also be impossible to lie as much as the actual situation would require, the ability of a medium must be in play, which helps such beings to come to terms through illusion with the things created by illusion.[203]

So both the use and abuse of language brings out Walsh's point that 'meaning can only be anchored in the relationship to transcendent mystery' (*GBM*, 123). We've already mentioned how Johannes Bobrowski applied that message to the human person's use of language in his last poem, '*Das Wort Mensch*' ('The Word Human'). It begins by speaking about his looking up the word 'Mensch' in the dictionary – in German, there are separate words for 'man' and 'woman,' while 'mensch' refers to any human being. He also hears the word used in ordinary speech, and

---

203 Eric Voegelin, *Hitler and the Germans*, Detlev Clemens and Brendan Purcell, eds., trs., Columbia: University of Missouri Press, 1999, p. 105, p. 109, p. 94.

repeated in the ideological anti-language of the German Democratic Republic. We've already quoted the last two lines where he laid down the criterion for its use, a criterion again going beyond any requirement of mere survival or material usefulness:

> *Wo Liebe nicht ist,*
> *sprich das Wort nicht aus.*
>
> Where there is not love,
> do not utter that word.[204]

1.3 Why must our affirmation of truth be beyond space-time conditioning?

As a seven-year old child, myself and my companions on the way home from school, despite the presence of the large public clock over Rathmines Town Hall, frequently asked people in the street had they got 'the right time, mister?' We weren't prepared to be fobbed off with mere opinions, we insisted on the 'right' time. And that seems to hold for every quest for truth – when a person claims their statement is true, they're claiming that it has fulfilled all the conditions required for it to be true.

This is so obvious to us that even those whose understanding of the human seems to require that sooner or later it's our genes or our emotions or social conditioning that determine us, themselves clearly seek the truth beyond any conditioning. Having several times been in dialogue with both Richard Dawkins and Daniel Dennett – whose views on the human certainly imply we're determined by our biological makeup – my most lasting impression of them was their passionate concern for the truth. Walsh speaks of us gaining our dignity as human beings whose fidelity to the truth transcends even our own existence:

> But isn't this what we mean by the touch of a higher reality? What is it that draws us in the direction of the transcendent truth, the resolution to strip away all falsehood? ... except the sense that this is the most real reality there is. In comparison with it nothing else – our comfort, our reassurance, our self-esteem – matters. (*GBM*, 42)

We've already mentioned Socrates' stance in the *Apology*, where he throws aside any possibility of surviving since it would involve him withdrawing

---

204 Johannes Bobrowski, in 'Das Wort mensch', *Wetterzeichen*, p. 83.

from what, for him, is the defining essence of his humanity: the search for truth. Aleksandr Solzhenitsyn has articulated and lived as well as anyone in our time that Socratic role, of being a witness to the truth, with full consciousness that that bearing witness could be at the cost of his life. Given the life-threatening circumstances in which his 1967 'Letter to the Fourth Congress of the Union of Soviet Writers' was made public, there was nothing rhetorical in its conclusion:

> I am of course confident that I will fulfil my duty as a writer in all circumstances – from the grave even more successfully and more irrefutably than in my lifetime. No one can bar the road to truth, and to advance its cause I am prepared to accept even death. But may it be that repeated lessons will finally teach us not to stop the writer's pen during his lifetime?[205]

Perhaps a few lines from his 1960 play, *Candle in the Wind*, conveys his consciousness of his duty to the truth. The play centres on the uniqueness of each human being particularly in the light of mortality. Alex, a 'biocyberneticist', is speaking with a fellow scientist:

> PHILIP: You have talent – but you can see no purpose for it!
> ALEX: No, I think I can see a purpose for it ... I'll tell you, only don't laugh. You remember you once said that you felt like a relay runner – that you would be proud to hand on the baton of Great Physics to the twenty-first century?
> PHILIP: Yes, I believe I did once.
> ALEX: Well, I'd like to help pass on to the next century one particular baton – the flickering candle of our soul.[206]

Solzhenitsyn had written a memoir about his unequal combat with the Soviet empire called *The Oak and the Calf*. But just how much the 'calf' had managed to shake the 'oak' was revealed when the relevant Soviet archives were printed. So, Yuri Andropov, then head of the KGB, wrote in February 1974:

---

205 Quoted in Leopold Labedz, *Solzhenitsyn: A Documentary Record*, Harmondsworth: Penguin, 1974, p. 116.

206 Aleksandr Solzhenitsyn, *Candle in the Wind*, London: Bodley Head, 1973, p. 134.

Leonid Ilyich! [Brezhnev] The ... Solzhenitsyn problem ... has currently gone beyond the framework of a criminal issue, and has been transformed into a problem of no small importance, having certain political characteristics ... The book by Solzhenitsyn [*The Gulag Archipelago*], despite our measures to expose its anti-Soviet character ... evokes a certain sympathy in some representatives of the creative intelligentsia ... In view of all this, Leonid Ilyich, I think it is impossible, despite our desire not to harm our international relations, to delay the solution of the Solzhenitsyn problem any longer, because it could have extremely unpleasant consequences for us inside the country. Y. Andropov.[207]

And as late as 29 November 1988, well into the Gorbachev period of 'glasnost', the then top party ideologist, Vadim Medvedev 'confirmed Solzhenitsyn would remain on the Soviet Union's blacklist of forbidden writers, saying that "to publish Solzhenitsyn's work is to undermine the foundation on which our present life rests"'.[208]

Solzhenitsyn concluded his 1972 Nobel Lecture with the Russian proverb, 'One word of truth shall outweigh the whole world.'[209] But even more than the word of truth is the person who utters it. Like Socrates, Solzhenitsyn communicated the truth as much or even more than his writings by how he lived it. Earlier, the Russian poet, Anna Akhmatova (1889–1966) chose to remain in the USSR when she could easily have left under a special concession by Lenin to intellectuals in 1922. Reflecting on all she'd endured – her first husband executed, her son jailed for ten years as a way of keeping pressure on her, various attacks by Soviet officials, and an almost complete ban on publishing – she wrote, still conscious of her duty to speak the truth to her own people:

> No, not beneath a foreign sky,
> Not sheltered by a foreign wing –
> I was where my people were,
> Where, alas, they had to be.[210]

---

207 Michael Scammel, ed.,*The Solzhenitsyn Files*, Chicago: Editions Q, 1995, pp. 342–4.

208 John Dunlop, 'The Solzhenitsyn Canon Returns Home', *Stanford Slavic Studies* (1992), 4:2, p. 429.

209 Alexander Solzhenitsyn, 'Nobel Lecture' in Edward E. Ericson and Daniel J. Mahoney, *The Solzhenitsyn Reader*, Wilmington, DE: ISI Books, 2006, pp. 512–26 at pp. 526.

210 Anna Akhmatova, 'Requiem', 1961, quoted in Amanda Haight, *Akhmatova: A Poetic Pilgrimage*, New York: Oxford University Press, 1976, p. 100.

She remarked to Isaiah Berlin (a British philosopher visiting her in Leningrad in 1945, when he was a minor diplomat there), that she felt 'it was important to die *with* one's country. Compared to this dying *for* one's country was easy.'[211] Similar witness has been borne by Nobel Peace Prize-winners Aung San Suu Kyi of Burma, who endured years of house arrest, or Liu Xiaobo, serving a punitive prison sentence for peaceful opposition to the Chinese government's repression of human rights.

It seems we'll always need men and women of their calibre to keep alive our own commitment to living the truth, since indeed the pressure is often on us to do what Shulubin, a character in Solzhenitsyn's *Cancer Ward*, accuses himself of doing. Quoting Pushkin, he concludes his examination of conscience with his own self-judgement – that he has betrayed himself and his society by settling on survival as his primary goal in life:

The people are intelligent enough, it's simply that they wanted to live. There's a law big nations have – to endure and so to survive. When each of us dies and History stands over his grave and asks 'What was he?' there'll be only one possible answer, Pushkin's:

'In our vile times
... Man was, whatever his element,
Either tyrant or traitor or prisoner!'

Shulubin wagged his great finger at him. 'The poet had no room in his line for "fool", even though he knew that there are fools in this world. No, the fact is there are only three possibilities, and since I can remember that I've never been in prison, and since I know for sure that I've never been a tyrant, then it must mean ... '[212]

In Shulubin's earlier life of conformism, Solzhenitsyn has anticipated the survival ethos of the sociobiologists. Only a scientistic ideologist, I believe – suffering from that odd spiritual blindness we saw von Doderer diagnose as the refusal to perceive reality – would try to explain away people like these dissidents in terms of the various determinisms rather than as outbursts of a desire for truth preferring physical to spiritual annihilation. And, to answer the question this section began with, only the coherence

211 See Haight, *Akhmatova*, p. 142.

212 Aleksandr Solzhenitsyn, *Cancer Ward*, New York: Farrar, Straus & Giroux, 2001, p. 438.

of our words and our life with what is ultimately real, and not what merely appears to be so, will answer our desire for truth in and for itself.

1.4 Etty Hillesum's choice of the other person as unlimited you

Voegelin notes how Aristotle attributes 'a higher degree of truth to concrete action than to the general principles of ethics'.[213] Because it is in and through what Lonergan called the 'effective freedom' of our actual willing that the 'essential freedom' of our capacity to will reveals itself, and also develops or matures. Without any attempt at hagiographical idealisation, I'll illustrate this from the writings of Etty Hillesum, a Jewish woman who discovers her freedom first assisting Jews interned by the Nazis at Westerbork camp in Holland, and then as an internee herself.[214]

We've already drawn on Walsh's insistence that we understand freedom only on its own level, where 'we choose to choose'. Hillesum shows rather clearly how decisions to do with the fundamental direction our lives will take involve a clear-sighted choice of moral existence over biological survival. She writes:

> They keep telling me that someone like me has a duty to go into hiding because I have so many things to do in life, so much to give. But I know that whatever I may have to give to others, I can give it no matter where I am, here in the circle of my friends or over there, in a concentration camp. And it is sheer arrogance to think oneself too good to share the fate of the masses. And if God Himself should feel that I still have a great deal to do, well then, I shall do it after I have suffered what all the others have to suffer. And whether or not I am a valuable human being will become clear only from my behaviour in more arduous circumstances. And if I should not survive, how I die will show me who I really am.[215]

---

213 Voegelin, *Anamnesis: On the Theory of History and Politics*, 148. The reference is to the *Nicomachean Ethics*, 1107a28ff.

214 Ria van den Brandt warns against hagiographical idealisation in her perceptive discussion of Hillesum's spiritual dimension, 'Etty Hillesum and her "Catholic Worshippers": A Plea for a More Critical Approach to Etty Hillesum's Writings, in *Spirituality in the Writings of Etty Hillesum: Proceedings of the Etty Hillesum Conference at Ghent University*, November 2008, Klaas A. D. Smelik, Ria van den Brandt, and Meins G. S. Coetsier, eds., Leiden: Brill, 2010, pp. 215–31. For this section, I've drawn on my 'Foundations for a Judgment of the Holocaust: Etty Hillesum's Standard of Humanity', in ibid., pp. 125–146. See Klaas Smelik, 'A Short Biography of Etty Hillesum (1914–1943)' in ibid., pp. 21–8; Meins G. S. Coetsier has an extended philosophical study on Hillesum in *Etty Hillesum and the Flow of Presence: A Voegelinian Analysis*, Columbia, MO: University of Missouri Press, 2008.

215 *Etty: The Letters and Diaries of Etty Hillesum, 1941–1943*, Klaas A. D. Smelik, ed., Arnold J. Pomerans, tr., Grand Rapids, MI: Eerdmans, 2002, p. 487. Further page references from Hillesum are to this text.

Etty's attitude is indicated not just by her words, but by her known deeds – particularly by her choice to remain with her own people, a choice she renewed even in the face of almost forcible removal by her friends, when it would still have been possible for her to withdraw from the camp under her protected status as a low-ranking member of the Jewish Council.[216] Her letters and diaries show a growth in her decision to choose what's absolutely good, a choice transcending any emotions either of withdrawal to fearful passivity or of revenge. Speaking of the SS camp guards she writes:

> They are merciless, totally without pity. And we must be all the more merciful ourselves. That's why I prayed early this morning: 'Oh God, times are too hard for frail people like myself. I know that a new and kinder day will come. I would so much like to live on, if only to express all the love I carry within me; carry into that new age all the humanity that survives in me, despite everything I go through every day. And there is only one way of preparing for the new age, by living it even now in our hearts. Somewhere in me I feel so light, without the least bitterness and so full of strength and love. I would so much like to help prepare for the new age and to carry that which is indestructible within me intact into the new age, which is bound to come, for I can feel it growing inside me, every day. (497)

It's no accident that the clearest examples of lived truth and freedom are those made in light of the threat of our biological destruction, since such a readiness to live out that truth and those decisions is like a crucial experiment on the human spirit. Similarly, that test can expose others as unready. Hillesum speaks of some of those imprisoned at Westerbork, who had previously belonged to the upper reaches of Dutch society:

> Their armor of position, esteem, and property has collapsed, and now they stand in the last shreds of their humanity. They exist in an empty space, bounded by earth and sky, which they must fill with whatever they can find within them – there is nothing else ... Yes, it is true, our ultimate human values are being put to the test. (590)

---

216 See Klaas Smelik's careful discussion, 'De keuze van Etty Hillesum om niet onder te duiken' in Ria van den Brandt and Klaas A. D. Smelik, eds., *Etty Hillesum in Context*, Assen: Van Gorcum, 2007, pp. 59–73.

Still, Hillesum refrains from judging anyone, since she's come to the realisation that each one is responsible for what they do. All she will do is judge herself – the *Letters and Diaries* include strict self-criticism, among other things, questioning her own participation in the Jewish Council's work (551, 645–6). Having done so, she set heights for her own freedom, heights which have nothing to do with self-preservation in the biological or utilitarian sense of the word, to ascend to a concrete love of humanity in each of its members:

> I suddenly came across a short quotation from Dostoevsky with which I shall end for today: 'It is wrong to judge people as you do. There is no love in you, only strict justice; that makes you unjust.' (178)

> More and more I tend toward the idea that love for everyone who may cross your path, love for everyone made in God's image, must rise above love for blood relatives. Please don't misunderstand me. It may seem unnatural – And I see that it is still far too difficult for me to write about, though so simple to live. (641)

From the perspective of political philosophy, Walsh would corroborate Hillesum's experience:

> Without any clear relationship to transcendent Being or any developed account of the human trajectory, one has difficulty sustaining the rationale for treating each human being as an inexhaustible centre of value in the whole universe. In a world defined by instrumental rationality why should man alone escape the iron necessity of efficiency?[217]

1.5 Albert Speer's choice of evil

No less than freedom, does our free refusal to live up to the level of its demands escape explanation by the usual determinisms – genetic, neural, emotional, sociological, even historic. As we've seen, Walsh roots the ideological holocausts of the twentieth century primarily in human will – mysteriously in our capacity not to choose the transcendent good and to prefer the more immediate satisfactions of hatred, anger, sadism

---

217 David Walsh, 'Are Freedom and Dignity Enough? A Reflection on Liberal Abbreviations' in Robert Kraynak and Glenn Tinder, eds., *In Defense of Human Dignity*, Notre Dame, IN: University of Notre Dame Press, 2003, pp. 165–91, at p. 175.

and revenge. Dostoevsky has explored the source of these modern hells through the well-known answer the monk Zosima in *The Brothers Karamazov* gives to his own question, 'What is hell?' by saying: 'The suffering of no longer being able to love.' Those condemned 'are sufferers by their own will'.[218] We can say then that human evil is the strange non-choice that arises from our willed refusal to take responsibility for ourselves and others, a reversal of the Golden Rule, so that we seek to undo others as we are undoing ourselves.

In a review of Hannah Arendt's *Origins of Totalitarianism*, Voegelin echoed some of Arendt's own observations, not only on the SS who ran the camp, but also of some of those imprisoned there. He refuses to allow that totalitarian movements are necessarily determined by social, economic or historic situations – these may be factors, but human freedom, or the refusal to exercise it, is the key component:

> The character of a man, the range and intensity of his passions, the controls exerted by his virtues, and his spiritual freedom, enter as further determinants ... Dr Arendt is aware of this problem. She knows that changes in the economic and social situations do not ... [make people] respond by necessity with resentment, cruelty and violence.[219]

Arendt is quite emphatic on this point. Reviewing Bernd Naumann's *Auschwitz*, an account of the Frankfurt trials of Nazi camp functionaries, she warned against indulging:

> ... in sweeping statements about the evil nature of the human race, about original sin, about innate human 'aggressiveness,' etc., in general – and about the German national character in particular ... [But] in any event, one thing is sure, and this one had not dared to believe any more – namely, that everyone could decide for himself to be either good or evil in Auschwitz ... And this decision depended in no way on being a Jew or a Pole or a German; nor did it even depend on being a member of the SS.[220]

---

218 Fyodor Dostoevsky, *The Brothers Karamazov*, Richard Pevear and Larissa Volokhonsky, trs., New York: Farrar, Straus & Giroux, 2002, pp. 322–3.

219 Eric Voegelin, *Published Essays 1953–1965*, Ellis Sandoz, ed., Columbia: University of Missouri Press, 2000, pp. 19–20.

220 Quoted in Elisabeth Young-Bruehl, *Hannah Arendt: For the Love of the World*, New Haven: Yale University Press, 1982, p. 368.

Highlighting the personal consequences of the refusal to actualise one's capacity for openness to others, Voegelin concludes his reflections on Plato's myth of judgement in the *Gorgias*: 'eternal condemnation means, in existential terms, self-excommunication'.[221] Whatever about the honesty of the former leading National Socialist Albert Speer's memoir, *Inside the Third Reich*, his examination of conscience regarding his capitulation to the desire for fame and power leads him to perform his own self-judgement in terms of an abdication of freedom. Speaking of Hitler, whom he considered a friend, he wrote:

> I felt, in Martin Buber's phrase, 'anchored in responsibility in a party.' My inclination to be relieved in having to think, particularly about unpleasant facts, helped to sway the balance ... I was ready to follow [Hitler] anywhere ... Years later, in Spandau [jail], I read Ernst Cassirer's comment on the men who of their own accord throw away man's highest privilege: to be an autonomous person. Now I was one of them.[222]

Walsh remarks that a person who radically fails to follow the attraction of the good, chooses to become evil (see *GBM*, 60). And that's how Speer became a morally 'hollow man'. He had in spades what Voegelin calls the 'secondary virtues' of orderliness, punctuality, politeness and incredible organisational skills: these bureaucratic habits were indeed the virtues essential for success in National Socialist Germany. To reverse Robert Musil's title, *Man Without Qualities*, Speer has the (secondary) qualities without man.[223] But he lacked the 'primary' or existential virtues by which we 'immortalise', as Aristotle called it. In terms of what we've said about our choice, 'immortalising', expresses the actualisation of our freedom in answer to the appeal of the good that surpasses material considerations.[224]

---

221 Voegelin, *Plato and Aristotle*, Baton Rouge: Louisiana State University Press, 1964, p. 45.

222 Albert Speer, *Inside the Third Reich*, London: Sphere Books, 1979, pp. 50–1, p. 88. In his *Spandau: The Secret Diaries* (London: Collins, 1976), Speer wrote how, in his *Buddenbrooks*, Thomas Mann gave 'an account of the disintegration of the German bourgeoisie's moral fibre'; having mentioned his architect father's own withering comments on what he, Albert, was doing for Hitler, Speer continues: 'how brittle all aesthetic and moral standards must have grown before Hitler became possible' (p. 390). Gitta Sereny examines Speer's honesty in *Albert Speer: His Battle with the Truth* (New York: Knopf, 1995).

223 Voegelin uses this phrase while discussing the 'spiritual disorientation' among the German elite in 'The German University and the Order of German Society: A Reconsideration of the Nazi Era' in his *Published Essays 1966–1985*, Ellis Sandoz, ed., Baton Rouge: Louisiana State University Press, 1990, pp. 1–35, at p. 16.

224 On the primary and secondary virtues, see Voegelin, *Hitler and the Germans*, pp. 102–5.

Given his position at the very summit of the power Hitler shared with his top subordinates, the failures Speer judges himself guilty of had enormous repercussions. He describes one of the most serious omissions, when advised not to inspect a concentration camp in Silesia by a friend of his who was Gauleiter there:

> I did not query him. I did not query Himmler. I did not speak with personal friends. I did not investigate – for I did not want to know what was happening there ... from that moment I was inescapably contaminated morally ... This deliberate blindness outweighs whatever good I may have done or tried to do in the last period of the war ... I still feel ... responsible for Auschwitz in a wholly personal sense.[225]

There's a range of ways by which I can deform myself as a person, from deliberate commission of destructive violence to culpable omission of responsible action. Speer's account focuses on culpable omission, a moral failure Albert Camus diagnoses in *The Fall*. In the story, Jean-Baptiste Clamence, a Parisian lawyer who'd become well known for defending the disadvantaged, addresses us in a monologue at Mexico City bar, Amsterdam. His audience is made up of 'professional humanists' – that large cohort of modern people, intensely sensitive to the ideals of human solidarity and love. We judge others by these ideals, yet are strangely remiss when responsible action towards a concrete human being is called for. Jean-Baptiste recalls the night in Paris he passed by a young woman in black leaning against the parapet of a bridge:

> I had already covered about fifty metres when I heard the noise – which, despite the distance, seemed tremendous in the silence of the night – of a body falling down into the water. I stopped dead, but without going back. Almost immediately, I heard a cry, repeated several times, going downstream, then suddenly dying out ... I wanted to run yet didn't budge. 'Too late, too far ... ' I kept listening, without moving. Then, gradually, in the rain, I drew away.

The lawyer ends his monologue with a question to the 'you' of each listener. Amsterdam is likened to the 'bourgeois hell' populated by those

---

225 Speer, *Inside the Third Reich*, p. 507. Even if we needn't credit Speer's own interpretation of these events, his version of what he failed to do is still damning.

who, despite their verbal idealism, will betray their neighbour by not being prepared to do anything for him or her:

> OK, tell us please, how you arrived one evening at the quays of the Seine, and succeeded in never risking your life ... 'O young woman, throw yourself into the water again so that a second time I may have the chance of saving both of us!' A second time, eh, what a risky suggestion! Just suppose ... we were taken seriously? We'd have to go through with it. Brr ... ! The water's so cold! But let's not worry! It's too late now. It'll always be too late. Lucky for us![226]

It is this 'not doing what I know I should do' that no determinisms within me or pressures from outside can justify. As Thomas Nagel said, we can't escape from moral reflection, nor, I would suggest, from our inbuilt orientations towards beauty, meaning, truth and goodness. Having focused on how our core orientations are to horizons irreducible to space-time categories only, though embodied in them, we can at last move on to explore the one whom Karl Kraus wrote of as 'coming from the origin', and who, because he always keeps the eternal in mind, 'is ever arriving at the origin'.[227]

---

226 Albert Camus, *La chute*, Paris: Gallimard, 1971, p. 98, p. 75, pp. 155–6.

227 Edward Timms, in his *Karl Kraus: Apocalyptic Satirist: The Post-War Crisis and the Rise of the Swastika* (New Haven: Yale University Press, 2005), ends with Kraus's poem, 'Zwei Läufer' ('Two Runners'), which concludes, '*Und dieser, den es ewig bangt,/ist stets am Ursprung angelangt*' – rather freely translated above (p. 613).

Part Five: Meeting you face to face – the human person as Communion

Chapter Eleven: From Big Bang to big mystery

To help us on our way to appreciating who a person is, I'd like to quote a 1954 reflection by Lithuanian-Polish poet, Czeslaw Miłosz. He's describing the enormous impact someone he saw on the Paris metro had on him. He named this reflection with the Latin word for 'to be', 'Esse':

> I looked at that face, dumbfounded ... And so it befell me that after so many attempts at naming the world, I am able only to repeat, harping on one string, the highest, the unique avowal beyond which no power can attain: I am, she is. Shout, blow the trumpets, make thousands-strong marches, leap, rend your clothing, repeating only: is! She got out at Raspail. I was left behind with the immensity of existing things ... [1]

For Miłosz, if we can presume he meant others to share in his reflection, each person is a unique, irreplaceable and unrepeatable miracle. We've already mentioned one of the earliest philosophical reflections on what it is to be human, Heraclitus' fragment, 'You could not find the limits of the soul even if you travelled every path so deep is its logos' (B45).

We've traced an answer to one of the questions we've been asking about human origins in the light of evolution in Parts Two and Three, and we've been leading up to an answer to the other of our origins, creation, over the last four chapters. What was interesting was how even that first, cosmic-evolutionary process of which we're a part was itself open to further questions as to its origin. What we'll be unfolding in this last chapter is how the same transfinite origin of the cosmic-evolutionary process and of humanity has had the courtesy[2] to invite the universe, and we'll see, ourselves, to take part in the immense single act of creation grounding everything. It's because our participation in that process and in that cooperation with creation is, as Kraus hinted, so freighted with our awareness both of coming from and ever arriving at our origin, that our coming into existence needs a separate inquiry.

---

1 Czeslaw Miłosz, *New and Collected Poems 1931–2001*, New York: HarperCollins, 2001, p. 249.

2 The word is Michelangelo's, who responded artistically more than most to that invitation, writing of the difficulty of focusing his thoughts, 'full of error', in the last years of his life, and exclaiming: '*Ma che poss'io, Signor, s'a me non vieni/coll'usata ineffabil cortesia.*' – 'But what can I do, Lord, if you don't come to me/with your usual ineffable courtesy.' *Rime*, p. 153.

Let's say there are three questions we can ask about the human person – a who question, a what question and a how question. While it'd be impossible here to give even the partial answer of an autobiography to 'Who am I?', we'll still keep as close to personal experience as possible. 'What am I?' is a question that's often been put in terms of human nature, what is it to be human, so the answer to the who question should be a big help here. Finally, we'll be in a position to discuss the question, 'How did I come into existence', the question of human origins we've been partly exploring in our chapters on evolution and the hominid sequence.

1. Who am I? The human person as Wewards

It's interesting how most academics (along with the rest of the human race) are convinced of the primacy of personal existence, even if it's not raised as a topic in their writings. In a discussion with Richard Dawkins on RTÉ radio some years ago,[3] I focused on the last section of his book, *A Devil's Chaplain*, 'A Prayer for my Daughter'.[4] This contains a letter he'd written to his young daughter warning her off religious belief as not based on evidence. I suggested that it could be seen as an expression of the love of a father for his child. Professor Dawkins agreed, and when I volunteered that the evidence for his fatherly love was quite different to the kind of evidence required by natural science, he also agreed. But that would imply he'd accepted Aristotle's point in his *Nicomachean Ethics*: that 'it is the mark of an educated man to look for precision in each class of things just so far as the nature of the subject admits' (1094b24–25). And, at least in the case of his daughter, Dawkins accepted that this also holds for our knowledge of persons too.

Another example comes from the physicist Stephen Hawking, who told interviewer Diane Sawyer that he's offered his children three pieces of advice – the third being the most relevant to our discussion: 'One, remember to look up at the stars and not down at your feet. Two, never give up work. Work gives you meaning and purpose and life is empty without it. Three, if you are lucky enough to find love, remember it is there and don't throw it away.'[5] It's hardly stretching things to suggest that both these public intellectuals find themselves more fulfilled as persons in and

---

3 On the Marian Finucane Show, RTÉ Radio 1 (11 December 2003).

4 Richard Dawkins, *A Devil's Chaplain*, London: Weidenfeld & Nicolson, 2003, pp. 241–8.

5 ABC News, 'Renowned Physicist Stephen Hawking Shares Thoughts on God, Fatherly Advice in an Interview With ABC's Diane Sawyer' by Ki Mae Heussner, 7 June, 2010.

through their relationships with others, without in the least denying the intellectual fulfilment their scientific work gives them.

1.1 The human person as intrinsically relational

I'd like to suggest three interrelated facets we can explore in our own personal existence: myself as intrinsically relational or youwards, how I live that youwardness by sacrificing myself for you, and how, if that self-giving is reciprocated, we become persons-in-communion, moving from youwardness to wewardness.[6]

As we've seen, this awareness of unlimitedness within Western culture has acquired a personal – or better, an interpersonal – dimension which comes out very clearly in Etty Hillesum's *Letters and Diaries*. They express her achievement of a perspective on personhood as intrinsically you-oriented or youwards.[7] In other words, for her, the unlimited quality of the openness of the human person as somehow 'containing' all the horizons of beauty, meaning, truth and goodness is only arrived at when it touches the boundlessness of another person. It's a boundlessness that's fully universal and fully particular:

> I have so much love in me, you know, for Germans and Dutchmen, Jews and non-Jews, for the whole of mankind – there is more than enough to go around. (569)

> I see more and more that love for all our neighbours, for everyone made in God's image, must take pride of place over love for one's nearest and dearest … (641)

And in what amounts to an interpersonal gloss on Heraclitus' 'The soul has a logos that augments itself' (B115), she speaks of how she's grown as a person in the concentration camp:

> Many people are still hieroglyphs to me, but gradually I am learning to decipher them. It is the best I can do: to read life from people. In

---

6 In what follows I'm drawing on my PhD thesis, 'Wewards: Theoretical Foundations for a Psychology of Friendship', University College Dublin (1980), and on my unpublished 'Piero Coda's theology of history as ongoing memory of humanity's participation in the trinitarian *kenosis*' (paper delivered at the Symposium on *Translatio Imperii*, University of Hong Kong, February 2010).

7 The page references to all quotations from Hillesum are to *Etty: The Letters and Diaries of Etty Hillesum*. I've borrowed from St Thomas More's 'Devout Prayer' written in the Tower of London just before his execution in 1534, where he speaks of 'my love to theeward' – so I hope the reader will forgive my bending his English with 'youwards' and 'wewards.'

> Westerbork it was as if I stood before the bare palisade of life. Life's innermost framework, stripped of all outer trappings. 'Thank You, God, for teaching me to read better and better.' (522)

She exposes the source of her understanding of this universal humanity in an effort-filled achieved experience of a transfinite personal ground:

> My life has become an uninterrupted dialogue with You, oh God, one great dialogue. Sometimes when I stand in some corner of the camp, my feet planted on Your earth, my eyes raised toward Your heaven, tears sometimes run down my face, tears of deep emotion and gratitude ... I am not challenging You, oh God; my life is one great dialogue with You ... Sometimes I try my hand at turning out small profundities and uncertain short stories, but I always end up with just one single word: God. And that says everything, and there is no need for anything more. (640)

That experience led to her intense consciousness of the youwardness of each person, each one a you-for-You:

> I love people so terribly, because in every human being I love something of You. And I seek You everywhere in them and often do find something of You. But now I need so much patience, patience and thought, and things will be very difficult. And now I have to do everything by myself. The best and the noblest part of my friend, of the man whose light You kindled in me, is now with You. (514)

In his study of Hegel, Italian philosopher and theologian Piero Coda understands Hegelian meta physics as 'a metaphysics of intersubjectivity, that is, of *being in relation*'. Coda agrees with Hans Urs von Balthasar that the notion of subsistent relation was not formulated by classic Greek thought, which proved inadequate for expressing the radically interpersonal dynamic of the Christian event. He goes on to quote Canadian theologian Jean Galot who makes the point that if the formal constitution of the Person in God is relation, then relation should also be constitutive of the human person created in the image and likeness of God. So he gives a dynamic meaning to the Thomistic notion of the divine persons as 'subsistent relations' when he suggests that each divine Person:

... precisely because *he is not, is*: because he is not a subsistence closed in himself, but a subsistence that is gift of self without remainder (and thus, in some way, renouncing self, he 'is not'), precisely because of this he is himself, he is a divine Person in unity-distinction with the other divine persons, in the unity-unicity of divine Being as Love.[8]

Etty Hillesum came to understand herself in and through her living out her relationship with the divine You and each of her friends and acquaintances – you could add, even those that would have been thought to be her enemies, like Westerbork's SS guards – as a you. Not unlike her experience, Coda sees the human person as both intrinsically eschatological (from e*schaton*, meaning an end that's beyond time) in its vertical dimension towards the divine, and intrinsically communional in its horizontal dimension towards the other.[9] Every 'you', whether human or divine, is an infinite horizon, so that there should be no trivial, and certainly no merely instrumental relationship.

1.2 My interrelationship with you by giving myself

But how do I relate to you as a person, from heart to heart? Even for non-believers, Hegel's view of the centrality of the death of Christ for philosophy may have relevance. Coda uses it to head his Hegel book, because he explains that death as an act of utter self-negation for the sake of the other. The quotation is: 'The death of Christ is the central point around which everything hinges' (*Lectures on the Philosophy of Religion*). For Coda, Hegel grasps that what a Christian would understand as self-sacrificing love is alone capable of 'uniting the "opposites" of God and the world, the infinite and the finite, the I and the you: the principle ... of unity in freedom-diversity', Hegel has understood 'the centrality of the moment of the *not*, of the negation of self out of love, in relation to otherness'.

However, Coda also points out that the subject's self-realisation occurs in and through his or her relation with another, a relation which might require for the fullness of self-realisation, 'the evangelical "losing one's life in order to find it"'.[10] More recently than Hegel, philosophers from Kierkegaard to Rosenzweig, Buber, Levinas, Derrida and Walsh have explored our experience of intrinsic responsibility towards the other through

---

8 Piero Coda, *Il negativo e la trinità: Ipotesi su Hegel*, Rome: Città Nuova, 1987, p. 142, p. 374, p. 402.

9 Piero Coda, *Evento Pasquale: Trinità e Storia*, Rome: Città Nuova, 1984, p. 192.

10 Coda, *Il negativo e la trinità*, pp. 356–7, p. 359, p. 376.

making an unconditional gift of ourselves. This experienced priority of the other, requiring me to sacrifice myself, is the lived 'language' of my being in relationship to the other. We can take an example from a South African-born doctor, Aubrey Hodes. In 1953, Hodes met Martin Buber in Jerusalem, and told him of his difficulties with a mentally sick relation. He writes how Buber:

> ... spoke of my involvement with my relative's illness as one of the crucial human encounters ... Her illness, he said, had a hidden significance for my own life. Only I could discover the meaning it held for me. But in order to do so I had to check my unconscious view of her as a person who was being drained of her human shape and becoming a thing, an object. I had to penetrate through the skin of her sickness to the basic unchanged humanity, enter her world, but with understanding, not with pity, concerning myself directly with her recovery. And, in doing so, I might discover the deeper meaning of my existence and my capacity for love. Otherwise I would not be able to reach her, and would not be able to unlock the riddle of my responsibility towards her.
>
> For I had a responsibility, he said. Love was responsibility for the loved person by the one who loved. Only by accepting this responsibility could I affirm my real self, my authentic personality. The situation called upon me to make a concrete commitment, to realise my responsibility in action – to see her as a single, unique, distressed individual, not just one of a depersonalised throng of mental patients.[11]

It is this requirement I have not to be just for myself, but for the other, and without conditions, that's the price of breaking out of what can become the prison of myself. Eugene O'Neill satirises the impossibility of assigning limits to our gift of self in an exchange in *Long Day's Journey into Night* between Tyrone and his son, Edmund, who is ill with consumption. Tyrone tells him to choose his sanatorium: 'Any place you like – within reason.'[12] What's missing here is the dimension of unconditional personal gift, which psychiatrist Ronald Laing focuses on from a clinical observation:

> Shortly after they had met, the nurse gave the patient a cup of tea. This chronically psychotic patient, on taking the tea, said, 'This is the first

---

11 Aubrey Hodes, *Encounter with Martin Buber*, Harmondsworth: Penguin, 1975, p. 15.

12 Eugene O'Neill, *Long Day's Journey into Night*, New Haven: Yale University Press, 1977, p. 148.

time in my life that anyone has ever given me a cup of tea.' ... It is the simplest and most difficult thing in the world for *one person*, genuinely being his or her self, *to give*, in fact and not just in appearance, *another person*, realised in his or her own being by the giver, *a cup of tea*, really and not in appearance. This patient is saying that many cups of tea have passed from other hands to hers in the course of her life, but this notwithstanding, she has never in her life had a cup of tea really given to her.[13]

Commenting on this some years ago, I wrote that 'All the things that are most central to who I am: my life, my capacity for feeling and imagining, for understanding and loving, my language, education and cultural background, are gifts to me from others. Obviously each person makes what he can of these gifts and talents, but whatever I have made of myself cannot alter the fact that my whole existence is a gift. If so, then like all gifts, it must be given. If giving means what it says, then the giver must part unconditionally with his gift. If I am to give myself to you I must lose myself to you.'[14] It's when we reflect on the fact that our own existence, along with all its 'grace notes', is itself a gift that we begin to get closer to the inner reason we feel morally obliged to offer our intrinsic giftedness to another person.

1.3 From interrelationship to communion

If we're mutually prepared to go through the self-negation we experience in making a gift of ourselves to another, we achieve what seems to be impossible, the reconciliation of our deepest need for personal fulfilment, through 'losing' our freedom in communion. What is that communion? Lonergan writes how a man and woman falling in love go beyond particular acts of loving to 'the prior state of being in love' which 'transforms an "I" and a "thou" into a "we" so intimate, so secure, so permanent, that each attends, imagines, thinks, plans, feels, speaks, acts in concern for both'.[15] We can call this relationship a we-relationship, which Buber comments on:

The We of which I speak is no collective, no group, no objectively exhibitable multitude. It is related to the saying of 'We' as the I to the

---

13 R. D. Laing, *Self and Others*, London: Tavistock, 1969, p. 89.

14 Brendan Purcell, 'Wewards', p. 228.

15 Lonergan, *Method in Theology*, p. 33.

saying of 'I'. Just as little as the I does it allow itself to be carried over factually into the third person. But it does not have the comparative constancy and continuity that the I has.[16]

In chapter one, we already spoke of the human person not only as intrinsically interpersonal, but as intrinsically oriented wewards in the simultaneous fulfilling yet transcending personhood that occurs in genuine communion. Intrinsic interpersonality is then discovered to be what we may call intrinsic 'co-personality', indicating a person's going beyond the difference between self and other in communion. As I concluded my reflections on 'The Person as Communion':

> The resolution of one of the greatest cultural tensions of our time, between being a person and being communion can be found here, in what Chiara Lubich has called 'the equilibrium of love': by going beyond myself to each you, a you also seen as a communion person. Then I am being most fully *I*, most fully *concrete*, most fully *person*, when I am being most fully *We*, most fully *universal*, most fully *communion*.[17]

So I'd suggest that the answer to our question, 'who am I' would be in the direction of, 'I am a being capable of communion with others.' Of course, as free, I can choose not to be in communion.

1.4 The refusal of communion

What then of the refusal to actualise my intrinsic capacity for communion? Hegel's acuity in the *Phenomenology of Spirit* in diagnosing this core deliberate failure of persons to exist as persons comes across in his describing it in the language of interpersonality, as the anti-relationship of Master and Slave. Even if Marx misunderstood Hegel's treatment of the Master/Slave relationship, he too was aware that depersonalisation through instrumentalisation is where the failure of humans to be human is most accurately located.

Commenting on Hegel's treatment of Master and Slave, Coda finds it to contain an unspoken echo of the lack of 'the evangelical love of the others "as" oneself'.[18] Although, and fortunately, as Buber remarks, 'Evil cannot be

---

16 Martin Buber, *The Knowledge of Man*, New York: Harper, 1965, p. 106f.

17 Brendan Purcell, *'La persona come comunione. Riflessioni in chiave psicologica'*, *Nuova Umanità*, 5 (1983) 30, pp. 87–98, at p. 98.

18 Coda, *Il negativo e la trinità*, pp. 146–7.

done with the whole soul,' its moral devastation is a powerful indication that the depths of the human spirit can't be reached only by considerations from biology, neurology or animal psychology.[19]

Dostoevsky articulates as well as anyone the profound derangement of relationships involved. To take an example of tyranny from his *Notes from Underground*, even as a schoolboy the Underground Man exorcised his own self-contempt by outrageous psychological bullying:

> I did once make a friend. But I was a tyrant at heart; I wanted unlimited power over his heart and mind, I wanted to implant contempt for his surroundings in him ... I frightened him with my passion for friendship; I reduced him to tears and nervous convulsions. He was a simple-hearted and submissive soul, but when he became wholly devoted to me I immediately took a dislike to him and repulsed him – just as though I had needed him only to get the upper hand of him, only for his submission.

As an adult, he tries to compensate for his rejection by his peers by delivering a high moral lecture to Liza, a prostitute he's visited, commenting afterwards that what chiefly attracted him was the power-play over her. And when she calls on him, presuming he'd meant what he'd said, to tell him she's giving up that way of life, he sees her moral strength and genuine love for him as a threat. So he deliberately sets out to undermine her newfound integrity:

> I could never fall in love, because, I repeat, with me to love meant to tyrannise and hold the upper hand morally. All my life I have been unable to conceive any other love, and I have reached the stage when I sometimes think now that the whole of love consists in the right, freely given to the lover, to tyrannise over the beloved.[20]

Liza grows in stature during the story, to the point of refusing to accept the role of prostitute to which – by paying for their final encounter – he wishes to reduce her. But the attempted depersonalisation can

---

19 Martin Buber, *Good and Evil*, New York: Scribners, 1953, p. 130. In the *Phaedo* (93c) Plato had already asked how one human being could be good, another evil, if, in our terminology, we're determined by our bodily components. The Irish proverb, '*briseann an dúchas trí shúilibh an chait*'– 'nature breaks out through the cat's eyes' – makes the point that animals act only according to their nature. Humans must choose to do so or not.

20 Fyodor Dostoevsky, *Notes from Underground* and *The Double*, Jessie Coulson, tr., London: Penguin, 2003, p. 69, p. 119.

be mutual, where tyrant and tyrannised are united by their reciprocal unlove. A milder form of this mutual depersonalisation is revealed in Max Frisch's play, *Biography: A Game*. Regarding his relationship with his wife Antoinette, the dying behavioural scientist Dr Kürmann sadly makes a diary annotation: 'We have belittled each other … I you, you me … We know each other only as belittled.'[21]

This consciousness of a willed incapacity to love is starkly stated by Inès in Sartre's *No Exit*: 'I can neither give nor receive', a state which leads another character, Garcin, to make the play's defining declaration: 'Hell is other people.'[22] He wonders how he can be in Hell if there are none of the traditionally imagined instruments of torture you'd find in an Hieronymus Bosch painting. Sartre's point is that the greatest human suffering is what accompanies our free choice not to love other persons, a torment we bring down on ourselves by our own uncompelled choice not to love.

2. What am I? The nature of the human person

After exploring the who-question we're better prepared to ask the what-question – what's the nature of the human person? Speaking of how what are called the human sciences also remain confined to the peripheral aspects of who we are, Walsh notes

> that we are ourselves the reality on which we seek to reflect. Our best access to the acting person is through our own acting personhood. Treating the individual as a specimen of a universal nature, they fail to acknowledge that the person in every instance exceeds the category of which it is an instance.[23]

The trouble with our attempt at articulating the nature of the human person is that words like 'nature', 'definition', or 'thing' have been developed to deal with the realities studied by the natural sciences, and generally bring their presuppositions with them. Still, if we bear Walsh's remark in mind, I think we can still try to articulate the what question without impugning what we arrived at in terms of the who question. So, I'll use here Lonergan's notion of the thing, and apply it to the human person, since it helps us make a few further clarifications about what we are.

---

21 Max Frisch, *Biografie: Ein Spiel*, Frankfurt: Suhrkamp, 1968, p. 105.

22 Jean-Paul Sartre, *Huis clos*, Paris: Gallimard, 1947, p. 64, p. 92.

23 David Walsh, 'The Person and the Common Good,' in Fran O'Rourke, ed., *Human Destinies: Philosophical Essays in Memory of Gerald Hanratty*, Notre Dame: Notre Dame University Press, 2011.

2.1 The person as unity-identity-whole

In *Insight* Lonergan has developed the notion of the 'thing', which he sees as 'the basic synthetic construct of scientific thought'. He writes that 'the notion of a thing is grounded in an insight that grasps, not relations between data, but a unity, identity, whole in data … ' These data are not considered abstractly but are taken 'in their concrete individuality and in the totality of their aspects' (*Insight*, 246). I'm quite aware that Buber in his *I and Thou* contrasts the 'I' and the 'Thou' with the 'It', but if we take the human person in his or her concrete individuality and as a whole, we've got what I think is an adequate framework for understanding the nature of the human person.

So each person is a 'unity' in the sense that they are completely unsubstitutable – one person can never be replaced by another. It's this inner conviction of our uniqueness that totalitarian governments have tried to eradicate, most clearly in their Stalags and Gulags. As Gabriel Marcel remarked:

> I understand by 'techniques of degradation' a whole body of methods deliberately put into operation in order to attack and destroy in human persons … their self-respect, and in order to transform them … into mere human waste products, conscious of themselves as such … [24]

Their 'identity' isn't only their consciously experienced and remembered identity – there are many aspects of our identity that depend on the memories of others, particularly our family, since few of us have memories of ourselves before we were three or four years old. Human beings come into existence months and years before they're conscious of themselves as persons, yet I'd argue that who they are later is identical with who they were before they were born. Robert George, a professor of jurisprudence, and philosopher Christopher Tollefson open their book, *Embryo: A Defense of Human Life* with the news story they call 'Noah and the Flood'. It tells how police saved Noah from the hospital where he was trapped during hurricane Katrina which devastated New Orleans in September 2006. Noah existed as a human embryo, frozen in one of several canisters of liquid nitrogen along with 1,400 other embryos. Sixteen months later, Noah was born, and his parents, Rebekah and Glen Markham named him in honour of the survivor of an earlier flood. If he hadn't been saved, Noah would have perished. The authors write:

---

24 Gabriel Marcel, *Man Against Mass Society*, Chicago: Gateway, 1967, p. 42.

Let us repeat it: Noah would have perished. For it was Noah who was frozen in one of those canisters; Noah who was brought from New Orleans by boat; Noah who was subsequently implanted in his mother's womb; and Noah who was born on January 16, 2008.

The writers say that if Noah were asked if it was he who was rescued that day, he would say 'Of course'. And they continue: ' ... what Noah would be saying in these two words – and his answer is confirmed by the best science – is that human embryos are, from the very beginning, human beings, sharing an identity with, though younger than, the older human beings they will grow up to become'.[25]

And, as Walsh points out, each person is a 'whole', not a part. As persons:

None can give only a part and none can be received only as a part. They are all wholes open to all other wholes and thus constituting a community of wholes. Not even the community as a whole outweighs such parts that, as Maritain expressed it, are themselves wholes.[26]

Where this outweighing of the social whole by each of the human persons who comprise it is lost sight of, or worse, subjected to systematic denial, then the way is opened to what we may call the 'depersonalisation from above'. This mass depersonalisation characterised the various totalitarian attempts at building a society treating humans as substitutable components of whatever value is considered greater than individual persons – the absolutised State, History, Race or Class. On the other hand, if the primacy of the concrete reality of the person over the different levels of components found in each of us – whether physical chemical, biological, neural or emotional – is lost sight of, then the way is opened for a 'depersonalisation from below' where these parts as seen as determining the whole that each human being is.

To return to the nature of the human person, we can say we can't be defined the way a galaxy, a tree or an animal, including a Neanderthal hominid, is. Because, unlike all the other things in the universe, as Aristotle put it, we immortalise, we exist in time yet participate in what's beyond time:

---

25 Robert George and Christopher Tollefson, *Embryo: A Defense of Human Life*, New York: Doubleday, 2008, pp. 1–3.

26 David Walsh, 'The Unattainability of What We Live Within: Liberal Democracy' in Anton Rauscher, ed., *Die fragile Demokratie – The Fragility of Democracy*, Berlin: Duncker & Humblot, 2007, pp. 133–56, at p. 147.

we're in, but not of the world. So we need an appropriate analogical method using negation to correct our tendency to speak of human persons as if we were material things, whether physical or chemical, biological or zoological.

But we can lay down the source of that indefinability in our capacity to reach out to the equivalent indefinability of the other person. Emmanuel Levinas entitled his masterwork *Totalité et infini*, where he contrasted the abstract and ruinous totalising of the human person to its innate 'asymmetry' that led it to its existing at the service of the similarly infinite Other. We can say, then, that a human person is a unique embodied identity intrinsically oriented to communion with others, where the authentic unfolding of that capacity for unlimited, self-sacrificing love requires a readiness to lose ourselves for the sake of the other.

3. How do we come into existence? The question of the origin of each human being

Right through the book, if I may borrow de la Potterie's metaphor, we've been circling, 'like a winding staircase always revolving around the same centre, recurring to the same topics at a higher level', where our topic is: what are the origins of humanity? As we've said, the use of the plural for 'origins' is deliberate. As well as the long path through the cosmic evolutionary sequence, there's another more direct one where every instant in our existence is open to eternity.[27] 'Phylogeny' is the name given to the evolutionary development of a species, so even though we'll be challenging both the presupposition that evolution alone suffices to explain the arrival of humanity, and that the category of 'species' is adequate to the kind of reality we find humanity to be, still we can call this the phylogenetic question. Similarly 'ontogeny' is the name given to the origin and development of an individual organism from embryo to adult. And though I'll argue that the individual human being can't adequately be classified as an organism, we can call this the ontogenetic question. Since we're a lot closer to it, it'll perhaps be more illustrative to approach the ontogenetic question first.

3.1 How does a human being come into existence?

We'll say a word on the first moment of every human being's existence as a zygote, then how the human zygote acts as a unity both in 'space' and

---

27 As Thomas More wrote, 'From all places it is the same distance to heaven' *The Complete Works of St. Thomas More, vol. 4, Utopia*, Edward Surtz and J. H. Hexter, eds., New Haven: Yale University Press, 1965.

in 'time'.[28] We'll discuss the objections that the human zygote or embryo only comes into existence with the first emergence of the nervous system at fourteen days, and that 'twinning' implies human existence begins later than the moment of fertilisation.

(a) **The moment of conception:** Maureen Condic, a neurobiologist and anatomist, notes 'the beginning of life as the point at which a new, single-cell organism with unique composition and behaviour is formed', and gives an up-to-date summary of research in this area.[29] Following sperm-egg fusion, the body of the new human being is the single cell that embryologists call a human zygote; thereafter cell division and differentiation get under way as the new human being undertakes the infinitely intricate and elegant self-development of the human embryonic body that contemporary imaging technology increasingly allows us to observe and wonder at.

The individual's unique genome is determined from the moment of sperm-egg fusion, with the caveat that for the first thirty minutes of life, every individual possesses a unique genome that contains roughly 1/3 more DNA than is characteristic of the mature state. The only thing that is different at the pronuclear stage (the nuclei of the formerly separate egg and sperm cells are called 'pronuclei') is that the two halves of the unique genome are in separate sub-cellular compartments; that is, there is a physical separation between the maternally derived and paternally derived components of the genome.[30]

---

28 We're a zygote for half an hour, and then an embryo for the following eight weeks.

29 Maureen L. Condic, 'When does human life begin? A scientific perspective', *National Catholic Bioethics Quarterly*, 9 (1), 2009, pp. 127–208, at p. 131.

30 'Based on universally accepted scientific criteria, a new cell, the human zygote, comes into existence at the moment of sperm-egg fusion, an event that occurs in less than a second. Upon formation, the zygote immediately initiates a complex sequence of events that establish the molecular conditions required for continued embryonic development. The behaviour of the zygote is radically unlike that of either sperm or egg separately and is characteristic of a human organism. Thus, the scientific evidence supports the conclusion that a zygote is a human organism and that the life of a new human being commences at a scientifically well defined "moment of conception".' Condic, personal communication, 24 January 2011; see her 'When does human life begin?' 136 n. 14; see also Günter Rager, 'Die biologische Entwicklung des Menschen' in Günter Rager, ed., *Beginn, Personalität und Würde des Menschen*, Freiburg: Karl Alber, 2009, pp. 67–122 at p. 82; Rager includes a photograph of the zygote, with its sealed zona pellucida containing the still separate maternal and paternal pronuclei on p. 74 – the 'zona pellucida' is the zygote's outer boundary guaranteeing its individuality before it's implanted in the womb; Condic considers the view that the zygote begins only with the breakdown of the two pronunclei's nuclear membranes (syngamy), in the section of her article entitled 'Why isn't syngamy the beginning of a new human life?', pp. 141–3, and concludes that the zygote's self-direction commences with the earlier fusion of the sperm and egg.

(b) **The zygote acts as a unity-identity-whole:** The zygote is not 'part' of the maternal womb. Rather, the mother's womb is where the embryo normally moves to, to implant itself and continue its development; the embryo, however, controls its own developmental program from the very beginning.[31] 'Indeed, this "totipotency", or the power of the zygote both to generate all the cells of the body and simultaneously to organise those cells into coherent, interacting bodily structures, is the defining feature of the embryo.'[32]

Condic points out that once sperm-egg fusion has occurred, 'a human zygote acts as a complete whole, with all the parts of the zygote interacting in an orchestrated fashion to generate the structures and relationships required for the zygote to continue developing towards its mature state'.[33] We can speak of this as the zygote's acting as a whole in its own space. What about its acting as a whole over time? Angelo Serra and Roberto Colombo refer to Hans Jonas' distinction between organismal identity and physical identity, where Jonas says biological identity 'is not the permanent identity of a static, synchronic form, but the evolving identity of a self-constructing and self-organised agent who realises this dynamic, diachronic form of itself and continually does so till death ... '[34]

(c) **Does human existence only begin at fourteen days with the emergence of the 'primitive streak'?** Condic's response to this is that:

... the primitive streak is a transient structure that marks the beginning of an embryologic process known as gastrulation. At gastrulation, important distinctions in developmental potency and fate arise between cells in different regions of the embryo. Gastrulation establishes the three 'germ layers': primitive tissues that give rise

---

31 See Günter Rager, 'Der Begriff "Individuum" in der Debatte um den Status des Embryos' in Jean-Pierre Wils and Michael Zahner, eds., *Theologische Ethik zwischen Tradition und Modernitätsanspruch*, Freiburg: Herder, 2005, pp. 145–54. We know from IVF procedures that since a zygote can get itself up and running in a Petri dish, it's self-directing its own growth. But there's also an all-important dialogue of incarnation between the mother and the zygote/embryo where who and what each is allows an appropriate interaction at each moment.

32 Condic, 'When does human life begin?', p. 145.

33 Ibid., p. 140.

34 Angelo Serra and Roberto Colombo, 'Identity and Status of the Human Embryo' in Juan de Dios Vial Correa and Elio Sgreccia, eds., *Identity and Status of the Human Embryo: Proceedings of Third Assembly of the Pontifical Academy for Life*, Vatican City: Libreria Editrice Vaticana, 1998, pp. 128–77, at p. 117. Authors' emphasis. Lonergan has a similar understanding of what he calls 'a developing whole that is present in the parts, articulating under each set of circumstances the values it prizes and the goals it pursues, and thereby achieving its own individuality and distinctiveness' (*Method in Theology*, p. 211).

to the structures of the mature body. Although it is difficult to put a precise date on the 'beginning' of the nervous system, due to the continuous and overlapping processes of development, the earliest components of the nervous system do not arise until approximately a week later, around day 20–21.[35]

Rager articulates the same critique from a philosophical perspective when he asks how 'a non-individual being can change into an individual' – since the claim is that before then, no human individual exists. But no 'qualitative jump' is observed at the time of the emergence of that 'primitive streak'; what occurs rather, is a 'continuous process'. Also, the zygote is 'a system as a whole', where a range of developments are occurring at different times, none of which can be singled out as the decisive one. Any attempt to link its beginning to gastrulation or the emergence of the nervous system is biologically unjustified.[36]

(d) **Does twinning mean there can't be a new life until after twinning could have occurred?** The argument most used against the humanity of the embryo from fertilisation is that, since twins can be born from an original single zygote, the zygote must be indeterminate until the moment when the twins can appear. Again, Serra and Colombo address this:

Firstly, this phenomenon ['of monozygotic twins'] is a real exception: 99–99.6 per cent of the zygotes develop as a unique organism. This logically means that the zygote is *per se determined to develop as a unique human individual*. Secondly ... recent studies ... support the hypothesis that in some part of the embryoblast [the early embryo's inner cell mass], because of some error ... occurring between the fourth and seventh day after fertilisation, a *new and independent plan of development* is determined so that a new individual being *initiates its own life cycle*. It seems, therefore, very reasonable to state there is one first human being from whom a second human being originates ... [And] it appears incorrect to state that *one undetermined system becomes two determined systems*. The concept itself of 'undetermined system' is, from a biological point of view, meaningless. Thirdly, the statement that there is a *first human being* who will continue its own way, and a *second human being* who originates from the first and then

---

35 Condic, personal communication, 24 January 2011.

36 Rager, 'Die biologische Entwicklung des *Menschen*', pp. 102–4.

continues its independent course, finds a strong confirmation – one might say nearly a proof – in many recent observations.

One of the observations they refer to is where one of monozygotic twins has Down syndrome, while the co-twin has a normal karyotype with forty-six chromosomes: 'It is evident that in both cases the first individual continues its own course of development, while the second starts its own life cycle as soon as the new plan becomes independent from the first.'[37] So, for Rager, before the formation of the twin there is one embryo acting as an individual, after twinning there are two embryos acting as individuals.[38]

Serra and Colombo write, 'The question is not "What does science tell us about the embryo?" but "What can science *legitimately* tell us about the status of the embryo?" Biology cannot say anything about the human embryo's personhood, since natural sciences do not have the person as the formal object of their inquiries'.[39] So after this brief survey of the embryological data, we can turn to the philosophical questions.

3.2 What does it mean to say that a zygote is human?

I've seen giant sequoia cones in Kings Canyon National Park, California, but there's no way I could ever have guessed what they might grow into without seeing the Park's various redwood groves. The same would go for the tadpoles we collected as children – they're only properly understood in terms of their fully developed stage, of being a common frog. Tadpoles belong to the second stage of frog development but while, as with the human zygote, these stages have to be studied in their own right, no one seriously tries to see them as other than stages in the life cycle of the frog.

In a similar way, I'd suggest that our use of the word 'human' in relation to the zygote brought into existence by a human mother and father poses a question. If it's undeniably a human zygote – since human parents couldn't give rise to a zygote of any other kind – then the word 'human' must be loaded with whatever we mean by that term. We've already mentioned how hominid studies are haloed about with the word 'human', attesting to the undeniable fact that the interest both of researchers and of their readers is in the relationship of the hominid sequence to ourselves. But

---

37 Serra and Colombo, 'Identity and Status of the Human Embryo', pp. 168–9.

38 Rager, 'Die biologische Entwicklung des *Mensch*en', p. 105.

39 Serra and Colombo, 'Identity and Status of the Human Embryo', p. 129.

that evolutionary relationship is between different genera, while what we're talking about here is the life cycle of an individual belonging to the human species.

The human embryo is undoubtedly human, but it cannot yet do all those things which mark us off as fully developed human beings. It cannot yet exercise those capacities which essentially involve transcendence of the material, the biological and the zoological, even though they do not operate independently of their being embodied. The question becomes all the more pressing when we include the specifically interpersonal and communional capacities of the person considered as a person, for what we've called youwardness and wewardness.

To answer these questions we have to deepen our understanding of the human zygote and embryo, to see that it is not a merely zoological reality. We have to widen out the context of the human zygote and embryo to the horizon of the fully realised human person. When we look at a human zygote and embryo, what we're seeing is the materially essential embodiment of a human being in the first stages of his or her life cycle. Of course I'm inclined sometimes to speak of 'my body' as 'something' 'I have', but what I mean is: 'this is me' – the same is true for these first stages of our life – each of us was once a zygote and an embryo, and when we were going through the zygotic and embryonic stages of our life, this is what our bodies were like, the essential exteriorisation of who we were in those early moments of our life.

Just as in later life, if my body is injured or killed, then I'm injured or killed, so at the beginning of my life, if my life was taken while I was an embryo I'd have been killed. As George and Tollefson wrote in their account of the fate of Noah Markham, 'it was Noah who was frozen in one of those canisters; Noah who was brought from New Orleans by boat; Noah who was subsequently implanted in his mother's womb; and Noah who was born on 16 January, 2008.'

When we're confronted with the unbearable lightness of Bach played by a Dinu Lipatti, it's almost beyond words to imagine how the pianist could once have been such a tiny speck of a living being. And yet that's exactly what Jonas is saying when he writes of 'the evolving identity of a self-constructing and self-organised agent'. The truly awe-inspiring photography in *A Child is Born* by Lennart Nilsson and Lars Hamberger illustrates a book that's been called 'a timeless masterpiece'.[40] Of course the real masterpiece

---

40 Lennart Nilsson and Lars Hamberger, *A Child is Born* [4th edition], New York: Random House, 2004.

is the child's actual journey from fertilisation to birth. It gives rise to the kind of wonder we called a boundary or threshold question, a wonder aptly expressed in the title of Nilsson's equally acclaimed TV series, *The Miracle of Life*.

In 2001, the BBC ran a series on the human body's *Incredible Journey from Birth to Death*, presented by Robert Winston, whose second programme, on human life in the womb, was called 'An Everyday Miracle' and accompanied by the comment, 'The drama of conception activates the most sophisticated life-support machine on earth.' It is this sense of the 'miraculous' even in presumably non-religious producers that invites us to apply the phrase 'Big Mystery' to the unborn human being – its tiny beginning makes it all the more mysterious. In these considerations of tininess, let's return for a moment to the Big Bang we began with.

Due to brilliant observation techniques using NASA's Hubble telescope, Rychard Bouwens, an astronomer from Leiden Observatory, has been able to penetrate back 13 billion years ago to what's captured in the deepest infrared image ever – what's known as Ultra Deep Field. He and his team have 'glimpsed a presumed galaxy' that may be the oldest ever seen, 'a small, hot affair that blazed to life during the childhood of the cosmos'. The press report continued:

This technique dates the galaxy to the childhood of the cosmos, just 500 million years after the Big Bang, the cataclysmic explosion that rocketed the universe into existence ... Observations from the new camera, and from another NASA space telescope called Spitzer, tell us that the first galaxies were small – less than one percent the mass of our own Milky Way – and hot, blazing with early stars that hungrily gobbled up the hydrogen fuel around them. 'They were forming stars as fast as they could,' Bouwens says. And although the new galaxy might be one of the first, an explosion in galactic growth soon followed. By 2 billion years after the Big Bang, the universe had grown out of its childhood, and galaxy formation slowed dramatically.[41]

It's important not to lose the sense of wonder astronomers, embryologists and mothers of unborn children constantly experience when confronted

---

41 Brian Vastag, 'Hubble spots presumed oldest galaxy: Hot, faint, and 13 billion years old', *Washington Post*, 26 January 2011.

with the tininess of the beginning of being[42] – of the Big Bang of the universe and of the Big Mystery of each unique human child.

The zygote is the personal concrete unity-identity-whole which includes the bodily life wondrously unfolding in the womb and the as yet dormant capacities for beauty, truth, meaning, goodness, youwardness and wewardness. The bodily part we see now; the other part we won't see until its bodily development reaches a stage that allows the self-transcending capacities to begin to operate. All due proportion guarded, it can no more be understood separately from the fully developed person than the redwood cone or the tadpole. The enormous difference between the human zygote and the zygote of another mammal or late pre-human hominid is that its whole *raison d'être* is to be the embodiment of a specifically human existence. We've already mentioned Adolph Portmann's understanding of growth patterns in childhood and adulthood as culture-oriented, not to mention the human brain and vocal tract and their significance for language, symbolisation and meaning. So its materiality is intrinsically meaning-, love- and you-oriented. In this light, S. J. Heany's interpretation of the zygote makes sense in terms of Aristotelian-Thomist philosophy:

> ... from the time of fertilisation the *conceptus* is matter properly disposed to be the subject of such a form as the rational soul ... a one-cell *conceptus* with the specific human genotype ... is matter well enough disposed to be the proper subject of the human intellectual soul in regard to first act, to be the matter for which such a soul is the substantial form.[43]

Now we can look more closely at the personhood of the earliest human being.

3.3 'It is only with one's heart that one can see clearly'
The fox tells the little prince in Antoine de Saint-Exupéry's fable that 'It is only with one's heart that one can see clearly; what is essential is invisible to the eye.'[44] Günter Rager speaks of the 'embryo-mother dialogue', of which one of the first indications is the child's implantation around day 5–6 after fertilisation (Rager uses the more evocative German word for

---

42 I've borrowed the phrase 'the beginning of being', as we'll see, from David Walsh.

43 Quoted in Serra and Colombo, 'Identity and Status of the Human Embryo', pp. 175–6.

44 Antoine de Saint-Exupéry, *The Little Prince*, Ware, Herts.: Wordsworth Editions, 1995, p. 82.

this, 'Einnistung', which can mean 'nesting') in the mother's womb without being rejected as a foreign body.[45] But how does the mother see with her heart?[46]

David Walsh has been writing about how our relationship with one another as persons 'always goes beyond the evidence available', and this holds for our response to the unborn child, whose unique existence is perhaps the biggest mystery directly available to us on earth.

Because so much of what makes us human can only be known from within, in a sense, 'only the mother can tell who the embryo is because it is in love that the otherness of the other is known'. Since our love for another, if it is love, is unconditional, the mother's love 'is not conditioned by the attainments of the earliest zygote'. Its incapacity to return that love is its greatest gift. 'None of its potential achievements can surpass the pure gift of itself that it radiates from the very beginning. Children are loved and make it possible for us to love before they are even known.'

Walsh goes on to say that the human zygote or embryo provides us with the purest instance of unconditional love there is, in the sense that we are loving the other for the other's sake alone:

Before we know who the other is, love must be called forth. This can only be when the other is present without being present. The unborn is in that sense the purest possibility of the person, of that which is without visible manifestation. It is not for us to determine the status of the embryo, for our own status as persons is determined by the embryo.

He beautifully continues: 'Of all the epiphanies of the person we might say that the vulnerability of the embryo is the one in which otherness

---

45 Rager, 'Die biologische Entwicklung des Menschen', p. 76.

46 Of course, ultrasound photography has revolutionised the awareness, not only of mothers but of everyone, to the awe-inspiring reality of the life of the child in the mother's womb. For example, a groundbreaking Italian study using 4D ultrasound discovered that for five sets of twins in the womb, between fourteen and eighteen weeks, the incidence of other-directed movements progressively increased to reach 29% of observed movements towards their sibling. The ultrasound pictures show the twins concentrating on one another's eyes rather than mouths, with greater accuracy towards the other's eyes and mouth than towards their own, so that 'other-directed actions are not only possible but predominant over self-directed actions' (p. 10). Not surprisingly, the researchers conclude by referring to Martin Buber's I and Thou as a relevant context for their research. See Umberto Castiello et al., 'Wired to be Social: The Ontogeny of Human Interaction', Public Library of Science PloS ONE, October 2010, Volume 5, Issue 10, e13199: pp. 1–10.

is most deeply invoked. Each birth is somehow the beginning of being itself.[47] And it's the source of this 'beginning of being itself' that we must now seek.

3.4 Creation and pro-creation

We've already noted how both Plato and Aristotle grounded their philosophical anthropology on their experience of human existence as both finite and transfinite. Writing around 350BC, Aristotle is aware there's a threshold question regarding the coming into existence of human beings in general, since they're endowed with reason, which, as we've seen, is for him a dynamic quest for the ground of existence. So in his treatise *On the Generation of Animals* he wrote:

> That is why it is a very great puzzle to answer another question, concerning Reason. At what moment, and in what manner, do those creatures which have this principle of Reason acquire their share in it, and where does it come from? This is a very difficult problem which we must endeavour to solve, so far as it may be solved, to the best of our power. (736b5)

He never returned to the issue, but he certainly knew there was a problem, since he later wrote a whole treatise on the difference between the organising principle or soul of plants, animals and human beings, insisting that humans have an intellectual soul that's essentially not determined by the body and even separable from it.

And the question hasn't become easier since Aristotle's time, as philosophy, theology and Western culture in general has developed our understanding of what it is to be human, particularly in terms of free, personal existence – following a whole tradition in philosophy that Walsh covers in his *The Modern Philosophical Revolution*, not to mention the development of Trinitarian theology over almost two millennia. In that light, despite his wonderful reflections on friendship in the *Nicomachean Ethics*, Aristotle didn't develop a philosophy of the person. That later movement in philosophy articulates each of us as intrinsically interpersonal.

(a) **Edith Stein on personal contingency and its necessary ground**

So Edith Stein's formulation of the question in her 1936 work, *Finite and Eternal Being*, catches the experienced contingency of the human being,

---

47 Walsh, 'The Person and the Common Good: Towards a Language of Paradox.'

conscious that, whatever the origin of our material embodiment, our self as personal must be grounded in a transfinite, personal source:

> So the riddle of the I remains. For the I must receive its being from Someone else – not from itself. I do not exist of myself, and of myself I am nothing. Every moment I stand before nothingness, so that every moment I must be dowered anew with being ... this nothinged being of mine, this frail received being, is being ... it thirsts not only for endless continuation of its being but for full possession of being.[48]

This would seem to me to be the key question, which can only be raised if I've come to an awareness of what it is to be a person. We've been saying throughout this chapter what that entails – self-transcendent, self-sacrificing youwardness. But if each of us is utterly unique, we're also, as Stein has said, utterly contingent. Yet, we've already mentioned Walsh's remark that 'contingency is not itself contingent'. In other words, contingency only makes sense in terms of what's not contingent, that is, of what's necessary.[49]

And Stein too has grasped this where the contingency applies to personal existence. As a matter of fact I do exist as a person. As another matter of fact, which Aristotle recognised, my parents' biological act of procreation couldn't adequately explain my existence as a person. But I'm aware both of the fact that I didn't have to exist (I remember walking some of the back roads of Cobh, Co. Cork that my parents would have strolled before they got married, and thinking: if they hadn't met here, I wouldn't be around!) and

---

48 I haven't been able to source the translation used above, which is more evocative than the version of Chapter 2, §7 in Edith Stein, *Finite and Eternal Being: An Attempt at an Ascent to the Meaning of Being*, Kurt F. Reinhardt, tr., Washington, DC: ICS Publications, 2002: 'My own being, as I know it and as I know myself in it, is null and void [*nichtig*]; I am not by myself (not a being *a se* and *per se*), and by myself I am nothing; at every moment I find myself face to face with nothingness, and from moment to moment I must be endowed and re-endowed with being. And yet this empty existence that I am is *being*, and at every moment I am in touch with the fullness of being ... The ego shrinks back from nothingness and desires not only an endless continuation of its own being but a full possession of being as such: It desires a being capable of embracing the totality of the ego's contents in one changeless present ... ' (p. 55f.).

49 Just to give a flavour of Emmanuel Levinas' rich exploration of the issue of finite personal contingency and its source in infinite personal giftedness, here's a remark from his *Otherwise than Being*: 'This antecedence of responsibility to freedom would signify the Goodness of the Good: the necessity that the Good choose me first before I can be in a position to choose, that is, welcome its choice. That is my pre-originary succeptiveness. It is a passivity prior to all receptivity, it is transcendent. It is an antecedence prior to all representable antecedence: immemorial. The Good is before being.' Quoted in David Walsh's chapter on Levinas in *The Modern Philosophical Revolution: The Luminosity of Existence*, New York: Cambridge University Press, 2008, p. 320 n. 19.

at the same time that I do exist as a you whose orientation is intrinsically transfinite.

The existence of such a contingent yet determinate transfinitely oriented reality can only be explained by a cause or ground that's capable of bringing it into being. That is to say: I can only exist as a person because You, the absolutely personal Other exist. Only if there exists an absolutely unconditional transfinite personal reality can a being with transcendent capacities for unconditioned truth and freedom come into existence. This has an enormously liberating consequence: both Edith Stein and Esther (to give Etty her full and still biblically evocative name) Hillesum were convinced that absolutely no human being can be eclipsed by ideology and force, since each one has the capacity to take up a dialogue, not just in words, but in existence, with the transfinite You, who safeguards us from personal annihilation, even if not from physical repression and death. Why? Because each one is a you-for-You, never a mere part of some greater political or economic or racial reality. Stein had discovered that her incarnate youwardness as oriented towards eternal communion was precisely what made her human.

Nor is there any danger of our freedom being crushed by such a ground. Since the way a person expresses their youwardness is through self-sacrificing love – as we saw when discussing Piero Coda's interpretation of Hegel – then the unconditional You's relationship with the contingent you is analogous to the love of a parent for his or her child: instead of controlling the other, the mature adult's love is precisely to will the other's freedom to be most fully free. If the locked-in-self's only form of relating to the other is, like Dostoevsky's Underground Man, by dominating, then certainly we can say with Sartre's Garcin, 'hell is other people'. But being loved by a transfinite reality is being made ever more free, not dominated.

(b) Creation and pro-creation: the intersection of the timeless with time

Thomas Aquinas was able to draw on a more differentiated notion of a personal God who is creator of everything than was available to Aristotle. As we noted in an earlier chapter, the act of creation is one single act in God; obviously this is not from the viewpoint of creatures (allowing that we're the only creatures in space and time who have a viewpoint), which come into existence over 13 billion years or so. And we've quoted Lonergan on how God is both the one cause outside space and time of the entire order of the universe, but that also 'he uses the universe of causes as his instruments in applying each cause to its operation and so is the principal cause of each and every event as event'.[50]

Where does that get our question about the origin of each human being? Because we're personal, so that the one who creates us must be personal too, it's possible to suggest that each individual human being and all of us together are loved into existence by a single act of unlimited love. The act of divine love is what Les Murray in his 'First Essay of Interest' called 'interest' in each of us:

> It is a form of love. The everyday shines through it
> and patches of time. But it does not mingle with these;
> it wakens only for each trace in them of the Beloved.[51]

And the first trace in us of the Beloved is when He, with our parents, loved us into our existence as a one-celled embryo. Because God acts through his own creatures, in this case, our parents.

So with Aristotle we can say, yes, human parents can't give rise to what he called 'reason', and what we're calling here transfinitely oriented persons. But we can also say yes to Aquinas' notion of caused causes – or of a primary cause working through secondary ones, though that language isn't really suitable for persons either – by which parents co-create with God in their act of pro-creation. Rather than that impersonal language I'd prefer, with Enrique Cambón, to speak of the 'reciprocal *kenosis*' between God as creator and his human personal creation.[52] As Giuseppe Zanghí puts it:

> When God enters into relationship with humanity, precisely because he is Love, he can only do it by giving himself completely, by 'not being' in order to make the other equal to himself (as Aristotle said, there can't be true love without equality). This is a kenotic discussion: God is present in the world but as one who has given himself completely … When God creates, he does so by loving. What does 'by loving' mean? By giving everything. When he causes me to be, he causes me to be like himself, that is, he makes me, like himself, 'absolute', complete.[53]

---

50 Bernard Lonergan, *Collection*, New York: Herder & Herder, 1967, p. 58.

51 Les Murray, *New Collected Poems*, Manchester: Carcanet, 2003, p. 166.

52 Enrique Cambón, *Trinità modello sociale*, Rome: Città Nuova, 2009, pp. 68–74. The use of St Paul's term for Christ's 'emptying' himself, *ekénosen* (Phil 2:7) has given rise to nouns like 'kenosis' and adjectives like 'kenotic', where it's used to express the self-emptying required by genuine love for the other.

53 G. M. Zanghí, '*Verso una cultura del post-ateismo,' Gen's 1* (1997), pp. 9–13, at p. 10.

In pro-creating, the parents' co-creation participates in the one act of divine love by which each and every human person is created.[54] My parents were the parents of me in time, and God created me from eternity. T. S. Eliot's famous phrase, 'the intersection of the timeless with time', paraphrased as the intersection of created with uncreated love, is one way of expressing what happened. God respects his creatures as others, who he allows to participate in the miracle of bringing a new human infant who'll live for eternity, into existence. And it's this miracle that father after father and mother after mother is confronted with in their amazement at seeing their child for the first time.

I'd add to those thoughts a metaphor of lower levels offering their existence as a 'gift' to the next highest level – which up to the zoological level could be more technically handled in terms of a dynamic sequence of emergence and correspondence. That is to say, the human parents offer as a gift their pro-creative act which co-occurs within an irruption of eternal being into the time of that act, so that it's simultaneously in time and beyond time. In that timeless moment, the parents and God co-create the embodied and infinitely youwards-oriented human being. We'll be looking at Genesis in a moment, but Eve's words seem to express this event perfectly: 'Adam knew his wife again and she bore a son whom she named Seth [meaning 'he has granted'], saying, "Because God has granted me another child … "' (Genesis, 4:25). If the Big Bang poses a boundary or threshold question about the coming into existence of the universe, then the conception of each new unique human being is the Big Mystery that gave our book the second part of its title, since as Aristotle declared, human conception cannot be explained within the categories of biology alone.

Aleksandr Solzhenitsyn wrote that 'The Universe has as many different centres as there are living beings in it. Each of us is a centre of the Universe … '[55] So we can say that each human being is a world of his or her own, far

---

54 A traditional way of expressing this was in terms of the parents generating a human body into which God infused a soul. The limitations of this way of speaking is that it could sound as if these were separate acts, with a human body 'waiting' for its soul. Aristotle would hardly have condoned that kind of picture thinking, with his heuristic definition of soul as 'the first actuality of a natural body which potentially has life.' (*De Anima*, 412a27–28) See his *De Anima* (On the Soul), tr. Hugh Lawson-Tancred, Harmondsworth: Penguin, 1986, p. 157.

55 Aleksandr Solzhenitsyn, *The Gulag Archipelago 1918–1956: An Experiment in Literary Investigation*, Vol.1, London: Fontana, 1974, p. 3. The 11th edition of the *OED* defines a singularity in mathematics and physics as 'a point at which a function takes an infinite value, especially a point of infinite density at the centre of a black hole'. If the Big Bang is a singularity, we can say that each human zygote is one too, a 'beginning of being' at the centre of a universe including yet far transcending that space-time universe. From its tiny beginning as a human zygote, it too is a 'point of infinite density' where the density is its capacity for communion with other persons and with the personal source of its existence.

outweighing in value and mystery the existence of the entire astrophysical universe, up to and including the last of the pre-human hominids. The answer to the question of human origins, then, is that each human being is constituted into existence as a you-for-You in one cooperative act: creation by an unlimited transcendent and personal source and of co-creation by the child's parents. Each human being outweighs the Big Bang; each human being is a new beginning of a new personal universe. Nothing less would be a sufficient answer.

(c) **Genesis on creation and pro-creation**

Since we've mentioned the Book of Genesis a few times already, it's interesting to see how closely it corroborates what we've just being saying about the link between creation and pro-creation. I'm drawing on Voegelin's discussion of Genesis 2:4 in *Israel and Revelation*, 'These are the generations [*toldoth*] of heaven and earth', The passage 'opens an account of the creation but uses the same phraseology as the genealogical registers'. For Voegelin this is 'an odd usage; for the noun *toldoth* contains the verb *yalad*, "to bear", "to bring forth", and thus unmistakably refers not to creation but to procreation. Hence, we must assume that the oddity was intended, precisely in order to reveal a deeper connection between creation and procreation.' Voegelin finds this interpretation 'confirmed by the sequel to the odd passage':

> For the account of creation (2:4–7) describes it as a sequence of generations, the earlier one procreating the later ones with the creative assistance of Yahweh:
>
> > These are the generations [*toldoth*] of the heavens and earth when they were created:
> >
> > On the day when Yahweh-Elohim made heaven and earth ...
> > ... there was no *adam* [man, Adam] to till the *adamah* [soil].
> > But from the earth rose an *ad* [mist] and watered the whole face of the *adamah*,
> > and Yahweh-Elohim formed *adam* from the dust of the *adamah*,
> > and breathed into his nostrils the breath of life,
> > and *adam* became a living being.

No modern translation can adequately render the innuendo of the Hebrew text that the first generation of creation, that is, the heavens and the earth, become procreative and co-operate with Yahweh in the work of creation. From the fertilisation of *ad* and *adamah* arises, under the forming and animating action of Yahweh, the second generation of *adam*, with the double meaning of man and Adam ... The authors intended the meanings of creation and procreation to merge in a co-operative process; the order of being is meant to arise from the creative initiative of God and the procreative response of his creation.[56]

Giving this cooperation a more strongly interpersonal dimension, and following the Jewish philosopher André Neher, Cambón writes on the use of the plural in Genesis 1:26, when the creator says, 'Let *us* make man in *our* image and likeness'. For Cambón, God's plan for humanity can't be achieved without the cooperation of man and God. 'This alliance is the basis of freedom, which has made every human being a partner of God, his 'you', and thereby a truly responsible protagonist and shaper of his own destiny and history.' Because true love helps the beloved to achieve their own autonomy.[57]

4. How did humanity come into existence? The question of human origins

4.1 Humanity as both continuous and discontinuous with cosmic and evolutionary process

What about what we called the phylogenetic question regarding the origin of humanity? We've already been exploring the hominid evolutionary sequence, and I would suggest there's no scientific doubt that human origins are partly to be found there. As embodied, we're rooted in the over 13 billion years natural history of the cosmos, and in the almost 4 billion years of biological evolutionary history on Earth.

Yet the theme of the later chapters of this book beginning with the notion of the 'human revolution' – what Richard Klein called 'the Big Bang of human consciousness' – have brought out a persistent discontinuity between humans and the later non-human hominids. As we move up the

---

56 Eric Voegelin, *Israel and Revelation*, Baton Rouge: Louisiana State University Press, 1969, pp. 169–70.

57 Cambón, *Trinità modello sociale*, pp. 60–1.

scale of the dynamic sequence of interaction between emergent materials and their corresponding higher syntheses, from atoms to compounds to bacteria, plants and animals, the higher syntheses are increasingly less dependent on their material basis. As we've seen, the specifically human level of existence is so 'independent' of its biological basis that a human being may sometimes rationally and freely decide to forego survival for the sake of a higher value like truth or freedom.

4.2 What is 'humanity' – a species or simply humankind?

A working definition for sexually reproducing animals is that a species is a group of organisms capable of interbreeding and producing fertile offspring. In his *Descent of Man* Darwin hesitated to apply the notion to human beings when discussing 'the question whether mankind consists of one or several species'. With what amounted to a presumption that human beings could be adequately understood by the methods of biology, he wrote that if an agreement on what a species is could be accepted, its 'definition must not include an element that cannot possibly be ascertained, such as an act of creation'.[58] He means what cannot be ascertained by the methods of the natural sciences. So he rules out anything relevant being ascertained by, say, a philosophical inquiry.

But that inquiry was carried out long before Darwin, nor has anything discovered by biology or zoology since his time managed to displace it. It's no harm to remind ourselves, as John Haught does, that the scientific knowledge acquired in the natural sciences only occurs because the scientists themselves are aware of themselves as knowing subjects and operating in terms of inner cognitive criteria – without which the science itself 'would be a completely untrustworthy enterprise'.[59]

Let's just list a few of the insights into what's central to humanity in classic Greek political philosophy. We've already mentioned Heraclitus' notion of the *xynon* – the common participation in the logos that unites all human beings. Aristotle uses the term homonoia or likemindedness, where what makes humans of the same nous is their participation in divine reality. We explored in some detail St John's understanding of *agape* or what we called co-personal love, as the basis for a realised humanity.

---

58 Charles Darwin, *The Descent of Man and Selection in Relation to Sex, Vol. I*, London: John Murray, 1871, p. 228.

59 John F. Haught, 'Emergence, Scientific Naturalism, and Theology' in Nancey Murphy and William R. Stoeger, eds., *Evolution and Emergence: Systems, Organisms, Persons*, Oxford: Oxford University Press, 2007, pp. 248–66, at p. 260.

Piero Coda indicates the clearly Christian origins of the political notion of fraternity, including the frequent use of *adelphos* (brother) for the disciples of Christ, with the substantive, *adelphotes* (brotherhood – cf. I Pt 2:17; 5:9), 'not referring to an ideal to achieve but to a reality acquired ... ' He notes how, in the Gospels, 'the root of fraternity is ... indicated in ... the universal fatherhood of God ... since the love of God, [when] received ... becomes the most formidable agent of transformation in [humans'] existence and relationships with the other'.[60]

Voegelin comments on this issue in the context of his own problematic of a philosophy of history: his reply is in terms of the nature not just of a single human individual but of the whole of humanity. As with Heraclitus, Aristotle and St John, for Voegelin what unites all human beings in the one humanity isn't primarily what we know from paleoanthropology: that we're genetically united since we first appeared some 150,000 years ago. What makes human beings human is their capacity to reach out to and be drawn by the transcendent. Voegelin spells out of the implications of our shared actualisation of this common capacity in terms of his insight into human universality:

> Without universality, there would be no mankind other than the aggregate of members of a biological species; there would be no more a history of mankind than there is a history of catkind or horsekind [in 1968 lecture notes he mischievously adds 'monkeykind']. If mankind is to have history, its members must be able to respond to the movement of divine presence in their souls. But if that is the condition, then the mankind who has history is constituted by the God to whom man responds.[61]

From the perspective of our biological origins, then, we belong to something like a species since we fulfil the requirements of the definition of a species. But what unites us into one humankind is our orientation to the same transcendent ground. However, as we've mentioned before, human capacities are by no means necessarily actualised – our real capacity for a common humanity (since we can have a vision of it) is also

---

60 Piero Coda, 'Per una fondazione teologica della categoria politica della fraternità' in Antonio M. Baggio, ed., *Il principio dimenticato: La fraternità nella riflessione politologica contemporanea*, Rome: Città Nuova, 2007, pp. 101–8, at pp. 101–2.

61 Eric Voegelin, *The Ecumenic Age*, Baton Rouge: Louisiana State University Press, 1974, p. 305.

an ideal, a calling to be concretely worked towards. Criticising the attempt to manufacture a common *liberté, égalité, fraternité* by force, Dostoevsky wrote:

> The Western man speaks of brotherhood as of the great moving force of humanity, and does not realise that brotherhood cannot come about if it does not exist in fact ... One should in fact become an individual to a degree far higher than has occurred in the West. A voluntary, absolutely conscious and completely unforced sacrifice of oneself for the sake of all, is, I consider, a sign of the highest development of individual personality ... How is this to be done? – what is needed ... is the principle of brotherhood and love – we must love. Man must instinctively and of his own accord be drawn towards brotherhood, fellowship, and concord ... [62]

Very much in tune with these philosophical, theological and literary insights into what unites human beings into the one human family are Karol Wojtyła's comments on the notion of 'neighbour', which 'takes into account man's humanness alone':

> It thus provides the broadest basis for the community ... it unites ... all human beings ... The notion of 'neighbour' refers then to the broadest, commonly shared reality of the human being and also to the broadest foundations of interhuman community ... Any community detached from this fundamental community must unavoidably lose its specifically human character.[63]

And because we live both within and beyond time, our task is to weave together a tapestry patterned from the timeless moments of past cultures so that their life enters into ours. As Pasquale Foresi puts it:

> The life of African peoples, often so little known, is a part of my history: I am something of what they are living and have lived through ... And the same with the Chinese, the Indians, all the oriental world, apparently so distant from the history of my European thought. They have brought with themselves and have developed a whole area of

---

62 Fyodor Dostoevsky, *Winter Notes on Summer Impressions*, in James M. Edie, James P. Scanlan and Mary-Barbara Zeldin, eds., *Russian Philosophy, Vol. II*, Chicago: Quadrangle Press, 1965, pp. 254–5.

63 Karol Wojtyła, *The Acting Person*, Dordrecht: Reidel, 1979, p. 293.

my humanity, in their wisdom, their symbols, their meditations, their asceticism, all things which I feel in need of. Their history, even if we have been separated for four or five thousand years, is part of my history. Their experiences are a day of my life spread out over the centuries ... But if, in a certain sense, it is from all these experiences of past history that I succeed in reconstructing myself and knowing myself, it is also true that each one of them was the experience of man, of mankind.[64]

4.3 So, what is the origin of humanity?

We've already suggested the basis for each human person's existence is our groundedness in a transfinite You. No less a ground can be suggested for universal humanity considered as one family, itself on principle capable of being united as a 'we'. Aquinas articulated what creation is with a distinction between creator and created not available to Aristotle. Piero Coda goes back to one of the sources of that differentiation when he refers to St Paul in Romans 4:17, who points out that God calls into existence what is not: 'God, who gives life to the dead and calls the things that do not exist [*ta me onta*] into existence [*ós onta*].' This calling into existence from non-existence is itself part of 'the permanent act of creation through which the reality other than God comes into existence' in terms of 'the well-known formula *creatio ex nihilo*'.[65]

But Coda has advanced this understanding of created contingency beyond the notion of ontological dependence in the direction of a continuous relationship. 'Creation out of nothing' may be applied to the creating subject as well as to the object created, as a kind of not-being in the creator so that the creation can be. As an expression of the self-sacrificing nothingness of the creator's love, he can be understood as 'losing' himself to let creation be.[66] When it's a matter of the creation of humankind, this richer notion of divine creation out of nothing lifts the metaphysical event at the level of being into the ethical event at the level of love and encounter.

Cambón's related notion of the relationship between creator and created as 'reciprocal *kenosis*' can be expanded here to the invitation into existence of the whole human family by the creator. Just as in the case

---

64 Pasquale Foresi, *Appunti di Filosofia: Sulla conoscibilità di Dio*, Rome: Città Nuova, 1967, pp. 134–5.

65 Piero Coda, *Il logos e il nulla: Trinità, religioni, mistica*, Rome: Città Nuova, 2003, p. 219.

66 Piero Coda, 'Dio e la creazione, I: Trinità e creazione dal nulla' *Nuova Umanità*, 115 (January-February 1998), 1, pp. 67–88.

of the coming into existence of each unique human being which calls on the parents' cooperation through pro-creation, we can say that the more than 13 billion years of cosmic natural history has cooperated in making the emergence of humanity possible. St Paul wrote: 'We know that the whole creation has been groaning in labour pains until now' (Rom 8:22). This could now be seen as the massive cosmic interplay of emergence and correspondence, from the Big Bang up to the last pre-human hominids, with each lower level 'losing' itself by gifting itself to the next level of existence, right up to that bewildering multiplicity of late hominid species Tattersall and Schwartz called 'a story of repeated evolutionary experimentation'. We've already quoted their comment on the entire almost 4-billion-years evolutionary sequence which culminated at that moment where 'clearly in the context of such experimentation rather than out of constant fine tuning by natural selection over the eons ... our own amazing species appeared on Earth'.[67]

And as we've seen, what breathes 'fire into the equations' is precisely this meaningful ascent towards the human. Jewish, Christian and perhaps Muslim believers have the Book of Genesis to put flesh onto the paleoanthropological narrative; however even at the level of reason, it seems possible to affirm this kenotic interaction between a personal You with his creation, leading up to the point when all of creation can through humanity say its yes to You, a reply leading to deeper co-personal recognition and cooperation. The astounding cooperative parallel is between the origin (i) of each individual human mystery through the cooperation between divine Creator and human parents, and the origin (ii) of the mystery of humankind through the cooperation of the divine Creator and of the whole of cosmic history from the Big Bang through the entire evolutionary sequence up to the first humans. Which leads us to our final consideration on the finality, if any, of the history of humankind.

4.4 What is the meaning of humanity in history?

(a) **Unity in diversity:** The question of ultimate meaning or finality isn't of course a question within the natural sciences, but as Voegelin remarked: 'The denial of meaning [to such ultimate questions] runs counter to the empirical fact that they rise again and again as meaningful from the experience of reality.'[68] We get a hint from Aquinas, who once asked

---

67 Ian Tattersall and Geoffrey H. Schwartz, *Extinct Humans*, New York: Westview Press, 2000, p. 9.
68 Voegelin, *The Ecumenic Age*, p. 316.

'Could God Make a Better Universe?' His answer is one which celebrates the diversity in unity of the cosmos, including ourselves:

> The perfection of the universe depends essentially on the diversity of natures by which the various levels of goodness are fulfilled, rather than on the multiplying of the individuals within one nature.[69]

So instead of the dull facticity some science writers seem to make a point of emphasising, for Aquinas this diversity in the created universe expresses the 'perfection' of the radical difference in unity characterising all of created reality. What happens when we apply this notion of greater perfection in diversity to the history of humanity? Earlier we mentioned Tarkovsky's insight into the implications for humanity of a Trinitarian vision: 'The concrete division of one alone in three and the triple union in one alone offers a wonderful perspective for the future still spread out across the centuries.' And it is this vision, in terms of the unique personhood of each one with the capacity to build relationships based on freedom and love with the other, that can extend Aquinas's notion of greater perfection from greater diversity to the specifically interpersonal level.

But that personal participation means going beyond any 'species' notion of humanity. Les Murray's Everyman, Fredy Neptune, remarks: 'My life, keeping out of the human race to stay in it.'[70] That is to say that the very lastingness of the matrix of cultures we mentioned earlier – mythic, philosophic, revelational, and various combinations and fallings away from these – is because individuals within them, and through them their cultures too, transcended the particular times and places where they flourished. The whole notion of an Everyman – the 'Here Comes Everybody' of *Finnegans Wake* – is that in the 150,000 years of humanity's existence there's been, along with the efflorescence of countless forms of mythic experience, what Voegelin calls the 'spiritual outbursts' of the great Eastern speculative-religious experiences of Zoroastrianism, Hinduism, Buddhism, Taoism and Confucianism. There have also been the more differentiated spiritual outbursts of Israel, Greek philosophy and Christianity, followed by the huge range of developments and regressions characterising Western culture. So that a deeper unity in diversity can also be envisaged, at least on principle, for the whole history of humanity.

---

69 Aquinas, *In Sent I.* 44.1.2, quoted in Norman Kretzmann, *The Metaphysics of Creation: Aquinas' Natural Theology in Summa Contra Gentiles II*, New York: Oxford University Press, 1999, p. 224 n. 106.

70 Les Murray, *Fredy Neptune: A Novel in Verse*, New York: Farrar, Straus and Giroux, 2000, p. 17.

(b) **The person as 'still point of a turning world' uniting both cosmic and human history into one narrative:** In fact, from a philosophical perspective, the human world – including of course our participation in the cosmos we're rooted in more deeply than redwoods – is far more amazing than anything science fiction or film has ever touched. After all, it's only because of persons that we know there is a cosmos. Nor could it be grasped by persons unless they went beyond the cosmic in order to do so: to paraphrase Solzhenitsyn, the truth of natural science outweighs the whole world it investigates. And it's only because of our existence as persons that we know that the personal being that grounds us, also grounds the cosmos.

Although less likely to use the language of the person, Voegelin too rejects the priority of astrophysical space and time, noting that the astrophysical measure by which:

> ... we refer the lasting of all other things, is not a 'time' in which things happen, but the time-dimension of a thing within the Whole that also comprises the divine reality whose mode of lastingness we express by such symbols as 'eternity'. Things do not happen in the astrophysical universe; the universe, together with all things founded in it, happens in God.[71]

So that we can say that the world of persons, which includes the astrophysical universe is less 'in time' than is the cosmos within the world of persons. Murray's Fredy Neptune is Everyman because he's outside of all history. As Walsh said at a Hong Kong conference whose theme was the meaning of history at the beginning of the third millennium:

> It is because each person is outside of all history that each one contains all of history and is therefore the still point of the turning world. They enter into history as not being in history, and it is this transcendence that enables them to reach across to one another through history ... We take for granted the mutuality of all persons within history but this is its most striking feature. We can hold in mind and in love persons long dead and they, in turn, can hold us before them before we are even born. History is the history of persons who are in history without being of it. They belong to one another before they belong to history.[72]

---

71 Eric Voegelin, *The Ecumenic Age*, Baton Rouge: Louisiana State University Press, 1974, pp. 333–4.

72 David Walsh, 'The Person as the Apocalypse of History', paper delivered at the Symposium on *Translatio Imperii*, University of Hong Kong, February 2010.

From a theological perspective, Piero Coda arrives at a similar conclusion, discussing the contemporaneity of all human beings in the divine in which they participate. 'Did not Jesus exclaim: "Abraham rejoiced that he was to see this day; he saw it and was glad." (Jn 8:56) ... What is needed ... is a new understanding of the relationship between eternity and time and of the meaning itself of eternity and time in light of the event of Jesus Christ.'[73] Equally strong on the copresence of all persons is Jesus' earlier remark that 'God is not the God of the dead but of the living; for all live to him' (Lk 20:38). Let's look at how we can come to experience this universal co-presence, at least in part.

(c) **The story of humanity in history as primarily a kenotic relationship:** Are we going beyond what philosophy or reason could tell us here? I don't think so, because once the discovery of the person has been made, these consequences for humankind seem to follow. In his forthcoming *The Politics of the Person*, Walsh speaks of Karol Wojtyła's 'incarnational personalism', whose foundation can be located within the inner experience of each one of us. Voegelin, as a philosopher of history, highlights the core of that incarnational personalism in his frequent returning to Augustine's reflection on the second exodus of Israel, from Babylon. Augustine comments that 'They begin to leave who begin to love.' Voegelin concludes his essay on 'Eternal Being in Time' with the comment:

> The Exodus in the sense of *incipit exire qui incipit amare* is the classical formulation of the substantive principle of a philosophy of history.[74]

So that for Voegelin too, the focus for a philosophy of history is on love, but a love that has exodus or self-sacrificing kenosis at its heart. In that light, every human society fully belongs to the one human family if and only if those within their various cultures undergo an exodus from their confinement within those cultures. Isn't that why we can still share in the experience of, say, in the Neolithic people who built Newgrange over 5,000 years ago? As we said, at the moment of midwinter dawn as the sun entered the long passage grave, there, 'in and through their loving-suffering struggle for attunement at the centre the cosmos the Boyne

---

73 Piero Coda, 'Creazione in Cristo e nuova creazione nella mistica di Chiara Lubich,' 6 (2010) *Nuova Umanità*, 192, pp. 659–72, at pp. 662–3.

74 Eric Voegelin, 'Eternal Being in Time' in *Anamnesis: On the Theory of History and Politics*, David Walsh, ed., Columbia: University of Missouri Press, 2002, pp. 312–37 at p. 337.

people touched ecstatically for a few boundless timeless moments the everlasting cosmic oneness at the heart of being'. Seamus Heaney wrote of this event which marks the first moments of the beginning of the new year:

> Inside the cosmic hill. Who dares say 'love'
> At this cold coming? Who would not dare say it?[75]

And in that truly Divine-Human Comedy lies the *trasumanar* (*Paradiso*, I:70), or 'transhumanising' of humanity in its long and painful journey from here to eternity that Dante gave us a word for.

Taking the hint from Augustine and Voegelin, then, I'd suggest we see a philosophy of history primarily in terms of relation – between each human person, between the communion of persons in each society and culture, and between persons and societies with the You that grounded them. At its core, such a praxis of universal humanity must be, in the language of Zanghí and Cambón, a will for kenotic relationship. Each participant must be prepared, as individuals and as societies and cultures, to lose themselves to the other individual, society and culture, in order, in Buber's language, to make their souls ours.[76]

(d) **Towards a truly universal dialogue:** As we've seen, that communion must expand out to the relation to all previous cultures before us, and in open and responsible anticipation to those to come. In these dialogues across the barriers of the present and past, we'll understand how each of the cultural matrices – including the matrix of natural science – is enriched by the others, even with the need to be purified by the at times immoderate critique of the others. And we'll appreciate that unless we're prepared to reach out to the genuine quest for truth, justice and love underlying the matrices different from, if not necessarily opposed to, ours, we'll be impoverished by the disappearance of any of them.[77] Of course

---

75 Seamus Heaney, 'A Dream of Solstice', *Irish Times*, 21 December 1999.

76 'Another thing we need is the ability to put ourselves in the place of the other man, the stranger, and to make his soul ours. I must confess that I am horrified at how little we know the Arabs ... As we [Arabs and Jews] love the country and together seek its welfare, it is possible for us to work together for it.' Aubrey Hodes, *Encounter with Martin Buber*, Harmondsworth: Penguin, 1975, p. 108.

77 See Chapter 4 in David Walsh, *The Third Millennium: Reflections on Faith and Reason*, Washington: Georgetown University Press, 1999.

this includes contemporary atheist viewpoints, which in their very denial of the Divine underline the importance of the question 'whose mystery very understandably forms the Alpha and Omega of all our speaking and questioning'.

(e) **Is there a way beyond humankind's failure to be human?** Can the weave of dialogue we've mentioned avoid being torn apart irremediably by the horrendously violent and murderous ruptures within humankind in the last and the present century? Hans Jonas' concluding remarks to his 'The Concept of God after Auschwitz' indicate how the weight of historical evil can be somehow borne. Jonas contrasts himself to Job, who

> ... invokes the fullness of the divine creative power, while mine is the renunciation of that power. And still – strange to say – both are praise: since renunciation is what makes it possible for us to be. This too, it seems to me, is a reply to Job: to know that in him, God himself suffers.[78]

Perhaps the only adequate 'answer' to the question of the meaning of humanity in history is that of Jonas: That in our suffering, in the suffering of hundreds of millions of innocent victims of twentieth-century political murder already spilling over into the twenty-first, the personal source of the cosmos and of humanity himself suffers too. It's not surprising that Coda writes about 'the cross: foundation of fraternity'. He sees the crucified One identifying both with the just brother Abel, but also with Cain, one who is 'outside the plan of God', with the accursed of Deuteronomy 21:23: 'Cursed be the one who hangs from the wood.'[79] No one can be finally excluded from the dialogue, except those who, as we've seen in Dostoevsky's *Karamazov*, obstinately refuse to make the kenotic exodus from themselves.

I'm reminded here of Annette Flynn's illuminating discussion, when she writes of a late poem of Jorge Borges, '*Cristo en la cruz*'. There Borges sees Christ hanging in the place of the good thief: 'With "*Cristo en la cruz*" there seems to occur a slippage from saviour (*Cristo en el medio*) to saved

---

78 Hans Jonas, *Le concept de Dieu après Auschwitz: Une voix juive*, Paris: Payot & Rivages, 1994, pp. 39–40.

79 Coda, 'Per una fondazione teologica della categoria politica della fraternità', p. 103.

(*el tercero*, the good thief).'[80] Borges somehow experienced how Jesus in his forsakenness is identifying with all who are excluded, including those who like Borges himself desired, but seemed to lack, faith. Still, it's not only lack of faith; the fact remains that we can all fall into the choice of evil. Les Murray catches this insight – already noted by St John: 'anyone who hates his brother [*adelphon*] is a murderer [*anthropoktonos*, human-killer]' (1 Jn 3:15) – in the snatch of dialogue towards the end of his *Fredy Neptune* saga:

> *That's not really mine, the Hitler madness* – No it's not, said my self
> It isn't on your head. But it's in your language.[81]

So the meaning of humanity in history includes not only our various cultures' thrust towards the You in whose light they achieve their youwardness and wewardness, and our terrible potential for self-willed waywardness, but also the possibility of something like a rediscovery of the face of the other, a kind of redemption. In fact, history sometimes witnesses to the reality of a society's or culture's painful recovery of its deepest soul.

Sophocles' Oedipus, in his earlier role as tyrant or king, thought he was like a god, the measure of all things. Deprived of kingship, sight and status, he gradually rediscovers love through the loyal care of his daughters Antigone and Ismene. At the point of death, he hears the call from the God beyond, evoking within him a life of communion he'd previously sought only on his own conditions. Like Job, having lost everything but love, the blinded and dying Oedipus finds he's invited into a We-relationship with the God. A guard relates to Oedipus' daughters, his final moments on earth:

> ... there was silence; and in the silence suddenly a voice cried out to him – of such a kind it made our hair stand up in panic fear: again and again the call came from the god: 'Oedipus! Oedipus! Why are we waiting? You delay too long; you delay too long to go.'[82]

---

80 Annette Flynn, *The Quest for God in the Work of Borges*, Continuum: London, 2009, p. 170.

81 Murray, *Fredy Neptune*, p. 254. Giuseppe Maria Zanghí has a powerful reflection on both a cultural 'dark night' and how it can be transcended, in his *Notte della cultura europea*, Rome: Città Nuova, 2007.

82 Sophocles, *Oedipus at Colonus*, in David Grene and Richmond Lattimore, eds. and trs., *The Complete Greek Tragedies II, Sophocles*, Chicago: University of Chicago Press, 1974, p. 1623.

Bernard Knox says of this last invitation to Oedipus: 'These strange, almost colloquial words are all that the gods say to Oedipus in either of the two plays ... The hesitation for which they must reproach him is the last shred of his humanity, which he must now cast off ... And the divine "we" completes and transcends the equation of Oedipus with the gods; his identity is merged with theirs.'[83] Or as Chiara Lubich has caught – in a few phrases at the end of a meditation on 'Life', including its moments of forsakenness – what we could see as the whole Youwards movement of cosmos and history:

> All,
> everything,
> always,
> has,
> has had,
> only one destiny:
> union with you.[84]

---

83 Bernard Knox, *The Heroic Temper*, Berkeley, University of California Press, 1964, p. 161.

84 Chiara Lubich, 'Life' in *Essential Writings: Spirituality, Dialogue, Culture*, Michel Vandeleene, Tom Masters and Callan Slipper, eds., Hyde Park, NY: New City Press, 2007, pp. 150–1.

Bibliography

Agamben, Giorgio. *The Open: Man and Animal*, Kevin Atell, tr. Stanford: Stanford University Press, 2003.

—. *The Sacrament of Language: An Archaeology of the Oath*, Adam Kotsko tr. Palo Alto, CA: Stanford University Press, 2010.

Alexander, Richard D. *How Did Humans Evolve?*, Ann Arbor Museum of Zoology, University of Michigan, Special Publication No.1, 1990.

Allport, Gordon. *Personality*, London: Constable, 1971.

Anati, Emmanuel. *I camuni: alle radici della civiltà europea*, Milan: Jaca Book, 1982.

Antoine, Jean-Philippe, Gertrud Koch, and Luc Lang. *Gerhard Richter*, Paris: Dis Voir, 1995.

Aristotle. *De Anima (On the Soul)*, Hugh Lawson-Tancred, tr. Harmondsworth: Penguin, 1986.

Arsuaga, Juan Luis, and Ignacio Martínez. *The Chosen Species: The Long March of Human Evolution*, Oxford: Blackwell, 2006.

Arthur, Wallace. *The Origin of Animal Body Plans: A Study in Evolutionary Developmental Biology*, Cambridge: Cambridge University Press, 1997.

Ash, Patricia J., and David J. Robinson. *The Emergence of Humans: An Exploration of the Evolutionary Timeline*, Chichester, West Sussex: Wiley-Blackwell, 2010.

Augros, Robert, and George Stanciu. *The New Biology*, Boston: New Science Library, 1987.

Aujoulat, Norbert. *Lascaux: Movement, Space and Time*, New York: Harry N. Abrams, 2005.

Baggio, Antonio M., ed. *Il principio dimenticato: La fraternità nella riflessione politologica contemporanea*, Rome: Città Nuova, 2007.

Balthasar, Hans Urs von. *You Have Words of Eternal Life: Scripture Meditations*, San Francisco: Ignatius Press, 1991.

Barden, Garrett, and Philip McShane. *Towards Self-Meaning*, Dublin: Gill & Macmillan, 1969.

Barrow, John D., and Frank J. Tipler. *The Anthropic Cosmological Principle*, Oxford: Oxford University Press, 1986.

Bellow, Saul. *Herzog*, London: Penguin Classics, 2003.

Bergh, Stefan. *Landscape of the Monuments: A Study of the Passage Tombs in the Cúil Irra Region, Co. Sligo, Ireland*, Stockholm: Riksantikvarieämbetet Arkeologiska Undersökningar, 1995.

Berlinsky, David. 'The Deniable Darwin', *Commentary*, June 1996, 19–29.

Bickerton, Derek. *Language and Species*, Chicago: University of Chicago Press, 1990.

—. *Language and Human Behaviour*, Seattle: University of Washington Press, 1996.

—. 'Did Syntax Trigger the Human Revolution?' in Mellars et al., eds. *Rethinking the Human Revolution*, 2007, pp. 99–105.

Binford, Lewis, R. 'Isolating the transition to cultural adaptations: an organisational approach', in Erik Trinkaus, ed. *The Emergence of Modern Humans: Biocultural adaptation in the later Pleistocene*, Cambridge: Cambridge University Press, 1989, pp. 18–34.

Bingham, Paul M. 'On the evolution of language: implications of a new and general theory of human origins, properties, and history', in Larson et al., eds. *The Evolution of Human Language*, pp. 211–24.

Blackmore, Susan. *The Meme Machine*, Oxford: Oxford University Press, 1999.

Blundell, Geoffrey, ed. *Origins: The Story of the Emergence of Humans and Humanity in Africa*, Cape Town: Double Storey Books, 2006.

Bobrowski, Johannes. *Wetterzeichen*, [East] Berlin: Union Verlag, 1968.

Botha, Rudolf P. *Unravelling the Evolution of Language*, Amsterdam: Elsevier, 2003.

Botha, Rudolf, and Chris Knight, eds. *The Cradle of Language*, Oxford: Oxford University Press, 2009.

Bower, Bruce. 'Stone Age figurine has contentious origins: Ivory female carving may be at least 35,000 years old, alter views of how Stone Age art developed', *Science News*, 20 June 2009.

Brandt, Ria van den. 'Etty Hillesum and her "Catholic Worshippers": A Plea for a More Critical Approach to Etty Hillesum's Writings', in Klaas A. D. Smelik et al., eds. *Spirituality in the Writings of Etty Hillesum* (2010), pp. 215–31.

Breinersdorfer, Fred, ed. *Sophie Scholl: Die letzten Tage*, Frankfurt: Fischer, 2005.

Brown, Raymond. *The Gospel According to John, XIII–XXI*, London: Chapman, 1971.

Buber, Martin. *Good and Evil: Two Interpretations*, Scribners: New York, 1953.

—. *The Knowledge of Man*, New York: Harper, 1965.

—. *I and Thou*, Edinburgh: T. & T. Clark, 1966.

Byrne, Richard W., 'Relating Brain Sizes to Intelligence in Primates', in Mellars et al., eds. *Modelling the Early Human Mind*, pp. 49–56.

Cambón, Enrique. *Trinità modello sociale*, Rome: Città Nuova, 2009.

Camus, Albert. *La chute*, Paris: Gallimard, 1971.

Carroll, Sean. *Endless Forms Most Beautiful: The New Science of Evo Devo and the Making of the Animal Kingdom*, New York: Norton, 2005.

—. *The Making of the Fittest: DNA and the Ultimate Forensic Record of Evolution*, New York: Norton, 2006.

—. 'Genetics and the Making of *Homo sapiens*', in Chiocon et al., eds. *The Human Evolution Source Book*, p. 630.

Cartmill, Matt. 'Oppressed by Evolution', *Discovery*, March 1998, pp. 78–83.

Cartmill, Matt, and Fred H. Smith. *The Human Lineage*, Hoboken, NJ: Wiley-Blackwell, 2009.

Cassirer, Ernst. *The Problem of Knowledge: Philosophy, Science and History Since Hegel*, New Haven: Yale University Press, 1969.

Castiello, Umberto, et al. 'Wired to be Social: The Ontogeny of Human Interaction', *Public Library of Science PloS ONE*, October 2010, Volume 5, Issue 10, e13199, pp. 1–10.

Cela-Conde, Camilo J. and Francisco José Ayala. *Human Evolution: Trails From the Past*, New York: Oxford University Press, 2007.

Chalmers, David J. 'Facing Up to the Problem of Consciousness', in Shear, ed. *Explaining Consciousness*, pp. 9–30.

—. 'Moving Forward on the Problem of Consciousness', in Shear, ed. *Explaining Consciousness*, pp. 379–422.

Chesterton, Gilbert K. *G.K.C. as M.C.*, London: Methuen, 1929.

—. *Collected Poetry, Part I*, San Francisco: Ignatius Press, 1994.

Chiocon, Russell L., and John G. Fleagle, eds. *The Human Evolution Source Book*, Second Edition, Upper Saddle River, NJ: Pearson/Prentice-Hall, 2006.

Chomsky, Noam. *Powers and Prospects: Reflections on Human Nature and Social Order*, London: Pluto Press, 1996.

Clément, Olivier. *L'espirit de Soljénitsyne*, Paris: Stock, 1974.

Clottes, Jean. 'Sticking bones into cracks in the Upper Paleolithic', in Colin Renfrew et al., eds. *Becoming Human* (2009), pp. 195–211.

—. *Cave Art*, London: Phaidon Press, 2010.

Coda, Piero. *Evento Pasquale: Trinità e Storia*, Rome: Città Nuova, 1984.

—. *Il negativo e la trinità: Ipotesi su Hegel*, Rome: Città Nuova, 1987.

—. 'Dio e la creazione, I: Trinità e creazione dal nulla', *Nuova Umanità*, 1, 1998, 115, pp. 67–88.

—. 'Per una fondazione teologica della categoria politica della fraternità', in Baggio, ed. *Il principio dimenticato*, 2007, pp. 101–8.

—. 'Creazione in Cristo e nuova creazione nella mistica di Chiara Lubich', *Nuova Umanità*, 6, 2010, 192, pp. 659–72.

Conard, Nicolas J. 'Palaeolithic ivory sculptures from southwestern Germany and the origins of figurative art', *Nature*, 2003, 426, pp. 830–2.

—. 'An overview of the patterns of behavioural change in Africa and Eurasia during the Middle and Late Pleistocene', in Francesco d'Errico and Lucinda Backwell, eds. *From Tools to Symbols: Early Hominids to Modern Humans*, Johannesburg: Witwatersrand University Press, 2005, pp. 295–332.

—. 'A female figurine from the basal Aurignacian deposits of Hohle Fels Cave in southwestern Germany', *Nature*, 2009, 459, p. 248.

Condic, Maureen L. 'When does human life begin? A scientific perspective', *National Catholic Bioethics Quarterly*, 9, 1, 2009, pp. 127–208.

Conroy, Glenn. *Reconstructing Human Origins: A Modern Synthesis*, New York: Norton, 1997.

Conway Morris, Simon. *The Crucible of Creation: The Burgess Shale and the Rise of Animals*, Oxford: Oxford University Press, 1998.

—. *Life's Solution: Inevitable Humans in a Lonely Universe*, Cambridge: Cambridge University Press, 2003.

—. ed. *The Deep Structure of Biology: Is Convergence Sufficiently Ubiquitous to Give a Directional Signal?*, West Conshohocken, PA: Templeton Foundation Press, 2008.

Cooper, Barry. 'The First Mystics? Some Recent Accounts of Neolithic Shamanism', Eric Voegelin Society paper, APSA Annual Meeting, Washington, D.C., September, 2010.

Corballis, Michael C. 'Did language evolve before speech?' in Larson et al., eds. *The Evolution of Human Language*, pp. 115–23.

Cowen, Ron. 'Solar system's edge surprises astronomers: New observations reveal a dense ribbon structure that current models don't explain', *Science News* Web edition, 15 October 2009.

Coyne SJ, George V. 'Science Does Not Need God. Or Does It? A Catholic Scientist Looks at Evolution', *Catholic Online*, 30 January 2006, pp. 1–3.

Darwin, Charles. *On the Origin of Species by Means of Natural Selection, or the Preservation of Favoured Races in the Struggle for Life*, London: John Murray, 1902.

—. *The Descent of Man and Selection in Relation to Sex*, Vols. I & II, London: John Murray, 1871.

—. *The Life and Letters of Charles Darwin*, ed. Francis Darwin, New York: Basic Books, 1959.

Davidson, Eric H. *The Regulatory Genome: Gene Regulatory Networks in Development and Evolution*, Burlington, MA: Academic Press, 2006.

Davidson, Iain, and William Noble, 'The Archaeology of Perception: Traces of Depiction and Language', *Current Anthropology*, 30, 2 April 1989, pp. 125–37.

Davidson, Iain and William Noble. *Human Evolution, Language and Mind: A Psychological and Archaeological Inquiry*, Cambridge: Cambridge University Press, 1996.

Davies, Paul. *The Goldilocks Enigma: Why is the Universe Just Right for Life?* Boston: Houghton Mifflin, 2008.

Dawkins, Richard. *The Selfish Gene*, Oxford: Oxford University Press, 1989.

—. *The Blind Watchmaker*, London: Penguin, 1991.

—. *The Ancestor's Tale: A Pilgrimage to the Dawn of Life*, London: Weidenfeld & Nicolson, 2004.

—. *A Devil's Chaplain*, London: Weidenfeld & Nicolson, 2003.

—. *The Greatest Show on Earth*, London: Bantam, 2009.

Deacon, Terrence. *The Symbolic Species: The Co-evolution of Language and the Human Brain*, London: Allen Lane/Penguin Press, 1997.

De Beaune, Sophie, Frederick L. Coolidge, and Thomas Wynn. *Cognitive Archaeology and Human Evolution*, New York: Cambridge University Press, 2009.

Dembski, William. *Intelligent Design: The Bridge Between Science and Theology*, Downers Grove, IL: InterVarsity Press, 1999.

Dennett, Daniel. *Darwin's Dangerous Idea: Evolution and the Meanings of Life*, London: Penguin, 1995.

—. *Freedom Evolves*, London: Allen Lane, 2003.

Denton, Michael. *Evolution: A Theory in Crisis*, London: Burnett, 1985.

—. *Nature's Destiny: How the Laws of Biology Reveal Purpose in the Universe*, New York: Free Press, 1998.

DeSalle, Rob, and Ian Tattersall. *Human Origins: What Bones and Genomes Tell Us About Ourselves*, College Station, TX: Texas A & M University Press, 2008.

Dillenberger, Jane. *The Religious Art of Andy Warhol*, New York: Continuum, 1998.

Dodd, C. H. *The Interpretation of the Fourth Gospel*, Cambridge: Cambridge University Press, 1970.

Donald, Merlin. 'Précis of Origins of the Modern Mind: Three Stages in the Evolution of Culture and Cognition', *Behaviour and Brain Sciences*, 1993, 16, pp. 737–91.

—. 'The roots of art and religion in ancient material culture', in Renfrew et al., eds. *Becoming Human*, 2009, pp. 95–103.

Donaldson, Mike. *Burrup Rock Art: Ancient Aboriginal Rock Art of Burrup Peninsula and Dampier Archipelago*, Mount Lawley, WA: Wildrocks Publications, 2009.

Dostoevsky, Fyodor. *Notes from Underground; The Double*, Jessie Coulson, tr. London: Penguin, 2003.

—. *Winter Notes on Summer Impressions,* in James M. Edie, James P. Scanlan, and Mary-Barbara Zeldin, eds. *Russian Philosophy, Vol. II*, Chicago: Quadrangle Press, 1965.

—. *The Brothers Karamazov*, trs. Richard Pevear and Larissa Volokhonsky, New York: Farrar, Straus & Giroux, 2002.

Dumbach, Annette and Jud Newborn. *Sophie Scholl and the White Rose*, Oxford: Oneworld, 2006.

Dunbar, Robin. *The Human Story: A New History of Mankind's Evolution*, London: Faber & Faber, 2004.

—. 'The social brain and the cultural explosion of the human revolution', in Mellars, et al., eds. *Rethinking the Human Revolution*, pp. 91–8.

Dunlop, John. 'The Solzhenitsyn Canon Returns Home', *Stanford Slavic Studies*, 1992, 4:2.

Dye, Melody. 'The Advantages of Being Helpless: Human brains are slow to develop – a secret, perhaps, of our success', in *Scientific American*, 9 February 2010.

Eccles, John. *The Human Mystery*, Berlin: Springer, 1979.

Eldredge, Niles. *Time Frames: The Rethinking of Darwinian Evolution and the Theory of Punctuated Equilibria*, London: Heinemann, 1986.

—. 'Species,' in Tattersall et al., eds. *Encyclopedia of Human Evolution and Prehistory*, pp. 537–9.

—. *Reinventing Darwin: The Great Evolutionary Debate*, London: Phoenix, 1995.

Eliade, Mircea. *Patterns in Comparative Religion*, London: Sheed & Ward, 1971.

—. *From Primitives to Zen; A Thematic Sourcebook of the History of Religions*, New York: HarperCollins, 1978.

Ellison, Ralph. *Invisible Man*, New York: Vintage, 1995.

d'Errico, Francisco et al. *Current Anthropology*, 39, June 1998, Supplement, S1–S44.

d'Errico, Francesco et al. 'From the origin of language to the diversification of languages: What can archaeology and palaeoanthropology say?' in Francesco d'Errico and Jean-Marie Hombert, eds. *Becoming Eloquent: Advances in the Emergence of Language, Human Cognition, and Modern Cultures*, Amsterdam: John Benjamins, 2009, pp. 13–68.

Fairbanks, Daniel J. *Relics of Eden: The Powerful Evidence of Evolution in Human DNA*, New York: Prometheus Books, 2007.

Fitch, W. Tecumseh. 'The faculty of language: what it is, who has it, and how did it evolve', in Larson et al., *The Evolution of Human Language*, pp. 14–42.

—. 'Three meanings of "recursion": key distinctions for biolinguistics', in Larson et al. *The Evolution of Human Language*, pp. 73–90.

Flynn, Annette. *The Quest for God in the Work of Borges*, Continuum: London, 2009.

Fodor Jerry, and Massimo Piatelli-Palmarini. *What Darwin Got Wrong*, London: Profile Books, 2010.

Foresi, Pasquale. *L'agape in San Paolo e la carità in San Tommaso d'Aquino*, Rome: Città Nuova, 1965.

—. *Fede speranza carità nel Nuovo Testamento*, Rome: Città Nuova, 1967.

—. *Appunti di Filosofia: Sulla conoscibilità di Dio*, Rome: Città Nuova, 1967.

Frisch, Max. *Biografie: Ein Spiel*, Frankfurt: Suhrkamp, 1968.

Gamble, Clive. *Origins and Revolutions: Human Identity in Earliest Prehistory*, New York: Cambridge University Press, 2007.

Gargett, Robert H. 'Grave Shortcomings: The Evidence for Neanderthal Burial', *Current Anthropology*, 30, 1989, 2, pp. 157–90.

Gay, Peter. *The Enlightenment, Vol. 2: The Science of Freedom*, New York: Norton, 1977.

George, Robert P. and Christopher Tollefson. *Embryo: A Defense of Human Life*, New York: Doubleday, 2008.

George, Robert P. and Patrick Lee. 'Acorns and Embryos', *The New Atlantis*, 7, Fall 2004/Winter 2005.

Gillespie, Neal C. *Charles Darwin and the Problem of Creation*, Chicago: University of Chicago Press, 1979.

Glaessner, Martin F. *The Dawn of Animal Life*, Cambridge: Cambridge University Press, 1984.

Gould, Stephen Jay. *Wonderful Life: The Burgess Shale and the Nature of History*, London: Hutchinson Radius, 1990.

—. 'Darwinian Fundamentalism'. *NYRB*, 44:10, June 12 1997, pp. 34–7.

—. *Rocks of Ages: Science and Religion in the Fullness of Life*, London: Jonathan Cape, 2001.

—. *The Structure of Evolutionary Theory*, Cambridge, MA: Harvard University Press, 2002.

Green, Richard E. et al. 'A Draft Sequence of the Neanderthal Genome', *Science* 328 (5979), 7 May 2010, pp. 710–22.

Griffiths, Bede. *River of Compassion: A Christian Commentary on the Bhagavad Gita*, Springfield, IL: Templegate Publishers, 2002.

Günz, Philipp, Simon Neubauer, Bruno Maureille, and Jean-Jacques Hublin. 'Brain development after birth differs between Neanderthals and modern humans', *Current Biology*, 9 November 2010.

Gyllensten, U., M. Ingman, H. Kaessman, and S. Pääbo. 'Mitochondrial genome variation and the origin of modern humans', *Nature*, 408, 7 December 2000, pp. 708–13.

Habel, Norman C. *The Book of Job*, London: SCM Press, 1985.

Haight, Amanda. *Akhmatova: A Poetic Pilgrimage*, New York: Oxford University Press, 1976.

Haught, John F. 'Emergence, Scientific Naturalism, and Theology', in Murphy et al., eds. *Evolution and Emergence* (2007), pp. 248–66.

—. *Making Sense of Evolution: Darwin, God, and the Drama of Life*, Louisville, KY: Westminster John Knox Press, 2010.

Hawking, Stephen. *A Brief History of Time*, London: Bantam Press, 1988.

Hawking, Stephen, and George Ellis. *The Large Scale Structure of Space-Time*, New York: Cambridge University Press, 1973.

Hawking, Stephen, and Leonard Mlodinow. *The Grand Design*, London: Bantam Press, 2010.

Hayek, Friedrich von. 'Scientism and the Study of Society', *Economica*, Vol. IX, 35, August 1942, pp. 267–91.

Henshilwood, Christopher. 'Fully symbolic sapiens behaviour: Innovation in the Middle Stone Age at Blombos Cave, South Africa', in Mellars et al., eds. *Rethinking the Human Revolution*, pp. 123–32.

—. 'Modern humans and symbolic behaviour: Evidence from Blombos Cave, South Africa', in Blundell, ed., *Origins: The Story of the Emergence of Humans and Humanity in Africa*, pp. 78–85.

Heschel, Abraham. *God in Search of Man: A Philosophy of Judaism*, New York: Harper & Row, 1955.

Hewlett, Martinez J. 'True to Life? Biological Models of Origin and Evolution', in Murphy et al., eds. *Evolution and Emergence*, pp. 158–72.

Hillesum, Etty. *Etty: The Letters and Diaries of Etty Hillesum, 1941–1943*, Klaas A. D. Smelik, ed. Arnold J. Pomerans, tr. Grand Rapids, MI: Eerdmans, 2002.

Hodes, Aubrey. *Encounter with Martin Buber*, Harmondsworth: Penguin, 1975.

Hogan, Maurice P. *The Biblical Vision of the Human Person: Implications for a Philosophical Anthropology*, Frankfurt: Peter Lang, 1994.

Horn, Stefan Otto, and Siegfried Wiedenhofer, eds. *Creation and Evolution: A Conference with Pope Benedict XVI at Castelgandolfo*, Michael J. Miller, tr. San Francisco: Ignatius Press, 2008.

Hughes, Glenn. *Transcendence and History: The Search for Ultimacy from Ancient Societies to Postmodernity*, University of Missouri Press, Columbia, 2003.

Hull, David L., and Michael Ruse, eds. *The Cambridge Companion to the Philosophy of Biology*, New York: Cambridge University Press, 2007.

Hurst, J. A., et al. 'An extended family with a dominantly inherited speech disorder', *Dev. Med. Child Neurol.* 32.4, 1990, pp. 352–5.

Jaki, Stanley. *The Origin of Science and the Science of its Origin*, Edinburgh: Scottish Academic Press, 1978.

—. *The Road of Science and the Ways of God*, Chicago: University of Chicago Press, 1978.

—. *Science and Creation: From Eternal Cycles to an Oscillating Universe*, Lanham, MD: University Press of America, 1990.

—. *Genesis 1 Through the Ages*, London: Thomas More Press, 1992.

—. *Is There a Universe?*, Liverpool: Liverpool University Press, 1993.

Johnson, Phillip. *Darwin on Trial,* Downers Grove, IL: InterVarsity Press, 1993.

Jonas, Hans. *The Phenomenon of Life: Towards a Philosophical Biology*, New York: Delta, 1968.

—. *Le concept de Dieu Après Auschwitz: Une voix juive*, Paris: Payot & Rivages, 1994.

Jones, Nicola. 'Weird wonders lived past the Cambrian: Moroccan fossils show that strange early animals were no flash in the pan', *Nature News*, online, 12 May 2010.

Jones, Stephen, Robert D. Martin and David R. Pilbeam, eds. *The Cambridge Encyclopedia of Human Evolution*, Cambridge: Cambridge University Press, 1994.

Joulian, Frédéric. 'Comparing Chimpanzee and Early Hominid Techniques: Some Contributions to Cultural and Cognitive Questions', in Mellars et al., eds. *Modelling the Early Human Mind* (1996), pp. 173–89.

Kasevich, Vadim B. 'On Universal Grammar and Cognitive Primitives', in Bernard H. Bichakjian, Tatiana Chernigovskaya, Adam Kendon, Anke Möller, eds. *Becoming Loquens: More Studies in Language Origins*, Peter Lang: Frankfurt am Main, 2000, pp. 273–92.

Keller, Helen. *The Story of My Life*, New York: Airmont Books, 1965.

Ker, Ian. *John Henry Newman: A Biography*, Oxford: Oxford University Press, 1990.

Kierkegaard, Søren. *Journals 1853–1855*, Ronald Gregor Smith, tr. London: Fontana, 1968.

—. *The Sickness unto Death*, Princeton: Princeton University Press, 1968.

Klein, Jan, and Naoyuki Takahata. *Where Do We Come From? The Molecular Evidence for Human Descent*, Springer: Berlin, 2002.

Klein, Richard G. *The Human Career: Human Biological and Cultural Origins*, Chicago: University of Chicago Press, 1999.

—. 'Behavioural and Biological Origins of Modern Humans', lecture at Stanford University, online, n.d.

Klein, Richard G. with Blake Edgar. *The Dawn of Human Culture: A Bold New Theory on What Sparked the 'Big Bang' of Human Consciousness*, New York: Wiley, 2002.

Knight, Chris. 'Language, ochre, and the rule of law', in Botha et al., eds. *The Cradle of Language*, pp. 281–303.

Knox, Bernard. *The Heroic Temper*, Berkeley: University of California Press, 1964.

König, Marie. *Am Anfang der Kultur: Die Zeichensprache des frühen Menschen*, Berlin: Mann, 1972.

—. *Unsere Vergangenheit ist älter*, Frankfurt: Krüger, 1980.

Koonin, Eugene V. 'The Biological Big Bang model for the major transitions in evolution', *Biology Direct*, online, 20 August 2007.

Kretzmann, Norman. *The Metaphysics of Creation: Aquinas' Natural Theology in Summa Contra Gentiles II*, New York: Oxford University Press, 1999.

Kuhn, Robert Lawrence. 'Does a Fine-Tuned Universe Lead to God?', *Science + Religion Today*, May 13, 2010.

Kuhn, Steven L. and Marcy C. Stiner. 'Middle Palaeolithic "Creativity": Reflections on an oxymoron?' in Mithen, ed. *Creativity in Human Evolution and Prehistory*, pp. 143–64.

Labedz, Leopold. *Solzhenitsyn: A Documentary Record*, Harmondsworth: Penguin, 1974.

Laing, R. D. *Self and Others*, London: Tavistock, 1969.

Laitmann, J. T. 'Speech (Origins Of)', in Tattersall et al., eds. *Encyclopedia of Human Evolution and Prehistory*, pp. 539–40.

Lake, Mark. '"*Homo*": The Creative Genius,' in Mithen, ed. *Creativity in Human Evolution and Prehistory*, pp. 125–42.

Larson, Richard K., Vivane Déprez, and Hiroko Yamakido, eds. *The Evolution of Human Language: Biolinguistic Perspectives*, Cambridge: Cambridge University Press, 2010.

Leakey, Richard, and Roger Lewin. *Origins Reconsidered: In Search of What Makes Us Human*, New York: Anchor Books, 1993.

Le Gros Clark, Wilfrid. *The Fossil Evidence for Human Evolution: An Introduction to the Study of Paleoanthropology*, Chicago: Chicago University Press, 1978.

Leroi-Gourhan, André. *Gesture and Speech*, Anna Bostock-Berger, tr. Cambridge, MA: MIT Press, 1993.

Levinas, Emmanuel. *Totalité et infini: Essai sur l'extériorité*, The Hague: Nijhoff, 1968.

—. *Etica e Infinito*, Rome: Città Nuova, 1984.

—. *Collected Philosophical Papers*, Dordrecht: Nijhoff, 1987.

Lenneberg, Eric H. *Biological Foundations of Language*, New York: Wiley, 1967.

Lewin, Roger. *Principles of Human Evolution*, Oxford: Blackwells, 1998.

Lewis, C. S. *That Hideous Strength*, London: Pan Books, 1963.

—. *The Abolition of Man*, London: Collins, 1981.

Lewis-Williams, David. 'Neuropsychology and Upper Palaeolithic Art: Observations on the Progress of Altered States of Consciousness', *Cambridge Archaeological Journal* 14:1, 2004.

Lieberman, Daniel E., and Ofer Bar-Yosef. 'Apples and Oranges: Morphological Versus Behavioural Transitions in the Pleistocene', in Daniel E. Lieberman, Richard J. Smith, and Jay Kelley, eds. *Interpreting the Past: Essays on Human, Primate, and Mammal Evolution in Honor of David Pilbeam*, Boston: Brill, 2005, pp. 275–96.

Lieberman, Philip. *Uniquely Human: The Evolution of Speech, Thought, and Selfless Behaviour*, Cambridge, MA: Harvard University Press, 1991.

—. *Eve Spoke: Human Language and Human Evolution*, New York: W. W. Norton, 1998.

—. *Human Language and Our Reptilian Brain: The Subcortical Bases of Speech, Syntax and Thought*, Cambridge MA: Harvard University Press, 2000.

—. 'The creative capacity of language, in what manner is it unique, and who had it?' in Richard K. Larson, et al., eds. *The Evolution of Human Language*, pp. 163–77.

Lonergan, Bernard. J. F. *Insight: A Study in Human Understanding*, London: Longmans, 1961.

—. *De Verbo Incarnato*, Rome: Gregorian University Press, 1964.

—. *De Deo Trino I, II*, Rome: Gregorian University Press, 1964.

—. *Verbum: Word and Idea in Aquinas*, Notre Dame: Notre Dame University Press, 1967.

—. *Collection*, New York: Herder & Herder, 1967.

—. *Method in Theology*, London: Darton, Longman & Todd, 1972.

Lorenz, Konrad. *Studies in Animal and Human Behaviour, Vol. 1*, London: Methuen, 1970.

Lubich, Chiara. *On the Holy Journey*, Hyde Park, NY: New City Press, 1988.

—. *Essential Writings: Spirituality, Dialogue, Culture*, Michel Vandeleene, Tom Masters and Callan Slipper, eds. Hyde Park, NY: New City Press, 2007.

Luria, Alexander Romanovich. *The Working Brain*, Harmondsworth: Penguin, 1973.

McBrearty, Sally, and Allison S. Brooks. 'The revolution that wasn't: a new interpretation of the origin of modern human behaviour', *Journal of Human Evolution*, 2000, 39, pp. 453–563.

McCarroll, Joseph. *Journey to the Centre of the Person*, Dublin: Radix Press, 1986.

McEvoy, James. *Robert Grosseteste*, Oxford: Oxford University Press, 2000.

McShane, Philip. *Plants and Pianos: Two Essays in Advanced Methodology*, Dublin: Milltown Institute, 1971.

Mann, Thomas. *Joseph und seine Brüder: Die Geschichten Jaakobs*, Frankfurt: Fischer, 1964.

Marean, Curtis. 'Earliest Evidence Of Modern Humans Detected', *Science Daily*, 17 October 2007.

Marean, Curtis et al. 'Early human use of marine resources and pigment in South Africa during the Middle Pleistocene', *Nature*, 449, 18 October 2007, pp. 905–8.

Márai, Sándor. *Memoir of Hungary 1944–1948*, Albert Tezla, tr. Budapest: Corvina, 1996.

Marcel, Gabriel. *Homo Viator*, New York: Harper, 1962.

—. *Being and Having*, London: Fontana, 1965.

—. *Man Against Mass Society*, Chicago: Gateway, 1967.

Marks, Jonathan. *What It Means to be 98% Chimpanzee: Apes, People, and their Genes*, Berkeley: University of California Press, 2002.

Marshack, Alexander. *The Roots of Civilization: The Cognitive Beginnings of Man's First Art, Symbol and Notation*, London: Weidenfeld & Nicolson, 1972.

—. 'The Berekhat Ram figurine: A late Acheulian carving from the Middle East', *Antiquity*, 71, 1997, pp. 327–37.

Mathews, William A. *Lonergan's Quest: A Study of Desire in the Authoring of Insight*, Toronto: University of Toronto Press, 2005.

Mellars, Paul. *The Neanderthal Legacy: An Archaeological Perspective from Western Europe*, Princeton, N. J.: Princeton University Press, 1996.

—. 'The Neanderthal Problem Continued', *Current Anthropology*, 40.3, June 1999, pp. 341–64.

—. 'The Archaeological Records of the Neanderthal-Modern Human Transition in France', in Ofer Bar-Josef and David Pilbeam, eds. *The Geography of Neanderthals and Modern Humans in Europe and the Greater Mediterranean*, Cambridge, MA: Peabody Museum of Archaeology and Ethnology, Harvard University, 2000, pp. 35–47.

Mellars, Paul, and Christopher Stringer, eds. *The Human Revolution: Behavioural and Biological Perspectives on the Origins of Modern Humans*, Edinburgh: Edinburgh University Press, 1989.

Mellars, Paul, and Kathleen Gibson, eds. *Modelling the Early Human Mind*, McDonald Institute Monographs: Cambridge, 1996.

Mellars, Paul, Katie Boyle, Ofer Bar-Yosef, and Chris Stringer, eds. *Rethinking the Human Revolution*, Cambridge: Short Run Press, 2007.

Meyer, Stephen C. *Signature in the Cell: DNA and the Evidence for Intelligent Design*, New York: HarperCollins, 2010.

Michelangelo. *Rime*, Milan: Rizzoli, 1954.

Midgely, Mary. *Evolution as Religion: Strange Hopes and Stranger Fears*, London: Methuen, 1986.

Miłosz, Czesław. *Emperor of the Earth: Modes of Eccentric Vision*, Berkeley: University of California Press, 1981.

—. *New and Collected Poems 1931–2001*, New York: HarperCollins, 2001.

Mithen, Steven. 'Domain-Specific Intelligence and the Neanderthal Mind', in Mellars et al., eds. *Modelling the Early Human Mind*, 1996, pp. 217–29.

—. ed. *Creativity in Human Evolution and Prehistory*, London: Routledge, 1998.

—. 'A Creative Explosion? Theory of mind, language and the disembodied mind of the Upper Palaeolithic', in Mithen, ed. *Creativity in Human Evolution and Prehistory*, pp. 165–91.

—. *The Singing Neanderthals: The Origins of Music, Language, Mind and Body*, London: Weidenfeld & Nicolson, 2005.

—. 'Out of the mind: material culture and the supernatural', in Renfrew and Morley, *Becoming Human: Innovation in Prehistoric Material and Spiritual Culture*, pp. 124–34.

Mochulsky, Konstantin. *Dostoevsky: His Life and Work*, Princeton, NJ: Princeton University Press, 1971.

More, Thomas. *The Complete Works of St Thomas More, Vol. 4, Utopia*, Edward Surtz and J. H. Hexter, eds. New Haven: Yale University Press, 1965.

Murphy, Nancey, and William R. Stoeger, eds. *Evolution and Emergence: Systems, Organisms, Persons*, Oxford: Oxford University Press, 2007.

Murray, Les. *Fredy Neptune: A Novel in Verse*, New York: Farrar, Straus and Giroux, 2000.

—. *New Collected Poems*, Manchester: Carcanet, 2003.

Nagel, Thomas. *The Last Word*, New York: Oxford University Press, 1997.

Newlands, Anne. *The Group of Seven and Tom Thomson*, Willowdale, ON: Firefly Books, 1995.

Newman, Cathy. 'The Uneasy Magic of Australia's Cape York Peninsula', *National Geographic* 6, 189, June 1996, pp. 2–33.

Newman, John Henry. *Apologia Pro Vita Sua*, London: Longmans Green, 1905.

—. *The Idea of a University: The Integral Text*, Teresa Iglesias, ed. Dublin: Ashfield Press, 2009.

—. *The Letters and Diaries of John Henry Newman*, Charles Stephen Dessain et al., eds. Vol. XXIV, Oxford: Clarendon Press, 1973.

Nilsson, Lennart, and Lars Hamberger. *A Child is Born* [4th edition], New York: Random House, 2004.

Noble, William, and Iain Davidson. *Human Evolution, Language and Mind: A Psychological and Archaeological Inquiry*, Cambridge: Cambridge University Press, 1996.

Oakes, Edward. 'Edward T. Oakes and His Critics: An Exchange', *First Things*, 112, April 2001, pp. 5–13.

Obrist, Hans-Ulrich, ed. *Gerhard Richter: 100 Bilder*, Ostfildern-Ruit bei Stuttgart: Hatje-Canz Verlag, 1996.

O'Hear, Anthony. *Beyond Evolution: Human Nature and the Limits of Evolutionary Explanation*, Oxford: Oxford University Press, 1997.

O'Neill, Eugene. *Long Day's Journey into Night*, New Haven: Yale University Press, 1977.

Opitz, Peter-Joachim. *Lao-tzu: Die Ordnungsspekulation im Tao-tê-ching*, Munich: Paul List Verlag, 1967.

Oppenheimer, Stephen. *Out of Eden: The Peopling of the World*, London: Constable, 2003.

Orwell, George. 'Notes on Nationalism' (May 1945), http://orwell.ru/library/essays/nationalism/english/e_nat.

Paley, William. *Natural Theology or Evidences of the Existence and Attributes of the Deity* [1802], Weybridge: Hamilton, n.d.

Pap, Arthur. *An Introduction to the Philosophy of Science*, London: Eyre & Spottiswoode, 1963.

Parker, Sue T., and Karin E. Jaffe. *Darwin's Legacy: Scenarios in Human Evolution*, Lanham, MD: AltaMira Press, 2008.

Pascal, Blaise. *Pensées*, Harmondsworth: Penguin, 1983.

Passingham, Richard. *What is Special about the Human Brain?*, Oxford: Oxford University Press, 2008.

Pennock, Robert T. *Tower of Babel: The Evidence Against the New Creationism*, Cambridge, MA: MIT, 1999.

Percy, Walker. *The Message in the Bottle*, New York: Farrar, Straus & Giroux, 1975.

—. *Lost in the Cosmos: The Last Self-Help Book*, New York: Washington Square Press, 1984.

—. 'Writing in the Ruins', interview with Robert Cubbage, *Notre Dame Magazine*, Autumn 1987, pp. 29–31.

Pezzimenti, Rozzo. 'Fraternità: il perché di una eclissi', in Baggio, ed. *Il principio dimenticato*, pp. 57–77.

Pfeiffer, John E. *The Creative Explosion: An Inquiry into the Origins of Art and Religion*, New York: Harper and Row, 1982.

Piattelli-Palmarini, Massimo. 'What is language, that it may have evolved, and what is evolution, that it may apply to language?' in Larson et al., eds. *The Evolution of Human Language*, pp. 148–62.

Pinker, Steven. *The Language Instinct: The New Science of Language and Mind*, London: Penguin, 2000.

—. *The Blank Slate: The Modern Denial of Human Nature*, London: Allen Lane, 2002.

Polanyi, Michael. *Personal Knowledge*, London: Routledge & Kegan Paul, 1969.

Portmann, Adolf. *Vom Lebendigen*, Frankfurt: Suhrkamp, 1979.

Postman, Neil. 'Science and the Story that We Need', *First Things*, 69, January 1997, pp. 29–32.

Potterie, Ignace de la. *Adnotationes in Exegesim Primae Epistulae S.Joannis*, Rome: Pont. Inst. Biblicum, 1967.

Powers, Thomas. *Heisenberg's War: The Secret History of the German Bomb*, London: Penguin, 1993.

Purcell, Brendan. 'Aspects of Method in Human Psychology', unpublished Master's thesis, University College Dublin, 1969.

—. 'Wewards: Theoretical Foundations for a Psychology of Friendship', unpublished PhD dissertation, University College Dublin, 1980.

—. 'La persona come comunione. Riflessioni in chiave psicologica', *Nuova Umanità*, 5.30, 1983, pp. 87–98.

—. 'In Search of Newgrange: Long Night's Journey into Day', in Richard Kearney, ed. *The Irish Mind: Exploring Intellectual Traditions*, Dublin: Wolfhound Press, 1985, pp. 39–55.

—. *The Drama of Humanity: Towards a Philosophy of Humanity in History*, Peter Lang: Frankfurt, 1996.

—. '*Amor amicitiae* in the *Bhagavad Gita*', in *Amor Amicitiae: On the Love that is Friendship*: *Essays in Medieval Thought and Beyond, in Honor of Professor James McEvoy*, Thomas Kelly & Philipp Rosemann, eds. Leuven: Peeters, 2004, pp. 347–77.

—. 'Foundations for a Judgment of the Holocaust: Etty Hillesum's Standard of Humanity', in Klaas A.D. Smelik et al., eds. *Spirituality in the Writings of Etty Hillesum*, pp. 125–46.

—. 'Piero Coda's theology of history as ongoing memory of humanity's participation in the trinitarian *kenosis*', paper delivered at *Translatio Imperii* Symposium, University of Hong Kong, February 2010.

—. 'Dawkins' Fear of Reason', in Fran O'Rourke, ed. *Human Destinies: Philosophical Essays in Memory of Gerald Hanratty*, Notre Dame: Notre Dame University Press, 2011.

Rabelais, François. *Gargantua and Pantagruel*, John M. Cohen, tr. London: Penguin, 1983.

Radhakrishnan, Sarvepalli, and Charles A. Moore, eds. *A Sourcebook in Indian Philosophy*, Princeton: Princeton University Press, 1967.

Raff, Rudolf A. *The Shape of Life: Genes, Development, and the Evolution of Animal Form*, Chicago: University of Chicago Press, 1996.

Rager, Günter. 'Der Begriff "Individuum" in der Debatte um den Status des Embryos', in Jean-Pierre Wils and Michael Zahner, eds. *Theologische Ethik zwischen Tradition und Modernitätsanspruch*, Freiburg: Herder, 2005.

—. ed. *Beginn, Personalität und Würde des Menschen*, Freiburg: Karl Alber, 2009.

Ratzinger, Joseph. *'In the Beginning ... ': A Catholic Understanding of the Story of Creation and the Fall*, Grand Rapids, MI: Eerdmans, 1995.

Renfrew, Colin. 'Situating the creative explosion: universal or local?', in Renfrew et al., eds. *Becoming Human*, pp. 74–92.

Renfrew, Colin, and Iain Morley, eds. *Becoming Human: Innovation in Prehistoric Material and Spiritual Culture*, New York: Cambridge University Press, 2009.

Richter, Gerhard. *The Daily Practice of Painting*, London: Thames & Hudson, 1995.

Robinson, Roxana. *Georgia O'Keeffe: A Life*, New York: Harper & Row, 1989.

Roebroeks, Wil, and Alexander Verpoorte. 'A "language-free" explanation for differences between the European Middle and Upper Paleolithic Record', in Botha et al., eds. *The Cradle of Language*, pp. 150–66.

Rondinara, Sergio. *Interpretazione del reale tra scienza e teologia*, Rome: Città Nuova, 2007.

Ross, Hugh. *Why the Universe is the Way It Is*, Grand Rapids, MI: Baker Books, 2008.

Ruse, Michael, 'Philosophy and Paleoanthropology: Some Shared Interests?' in G. A. Clark and C. M. Willermet, eds. *Conceptual Issues in Modern Human Origins Research*, New York: Aldine de Gruyter, 1997, pp. 423–35.

—. *Can a Darwinian be a Christian? The Relationship Between Science and Religion*, Cambridge: Cambridge University Press, 2001.

—. *The Evolution-Creation Struggle*, Cambridge, MA: Harvard University Press, 2005.

Saint-Exupéry, Antoine de. *The Little Prince*, Ware, Herts: Wordsworth Editions, 1995.

Sartre, Jean-Paul. *Huis clos*, Paris: Gallimard, 1947.

Scammel, Michael, ed. *The Solzhenitsyn Files*, Chicago: Editions Q, 1995.

Schick, Kathy D., and Nicholas Toth. *Making Stones Speak: Human Evolution and the Dawn of Technology*, New York: Simon & Schuster, 1993.

Schnackenburg, Rudolf. *The Moral Teaching of the New Testament*, New York: Herder & Herder, 1971.

Scholl, Inge. *The White Rose: Munich 1942–1943*, Wesleyan University Press: Middletown, CT, 1983.

Schwartz, Jeffrey H. et al., eds. *The Human Fossil Record*, 4 Vols, Hoboken, NJ: Wiley-Liss, 2002–5.

Schwartz, Jeffrey H., and Ian Tattersall. *The Human Fossil Record, Volume 4: Craniodental Morphology of Early Hominids and Overview*, Hoboken, NJ: Wiley-Liss, 2005.

Sereny, Gitta. *Albert Speer: His Battle with the Truth*, New York: Knopf, 1995.

Serra, Angelo and Roberto Colombo. 'Identity and Status of the Human Embryo', in Juan de Dios Vial Correa and Elio Sgreccia, eds. *Identity and Status of the Human Embryo: Proceedings of Third Assembly of the Pontifical Academy for Life*, Vatican City: Libreria Editrice Vaticana, 1998, pp. 128–77.

Shear, Jonathan, 'The Hard Problem: Closing the Empirical Gap', in *Explaining Consciousness*, Shear, ed., pp. 359–75.

—. ed. *Explaining Consciousness*: '*The Hard Problem*', Cambridge, MA: MIT Press, 1997.

Shubin, Neil. *Your Inner Fish: A Journey into the 3.5-Billion Year History of the Human Body*, New York: Pantheon Books, 2008.

Smelik, Klaas A.D. 'De keuze van Etty Hillesum om niet onder te duiken', in Ria van den Brandt and Klaas A. D. Smelik, eds. *Etty Hillesum in Context*, Assen: Van Gorcum, 2007, pp. 59–73.

—. 'A Short Biography of Etty Hillesum (1914–1943)', in Smelik et al., eds. *Spirituality in the Writings of Etty Hillesum*, pp. 21–8.

Smelik, Klaas A.D., Ria van den Brandt, and Meins G. S. Coetsier, eds. *Spirituality in the Writings of Etty Hillesum: Proceedings of the Etty Hillesum Conference at Ghent University, November 2008*, Leiden: Brill, 2010.

Smith, Ben. 'The Rock Arts of Southern Africa', in Blundell, ed. *Origins: The Story of the Emergence of Humans and Humanity in Africa*, pp. 97–117.

Smith, Kerri. 'Evolution of a single gene linked to language: Mutations in the FOXP2 gene could help explain why humans can speak but chimps can't', *Nature News*, 11 November 2009.

Smoot, George, and Keay Davidson. *Wrinkles in Time*, New York: Morrow, 1993.

Solzhenitsyn, Aleksandr. *Candle in the Wind*, London: Bodley Head, 1973.

—. *Cancer Ward*, New York: Farrar, Straus & Giroux, 2001.

—. *The Gulag Archipelago 1: 1918–1956, Parts I and II*, London: Collins, 1974.

—. *The Gulag Archipelago 2: 1918–1956, Parts III and IV*, London: Collins, 1976.

—. 'Nobel Lecture', in Edward E. Ericson, Jr, and Daniel J. Mahoney, eds. *The Solzhenitsyn Reader: New and Essential Writings*, Wilmington, DE: ISI Books, 2006, pp. 512–26.

Sophocles. *Oedipus at Colonus*, in David Grene and Richmond Lattimore, eds. and trs. *The Complete Greek Tragedies II, Sophocles*, Chicago: University of Chicago Press, 1974.

Speer, Albert. *Spandau: The Secret Diaries*, London: Collins, 1976.

—. *Inside the Third Reich*, London: Sphere Books, 1979.

Sperber, Dan, and Gloria Origgi, 'A pragmatic perspective on the evolution of language', in Larson et al., eds. *The Evolution of Human Language*, 124–31.

Spicq, Ceslas. *Agape dans le nouveau testament I*, Paris: Gabalda, 1965.

Stein, Edith. *Finite and Eternal Being: An Attempt at an Ascent to the Meaning of Being*, Kurt F. Reinhardt, tr. Washington, DC: ICS Publications, 2002.

Stevens, Wallace. *Opus Posthumous*, New York: Vintage, 1990.

Stoeger, SJ, William R. 'Reduction and Emergence: Implications for Theology', in Murphy et al., eds. *Evolution and Emergence* pp. 229–47.

Stoneking, Mark, and Rebecca Cann. 'African *Origin* of Human Mitochondrial DNA', in Mellars et al., eds. *The Human Revolution*, pp. 17–30.

Stringer, Chris, '*Homo sapiens*', in Tattersall et al., eds. *Encyclopedia of Human Evolution and Prehistory*, pp. 267–74.

—. 'Modern Human Origins: Progress and Prospects', in Chiocon et al., eds. *The Human Evolution Source Book*, pp. 512–28.

—. 'Out of Ethiopia,' *Nature,* 423, 2003, pp. 692–4.

Stringer, Chris, and Clive Gamble. *In Search of Neanderthals: Solving the Puzzle of Human Origins*, London: Thames & Hudson, 1993.

Stringer, Chris, and Robin McKie. *African Exodus: The Origins of Modern Humanity*, London: Pimlico, 1997.

Tattersall, Ian. *Becoming Human: Evolution and Human Uniqueness*, New York: Harcourt Brace, 1998.

—. *The Last Neanderthal: The Rise, Success, and Mysterious Extinction of Our Closest Human Relatives*, Boulder, CO: Westview Press, 1999.

—. 'The Place of the Neanderthals in Human Evolution and the Origin of *Homo sapiens*', in Donald C. Johanson and Giancarlo Ligabue, eds. *Ecce Homo: Writings in Honour of Third-Millennium Man*, Milan: Electra, 1999, pp. 157–75.

—. *The Monkey in the Mirror: Essays on the Science of What Makes Us Human*, New York: Harcourt, 2002.

—. *The World from Beginnings to 4000BCE*, New York: Oxford University Press, 2008.

—. 'Language and the *Origin* of Symbolic Thought', in De Beaune et al. *Cognitive Archaeology and Human Evolution*, pp. 114–15.

Tattersall, Ian, E. Delson, and J. Van Couvering, eds. *Encyclopedia of Human Evolution and Prehistory*, New York: Garland, 1988.

Terrace, H. S., L. A. Petitto, R. J. Sanders, T. G. Berer, 'Can an Ape Create a Sentence?', *Science*, 23 November 1979, pp. 891–902.

Timms, Edward. *Karl Kraus: Apocalyptic Satirist. The Post-War Crisis and the Rise of the Swastika*, New Haven: Yale University Press, 2005.

Tinbergen, Nikolaas. *The Study of Instinct*, Oxford: Clarendon Press, 1951.

Vandermeersch, Bernard. *Les homes fossiles de Qafzeh (Israel)*, Paris: Editions du Centre National de Recherche Scientifique [CNRS], 1981.

Voegelin, Eric. *The World of the Polis, Vol. 2 of Order and History*, Baton Rouge: Louisiana State University Press, 1964.

—. *Plato and Aristotle, Vol. 3 of Order and History*, Baton Rouge: Louisiana State University Press, 1964.

—. *Israel and Revelation, Vol. 1 of Order and History*, Baton Rouge: Louisiana State University Press, 1969.

—. *The Ecumenic Age, Vol. 4 of Order and History*, Baton Rouge: Louisiana State University Press, 1974.

—. *In Search of Order, Vol. 5 of Order and History*, Baton Rouge: Louisiana State University Press, 1987.

—. *Autobiographical Reflections*, Ellis Sandoz, ed. Baton Rouge: Louisiana State University Press, 1989.
—. *What is History? and Other Late Unpublished Writings*, Thomas A. Hollweck and Paul Caringella, eds. Baton Rouge: Louisiana State University Press, 1990.
—. *Published Essays 1966–1985*, Ellis Sandoz, ed. Baton Rouge: Louisiana State University Press, 1990.
—. *History of Political Ideas, Vol. I: Hellenism, Rome, and Early Christianity*, Athanasios Moulakis, ed. Columbia, MO: University of Missouri Press, 1997.
—. *History of Political Ideas, Vol II: The Middle Ages to Aquinas*, Peter von Sivers, ed. Columbia, MO: University of Missouri Press, 1997.
—. *History of Political Ideas, Vol. IV: Renaissance and Reformation*, David L. Morse and William M. Thompson, Columbia, eds. MO: University of Missouri Press, 1998.
—. *Hitler and the Germans*, Detlev Clemens and Brendan Purcell, eds. and trs., Columbia, MO: University of Missouri Press, 1999.
—. *The New Science of Politics* in *Modernity Without Restraint*, Manfred Henningsen, ed. Columbia, MO: University of Missouri Press, 2000.
—. *Science, Politics and Gnosticism*, in *Modernity Without Restraint*.
—. *Published Essays 1940–1952*, Ellis Sandoz, ed. Columbia, MO: University of Missouri Press, 2000.
—. *Published Essays 1953–1965*, Ellis Sandoz, ed. Columbia, MO: University of Missouri Press, 2000.
—. *Anamnesis: On the Theory of History and Politics*, David Walsh, ed. Columbia, MO: University of Missouri Press, 2002.
—. *The Drama of Humanity and Other Miscellaneous Papers, 1939–1985*, William Petropulos and Gilbert Weiss, eds. Columbia, MO: University of Missouri Press, 2004.
—. *Selected Correspondence 1950–1984*, Thomas A. Hollweck, ed. Columbia, MO: University of Missouri Press, 2007.
Vonnegut, Kurt. *Cat's Cradle*, London: Penguin, 1973.
Walsh, David. *After Ideology: Recovering the Spiritual Foundations of Freedom*, San Francisco: HarperCollins, 1990.
—. *Guarded by Mystery: Meaning in a Postmodern Age*, Washington, DC: Catholic University of America Press, 1999.
—. *The Third Millennium: Reflections on Faith and Reason*, Washington, DC: Georgetown University Press, 1999.
—. 'Are Freedom and Dignity Enough? A Reflection on Liberal

Abbreviations', in Robert Kraynak and Glenn Tinder, eds. *In Defense of Human Dignity*, Notre Dame, IN: University of Notre Dame Press, 2003, pp. 165–91.

—. 'The Turn Toward Existence and Existence in the Turn', in *Philosophy, Literature and Politics: Essays Honoring Ellis Sandoz*, Charles R. Embry and Barry Cooper, eds. Columbia: University of Missouri Press, 2005, pp. 3–27.

—. 'The Unattainability of What We Live Within: Liberal Democracy', in Anton Rauscher, ed. *Die fragile Demokratie – The Fragility of Democracy*, Berlin: Duncker & Humblot, 2007.

—. *The Modern Philosophical Revolution: The Luminosity of Existence*, New York: Cambridge University Press, 2008.

—. 'The Person as the Apocalypse of History', paper delivered at *Translatio Imperii* Symposium, University of Hong Kong, February 2010.

—. 'The Person and the Common Good', in Fran O'Rourke, ed. *Human Destinies: Philosophical Essays in Memory of Gerald Hanratty*, Notre Dame: Notre Dame University Press, 2011.

Wells, Spencer. *The Journey of Man: A Genetic Odyssey*, London: Allen Lane, 2002.

White, Randall. 'Reply to Robert G. Bednarik's "Concept-Mediated Marking in the Lower Paleolithic"', *Current Anthropology*, 36.4 August–October 1995, pp. 605–34.

White, T. D. et al. 'Pleistocene *Homo sapiens* from Middle Awash, Ethiopia', *Nature,* 423, 2003, pp. 742–7.

Whitehead, A. N. *Science and the Modern World*, London: Cambridge University Press, 1953.

Willermet, Catherine M., and Brett Hill. 'Fuzzy Set Theory and its Implications for Speciation Problems', in *Conceptual Issues in Modern Human Origins Research*, G. A. Clark and C. M. Willermet, eds. New York: Aldine de Gruyter, 1997, pp. 77–88.

Willoughby, Pamela R. *The Evolution of Modern Humans in Africa: A Comprehensive Guide*, Lanham, MD: Altamira Press, 2007.

Wittgenstein, Ludwig. *Tractatus Logico-Philosophicus*, London: Routledge & Kegan Paul, 1963.

—. *Culture and Value*, G. H. von Wright, ed. Chicago: University of Chicago Press, 1984.

Wojtyła, Karol. *The Acting Person*, Dordrecht: Reidel, 1979.

Wolin, Richard. *The Heidegger Controversy: A Critical Reader*, Cambridge, MA: MIT Press, 1993.

Wolpoff, Milford H. 'Multiregional Evolution: The Fossil Alternative to Eden', in Mellars et al., eds. *The Human Revolution*, pp. 62–108.

Wood, B. A., 'The History of the Genus *Homo*', *Human Evolution* 15.1–2, January–June 2000, pp. 39–49.

Wynne, Clive D. L. *Do Animals Think?*, Princeton: Princeton University Press, 2004.

Wynn, Thomas. 'Whither evolutionary cognitive archaeology: Afterword', in De Beaune et al. *Cognitive Archaeology and Human Evolution*, pp. 145–50.

Wynn, Thomas, and Frederick L. Coolidge. 'Implications of a strict standard for recognizing modern cognition in prehistory', in De Beaune et al., *Cognitive Archaeology and Human Evolution*, pp. 117–28.

Young-Bruehl, Elisabeth. *Hannah Arendt: For the Love of the World*, New Haven: Yale University Press, 1982.

Zaehner, R. C. *The Bhagavad Gita*, New York: Oxford University Press, 1973.

Zanghí, G. M. 'Verso una cultura del post-ateismo', in *Gen's 1*, pp. 9–13.

—. *Notte della cultura europea*, Rome: Città Nuova, 2007.

Życiński, Józef. *God and Evolution: Fundamental Questions of Christian Evolutionism*, Washington DC: Catholic University of America Press, 2006.

Author Index

Acknowledgments

For many of my friends, the big mystery of the book's title was 'what took you so long?' The introduction tells that story, but here I'd like to say how grateful I am to a wonderful cast of characters who cheered me along to the finishing line. In the School of Philosophy at University College Dublin, Professors Dermot Moran, Ger Casey and Brian O'Connor were the best departmental heads I could have wished for, along with all my colleagues in a wonderfully friendly department, especially Professors Teresa Iglesias and Fran O'Rourke, and at the heart of the School, Margaret Brady and Helen Kenny. Then there were the long-suffering UCD philosophy students who patiently endured various half-cooked versions of this enterprise. A small group of students at UCD – Eamonn Barron, Norella Broderick, Robbie Butler, Ruth Cabero and Dušan Sabol – with UCD's Head Chaplain, Fr John McNerney, made my last years among my happiest at UCD. I owe so much to Professor Richard Rosengarten, then Dean of the Divinity School at the University of Chicago, and to Professor Paul O'Hara of Northeastern Illinois University, together with all the staff at St Thomas Apostle Rectory, who made my several stays at the University of Chicago – where this book really got started – possible.

Dr Joseph McCarroll read every line of the text and made it a lot less mysterious than it might have been – his positive contributions and corrections run right through the book: I couldn't have had a more magnificent partner in the dialogue. The other most deeply appreciated partner in the dialogue was Professor David Walsh at Catholic University of America, who is giving philosophical expression to the mystery of the human person in political existence in a spiral galaxy of publications, from which I've freely borrowed. And just when I needed expert help the most, Professor Maureen Condic of the University of Utah checked over what I'd written on the human zygote and found it wanting: it's an honour to have had her as a collaborator. Fr Hugh Kavanagh and Professor Brendan Leahy read and commented on the earlier chapters, and with Frs Fergus McGlynn, John McNerney, Tom Norris and Michael O'Kelly, along with Fr Tom McGovern, provided me with the warmth, support and wisdom I needed all through the period the book was being crafted.

Wallace Stevens writes about tradition in terms of the relationship between a father and his son, where the son bears his father on his back: 'But he bears him out of love,/His life made double by his father's life.' Well, my life has definitely been 'made double' by all those who have entered into this book, directly and indirectly. But the credit for any mistakes in the text is all mine.

I'm also tremendously grateful to my publishers, Veritas, for staying with a project that missed more deadlines than the inhabitants of Boot Hill Tombstone. The book became something quite different to what both Veritas and I expected – so, many thanks to Donna Doherty, whose consistent and cheerful encouragement was a tonic, and to Caitriona Clarke and Julie Steenson for patiently and painstakingly shepherding the text through to publication. And I've deeply appreciated the kind support both of Archbishop Dermot Martin of Dublin and of Cardinal George Pell of Sydney.

I'm dedicating the book to the memory of two great friends, Dr Gerry Hanratty and Professor Jim McEvoy. *Ar dheis Dé go raibh a nanamacha.*